DAT

FE 7 7 10			

The Gender of History

The Gender of History

Men, Women, and Historical Practice

Bonnie G. Smith

Harvard University Press

Cambridge, Massachusetts

London, England

1998

Library of Congress Cataloging-in-Publication Data

Smith, Bonnie G., 1940–
    The gender of history: men, women, and historical practice /
Bonnie G. Smith.
        p.   cm.
    Includes bibliographical references and index.
    ISBN 0-674-34181-3 (alk. paper)
    1. Historiography. 2. Historians. 3. Women historians.
I. Title.
D13.S567   1998
907'.2—dc21   98-11926

For Natalie Zemon Davis and Donald R. Kelley

Acknowledgments

After listening to an oral presentation of the section in this book that deals with male historians' fantasies, David Schalk of Vassar College reported he had once had a vision in which Clio swooped into his presence and predicted he would never make it as a scholar. Many years before this confession, David had presented me with two volumes by Lucy Maynard Salmon—a prominent character in these pages. Because *The Gender of History* has taken so long to complete, generous colleagues like David have had the opportunity to make wonderful contributions for nearly two decades.

Students and faculty at Rutgers and the University of Rochester provided a host of ideas and were extraordinary colleagues. In particular I thank Mary Young, Stewart Weaver, Bette London, Brenda Meehan, Thomas DiPiero, and Lynn Gordon for sharing their work or providing thoughtful critiques of my own. Colleagues at Rutgers are at the forefront of investigations in the field of gender, and many deserve thanks for their personal and intellectual support, especially Suzanne Lebsock, Alice Kessler-Harris, Dee Garrison, John Gillis, Jennifer Jones, Belinda Davis, Deborah White, Barbara Balliet, and Mary Hartman. Graduate students at both institutions were important critics. Among them, Todd Shepard also assisted with research, and Tamara Matheson and Scott Glotzer helped with final details.

Colleagues at other institutions had a variety of responses to this book as a work-in-progress. In particular I thank fellows at the Shelby Cullum Davis Center in 1992–1993 and faculty in the Department of History at Princeton, especially Elizabeth Lunbeck, Peter Brown, Christine Stansell, Philip Nord, and Suzanne Marchand, for their support and generous help. Ann-Louise Shapiro, Jo Burr Margadant, Isabel Hull, Stephen Kaplan,

Joan Scott, and Elizabeth Faue provided acute and extensive comments on various segments. Beate Popkin tipped me off to boys and fighting; Margaret Higonnet to complexities in de Staël; Judith Bennett to medievalist women. My arguments were also sharpened through my exchanges with European colleagues, including Gisela Bock, Maria Grever, Mineke Bosch, Francisca de Haan, Josine Blok, Berteke Waaldijk, Janet Sondheimer, Constance Blackwell, and Christiane Klapisch. The American Council of Learned Societies, the National Humanities Center, and the John Simon Guggenheim Foundation provided crucial fellowships.

Portions of this book were previously published, in somewhat different form, by the *American Historical Review, French Historical Studies, History and Theory,* the *History of Education Quarterly,* and Brepols, S.A. (Belgium).

Joyce Seltzer and Maria Ascher of Harvard University Press gave the manuscript expert editing. I am extremely grateful for their encouragement, for the many improvements they made in the text, and for the many ideas they provided. Joyce Seltzer also found two anonymous critics whose comments were invaluable.

I thank Susan Kingsley Kent, Karen Ordahl Kupperman, and Joel J. Kupperman for ideas that shaped specific sections. Beyond that, they know how I treasure each of them and their friendship. Honoré Sharrer and Perez Zagorin, loyal friends and charming companions, nudged the manuscript toward completion. Patience H. Smith contributed important insights to the material on trauma and writing. She, John R. Kelley, and Patrick W. Smith have supported my work beyond what anyone has a right to expect—even of one's family.

This book took shape in my mind as I witnessed the force of historiographic dialogues over several decades. Early in the 1970s, Natalie Zemon Davis gave a pioneering lecture about women historians and some of the men who supported them. Since then, her gift for dialogical engagement has advanced the gendering of historiography, as it has advanced so much other historical scholarship. Hearing Natalie Davis and Donald R. Kelley discuss historiography together has been a further source of dialogical appreciation. And in still another dialogue, Donald Kelley has proffered endless support, bountiful information, and patient correction to the historiographic detail presented here. In the spirit of dialogue, and as a token of my gratitude for the inspiration they have given me, this book bears a twofold dedication.

Contents

The Gender of History

Introduction
Gender and the Mirror of History

> I am not partisan . . . Why? Because in
> history I see nothing but history.
>
> —Lucien Febvre, *Combats pour l'histoire*

This book inserts the term "gender" into an account of historiography in
the Western world.[1] It proposes that the development of modern scientific
methodology, epistemology, professional practice, and writing has been
closely tied to evolving definitions of masculinity and femininity. In so
doing, it seems to go against the grain of professionalism itself: for more
than a century and a half historians have prided themselves on the way in
which their training allows them to overcome contingencies of religious
creed, national origin, class, race, ethnicity, and gender through scrupulous adherence to the scientific method. When people's biases do appear,
historians point these out and correct them in order to come as close as
they can to "value-free" science. Although their personal lives may be very
much influenced by issues of gender, their methodology helps them arrive
as close as humanly possible to an ungendered historical truth. Only bad
history would work to promote a religious, racialized, or class-based version of the past that flew in the face of accepted evidence.

Changes in the profession since the early 1970s have been based on these
beliefs. Trained in scientific methods, historians of both women and people
of color have assumed that their scholarship would eventually fit into the
field of history as a whole. Their findings fill out the picture, making the
scholarship of the past finally truthful because more complete and up-to-
date. Of course, many have also believed that ingredients such as periodiza-
tion would change as matters important to women displaced men's events,
and that the cast of historical characters and many traditional interpretations would alter too. But the profession's rationality and fairness, it was
thought, would ultimately allow the findings of women's history and the

1

accomplishments of women historians their full influence and dignity in the academy. Meanwhile, some male historians welcomed the arrival and development of women's history and, later, gender history as a corrective.[2] When, in the mid-1980s, one prominent social historian announced that historical research about women had gone far enough and should stop, it was in the belief that history's claims to lack of bias could be vitiated by an excess of such information. The history of women and blacks, it was said, would politicize the field. Or these subdisciplines—being "sexy, fashionable, and hot"—could undermine the truth value of real history by exposing it to influences (such as ideology and rampant market forces) that operated outside professional standards for what was important.[3]

We hold such beliefs because we trust in the mirror of history—a metaphor that has long been indicative of how scholars in the West envision historical truth. Held up to the past, the mirror supposedly reflects bygone events more accurately than any other instrument or tool, showing nothing fanciful or imaginary. While faithfully reflecting the past, the mirror can also show fleeting images and provide a sense of change and movement. The mirror is also a theme relevant to the modern rational subject, whose self-scrutiny is the first step toward understanding and toward the construction of an unbiased scientific mindset. As a consequence of knowing himself and his biases and faults, the historian is better equipped to analyze the historical objects that appear in the mirror.[4] This theme has other aspects, especially in the Hegelian idea that reaching a higher truth comes only with the deliberate transcendence of the relationship between the knowing subject and the object of scrutiny. The result, as Lucien Febvre suggests when he claims to see nothing in history but history, is that the figure of the individual historian becomes spiritualized and invisible. His self, which includes prejudices and preferences, disappears from the mirror along with the flawed minutiae of the reflected object, to be replaced by a "true" vision of historical reality recounted by an invisible, omniscient narrator.

In Western iconography the knowing subject—along with the historically important objects the mirror serves up for scrutiny—is usually male, adding complexity to what seems a simple image. When we envision a great historian, we instinctively imagine him as male; we accept as natural such titles as *The History Men* (as a recent book of historiography was called) because professionalization and historical science developed at a time of separate spheres, when middle-class women mostly stayed at home.[5] Thus, for historically explicable reasons, it is said, the profession was virtually all male. Only men had the time to engage in the activities (archival research, teaching in universities) on which the founding of professional history depended. Historical common sense should also explain why the most well-regarded histories were about men: focusing on political history, professional history would naturally choose great men to study. Moreover, the nation-state, which inspired and financed so much of the new historical science, allowed men alone the full rights of citizenship during this time. Evidently, then, they would be most likely to champion its history. History, as Jack Hexter maintained some fifty years ago, "has mostly been stag affairs," gendered male by tradition, accident, and circumstance.[6] According to these views, there is little to be gained from looking at gender in historiography and historical practice.

But let us consider another image in the mirror of history. When the person before a mirror has been a woman, her self-regarding has appeared repetitive, even obsessive, and indicative of vanity or love of luxury—connoting the sensual rather than the rational. The iconographic mirror in women's case has occluded reflexive depth and yielded only superficiality—a dramatic change in the mirror's signifying work. So fixated on the surface, women have been seen as incapable of reaching the requisite profundities of either history or self-knowledge. They occupy a lower rung on the ladder of cognitive being—poor practitioners indeed, as the many women amateur historians are often said to have been, even by women professionals themselves. On the one hand, the mirror can produce universally true, important, and objective reflections of reality; but on the other, it has traditionally worked best if the observer is male. We might argue that these often-invoked images of the mirror are merely metaphorical; but historicizing the metaphor shows that, for centuries, it in fact has had not just decorative but explanatory force. The adjectives "sexy," "fashionable," and "hot," which are used to designate bad history (or the history of people of color and women), are likewise rich with gendered efficacy and form part of a long tradition of imaging the historian's work in gendered ways. Thus, because the mirror of history resists some efforts to reach gender neutrality, its multiple images of gender's relationship to professional practices and historical science are intriguing enough to merit further exploration, if only to clear the air.

Embedded in these preliminary images of superficiality and depth, gendered versus universal truth, the metaphorical and the real are some historical knots that we have devoted little attention to because we automatically favor "depth" in our scholarship and hope to provide "real" accounts and "universal truth." We concomitantly reject as goals the superficial, gendered, and metaphorical. Many disciplines share history's claims to attain universal truth or beauty, either of which can be verified by a set of rigorous standards that are beyond such contingencies as race, gender, religion, and ethnic background. Although musical, scientific, and philosophical geniuses, for instance, are nearly always men, their genius soars beyond such contingent or ultimately insignificant matters as gender to reach the heights of philosophical insight or the musical sublime. Great artists and philosophers are geniuses above all, and men only accidentally.

Scholars in other disciplines, however, are probing these foundational claims to understand how their fields are gendered. Feminist scholars in music and philosophy have been among the first to explore the functioning of such claims, showing how gender operates inexorably in even the most abstract, nonrepresentational work and in the standards applied to judge it. Susan McClary has compared the formal elements in music that critics discuss as "masculine" and therefore of high quality with those that are considered "feminine" and therefore inferior. The "masculine" in the sonata and several other forms is seen as a series of ascending phrases of notes competing to reach ever higher until their competition is utterly exhausted. The "feminine" is often taken to be any "large-scale dissonance" needing to be resolved in a piece.[7] Londa Schiebinger has pointed to the ways in which modern science has often claimed to be value-free even as it has been inhospitable to women scientists. Further, she has described the male fantasies at work in the naming of animal species and in portrayals of plant functioning.[8] Both authors show how claims of universality were accompanied by the elevation of men and the concomitant devaluation of women—were enabled, that is, by gender hierarchy.

The philosopher Michèle Le Doeuff has discerned two roads to the masculinization of philosophical study—roads that might also be suggestive for historians.[9] The first involves the metaphors by which philosophers have described their perfect societies and through which they have been able to come up with new answers to epistemological, ontological, aesthetic, and ethical dilemmas. These metaphors are often highly gendered, meaning that the road to universal truth—what it is that allows male genius-philosophers to think—is sex and gender. Le Doeuff does not present gender at work in every theoretical advance. But Andrea Nye finds that metaphors of femininity and sexuality have been essential to the breakthroughs of great logicians from Parmenides to Frege. Logic is not a kind of mathematical abstraction devoid of social content; rather, Nye demonstrates, logic has historically been constituted out of gendered thinking—a gendered thinking based on a hierarchy that privileges men as intellects and sexualizes women.[10]

Le Doeuff further elaborates how gender hierarchy makes philosophy work both intellectually and sociologically. Jean-Paul Sartre's *Being and Nothingness,* the central example in Le Doeuff's book, took the female body as an image for all that is inauthentic, for the filth of nature that humans must transcend in their quest for philosophical truth. "There is a possibility that the In-itself might absorb the For-itself . . . Slime is the revenge of the In-itself. A sickly-sweet feminine revenge . . . [It] draws me, it sucks at me . . . It is a soft, yielding action, a moist and feminine sucking . . . In one sense it is like the supreme docility of the possessed, the fidelity of a dog that *gives* itself."[11] As this example begins to show and as Merleau-Ponty pointed out in detail, Sartre could explain the main point of phenomenology only as the work of a male subject needing to annihilate female subjectivity. He described the entire process of self-creation in terms of disgust at sexual engagement with a woman.[12]

According to Le Doeuff, these philosophically enabling sketches of overcoming the "disgusting" other accompanied the exploitation of Sartre's partner, Simone de Beauvoir—an exploitation verified in many accounts of their relationship. As university students, Sartre and de Beauvoir were virtually identical in their accomplishments. Sartre ranked first and she second on the *agrégation,* but evidence shows he had flunked so many times previously that the examiners felt sorry for this man who had convincingly advertised himself as a genius. De Beauvoir, by contrast, finished the same arduous course of study in two years instead of three, and was acquiring her lifelong name of "Beaver" for the hard work she put into philosophy. Throughout their lives together, Sartre insisted to de Beauvoir and others that hers was a far lesser but hardworking mind, all the while employing her to spend most of the day writing his projects.[13]

But how can such sordid stories advance our understanding of scientific history and its professionalization, especially when the profession ultimately allowed women entry into the field? While this book explores the development of historical science as a complex endeavor undertaken by young scholar-adventurers in the nineteenth century, it is also centrally preoccupied with all those terms like "superficiality," "metaphor," and "women" that supposedly became irrelevant to received historical techniques and to the scientific communities that practiced the new history. It thus looks at female personalities and gender issues that historiography generally shuns.

For example, despite the thrust of most historiographic accounts, history for the past two centuries has *not* been mostly written by men or even been concerned mostly with men. Women in the West have had a lively, productive, and growing interest in the genre since at least the end of the eighteenth century. Their careers and rewards have been different, however. For one thing, although by the end of the nineteenth century some English and American women had satisfying careers in higher education, thousands of women historians pursued their calling as amateurs, without the institutional affiliations of male professionals.[14] For another, women often chose different historical subjects: the history of women, of social life, and of high and low culture. Prestigious professional history based on deep reflection and weighty political topics was for men, while "amateurish" women pursued a more "superficial" kind of writing about the past.

This book looks precisely at naive tales of queens and famous ladies in order to chart the superficial, literary, trivial, and "feminine" side of amateurism. It does so not to deny such characterizations but rather to explore this type of historical production as it existed in the early nineteenth century, before university-based, scientific practice surpassed it. Departing from the rich historiographic tradition of seeing canonical male writers at the center of the story is risky, but it seems important to address from the outset women's superficial, trivial, yet ardent relationship to history. I analyze women's amateur status not only because their work became synonymous with the "amateurish," but also because the connection between the woman amateur and professionalization has been far from clear, even unexplored, although the historical subject matter—"the past"—is similar for both male and female writers.[15] For instance, given that amateur writing of history antedated professionalism, is women's practice the more authentic and natural one, preceding the creation of scientific history, with its copious rules and procedures? Constantly excoriated by university men, amateur writing in the nineteenth century might additionally be seen as a kind of impurity that the professional eliminated—a thicket of falsehoods he cleared away in order to find an authentic past and objective truth. Or, again, was the concept of the amateur only a result of professionalization, a weak and less worthy ("amateurish") imitation of the scientific practitioner embodied by those not up to being professional historians? If any of these notions is true, then how did the "impure" or "false" historical productions function? We think we know what superficial, amateurish history is. But do we really?

Two senses of the "trivial" and "low" inform this discussion. Amateur writing came to be seen as in some way fit for women—women who made their living by writing for the marketplace, outside the more exclusive professional institutions of history. This kind of market-driven work was interpreted by later professionals as base, catering to low reading tastes, and distinct from the high-quality work of well-off men outside the academy. Women were the quintessential amateurs, who dealt with the market; men, the appropriate professionals, who served more lofty ends.[16] The distinction between these juxtaposed terms was crucial to the ability of professionals to fashion themselves as part of the elite power structure, discrete from the untutored views of ordinary people. But how exactly did this happen, on what terms, with what moves and countermoves? Women's amateur history has served as a gendered ground for professionalization, though one thus far lacking historical specificity, just as the historiography of professionalization has lacked much sense of this interaction. Women's connections with the market permitted a more transcendent, professionalized, male realm of history writing to arise.

Professional writing rose to importance in times of economic and political modernization, beginning very slowly in the mid-eighteenth century and accelerating in the mid- to late nineteenth century. Women's amateurism, however, had taken off several decades earlier. From the French and

American Revolutions on, women amateurs like Mercy Otis Warren, Louise Keralio, Germaine de Staël, Johanna Schopenhauer, Caroline Pichler, and Anna Jameson lived in a climate of violent bloodshed, drastic social turmoil, and increasing discrimination against women. Their intellectual vision traveled through a contemporary landscape of horrendous wounds and massive losses on its way to the past. Although many amateurs studied manuscripts and other archival sources, the vast numbers who wrote did so in a period before history was tamed into a kind of professional knowledge and in an age of new mass armies and interminable violence, when life itself precluded dispassionate objectivity on issues of social life or politics. Constructed amid the modernity spreading across ever larger sections of the West, amateur history by women often throbbed with vivid description and heightened feeling—the heart of what has come to be called the "low" and "superficial."

What was first called women's "amateurism" is symptomatic of a relationship to the past similarly filtered through trauma. Revolutionary times brought unbearable pain, and the resulting modernity led to disorientation. The political climate promoted equality and universal rights, but at the same time there was increasing denigration and legal despoliation of women.[17] Written largely by women, who often had no right to keep their earnings, amateur history was a complex expression of this world. Like many men of the time, women writers—notably Germaine de Staël—saw the past as a point of mournful remembrance and loss for them as women, and often for society as a whole. Legitimate heightened feeling connected with memory work is most often associated with men's experience of such events as World War I and the Holocaust.[18] We are accustomed to the trauma motivating the drug-sated Romantic genius of the early nineteenth century, as well as to the sufferings of writers such as Baudelaire and Mallarmé in response to the trials of modernity. In the case of women, drugs also helped someone like de Staël work through to the past, yielding what I will investigate here as "narcohistory." Other women writers, similarly positioned in the field of trauma, devised different but no less important strategies that yielded well-read histories of queenship and notable women, of culture, travel, and social life, as part of a major, uncharted, and gendered tradition.

Leading historians have suggested that good, even analytic history inspires emotion and that in so doing it may serve important psychological functions. Because the past serves up accounts of violent events that are over, Hayden White claims, readers (including scholars) can let their violent fantasies roam freely when doing history.[19] In a somewhat different set of observations, Dominick LaCapra maintains that cognitively dealing with traumatic events can help "work through" the disabling emotions associated with them.[20] Just as these scholars have recently come to problematize our relationship to the history of war and the Holocaust, so we might look at the work of women amateurs in the context of new ideas about the relationship among cognition, emotion, and the psyche. Incessant writers often to the point of graphomania, indefatigable gatherers of information during perilous times, overworked and exploited contributors to flagging household economies, deprived of political and property rights, women historians produced a stream of cultural and social histories and accounts of queenship and notable women. This repetitive historical focus on superficial subjects needs investigation in epistemological and psychological terms.

What has prevented us from considering the work of women amateurs and their relationship to the development of intellectual and political womanhood is a historiography that eradicates amateurism to tell a singular story of professionalism's high accomplishments. In contrast, interlacing men's and women's historical work shows how professionals constructed their standards of excellence by differentiating themselves from a low, unworthy, and trivial "other."[21] Several generations of young classicists, expert in Latin and Greek and brutally trained to appreciate the nuances of words, laid the foundations for reform of the field. Beaten in school for mistakes with words in the recondite classics, professionalizers came to fetishize the written document, devaluing everyday objects and artifacts, and emphasizing their shared, lofty male identity as experts who were beyond ordinary life, just as their work was beyond the comprehension of the ordinary intellect and beyond domestic, feminine matters. Historical "scientists" set up polarities between professionalism and amateurism, between political history and cultural trivia, between the spirit and the body—polarities in which the latter term was always inferior to the former.[22] It was in dialogue with the more popular amateur vision—that is, with femininity, everyday life, and their attendant superficiality—that historical science took shape as a matter of national importance, as gender-less universal truth, and simultaneously as a discipline mostly for men.

Until recently, the idea of a universal truth reflected by the mirror of history has been compelling in Anglophone circles. Historians of science, however, provide evidence that the sciences do not just reflect in some neutral way but that practices and tools (such as looking in a mirror, and the very mirror itself) help shape the discipline, its ideas of truth, its practitioners, and its readers.[23] Procedures, professional behavior, and scholarly practices have been definitional, and never more so than in the creation of professionals in the field of history. Women wrote endlessly, managed childbirths, families, and political catastrophe while doing so, and haggled with publishers for terms; they acted out history in *tableaux vivants,* canvassed an odd assortment of documents, repositories, and informants for material, and tried to make this material vibrant in travel books and historical novels. Professionals, in contrast, focused on seminar training and imaged themselves as archival researchers interacting with authentic, if dusty, documents. These male adepts also practiced history more privately at home, enlisting mothers, wives, children, sisters-in-law, cousins, and other female relatives to do the work of researching, filing, editing, and even writing. All credit went to the male author. These works by the singular male professional as the most credible narrator of the past, and the attendant erasure of contributions by their women relatives and women amateurs, are another part of the gendering of historical science. A historian is often seen as unproblematic: a well-trained expert. In this book I will look at the professional historian's connections to suppressed work and "inferior" accounts. In the process, I will explore the hypothesis that professionalism is a relationship dependent on discredited voices and de-valued narratives.

Insights borrowed from anthropology, literary criticism, and philosophy have guided contemporary inquiries into the linguistic and methodological development of the new science and profession of history. Since Wittgenstein, we have known that language and understanding are fragmented into linguistic communities, and more recently the philosopher Mary Hesse has shown in great detail how metaphorical thinking has helped scientists to make their breakthroughs and advance their careers. These metaphors nourish the formulation of new ideas, providing a language in which scientists can reconceptualize problems or settle issues.[24] The mirror has been a helpful metaphor for explaining how history operates, and gender was necessarily involved as part of defining professionals against the low and amateurish. Images of femininity and sex served, surprisingly, to advance historical work, untangle historical knots, and incite fantasies about the past. Thus, I will look particularly at the way in which both the language of the body and sexuality became crucial to establishing the coherence-conditions for breakthroughs in the field. Even such important but simple terms as "facts," "detail," and "reality" were explicitly interwoven with sex and gender.

Since the profession has evolved on such a gendered basis, questions arise about the first women professionals who received university training in Britain and the United States, from the 1870s on. Would they perform as professionals and thus as "men"? Could they somehow makes themselves disembodied, despite women's collective persona in the Victorian period as "the sex"? Could they avoid the taint of amateurism, especially since amateurism was flourishing by the end of the century? Most of these women stayed single, disassociated themselves from the personal and financial dependency that marriage automatically brought, and consequently had to carry on their work without the vast household support that helped produce the male professional. Simultaneously during the second half of the century, amateur history written by women flourished, and not only expanded its range of travel literature, social history, and cultural accounts but also adopted new fields such as the cultural study of the Renaissance. Many of these developments have been interpreted as part of various national traditions stemming from ethnic anxiety, cultural malaise, and the like. I read them differently: as continuing the traumatic figurations of earlier work, while molding them into a distinct genre. More dramatically, suffragists and other feminists, social investigators, and reformers began probing the past to produce accounts of women's lesser economic and political experience and to chart the rise of movements for change.

This is the story of women professionals' intriguing and still-uncharted relationship both to amateurism and to historical science's bodily tropes, sexual metaphors, and gendered values—correlates of the archival research they undertook and the objectivity they valued. Did professional women historians and those with university training have a deep or superficial regard in the mirror of history? Was their work inflected by the status of the private sphere and its attendant demands for propriety and virtue? The account of women's performance as historians in the late nineteenth century, amid the development of professionalization and feminism, will start to blur the story.

Assuming a malleable, plastic identity, women historians played as great a part in historical modernism as gender did in the construction of modernism in general. Professionalism had involved control of the mirror of history by university men, whose founding practices depended on discrediting the historical vision of outsiders as feminine and thus "low." What would happen when different practitioners—including those from the "inferior" sex and the "inferior" races, backed by considerable professional expertise—came to engage history in a noticeable way? For much of the nineteenth century, at a time of minimal electoral participation, historical subject matter had concentrated on elites and on the functioning of government at the highest levels. But in the years prior to World War I, the white male electorate in the West rapidly expanded, while growing consumerism and advances in communications media furthered the development of mass society. A mass suffrage movement, the attendant repeal of laws that had awarded women's wages and property to men, and a rapidly falling birthrate were all challenges to traditional ways of producing gender. Commitment to certain hallowed aspects of professional male identity unraveled as a result of these changes. Redefining themselves, such disparate male historians as Benedetto Croce, Karl Lamprecht, Johan Huizinga, Henry Adams, and Henri Berr expanded their range to include the history of culture, economic life, and a commitment to "synthesis" and "aesthetics" instead of facts and details. Their work became modernist, but no less sexed and gendered than that written in previous eras, even though they questioned the centrality of facts, archival research, and elite political history. They helped construct the modern historian's persona, making it far more visible in the mirror of history.

Women historians performed no differently, becoming modernist in their turn. Literary critics have seen in modernist metaphors and concerns both gender definition and a gender blurring that offered the possibility for more equitable literary, social, and professional practices.[25] Women, according to such scholars, are emblematic in a way that is more liberating than that offered by Victorian concepts of separate spheres. Technology, primitivism, parody, and other aspects of modernism provided openings that women scholars took, with varying degrees of success. Lucy Maynard Salmon, Eileen Power, Jane Ellen Harrison, and Mary Beard were unique historians, but each produced history and historical personae that constitute a hitherto neglected element of our profession's modernism.

Although studies of history as a profession often follow fantasies of male historiographic parthenogenesis, of an exclusively male subject of historical truth, and of the importance of male-defined procedures and topics, this book explores multiple practices, impulses, cognitions, and subject matter that men and women have interactively devised out of a socially built and cognitively expressed alterity.[26] It examines how, between 1800 and 1940, they struggled over definitions of historical significance; how they variously imagined historical topics and meaning; and how they produced scholarly selves out of historical practices and the iteration of historical rules. There was no "one" without the "other." Nonetheless, despite the contentious centrality of gender, the "singular" tale of historiography, historical reality, and professional advance endures and remains a staple for most of us. It is time for a version of historiography that acknowledges gender—a version that will allow us to refurbish our mirror on the past.

The Narcotic Road to the Past   1

Historiography crystallizes around the figure of a historian and his work, mapping a cluster of distinguishing themes, strategies, and breakthroughs. He himself serves as an intellectual hero, whose unified character has been purged of contradictory or confusing material. The virtues of such a presentation are legion, allowing us to identify with a great character, to find coherence in vast amounts of written work, and to imagine so vividly that we are intellectually inspired to innovations of our own. History by and about women, however, has called into question the focus on "worthies" as jejune and elitist, and these criticisms are important.[1] Because one such "worthy"—Germaine de Staël—figured so large in the North American and European historiographic imagination, it nonetheless seems essential to deal with her and in so doing introduce the historiographic, biographical, and "worthy" contours of our science.

In de Staël's case the unity imputed to her writing centers on the enlightened constitutionalism and liberalism she championed, both of which are bound up with the proclivities of her parents and manifested in her own activism.[2] Such a unity can have its pitfalls, however, by encouraging us to imagine someone in inappropriately clear ways that do a real disservice to complexity.[3] Historiography advances by charting coherent selves and their coherent sets of ideas. But there may be instances when it should not: de Staël, credited with shaping an early liberal trajectory for the history of the French Revolution, had a far more problematic set of historical values than is generally assumed. For one thing she unabashedly promoted herself as a "genius" at doing history, and then deployed this identity in a number of remarkable books that were grounded in historical work: *Corinne, ou l'Italie* (*Corinne, or Italy*); *Dix années d'exil* (*Ten Years of Exile*); *De l'Allemagne* (*On Germany*); and even *Considérations sur les événements principaux de la Révolution française* (*Considerations on the Principal Events of the French Revolution*). For almost the entire nineteenth century this model of "genius" inspired women writers and feminists, who modeled themselves and many of their fictional protagonists after de Staël. But "genius" is a word rarely associated anymore with good history, whose watchwords are "research" and "facts." The hardworking researcher, sometimes crabbed by archival toil but wielding a wealth of knowledge, is supposed to disappear in scholarly discourse, allowing scientifically constructed truth its day. In contrast, a genius, flashing inspired insights, is far more intrusive—to the professional mind, unpleasantly so. We might have even more difficulty imagining genius when it comes to women historians: genius implies uniqueness, originality, and unprecedented creativity, whereas women have traditionally been characterized as derivative, secondary, and merely competent. At the time de Staël wrote, this meaning of "genius," "an inexplicably and uniquely creative individual," was replacing its older sense, "a presiding spirit," as in Chateaubriand's *Génie du Christianisme* (*Genius of Christianity*). Moreover, in the late eighteenth century "genius" reacquired its ancient overtones of divine madness and frenzy; thus, it became increasingly dangerous for professional women to adopt the pose of genius, once the field of psychology came to characterize femininity as the prototype of madness.[4] De Staël's genius offers challenges to the historiographic tradition that make her case instructive in our effort to understand the dynamics of gender.

In 1807 Germaine de Staël, most often associated with constitutional and rational political aspirations, published her novel *Corinne*—a striking depiction of historical sensibility constructed around a woman's genius. In one scene, the heroine, a poet and patriot whose eloquent accounts of the glories and misfortunes of the Italian people move even the hardest hearts, orates at the Capitol on the history of Rome. In de Staël's rendering, genius soars beyond special giftedness or quantifiable intelligence: it is the ineffable in human form, publicly and responsibly acted out, but often troubled and at times deadly. The Roman intelligentsia—just as it once did with Petrarch and Tasso—crowns Corinne with laurels, launching her into the tumultuous multitude in the surrounding streets to receive tribute for her insights into Italian character, history, and civic traditions. A Scottish lord, Oswald, happens to be in the crowd, and he too falls under Corinne's spell. She travels with him throughout Italy, all the while continuing her narrative of Italian history. Eventually Oswald returns to England and marries someone more conventional, thereby contributing to Corinne's death. In this work, de Staël claimed historical genius for women and herself, showing both for better and for worse how it operated in recounting the past.

Even for a historian the consequences of choosing an identity can be dramatic, and in this regard *Corinne,* in which a celebrated woman recounts history as a self-proclaimed genius, is one of the fateful books of early nineteenth-century Europe. On the one hand, it personified genius, situating it in a life, and made Germaine de Staël lionized internationally: "Corinne" and "de Staël" were associated with genius for much of the century.[5] On the other hand, the conflation of genius and woman writer made for a variety of other emotional responses, including the kind of anger and confusion that often result from claims to outstanding accomplishment by women. De Staël was labeled with the unflattering epithet *homasse* ("man-woman"), while her works, though lauded by many, were sometimes denigrated as chaotic, neither history nor fiction. With the publication of *Corinne,* de Staël became further hated by Napoleon, who liked his history (and presumably his geniuses) unambiguously military and manly. Even in exile on Saint Helena, the defeated emperor felt a compulsion to reread the novel, but it merely reinforced his anger: "I detest that woman."[6]

The depiction of this anomalous woman genius has been a conflicted legacy to women historians ever since. For almost a century, biographies of de Staël poured off the presses, from Norway and Germany to the United States. Many of these biographers agreed with the American writer Lydia Maria Child: de Staël was "intellectually the greatest woman that ever lived."[7] In this reading of de Staël, she was an exemplar whose memory was powerful long after her death, a resonance that could fuel women's ambition. In the twentieth century, however, that appreciation was muted as women became more professionalized: "Let us try to take *Corinne* seriously," Ellen Moers wrote in her cruel analysis of what the portrait of Corinne and her creator meant to women intellectuals in the nineteenth century.[8] To contemporary women like Moers, the performance of genius was an embarrassment, a display of narcissism, an exaggeration. Not only do many women today still equate history with rationality and men, but as professionals occupying serious places in the academy they quite understandably find the term "genius," especially as de Staël embodied it, difficult to accept.[9]

Still other contemporary historiographers *ignore* the inspiration that the depiction of women's historical genius might have provided for early nineteenth-century writers. Suppressing evidence of the "divine frenzy," they insist on republican commitment as the common ingredient in women writers' biographies. Not genius but virtue, they claim, provided the salutary vantage point from which to write history, because it valorized women's disinterested position outside the political sphere.[10] Such an explanation of women's historical work in the so-called "age of revolution" is persuasive: republicanism allowed them to envision themselves as important truth-tellers and witnesses. But why has the notion of women writers as improvers and republican mothers been so compelling as to erase the dramatic portrayal of women as absolute geniuses at history?

By today's standards, de Staël was too bizarre as a historian. To put it bluntly, drugs and the body were two of her chosen vehicles to historical truth; and she wrote not in some well-appointed private study but on the road in the chaos of flight and exile. Moreover, de Staël—like Corinne—was profligate, not chaste; excessively rich, not poor. So although nearly from the beginning many wanted to claim de Staël for intellectual womanhood, her narcotic and erotic approach to the past makes it difficult for professionals today to identify with her in any conventional sense. Women's historical genius as depicted by de Staël may be so incomprehensible and unpleasant a notion as to prevent our access to it, once professionalism has defined our methodology. On the one hand, she wrote before our modern historiographic paradigms had taken shape; but on the other, she has been most susceptible to interpretations devolving from our rational practices. In de Staël's case, finding a unified historiographic approach may be simply impossible.

De Staël partially situated herself in the mad world of geniuses, in the pulsating climate of sensual knowledge, and in the traumatic ferment over post-guillotine politics and history. In the guise of Corinne, or in her own authorial voice, she *acted out* what it meant for women to do history and for them to be considered its central practitioners. In her writing, history explicitly confronted the gulf between the living and the dead; it dealt with ghosts and tombs, but also with liberty and community, while it floated along on huge doses of opium. It confronted history with art, music, poetry, and literature and brought men and women together, but also distanced them through that gap called interpretation. History was a mode of comprehension we have left behind in favor of unambiguous knowledge, professionalism, and historical science. Nonetheless, this virtually unique performance of women's genius at work doing history constitutes a specter that must be situated, contextualized, and closely examined as a vestige from a time when gender was seen as explicitly connected to history and when history itself was something other than professionalized knowledge.

A Blurred Genre: Genius and Narcohistory

De Staël fashioned her historical genius from the materials of her time, and Charlotte Smith's "Ode to the Poppy" (1803), which inspired De Quincey and Coleridge, was among them:

> Hail, lovely blossom!—thou canst ease
> The wretched victims of Disease;
> Canst close those weary eyes in gentle sleep,
> Which never open but to weep;
> For, oh! thy potent charm
> Can agonizing Pain disarm!
> Expel imperious Memory from her seat,
> And bid the throbbing heart forget to beat.

Smith alluded to a human psyche so pained by history that it needed an antidote to quiet its torment. In this regard, the poem opened onto the ingredients of history before its practitioners had fashioned themselves as professional knowers in control of their data. In those days, history often bespoke an intense sensibility, shrouded overpoweringly bitter memories, and saw itself in relation to the dead, not to past time in the form of professional knowledge. Michel Foucault has shown how, during the revolutionary period, the human sciences developed as a form of knowledge that itself enables the exercise of power by knowers.[11] But this was not the history practiced by de Staël, or by any of the other self-styled geniuses of her day who have been described inadequately as Romantic.

As the nineteenth century opened, archival research was by no means the universally accepted road to historical truth, nor was the seminar the premier way of instilling sophisticated historical knowledge. Between 1750 and 1830, male historians were most likely to have been trained as jurists and theologians; or they were bankers and bureaucrats who wrote merely as an avocation. Moreover, historical practices and impulses were expressed in a variety of ways that had not been reduced to a formal method, and historians themselves had, as yet, little institutional power. Alongside the meticulous research of the Benedictine monks and the development of scholarly methods and pedagogy at the University of Göttingen, for instance, were the colorful historical novels of Walter Scott, the Porter sisters, and Sophie Cottin.[12] Scholarly editions of texts at one end of the spectrum and novels at the other were both considered history.

Thus, in its pedagogy, audience, methodology, and practices, history was less disciplined in the early years of the nineteenth century than it was in later generations, because in this age of revolution the content and focus of history were less settled. German Romantics found historical traces in monuments, folktales, language, and ancient ruins, while another cohort of historians emphasized written evidence. For still others, evidence hardly mattered at all. The style of historical writing was also undetermined. History could take the form of epic poetry, as in the work of Lucy Aikin; the historical play was a popular form; and a few proto-professional historians were even coming to see journalism as a historical medium, as well as a rival. Many of these conventions, procedures, and tendencies remain vital to certain historical writers even today.[13]

Just as unsettling, the nineteenth century opened amid painful memories of revolutions, confusion about the terms of historical representation, and uncertainty about which past would be written. History's representations were at once ceremonial and performative, both artistically presented (as in the great neoclassical paintings that were popular both before and during the revolutions) and part of everyday life (when historical and patriotic scenes appeared on dishes and buttons, connecting artisanal production with politics). Historical writing sometimes took the form of sober tracts, paeans to heroes like Washington, or (Napoleon's favorite) thumping histories of battles and bygone military leaders.[14] But like memoirs of the U.S. loyalists, the Vendéens, or old courtiers, much of the past remained haunted, immanent in the present, even bitterly intrusive.

In those tumultuous and uncertain days, historical authorship for de Staël encoded a particular relationship to a difficult past that was not "knowledgeable." Dealing with the past always involves a relationship to what is gone or lost, but this can differ wildly, depending on authorial positionings. Writing in the midst of unprecedented war and revolution, de Staël shared with many in her generation a sensibility connected not only with the times but especially with the use of opium. Although writers chronicled the use of morphine, opium, and laudanum as part of Romantic genius, few folded it so tellingly into historical practice as she did.[15]

Corinne tells the history of Italy, defeated and dismembered like Germany and ultimately France, whose histories de Staël would chronicle as well. In those days the past afforded only traumatic mysteries—incomprehensible and uncanny—of which the greatest was precisely the status of the dead.[16] Standing near the ruins of Pompeii, Corinne observes: "What a long time has man existed! What a long time has he lived, suffered, and perished! Where can his feelings and thoughts be found again? Does the air we breathe in these ruins still bear their trace, or are they forever lodged in heaven where immortality reigns?" (204).[17] The historian did not search for knowledge and facts but rather undertook to bridge a gap, to tend a painful wound that came from suffering and death. Italy's history, for example, revealed a past grandeur, and according to de Staël its future (because of this past) promised greatness as well. But between the past and the future came the near-past and the present, which constituted a string of misfortunes, an unfathomable abyss blocking access to the splendid lives of the dead Italians. It was here that de Staël situated herself in the quest for understanding. "Mystery" and "misfortune" such as Italy's would be "understood through imagination rather than through . . . critical judgment" (17). Bridging the gap and probing misfortune required the powers of emotion and imagination—the genius of the interpreter. "Of all my gifts," says Corinne, "the most powerful is the gift of suffering" (75).

Historical genius entailed a set of emotions, psychic states, and bodily feelings that present-day historians have rejected in their well-trained quest for historical knowledge. De Staël acknowledged the realm of historical erudition when she had Corinne elaborate the virtues of written history and scholarship and the "pleasure found in research both learned and poetic" (72). But erudition alone was simply inadequate. Although instructed in books herself, Corinne supplements them with the study of music, monuments, architecture, horticulture, the visual arts, tombs, and many other artifacts. She makes Oswald listen to the sounds of Alfieri and Tasso, look closely at the Colosseum and the Bridge of Sighs, and explore the hues in her collection of historical paintings. "Readings in history, the thoughts they provoke, do not act upon our souls like these scattered stones, these ruins interspersed with buildings," Corinne explains as they take in the panorama of Rome from the Capitoline hill. "Eyes are all-powerful over the soul; once you have seen Roman ruins, you believe in the ancient Romans as if you had lived among them" (64). To Corinne, seeing in this way is also a matter of contrasts, for the uncanny spectacle of Rome is one in which ruins of ancient monuments stand beside a peasant's cottage, thus evoking "an inexplicable mixture of great and simple ideas" (65). The immense baths, aqueducts, and obelisks serve both as ways to access the past aesthetically and as symbols of the past as difference and gap: "The genius of ideal beauty seeks to console man for the real and true dignity he has lost" (67).

For de Staël, history depended on the genius' painful perception of irreconcilability and incommensurability, and on her constant endeavor to bridge the unbridgeable. "These great Roman lords are as distant now from the luxurious pomp of their ancestors as their ancestors were from the austere virtue of the Romans under the Republic" (86). Thus, a deep sense of difference drove the genius' historical sensibility—a sense of the difference between the humble and the mighty, the vanquished and the victors, the dead and the living. This irreconcilable disparity was not tamed by knowledge or made "real" by a convincing narrative, but was manifested in the presence of ghosts, specters, and other haunting apparitions. The atmosphere of Italy, as Corinne explains, is charged with death: "The air you breathe seems pure and pleasant, the earth is cheerful and fertile, the evening is deliciously cool and refreshing after the burning heat of the day—and yet all of that is death" (88). In the early nineteenth century, death, representing history's immanence, was always on hand.

One saw it in the tombs that depicted ancient Romans and their customs, in the prophets and sibyls painted on the ceiling of the Sistine Chapel, looking "like ghosts enshrouded in the dusk." The "funereal," the "ghostly," "cold sensation," images of "those who will precede us on our way to the grave" (180) infused not only the content of monuments, buildings, literary texts, and the arts but their evanescent or partial (ruined) form as well. History pulsated with death.

The historical genius of Corinne imbibes the past as painful, funereal loss in the ordinary course of life in her time. De Staël was not alone, however, in offering this historical vision. "One moonlight night . . . I was walking in the Colosseum full of sublime thoughts [when] a voice, distinct, but like that of a flute, said 'I am one of the Roman deities!'" This particular experience was reported in the 1819 journal of Humphrey Davy—a brilliant chemist, a friend of de Staël's, and, like her, a regular user of opium.[18] The sense of history as a ghostlike immanence or sensual presence (a flute-like voice) ran like a current through a certain elite experience. Davy noted other reflections similar to those animating *Corinne* as he gazed at the ruins of Tintern Abbey: "Thousands of thoughts . . . had rolled through the minds of a hundred intelligent beings—I was lost in a deep and intense social feeling . . . Nothing remains of them but mouldering bones; their thoughts and their names have perished. Shall we, too, sink in the dust?" Yet Davy's reflections, like those of de Staël, led him to conclude hopefully that the dead lived on in those "deep and intense feelings" which one had for society and nature and which ultimately produced an exalted historical sensibility.[19] One got this refreshment from opium: it created a prosthetic relationship to the past, played out as the complexity of genius.

Drugs relieved the pain of loss felt by geniuses like de Staël, while simultaneously enhancing the vision that was so critical a part of their powers.[20] It was in the opium dream that brilliant experiences of mnemonic truth often occurred. Indeed, addicts touted the dream's superior insights and greater reliability. The intellectual dreamer penetrated the heart of misfortune, sorrow, and suffering and then awoke to note the dream's insights, which would later be incorporated into the work of art or history. (Sir Walter Scott was said to have created brilliantly true characters in *The Bride of Lammermoor* because he composed it while taking massive quantities of laudanum—an opium-based narcotic.) But if opium provided access to the historical spirit, allowing one to narrate more vividly, it did so under specific conditions that colored the written work. Most notably, the opium dreamer accessed truth with the help of a guide, a deity, a double, or, as Davy found, a "genius" of the times (an Ancient Mariner, a Kubla Khan). Thus, the genius Corinne, like the vision in an opium dream, takes Oswald (and likewise guides the reader) through Italian history. Under the influence of opium, the dream produced an authority about the past—the historian—whom one followed and even questioned about the meaning of history.

Accompanied and aided by his authority or genius, the opium dreamer thus saw himself touring, seeing, stretching closer to truths that seemed beyond his grasp or his capacity to endure. Indeed, Oswald constantly marvels at the inspired way in which Corinne explains the past, how she sees higher to track human aspirations and reaches deeper into history's foundations than he can. But it is the doubling of the historical process that we need to consider, alongside the creation of a visible historical genius. Corinne is a historical authority who is a woman, and female authorities were not unusual in opium dreams. She is also a genius with a pupil, an audience, and thus a society—all of them necessary for plumbing the depths of historical understanding. The opium dream made visual what was less often the case in reading and writing: it intertwined materializations of the scholarly writer and the reader, the authority and the unlettered. As modernity encroached, these entities increasingly operated in discrete realms, separated by the book, and associated not bodily but mentally. In the opium vision, by contrast, the authority and the unlettered, pain and relief, the living and the dead were fully immanent as the embodiment of difference, of an other, that could both comfort and dismay the dreamer.

In an opium dream, De Quincey and other addicts maintained, one sees only what one is already predisposed to see. The envisioning of a community of intellectuals—a public—was an established ingredient of Enlightenment thought and, like salon life and opium, a critical part of de Staël's biography.[21] Corinne's oratorical eloquence in reciting history brings the community into being, making culture the foundation of the national and the political. *Corinne* reproduces an ancient republican scenario by rejecting the isolation of a modern reading public and evoking instead a polite sociability in which eloquence aggregates individuals and moves them beyond their petty and isolated passions into a realm of heady public virtue. For de Staël, the declamation of history built community and understanding based not on Napoleonic force but on a visualized reciprocity and politeness. "Reasoning and eloquence," she had proposed in an earlier work, "are the natural bonds that hold together a republican association . . . Those who cannot convince must oppress."[22] As in Goya's depictions of the peasant countryside, however, dark forces and mystery now contrasted with the bright rational and republican vision of an earlier time. Davy's opium dream also evoked the republican aggregate in which "thousands of thoughts . . . had rolled through the minds of a hundred intelligent beings—I was lost in a deep and intense social feeling."[23]

The public, however, also produced its other—the historian—in a visceral and visual way, summoning her into being. The audience, in listening to and making great demands on its intellectuals, drove them to mental and oratorical heights impossible to the solitary thinker or isolated author. Indeed, the lack of audience led to intellectual sterility: "When thought is no longer nourished from without, it turns upon itself, analyzing, shaping, burrowing into the inner feelings." By contrast, "encouragement" and "emulation" fueled creativity. "The common run of men gloried in their ability to admire, and so the cult of genius was served by the very people who had no hope of aspiring to its crowns" (143). Corinne's historical powers come from her genius, but that genius flourishes only with an other—an actual audience. Thus, *Corinne* abounds in historical performances in which the genius is fully conscious of her own visualization; she stars in a series of *tableaux vivants*—a form that later in the century became popular for home dramatizations of history. The opium dream enacted this visualization in which the instructing self and the instructed self were doubled and observed by the dreaming self, the creation of the republic and its citizenry resting on a thick layer of theatricality rather than the transparency that theorists have heretofore posited.[24]

Addiction responded to the uncanny, helping re-member the dreadful fragments of the dead. No longer uprooted, Corinne herself joins an associative train of truth-telling geniuses whose stories she intertwines with her own as part of the history of Italy. Sappho, the female Italian professoriat, Corilla, and the Sibyl in whose house Corinne lives provide a lineage for the woman historian. They are the substance from which she springs; they produce and thicken her, instead of making her transparent. Corinne as historian takes on additional density acting amid her historical material, surrounded by a retinue of pupils and an audience, and serving as a link in the chain of women geniuses. Reticulative thinking—typical of a narcotic epistemology—makes history and in this case the historian spring from a web of associations and analogies rather than from a knowledge of dates, details, and facts. This historical genius, fully visualized and enmeshed, is not a slayer of the father, as historians would later become by showing a knowledge superior to that of the preceding generation. Instead, a genealogically cast persona depended on a train of performing women geniuses for her identity.[25]

Reticulative, theatrical, and dreamlike, de Staël's other histories also eschewed the realistic, linear chronicling of war, preferring the world of monuments and tombs, song and poetry. Characters such as Mirabeau, "whose passions enveloped his entire body like Laocoön's snakes," lived in the world of myth, leaving analysis to another generation. Even after the fall of Napoleon, each bloody moment of the French Revolution and subsequent wars was "an abyss" upon which "no one should fix his attention." Wherever these might have come in her narrative, de Staël substituted excerpts from her father's writings or analyses of political fanaticism, making a better, less bloody story. Instead of an account of the gruesome march of the royal family to Paris after the events of October 6, she told of her own family's parallel progress to the capital: "We reached Paris by another route, which spared us the dreadful sight: we went through the Bois de Boulogne, and the weather was uncommonly beautiful: a breeze barely stirred the trees, and the sun was bright enough to leave no shade on the landscape." The unthinkable—the heads and body parts on pikes, the blood flowing at Versailles, the Terror—is not yet recuperable as knowledge: "We looked at the sky and the flowers and reproached them for brightening and perfuming the air at a time of so many sacrifices." Rather, narcohistory generated poetic masks, articulated the unthinkable as romantic difference: "No exterior object corresponded to our grief. How often does the contrast between the beauty of nature and the suffering inflicted by others reappear in the course of one's life!"[26] Sometimes aestheticized and often dreamed about, narcohistory sprang from and displayed the frenzied genius, who lived the unthinkable in her addiction and displayed it as her work.

Historical Erotics

"My coarse imagination has never been able to imagine a creative genius without genitals," Johann Georg Hamann wrote to the historian Johann Gottfried Herder. De Staël, too, attached genitals and a body to genius, in no way prefiguring narcohistory as the transcendent universalism of later scientific history. Corinne's imagination, presenting Italy's mysteries to an audience, was graphically embodied: Corinne's eyes took in the past's monuments, her ears feasted upon its sounds, her body shuddered as she contemplated despotic rulers, and she sighed at tombs and ruins. As Martin Heidegger said about the addict, she lived the outside world—but with this addition: explicitly through the body.[27] The historian's body located the important aspects of the Italian past. Physically, Corinne the historical orator provided the means to bridge all those gaps, reaching across them and filling them in sensually. The embodied historian, perceiving and performing the past, became the missing link that made ruptured oppositions into a recognizable continuum, most importantly by connecting the past to the present. Even in so late a work as her history of the French Revolution, de Staël consistently put herself into the scenario, talking to the (dead) queen, escaping or going into exile with her (dead) parents, and personally experiencing the terrors of August 10, 1792, as had so many others of her class who were massacred while she was spared. In *On Germany*, she was always on the scene with Goethe, Kant, or Hegel, an insistent questioner and irrepressible presence. In this presentation, the past and present, the living and the dead, the real and the imaginary, the French and the German formed a panorama only when the historian physically stepped in to resuture time and space. The self-represented body of genius bridged epistemological irreconcilables and existential horrors.

In *Corinne,* genius physically presenting history allows the Italians to reconstitute themselves into a social and public entity. Corinne's voice employs "a variety of tones that did not destroy the sustained charm of the harmony," thus awakening the emotions and establishing a rapport between historian and audience. Her history executes the Romantic project of attaching affect to the narrative of the past, but with a constitutive purpose. Instead of analyzing or recounting, it aims at a poetic summoning of images that will produce physical sensations in the hearer. The physical sound of Corinne's voice reciting history then "sets off an emotion in the listener as vivid as it is unexpected," and creates a further tie between historian and audience, but also among the individuals who make up the audience (31–32). In addition, the enacted and embodied epistemology of her performances ultimately persuade her Italian audience of their (and her) own genius. Italians visually and aurally drink in, comprehend, and approve her recapitulations of the past. The community (the nation) physically materializes around its reception of the physical performance of the past, as Corinne's body not only reenacts but recirculates the past to a like-minded audience of Italians. History as rhetoric, as performance, as embodied immanence fills the interstices among individuals, gluing them into a sensible unity. Bodies replace an imagined readership, a transparent citizenry, and a disappearing narrator in this still-unexamined and unique depiction of the republic.[28]

The history of Italy figures not only bodily but erotically as part of a struggle over historical interpretation. The horizon of historical understanding of Oswald, Corinne's English lover, diverges from hers. Here is another abyss in which history, nationality, gender, and epistemology are intertwined in one way for Oswald and in another for the genius Corinne. Oswald proposes that reason alone shows the fundamental superiority of English institutions as they have developed over time. Whereas Corinne gives each culture (French, Greek, Italian, and so on) its due by marking out its distinctive national history and character, Oswald remains locked for the most part to a reasoned, singular identity by using political institutions as the sole standard for historical evaluation. Corinne, in contrast, gives historical weight to a cornucopia of successes (in the arts, religion, sociability). The tension in their relationship stems precisely from their competing historical standards, and as they travel throughout Italy, each looks at the Italian past and then tries to persuade the other of the virtues of his or her interpretation.

History, in *Corinne*, is thus erotic, consisting in an intense relationship of telling-to-the-other, and negotiating different understandings of the past with an other, without necessarily producing resolution. For de Staël, as for many Romantics of her age, history involved a kind of interpretation or hermeneutics based on establishing an association with the past that was not necessarily one of identity. The past as "other" fit into a necessarily imperfect I-thou association of subject-object distinctions in which gaps and disaggregations abounded precisely because of differentiation between the self and the other. But the hermeneutical situation extended to personal situations too, according to Romantics and philosophers, and indeed the hermeneutic was explained in personal terms. Individuation or the distinct person or subject materialized only in relationship to someone else—an other—who was exemplified most often as a sexual partner.[29] Further subject-object relations existed—those between the self and society, the self and the state, the self and the family, the present and the past, and so on. Thus, de Staël drew on and compounded subject-object oppositions—Corinne and Oswald, the living and the dead, history and fiction, men and women—making an intensely charged hermeneutical (that is, erotic) situation, and at the same time one in which individuation resided in a complex web of multiple "others."[30]

Such an erotics structured most of de Staël's writing. In *Considerations on the Principal Events of the French Revolution,* her descriptions of great historical actors consisted of tense interrogations of their motives and character in a dizzying back-and-forth movement of narrative and evaluation, their words against hers. *On Germany* reported her probing conversations with philosophers, historians, and other intellectuals. The tension in these works, the disaggregation, and the manifest erotic charge they produced in readers, from Napoleon to Elizabeth Barrett Browning, remained effective in the West until the late nineteenth century. Male and female pitch their differences to each other, anxious for understanding and definition. The state and the individual, as well as history and fiction, vie for control of the narrative: Will it be dominated by the study of Italy, or by the love story? In hermeneutical history, the relative identity of entire nations entered into play. Readers came together to form de Staël's community, aroused not just by virtue but by her erotic genius.

In *Corinne,* the perpetuation of the hermeneutic, including cultural plurality, cosmopolitan heterosexuality, generic indeterminacy, and the reconciliation of life and death, means that one must accept incommensurability, or difference: one must accept that loss will never be totally recuperated, though one might enjoy a vision of the panoramic sweep of things in dramatic reinterpretations. Both the paradoxical situation and the suspension of determinacy further entail the cohabitation of reason (that is, Oswald's historical reality) with Corinne's own embodied, sensual epistemology. So long as the couple focus on the telling of history and the conduct of their relationship along these complex, argumentative, and unsettled lines, narrative has endless possibilities. By contrast, it is always clear that the triumph of Oswald's absolute standards will mean his withdrawal from her eclectic hermeneutic, leading to the couple's separation—an end to erotics. Indeed, this happens when Oswald finds his dead father's letter portraying Corinne, whom the father had once met, as a poor marriage choice. Oswald endows this document, foreshadowing the grip of written evidence on historical science, with ultimate force. Immune from interpretation or questioning, it is the voice of authority and reason, factual history, patriarchy, smug insular nationalism, and the military caste.

In these daunting circumstances, the genius as sensible body offers the only remaining ground of freedom. It alone opens onto the hermeneutic and is posed against blind obedience to disembodied reason. Through the physically present historian, de Staël, the so-called constitutionalist or liberal, questions Cartesianism and the disembodied rights-bearing acquisitive individual as the fundament of either history or the nation. Ecstatic and free in the moment of historical performance, Corinne's history of Italy draws attention to the female body in the construction of the nation.

One insists that Corinne's genius situates freedom on gendered ground because the hermeneutic is an explicit articulation of difference. In discussing the artistic past, Corinne cites classicism in the historical painting of the eighteenth century as an example of unfreedom. If genius slavishly followed classical principles, "how could genius soar?" she asks. Because the Greeks and Romans are different, she maintains, "it is impossible for us to create the way they did, to invent new ideas in what might be called their territory" (147). In other words, if artists used history to occupy the identical historical space as their forefathers did, they would find themselves fettered and produce mere imitations. Instead, genius and freedom demand difference—the difference in the hermeneutic of genders, nations, the living and the dead. Erotics blocks the singular rule of authority, of a transcendental truth, and of patriarchy because an embodied and performing feminine—its voice, movements, sighing—displays difference just as surely as a disembodied universalism hides it. This de Staël counterposes to any generic or unitary solution to politics and history in terms of "the real," written evidence, and the military hero.

The world of imaginative and cultural history creates a physically manifest republic of letters, where men and women can come together in a hermeneutical quest and where superior women—not just men—can fulfill their destinies. Corinne's genius for history initially uses male-female differences to draw Oswald to her. As they travel to see Pompeii and Vesuvius, he recognizes "the generous thoughts that nature and history inspire" (206), while she comes to appreciate "the northern way" of English customs (301). Ultimately, however, his adherence to traditional English beliefs, especially the notion that women should be silent, blocks the "I" of Oswald from truly engaging the "Thou" of Corinne.

A different community takes shape, built on disaggregation, segregation, and thus the end to genius. As historical storytelling ends, Corinne becomes what Julia Kristeva calls the abject, one who is beyond the community's borders.[31] The ending, in which Corinne dies, shows the difficulties in embodied knowledge: it cannot transcend death but merely reiterates it. This reiteration may have stoked the emotions of several generations of readers, allowing them to mourn more successfully than they could have with professional history. Current debates over writing, addiction, trauma, and melancholy have never figured de Staël in the vast panorama of addicted, embodied, and compulsive writers.[32] One thing, however, is certain: at the end of de Staël's work, death is as irrational as it had always been. Evocations and poetry do not make for a modern knowledge of death and the past; rather, they allow us to drink an overflowing draught of loss.[33] In the early nineteenth century, a reveling in death and loss, along with a drugged, erotic epistemology, became utterly foreign to modern ways of doing history, constituting a negative ground for professionalization.

Exiled from History

De Staël's narcohistory and her erotic epistemology sit uneasily with any conventional understanding of her enlightened liberalism, and perhaps this is why the many analyses of her work have ignored the way both the body and drugs figure in her writing. Even her approach to political history—which is usually attributed to her "natural" interest in politics as the daughter of Jacques Necker (reforming banker and minister to Louis XVI) and Suzanne Curchod Necker (a serious *salonnière*)—has bizarre, even incompatible ingredients that have been written out of her life.[34] Holding her own salon, like her mother ("I raised my daughter to be Emile, not Sophie," Suzanne Necker announced), she knew everyone from Talleyrand to Bonaparte and thus appears to have participated normally in the world of high politics. De Staël, it is thought, was close to power and wrote about it from that position: an insider, a republican advocate, a citizen.

Such interpretations barely take into account the overwrought and gendered context in which her work was produced. The Age of Revolution traced citizenship, nationality, and national borders with bold, gendered strokes. From the Terror through the time of Napoleon, women's access to the rights of citizenship was sharply curtailed. De Staël was in her early thirties when a serious move was made legally to prohibit women from learning to read and write.[35] Although the attempt failed, the elaboration of male citizenship blossomed with the delineation of nationality as, theoretically, a universal prerogative open to all people. Almost simultaneously with the prohibitions on women's political activity during the Revolution, Mary Wollstonecraft, in her posthumous novel *Maria,* wondered "if women have a country."[36] The case of Germaine de Staël vividly raised the issue of women's citizenship. Born of Swiss parents, emphatically identifying herself as French, married to a Swedish ambassador, exiled from Paris and eventually from many areas controlled by Bonaparte, she in fact often wrote while far from the center of politics and power. A vigilant manager of her family's fortune, de Staël loved the stuff of politics but, constantly in flight from Napoleon's police, was forced to view it from an extreme distance. Thus, while her history showed opium insights and espoused an erotic hermeneutic, it also positioned itself in a geographic and national extraterritoriality unusual for historical writing in the modern period. More often, writers, even when they wrote the history of another country, did so naturally—that is to say, nationally situated in an unnoticeable position.[37]

Such was not the case with de Staël: her historical work conspicuously draws attention to exile and foreigner status. *On Germany* and *Corinne* do not just describe and analyze the accomplishments of foreign countries to pique the reader's interest; both are dramatized as written amid foreign *encounters.* The former explicitly interprets German history and culture to non–Germans, drawing clear boundaries between national groups. As interpreter, present on the scene and self-dramatizing, de Staël comments as a foreigner in their midst. *Corinne* portrays a variety of national observers attesting to the history of Italy: Oswald, his English relative Egermond, his wife and daughter, his dead father, and several minor characters all make observations about the nature of the Italians they have met; the French count d'Erfeuil constantly compares Italy to France on the basis of his travels; even Corinne herself is of two nationalities, and bases her acuity in part on that bifurcated origin when she discusses the histories of Dalmatia, England, Italy, Africa, and other regions. De Staël laces all her works, including these two, with extensive descriptions of travel by coach and on foot.

The narrator de Staël, like her protagonists, initially crosses geographic borders that mark the frontiers of the state. But the more important boundaries are those that come to separate and define populations mentally and culturally. In this regard, de Staël's work contributed to filling in the political boundaries of Europe with cultural markings and thus to furthering national definition. Despite our sense that mental and cultural distinctions are somehow intangible, nonetheless, like most other aspects of her historical writing, nationality for de Staël was a staged and embodied proposition. Her visits to German states and cities to research her book provoked a sensation. Arriving in Weimar in 1803, she inspired extreme admiration in court women and the intelligentsia—so much so, that Schiller initially reassured Goethe that "she is of a piece and has nothing of the strange, false, or pathological about her . . . One can say of her that she perfectly and interestingly represents French intelligence." Her insistent probing and interviewing, however, soon turned her from an object of curiosity representing the French spirit into a troublesome example of the "superficial nature of the French." Goethe, questioned and cajoled in turn, found that "she behaved coarsely, like a traveler sojourning among the hyboreens."[38] Although de Staël could portray herself as a simple, transparent republican with no excessive wants as a guest ("I need only two rooms," she often wrote her hosts), others indeed saw her as a baroque, excessive presence, a performer ostentatiously staged and separated from her natural audience. This foreignness was further visualized in long descriptions of flight and traveling. In *Considerations on the Principal Events of the French Revolution,* she dwells on her own and her family's hasty departures from Versailles, Paris, the Paris suburbs, Belgium, Switzerland, and other venues: "The joy of the entire people that I had just witnessed, my father's carriage pulled by the inhabitants of cities we passed through, women kneeling in the countryside as they saw us pass—nothing makes me feel such vivid emotion." *On Germany* opens with a coach traversing the German countryside, gray and melancholy in its aspect.[39]

So embodied, so staged, and so situated, history invoked the nation as an absence, something that one had lost in one's travel and exile, thus connecting history and nationality differently from scientific narratives. The nation and the dead were located together in a beyond, a realm of difference from which both became haunting presences and ghosts, a realm from which the living were excluded. From this gothic, inverted position, women like de Staël wrote history or staged themselves writing it. Virtuous but never transparent narrators, they wrote in flight, haunted while also chased into exile, treated as pariahs (de Staël certainly was a pariah to Napoleon, and Flora Tristan later used this metaphor to characterize the situation of women in general).[40] Outside, de Staël allowed her adoring women readers to gain a new perspective on their own position as outsiders lacking the stability of a political identity. Thus the use of travel, in which perspective is refocused minute by minute to accommodate the traveler's place in the passing scene.[41]

From this constantly shifting position, national history appeared in another form: not political but cultural, based not on military power but on artistic and intellectual achievement. Outsiders always need to get a grip on culture, and de Staël adduced cultural difference in minute detail. If one could not have political rights, one might still enter the cultural community. The everyday life that one led while in exile, that one had to deal with more deliberately as a stranger, was also foregrounded in de Staël's comments on dress and appearance, the status of women, the comfort of accommodations, and on standards of etiquette. Indeed, in de Staël's history the nation became a more ephemeral presence as compared to its other historical incarnations—a shifting, different cultural entity that one sensed with the body and according to the body's state, in flight and drugged to blot out the pain of exile. The addict, wrote Martin Heidegger, is always ahead of Being; the hermeneuticist must enter into another's horizon of knowledge. So, too, the exiled genius was beyond the ground of her identity.

This version of de Staël as drugged, erotic, and baroque is offered as a fragment—one that must be held in tension with the more familiar depictions of her life and work as rationally and constitutionally inspired. It is part of a constellation that might comprise a Staëlian propsopography of her multiple selves.[42] It seems in de Staël's case that tension and ambivalence among interpretations and fragments is the better alternative: women, she once wrote, are "indeterminate."[43] Too staged to be transparent, she is also too opium-sated, erotic, and conspicuously exiled for her work to be fully reconciled with the rational, republican, and insider de Staël. Moreover, these conflicting pictures, each of them perfectly possible, do not align convincingly enough to form the basis of a knowledge-based or biographical truth. Often unbelievable in her writing and in the baroque, even grotesque aspects of her life, she does not as a character meet the historiographic requirement of miming the real. These excessive, unbelievable qualities made de Staël and her central character, Corinne, embarrassments to Ellen Moers as the contemporary feminist movement began to heat up.[44] Better, she thought, to fix on virtue, rationality, republicanism, and the "achievements" of de Staël in inspiring women writers of the nineteenth century.

It is an irony of de Staël's life that she launched the feminine intellectual hero—that subsequent portraits established her as the quintessential woman worthy, and as the model of female accomplishment. For several decades talented women tried to *be* Corinne, and one senses that they better grasped the complexity of what that meant. Meanwhile, de Staël's descendants began managing the family archives in such a way as to shroud her personal life—with its love affairs, adulterous children, and clandestine marriage—in secrecy. She ultimately became a figure that one had to discover and unmask in order to constitute her as a subject of knowledge, importantly contributing to women's political imaginary as a model. Or she could be read as a familiar type: an eternal return of the sensitive woman of genius, the experienced aristocratic woman, the *salonnière* at the center of international culture. But for all the advantages, the move to a model exemplarity replaced the historical hermeneutic with the dangerous vision of a unique historical character—a female worthy. Despite its political energy, it was simultaneously fraught because a woman author would, like Oswald, reinsert herself into a patriarchal kind of history based not on hermeneutics but on authority, based not on difference but on identity.

An alternative would be to see that, like the history de Staël wrote, some of the lives she led are too inaccessible and too excessive in terms of historiographic models to be comprehensible for us today. Can we begin to appreciate what a narcotic, erotic, and baroque history actually entails, despite initial attempts here to outline its contours? And the word "genius"—doesn't it always serve to describe the indescribable, getting us past the limits of our own understanding to the ineffable? The lack of reconciliation is not the world of historical or biographical modernity, and I do not invoke it in any sentimental way. Rather, it serves for us as the world of the unintelligible, the archaic—which, as Homi Bhabha points out, is a world of the other that both blocks and launches scientific discursivity.[45] Thinking about de Staël can serve to locate that important point where intelligibility has been established, but where it also disappears.

Thus, a search for closure returns us to the hermeneutical studies of Hans-Georg Gadamer, which seem appropriately to point in de Staël's direction: "Only if all these movements which make up the art of conversation—argument, question and answer, objection and refutation . . . —are in vain will the question recur; only then does the effort of understanding become aware of the individuality of the 'Thou' and take account of his [sic] uniqueness."[46] Genius was, according to the hermeneuticists of de Staël's day, that which one always strove—unsuccessfully—to interpret. Before professionalization, historical work was thick with unanswerable questions, contradictory layerings of the progressive and the mysterious, gender and race, imagination and reason, the written and the oral. Invoking these alterities may suggest to some that we can read them both with and against the grain for their sense and contradiction. Such reconciliation, however, would still nod to the world of the comprehensible, which is different from what the preprofessionalized historical writers recognized—that is, an extensive realm of the misunderstood where meaning itself went beyond the tools of well-intentioned minds. Thus, genius, because of the constant state of misunderstanding and final incomprehensibility, launched discursivity, questions, and instability.[47]

Today's informed historian might see a final, alternative ground for definitively interpreting de Staël: colonialism, slavery, and race. Sometime before she reached twenty (around 1785, it is estimated), young Germaine Necker wrote the short story "Mirza," a work with several ingredients familiar to readers of *Corinne:* a misunderstood, exceptional heroine (Mirza) who speaks wisdom in several languages, and a lover who ultimately fails to appreciate her. Only this time the history of gender difference and the horrors of war occur among African ethnic groups; defeat brings enslavement, as the losers are sold by the winners to European traders. The historical trauma resides in the institution of slavery, while the hero, whose sexual unfaithfulness causes Mirza's death, enacts his multiple traumatization through the deterioration of his body, which is brought on both by his enslavement and by his lover's death.[48] His obsession with her tomb, ghost, and other apparitions suggests yet another register in which the archaic played for de Staël.

The reader resists an exclusively imperialist interpretation here as well, although Homi Bhabha's equation of the archaic or unimaginable with imperialism suggests one. It is possible that, long before *Corinne* was written, its extraordinarily wealthy author had already constructed her imaginary archaic in racial, colonizing terms, that race was the ultimate propellant of her historical speech about culture, nationality, and gender, and that *Corinne* was a mere cover for this imperial origin of modern history and heroism. Yet it also seems unnecessary to elide the multiple traumas that launched history in those days, to narrow and thus conquer meaning instead of locating its limits, and in the name of professional knowledge to dispose of the concept of genius.[49] The narcotic, erotic, and painfully wandering road of genius through the land of the dead and their ghosts constitutes a border to the subsequent practices that we employ, marking a place from which rationalism could begin. As such, it is an enticing conquest, but in the long run it still serves as an important limit and control against which professional history would write itself—for good and for ill.

The Birth of the Amateur

2

De Staël's achievement provided some of the definition for a new category of writer—amateurs—who looked to the past. She was their heroine, their model, the genius to which they aspired. In the beginning, many felt the full import of "genius" as she had made it unfold. Margaret Fuller, for example, thought of herself and was known as "the Corinne of New England." Unlike their model, however, many amateurs needed to earn a living, and strove to do so with their essays, biographies, novels, and other historical writings. The Strickland sisters in Britain, Lydia Maria Child in the United States, and many women on the Continent were among the writers since called amateurs. Schooled in professionalism, we have a more or less intuitive sense of what their amateur history consisted of: dramatic narratives, flawed if not wholly inaccurate accounts, often moralistic characterization and emplotment. Amateurs, in our mind, are lesser writers, people whose work holds little interest because it seems so casually or commercially done. The only thing amateur history possibly had to offer, we might hypothesize, was a negative springboard from which such professionalizers as Leopold von Ranke, Lord Acton, Gabriel Monod, and Herbert Baxter Adams could launch a more valued history based on scientific methods. It represents all that we well-trained writers and readers have happily left behind.

Superseded, superficial, and associated more with scribbling women than with men, amateur history from the nineteenth century has been so cloaked in professional disdain as to have drawn relatively little scholarly attention.[1] In order to ignore this embarrassment, most professional women scholars have chosen to see women's history as beginning only in the 1970s: "We invented it," one noted professional said recently, claiming credit for the birth of the field. Where women's writing *is* positively treated, it is done so mostly by literary critics, who continue to emphasize the virtuous, patriotic, religious, and moral inspiration behind such work, connecting it to republicanism and civism in an effort to make it intelligible and worthy in its own right.[2] Amateurs' interest in good government, religion, and domestic probity is sometimes seen as a consequence of a father's, husband's, or brother's political alignment, something natural, derivative, and thus less interesting. Constructing a scenario similar to that used for de Staël, these scholars interpret women's historical writing as aiming to advance the influence of the domestic sphere, and thereby that of women. Even this more positive assessment makes such amateur writers tepid in comparison to women of the barricades, to escaped slaves who fought for their people, and to the active feminists who started building a mass movement.

Depictions of the earnestness and virtue of amateurs have merit, but, as in the case of de Staël, multiple impulses may have shaped their writing, at least in the first half of the nineteenth century. Like de Staël, Stéphanie-Félicité de Genlis, Victorine de Chastenay, Lucy Aikin, Lydia Maria Child, Cristina Belgiojoso, and Johanna Schopenhauer wrote in perilous, traumatic, unsettled times. Few of them, however, were as insulated by wealth and political clout as de Staël was; and we have already seen how feebly these could protect even a woman like her. One cannot write the historiography of the years 1800–1860 without considering the ongoing turmoil that inflected historical work. But a more symptomatic reading of amateurism reveals that amateur history consists of something quite extraordinary: the writing of multiple traumas, and not only those of war and revolution. Considering amateurism along these lines advances our understanding of the gendered nature of modern historiography in the West.

In using the term "trauma," I do not mean to invoke feelings of dismay over victimhood but to suggest a situation, a social, cultural, and political location, from which women wrote. Trauma in most studies is a historical category almost exclusively applied to white men—their experience of war, of the Holocaust, of train (and later automobile and car) voyages and train collisions, and even of such intangible shocks as "modernity." Most historians refuse to concede that the rapes, beatings, incest, and other acts

of violence perpetrated on racial minorities and women have been traumatic, because the abuse is so usual. Arguing to the contrary, the psycholo-
gist Laura S. Brown expands the category "trauma" to include situations
of constant coercion, denigration, and inequality, where the announced
value of the society is equality.[3] If we look at the condition of women from
the American and French revolutions to roughly 1860, we see that articulations of universal equality along with the codification of women's inferiority became particularly acute, that the extreme violence of political
warfare and revolution occur in women's midst and with great effect on
their lives, and that personal violence in institutions such as marriage and
slavery persist.[4] Incidents of traumatic shock, as Freud described them,
leave memory traces that the subject deals with in a variety of ways in an
attempt to reestablish control and wholeness. Vestiges of these excitatory
phenomena in art, language, and behavior manifest linkages to trauma.

A powerful cluster of conditions informed women's historical amateurism, ordering its cognitive boundaries, language, and psychic manifestations. "Perhaps, if this page ever has readers, they will be astonished at the
terror that gripped us," the French historian Victorine de Chastenay
scrawled almost illegibly in her diary of the Napoleonic and revolutionary
years. Mercy Otis Warren filled her account of the American Revolution
with repetitive though unanalyzed allusions culled from her friends' letters
describing bloodshed, conflagrations, and rapes. "It was poverty . . . that
first induced me to become an author," admitted Hannah Adams, the first
published woman historian in the United States.[5] These testimonies draw
attention to the fact that women's published historical writing often served
as a counternarrative or cover to what went on in the violent, tumultuous
lives they led—lives marked by poverty, adultery, out-of-wedlock childbearing, violence, abandonment, and abuse; lives inflected by the twin context of a political discourse of rights and equality and a legal one enslaving,
impoverishing, and despoiling women. This situation produced a particular
historical timbre, a specific methodology, and a rigorous writing for the
market that created a distinctive and influential genre called amateurism.

But where is the trauma in the more well-known histories by amateurs?
There were thousands of engaging, amusing histories of queens (for in-
stance, Elizabeth Benger's biographies of Queen Elizabeth and Anne
Boleyn) and notable women (with Germaine de Staël constituting the

favored subject and with Lydia Maria Child performing as one among many biographers), and prosopographies of them all. And there were lively portraits of social life (for example, the histories by Elizabeth Ellet or Sarah Taylor Austin) and culture, many of which, such as those by Johanna Schopenhauer, took a form variously resembling travel literature. Amateurs also wrote informatively and entertainingly of court life and sometimes, more solemnly, of political events, trying in most cases to sell their works as advantageously as possible to publishers, whose terms often provided their sole means of support. Most early amateurs did *not* turn their work into sober, professional knowledge produced through a set of procedures and practices and based in institutions such as universities, academies, and professional societies.

Recently, scholars have interpreted writing containing repetitive themes, jokes and laughter, and everyday detail as part of a relationship to traumatic experience. But because the term "amateur" has come to connote an accidental state and an inferior literary vocation, an occupation arrived at *faute de mieux*, anything but amateurism's ultimate purposelessness is hard to see. The evidence nonetheless suggests something else for the early nineteenth century: a special initiation into historical practices, a quest for a métier, a constructed tradition, an intelligible epistemology, a politics, a committed striving for public voice—all of this part of the writing of trauma in the Age of Revolution. Whereas in the eighteenth century only a handful of women wrote historical works, this number greatly increased in the first half of the nineteenth century, when hundreds of women—excluded from the growing bureaucracy, the learned and other professions, and an expanding university system that was coming to be based on professional credentialing—wrote and sold books, supported themselves and their families, and were often momentarily lionized for their work. Their story shows how amateurism's superficiality became an integral part of the gendering of history.

Blood of Politics, Bonds of Love

Claims for amateur women's highmindedness has blotted out a more piquant function of their work, taking for inspiration what their writing produced, making effect into cause, and smoothing out a practice that was often frenzied, distraught, and set in the trauma of war, revolution, and the struggle for survival. Victorine de Chastenay (1771–1855), besides her published histories of the Normans, classical civilization, and Asian culture, left a disheveled manuscript of memoirs written in an increasingly stressed and illegible hand. It was begun in 1817, pieced together from notes and other bits of memoirs that had been lost or destroyed amid political chaos and danger. Chastenay included chilling details: pikes bearing heads whose hair was curled with fresh blood; a summons by a stern and ascetic Jacobin official whose words had life-or-death power; Napoleonic bureaucrats threatening dire punishment for royalist friendships. "I enter into personal details only to give a better idea of the situation in France, which participated in an immense struggle."[6] Mercy Otis Warren agonized when her son's leg had to be amputated because of a wound sustained during the American Revolution, when another son died en route to Europe, and when still another was killed in a frontier battle against Indians.[7] Johanna Schopenhauer, whose son blamed her for somehow causing her husband's suicide, wrote grim stories of the invasion of Danzig during the revolutionary and Napoleonic wars.[8]

Some, like the English writer Helen Maria Williams, sought out the excitement: Williams settled in Paris to compose journalistic accounts of the French Revolution.[9] After producing a respectful biography of Queen Elizabeth and a fourteen-volume anthology of women's writings in the 1780s, Louise Keralio-Robert edited her own newspaper and authored the sanguinary *Les crimes des reines de France* (*Crimes of the Queens of France*, 1792) at the height of the revolutionary fervor.[10] Late in the 1820s the Italian activist Cristina Belgiojoso escaped the police, and wrote her many histories from exile in Paris and other parts of Europe.[11] In 1848 the American writer Margaret Fuller, like Jessie White Mario and Belgiojoso, journeyed to Italy and sent back reports from Rome of the way French troops were spilling blood in the streets and killing women and children in their beds. The wounded were dragged into airless basements, and homes were brutally invaded in the search for suspected revolutionaries. "I could not feel much for myself, though now the musket balls and bombs began to fall around me also."[12] Participating in the abolitionist movement, Lydia Maria Child was roughed up more than once by bullies among the opposition, who seemed to relish beating up women. Few women analyzed the particular violence in which they were enmeshed, but most of them could not avoid the tumult, whether of Luddite riots, war, political revolution, or the extreme social dislocation that accompanied industrialization and economic modernization. American women's poetry was one type of "memorializing" that covered the American Revolution, the War of 1812, the forced relocation of the Cherokees, war with Mexico, struggles against slavery, and the ongoing violence involved in pushing westward. It contained images of "clotted gore," burning homes, flowing blood, filth, stains, swords, rapes, and perishing children.[13]

At the same time, revisions in the rules for gender in Western society were taking place—revisions that further contextualize the work of intellectual women. The cultural, economic, and political disabilities of women mounted and became strikingly clear in the early decades of the nineteenth century, when the rhetoric of equality echoed across revolutionary and postrevolutionary society. As the language of rights resonated ever more loudly, new legal codes stripped women of their property, the independent right to work, the wages of their work, their civil status as plaintiffs and witnesses, custody of children, sexual autonomy, and even the right to determine where they would live. "One can tell by its laws on women," went the complaint against the influential and highly coercive Napoleonic Code (1803–1804), "that it was written by a man."[14] If women were not deliberately kept uneducated, the French newspaper *Athénée des Dames* noted in 1808, "one would see them marching in the same ranks as men."[15] Mary Wollstonecraft was writing a series of works bitterly chronicling the legal disabilities of women, while Judith Sargent Murray was urging improvement through education.[16] In a rare show of pique, Agnes and Elizabeth Strickland commented on the good fortune of Queen Katherine Parr and her charges, the princesses Mary and Elizabeth, not to have lived as vilified "bluestockings" in the nineteenth century. "The acquirements of ladies were regarded as their glory, not their reproach . . . In later centuries individual ignorance has succeeded in flinging the brand of vulgar opprobrium on such women as Sir Thomas More, Erasmus, Udall, and Ascham all but deified."[17]

A few historians joined the Stricklands in articulating how deeply they felt these disabilities. The English author Mary Berry edited the papers of Horace Walpole, wrote biography and history, and traveled extensively, thus keeping a sharp eye on sites where naval battles were about to occur in the early decades of the century. She sensed national peril in the persistence of revolutionary movements ("my country tottering on its basis"), and was often on the spot for violent events such as the destruction of all the trees in the Tuileries by allied troops, or the assassination of the duc de Berri. Yet virtually throughout her life, and despite her adequate means, she also felt the double blow of her father's lost inheritance and of being born a woman. "I suffer from what I am, from what I have been, from what I might have been, and from what I shall never be."[18] Born four decades after Berry, Margaret Fuller suffered intense migraines, and lamented that she would never have a good life because of her "man's ambition with a woman's heart." "How can a woman of genius love and marry?" she asked. "A man of genius will not love her; he wants repose."[19] Although the frustration was not always expressly articulated, men's privileges and women's disadvantages battered female intellectuals.

Legally induced poverty provoked much amateur writing, and this further distanced these writers from the leisured gentility that was taken as the norm for middle-class women. Catharine Macaulay, Germaine de Staël, Mercy Otis Warren, and Daniel Stern were all patricians of varying wealth, birth, and social position, but most other amateurs lacked funds and desperately sought them with their writing. Women's historical writing was situated in the developing market in books, whose publishers took advantage of these authors' social and legal disabilities to lower the costs of expansion. The abuse of women writers at the hands of publishers, in terms of generally disadvantageous financial arrangements, became the stuff of nineteenth-century literary lore. Anna Jameson exchanged the rights to *Diary of an Ennuyée*—an incredibly popular imitation of *Corinne*—for a guitar, even though the need to support her parents kept her working as a governess as well as a writer.[20] The Strickland sisters sold the twelve-volume *Lives of the Queens of England* for 150 pounds; the work was reprinted incessantly throughout the nineteenth and twentieth centuries, and the rights were purchased, sold, and auctioned several times before 1900. The story of Lydia Maria Child's literary finances would make an entire volume, so full was her life of deals for books, articles, and journal editorships, as she struggled to pay her husband's vast and constantly accruing debts. Eventually Child left a substantial estate, but only after she had settled with large numbers of creditors and separated her finances from those of her husband.[21]

Many women writers were from prosperous if not rich families, but the legalities of marriage and sometimes unfortunate unions stripped them of their prosperity, while publishers treated them as hacks. Although most succeeded in maintaining some semblance of a respectable lifestyle, they often did so by moving to foreign countries or rural areas where living was inexpensive. In most cases the experience was exhausting, pressing the limits of endurance, self-esteem, and the social conventions of gender. Often racked by long hours of poorly paid work, responsible for more than their share of family affairs, including the education of children, most were not what historians have come to see as "proper ladies."

The same could be said of their personal, affective lives: Daniel Stern as Liszt's mistress; Hortense Allart as Chateaubriand's, Sainte-Beuve's, and Henry Bulwer-Lytton's; Margaret Fuller as the pursuer of Emerson; Johanna Schopenhauer as a too-vivacious German matron.[22] Details of their eroticism have been sought out by male writers in the past, but suppressed by the women's families and by feminist critics. For many women, de Staël was a model and guide, one whose rules they iterated in constituting their lives and work. They *were* Corinne. And many of de Staël's contemporaries lived the sexually full life she did.

Under these rules, passionate love was never far removed, and was often closely intertwined with the intellectual work of history. "Thank God you do not yet know how ceaselessly my thoughts are with you—how tender, how passionate my longing for you," wrote Sarah Taylor Austin to a German prince, whose bawdy accounts of his tour of England she translated and edited into a best-seller of the early 1830s.[23] Austin was unhappily married to the domineering and brilliant jurist John Austin, whose "genius" reputedly prevented him from performing such ordinary tasks as work.[24] His wife's secret correspondence was symptomatic of the tumultuous love lives or erotic longings that early nineteenth-century intellectual women experienced, and that their embarrassed families later hid. For several generations Austin's family sought to destroy the evidence that, while she translated Ranke, Cousin, and many other respected writers and wrote biographies and histories, she burned with sexual passion for a philandering German cynic. Often when she wrote to her epistolary lover, her hand would race over the paper, filling ten and twenty pages. Called an "authoress" or a "learned woman" in her day, Austin displayed what has since been seen as behavior unbecoming to a learned woman, appearing as a fashionable hostess at one moment and riding horses wildly at another. She supported her family with her prodigious writing and translating, yet disdained official recognition of her intellect. Instead, she claimed that writing was an effective means to "deaden the capacity for love . . . A character so strong and energetic as mine—feelings so warm and acute—must be employed somehow."[25] Again, following de Staël's lead, women authors maintained that writing helped them work through issues, providing employment and control; they billed it as something that overcame daily life in more ways than one.

Although these authors were often chastised, and chastised themselves, for their passionate lives and intellectual aspirations, they also sought ways to facilitate them. "Your Unfaithfulness" or "Your Sublime Unfaithfulness" was how Chateaubriand addressed Hortense Allart, whose book production was as plentiful as her lovers. Allart's first works, written in her early twenties, included a history of the Amboise conspiracy of 1560 and an appreciation of Germaine de Staël. Soon thereafter she moved to Italy to bear her first illegitimate child. Marriage, she later maintained, was "a yoke, unbearable and degrading, which enslaved women,"[26] and she invited Marie d'Agoult, pregnant by her lover Franz Liszt, to come give birth in Italy. "It's time that women were able to deliver where and when they choose." Motherhood out of wedlock further intensified Allart's social and political contacts with men, for being shunned by many respectable women made men her most accessible companions, apart from intellectuals like d'Agoult and George Sand. Ostracism from certain social rituals thus left plenty of time for a vast range of learning—Chinese, Asian history, theology, and classical civilization, not to mention the history of the Amazons. History formed a companion to love, providing long periods of solitude. Separated from Bulwer-Lytton, but nursing an infant by another lover, Allart wrote of working on "three books at once, and I am very happy, living philosophically, occupied only with my baby . . . and completely enjoying my liberty and my chastity."[27]

These historians—contrary to the bland personas that have come down to us—did not live their lives according to the evolving portrait of how respectable women were to comport themselves. Mercy Otis Warren and Stéphanie de Genlis produced biting political satire, though Warren's was often anonymous and she suppressed her history of the American Revolution for seventeen years. Driven into exile during the Revolution, de Genlis supported herself in a variety of ways, most notably by copious argumentative and partisan writing. Intellectual accomplishment was forged out of promethean, prodigious undertakings, and eccentricity. Marie d'Agoult, according to her husband, was an inconsiderate graphomaniac whose need for huge trunks of writing materials and insistence on constant writing inconvenienced the entire household. After her notorious liaison with Liszt had ended, she ran a well-attended salon and entertained numerous suitors, while producing a torrent of publications. This is not to invert the accepted depiction of the amateur as colorless and virtuous by making her out to be a "bad girl," or to suggest that she was merely (as Christopher Herold called de Staël) "mistress to an age." Rather, it looks to an enactment of amateurism as at once more resistant and more constrained than has been claimed.

Feats of love and feats of writing matched other behavioral extravagances. Harriet Grote—biographer, historian, and wife of the classicist George Grote—was known for her wild clothing, her reckless driving of carriages, and her lively intelligence. She was conspicuous: "One of the cleverest women I ever met," reported Sir William Molesworth.[28] The exotic dress of Lucie Austin—who was the daughter of Harriet's friend Sarah Taylor Austin and who, like Sarah, translated Ranke, in addition to writing several books on Egypt—went hand-in-hand with her cigar smoking and her adoption of cast-off African and Asian children whose patrons had wearied of them.[29] In the United States, Lydia Maria Child refused to dress according to codes of high New York or Boston society, and became so neglectful of her apparel that concerned friends sent her clothes. Child was a frantic writer, partly out of ambition but also because her husband was extremely impractical and forced her to endure the humiliation of bankruptcy. Believing herself to be George Sand's twin, she would have preferred to "tramp through the forests to the sound of a tambourine, with my baby strapped to my strong shoulders, than to live amid the constrained elegances of Beacon Street."[30] Poor clothing ultimately became a disguise that allowed Child to investigate social conditions for her writing without exciting the suspicion that a well-dressed society woman might arouse. Her younger colleague Margaret Fuller also had a reputation for obsessive work habits, oversexed behavior (at least in her teens), and limitless intelligence. But the most eccentric of all may have been the aging Berry sisters of London. Heavily rouged cheeks and vulgar conversation had been acceptable to their upper-class status in the eighteenth century, but by the 1830s and 1840s such habits in elderly ladies, who were also accomplished intellectuals, shocked more than one Victorian.

Amateur women often acknowledged that their sexual relationships were a school for the mind that added their lover's intellectual drives to and even initiated their own. At the time of her engagement in 1817, Sarah Taylor was already proficient in Latin and several modern languages. But her fiancé, John Austin, drew up long reading lists, including the works of Cicero, Machiavelli, Hume, Adam Smith, and many other classics, which she studied and regularly reported on during their five-year engagement. George Grote composed a similar reading list for his fiancée, Harriet. Hortense Allart enlisted one of her lovers, Chateaubriand, to read the proofs of her works, and he always had good authorial and publishing advice. Mary Wollstonecraft and Helena Maria Williams gained eyewitness information on the French Revolution for their subsequent works, while pursuing lovers on the Continent. Similarly, three decades later, Allart's travels with Henry Bulwer-Lytton provided her with first-hand accounts of politics in England and Belgium for her historical writing and political commentary. Her lovers and her other male intimates were the ones who first persuaded her to drop the successful novels she had been writing late in the 1820s and early in the 1830s, and to pursue exclusively the "virile" study of history. The comtesse d'Agoult wrote her first articles with the help of her lover Liszt, who signed them for publication. The early preparation for becoming an intellectual was explained as wrapped up in love and even sex. Few of these scholars articulated their connection with history as part of a burning vocational drive inherent in their natures; rather, history came later, as part of the development of a female persona set in a network of complex relationships. Thus, their performance of historicalmindedness was a Staëlian one, claimed as hermeneutical, erotic, and even imitative, instead of natural or transparent. Less the *result* of virtuous social goals, their work ultimately *produced* more regular, disciplined conduct out of prodigious lives.

Eros was a place where understanding began, but it could also be connected with a sense of confusion, as boundaries between self and other weakened. A normal or normative sense of identity was often expressed as attenuated or weak, thus departing from nineteenth-century ideas of the autonomous, rational self. Some of these historians not only flouted but professed to be estranged from the ideals of nineteenth-century womanhood prescribed by the code of middle-class conduct. Fuller characterized her estrangement as inborn, gripping her when young: "From a very early age I have felt that I was not born to the common womanly lot."[31] For Daniel Stern, the uncommon life was one taught by her grandmother—a remnant of aristocratic womanhood who steadfastly upheld the *vie du château.* Her legacy to Marie and all other protégées entailed "protecting [them] from the pruderies of 'respectable women' [*femmes comme il faut*])."[32] Against the "languor, boredom, and intellectual vagueness" associated with the new female gentility, Allart maintained, one needed to "impose forced labor . . . After an hour of application, one's mind hardens."[33] Lydia Maria Child felt that something wrong though indeterminate had happened to her at birth, putting her perhaps into the wrong family. Ultimately, she expressed this sense of malaise by making people call her Maria instead of Lydia, as her family had done. Historical writing and the assumption of new identities went in tandem, as female writers often invoked intellectual women and other heroines from the past. Allart called d'Agoult "Hypatia," and rejected "Marie the lovable, Marie the beautiful," preferring instead "Marie the highly cultivated, Marie the savant."[34]

Changing class, changing names, many played with gender. Well-known amateur historians with male-sounding names like Daniel Stern and Blaze de Bury were women, and thus their work became a place where an ambivalent gendered identity took shape. Literary critics have generally interpreted women's adoption of male pseudonyms as a means of protecting their middle-class femininity. But some of it resulted from out-and-out coercion. In the 1860s François Buloz, editor of the *Revue des Deux Mondes,* made Rose Stuart Blaze de Bury sign all her historical articles with her husband's surname alone; he would not allow "the feminine in such writings."[35] In contrast, the practice of hiding one's identity through multiple changes of name was common among Native Americans who had to deal with Europeans. A new name protected the self from harmful forces, repackaged it, and thus multiplied or guarded its force.[36] From Stéphanie de Genlis, who wrote under several names during the Revolution, to Charlotte Carmichael at the turn of the twentieth century, amateurs adopted women's names and not just men's to shroud and embellish their authorship.

Opinion was uncertain about what women actually were, when it came to undertaking intellectual work. They could not be great "astronomers or geologists, or metaphysicians," Margaret Fuller told her pupils at the Greene School in Providence, "but they could and are expected to be good historians."[37] "Society is so much the province of women," wrote Sarah Taylor Austin, that it seems as if they were the natural and proper historians."[38] Only late in her life, however, did she turn from editing and translating to writing history. Lydia Maria Child felt that hers "was the heart of a man imprisoned within a woman's destiny,"[39] and for Hortense Allart, history was "virile" work. But when one of her lovers, the critic Sainte-Beuve, praised her writing, he did so by calling her "my Mademoiselle Lézardière," after a celebrated woman whose four-volume, document-based history of French institutions written during the French Revolution had been the rage in the 1840s. At other times, these amateurs wrote of themselves as "men" and offered unapologetic explanations for their writing. When a woman was self-made outside the norms and when circumstances such as talent or chance propelled her into the limelight, Daniel Stern maintained, "at that very moment she contracted virile responsibilities."[40] Before the 1850s history was not yet clearly gendered, nor were women intellectuals fully situated as part of womanhood. As women, they were beyond the circle of citizenship, yet as intellectuals they were excluded or removed themselves from the developing definitions of womanhood. At this indeterminate moment, one could simultaneously take inspiration from Corinne, the histories of queens and courts, the heart-thumping works of Walter Scott, and even the studies by Thierry, Ranke, and Sparks.

As with the poetry of Sappho or the writing of their many other exemplars, women intellectuals construed work as providing refuge from the sorrows, inequities, and trauma of love, a place where the self was restored, the lover forgotten, a better narrative of one's activities forged. Losing a lover, Allart searched out her friends and redoubled her scholarship: "I returned to public issues, to my country, to the intellect; I interested myself in everything."[41] Sarah Taylor Austin, who wrote articles and one major historical work, preferred translating. Even though it brought in less money and provided less glory, "I welcome the forced absorption in drudgery as a potent reason against painful meditations. My nouns and my adverbs keep me out of myself."[42] The idea of the amateur as a form of personal consolation and a desperate solution to personal want was born early in the nineteenth century. It did not fit in with men's narratives, which told of heroically coming to a historical vocation through a process whereby a developmental self discovered the transcendent world of ideas and science in adolescence. But the idea of consolation, implying some sort of self-pity, does not capture the right tone. Women confounded themselves and others: shown an important new archival document, the Stricklands "set to work for two hours in earnest, to the evident surprise of the French officials."[43] Amateurs presented their vocation as a part of their selves, including the hard intellectual work they did while enmeshed in love and the struggle for money. They wrapped themselves in productive memories of other formidable and impressive women—memories that helped them work through definitional issues surrounding their lives. Most of the time, they confronted the emerging standards and laws governing an increasingly normative femininity with frenzied intellectual labor.

The Amateur Vision

This complex performance of amateurism that could weave itself around and beyond feminine roles encourages us to rethink amateur historiography: first, the interpretation that these amateur historians merely hewed to one of the competing male political biases, especially republicanism or constitutional monarchism; and second, that they did so in some kind of bland imitative way. There is little doubt that a powerful fascination with the history of political and civic life during those tumultuous times fueled women's work. Mercy Otis Warren on the American Revolution; Helena Maria Williams, Mary Wollstonecraft, and Germaine de Staël on the French Revolution; Daniel Stern on the Revolution of 1848; and Cristina Belgiojoso on Italian nationalism were but the most celebrated of political historians. Theirs were critical, informed, and detailed analyses of men and revolutionary politics. Yet by far the more common topic was that of queens and famous or noble women—what came to be called "the woman worthy." Extremely popular in the early nineteenth century were biographical dictionaries of famous women, such as Fortunée Briquet's massive *Dictionnaire historique, littéraire et bibliographique des Françaises (Historical, Literary, and Biographical Dictionary of French Women;* 1804).[44] Biographies and prosopographies also flourished: Elizabeth and Agnes Strickland's *Lives of the Queens of England,* Anaïs Bassanville's *Salons d'autrefois (Salons of Yesteryear,* 1862–1864), and Elizabeth Ellet's *Women of the American Revolution* (1849) were accompanied by numerous individual biographies of famous women, especially Madame de Staël.

Repeated writing about women who had mostly acted in public and been influential beyond the purview of the nuclear family gave readers an alternate account of political and public life, and one far more problematic than the history of queenship is envisioned as being. Their subjects were important, worthy women whose histories offered more identities and demonstrated unparalleled superiority. Traumatic writing, according to theorists, avoids conscious observation and full articulation of conditions such as victimization or pain. Instead, with the traumatic moment or condition overtly absent, a traumatic narrative—in this case amateur history—provides a better story, one that smooths over and improves on the condition of shock, torment, persecution, or persistent misuse. Touting Old Regime aristocratic identity, the Stricklands announced that "a queen is no ordinary woman."[45] For amateurs, queens were amazons and powerful leaders, or, like Martia Proba (wife of King Gutiline), they performed unacknowledged deeds. Martia Proba devised the common law in its first incarnation—the Martian statutes. Even in a republic, however, the queenly motif had force, as in Elizabeth Ellet's *Queens of American Society* (1867). In this half-century of early amateurism, trauma largely blocked the history of women's inferior, denigrated, propertyless position. This was one history early amateurs did not explicitly research and write.

Repetition, too, is said to characterize traumatic narrative, making for a kind of account that does not quite fit with the alleged measure and restraint of scientific analysis. Between the late 1830s and the 1860s, the Stricklands wrote not only their sixteen-volume history of the English queens but also eight volumes on the queens of Scotland and English princesses, a volume on the Tudor princesses, another on the last four Stuart princesses, and a five-volume edition of the letters of Mary Queen of Scots (thirty-one volumes on women royalty alone). But their way had been paved during the previous thirty years by such productive historians as Lucy Aikin and the impoverished Elizabeth Benger. For the first half of the century, the most studied woman of talent was Germaine de Staël—"intellectually the greatest woman that ever lived," as Lydia Maria Child characterized her. Biographies of de Staël, penned by an international panoply of authors, numbered in the dozens. Since Sappho was sometimes elided with her, she received treatment such as Bianca Milesi Mojon's *Vita di Saffo* (*Life of Sappho;* 1824). Prosopography also allowed for a repetition of the theme of women's stature. Examples here are the prosopographies by Dora d'Istria (Romanian author Elena Ghika) of worthy women in eastern Europe, including Princess Lioubitza, Madame Küdner, and Princess Dashkova, who headed the Russian Academy of Sciences and Fine Arts and edited a major Russian dictionary; Julia Kavanagh's studies of the eighteenth-century French noblewoman; and Elizabeth Ellet's *Pioneer Women of the West* (1852) and *Women of the American Revolution.*[46]

Great ladies and queens appeared in ghostly form, symbolic apparitions of benefits lost. "Alas! The Civil Code was passed and the great lady died," wrote Anaïs Bassanville of the French Revolution's historic import, "with the powder, the beauty marks, the high-heeled slippers, the curvaceous [*busqué*] corset decorated with ribbons, pompoms, and lace—all things that women try to recapture today."[47] She reported Talleyrand as saying, "The death knell of high society rang out, . . . and the first note that it struck was the modern phrase 'the proper lady.'" Modern society meant the death of queenship, the *salonnière,* and the noblewoman's prerogatives. Far from universally appreciating progress, many of these nineteenth-century historians fixated on the Old Regime aristocrat. De Genlis remarked on the sad end of the mincing, preening, affected woman who had ruled châteaus and courts, while Schopenhauer mourned the multishaped beauty marks that had once adorned the fashionable woman's face. The invocation of loss mimed the death of Corinne, for the aristocratic woman had been amusing, engaging, and ripe for adventure. Julia Kavanagh's *Woman in France during the Eighteenth Century* (1850) depicted the eighteenth century as a time when French women had held extraordinary power, and as Dora d'Istria remarked, only in Russia could one still find the type of forceful upper-class woman that successive revolutions had destroyed in the rest of Europe. Unlike men, who wrote about the "Orient" to justify the enlightened rule of imperialism, these writers used the example of women in Turkey, whom they saw as having a privileged history, as a foil for their own contemporary political situation. History for these writers was a locus of overpowering loss, where oblique, hesitant traces of former power remained in Asia, in Russia, and in contemporary women's futile attempts to recapture it.

Trauma can involve the inability to mourn, to dispatch the dead or accept traumatic consequences by working them through to closure. In this respect, amateur literariness did not entail closure or objectification of its subjects, but rather promoted the immanence of its great women characters. That is, the narrative and analytic work of amateurs did not depend on studying characters to find their truth but summoned them to existence as vividly as possible in the narratives, finding reality in the body and the details of physical appearance. Amateurs stressed the importance of the surface: historical actors gave forth their truth in their physiognomy, comportment, and general aura. Of the prince de Joinville, Daniel Stern wrote:

> In spite of an affected brusqueness, which he thought necessary for his role in the navy, a sweetness suffused his melancholy face. His bearing lacked neither firmness nor nobility. People who came close enough to penetrate his character said that under a frank and simple demeanor the prince de Joinville hid a hereditary charlatanism and a desire for effect that drove him in a thousand different directions. But ordinary people, who had not this fine discernment, contented themselves with appearances.[48]

So it was with all of Stern's characters, whether Lamartine or Ledru-Rollin. Historical protagonists revealed motives, weaknesses, and the strengths that would allow them to make an impact in politics. The narrative, in portraying men, revealed to readers a truth that had been immanent at the time. Events, too, displayed surface meanings: "This ferment of discord, these passions contained with such difficulty by the despotic hand of the king, presaged a tempestuous regency for the country" (47).

What is more important, amateurs tried to depict the vital remains of dead worthy women in a number of ways. Critic Richard Garnett cited British writer Anna Jameson's historical essays as storehouses of "delightful knowledge," with "The House of Titian" serving as a model for this kind of production, "saturated in Venetian feeling."[49] Jameson, who opened up art history as well as amateur history proper, invoked Titian's Saint Catherine and Saint Barbara as still present in Italian society: "Such I have seen as I well remember at a *festa* on the Lido; women with just such eyes, dark, lustrous, melancholy,—and just such hair, in such redundance, plaited, knotted, looped round the small elegant heads." In providing this overview of history, Jameson was not nostalgic—was not sentimentalizing the art of the "good old days" by showing Titian's heroines in contemporary Venice and hoping for the appearance of a new genius to recapture the glories of the past. Hers was a history of immanence: "Is it not *here*, beside us, a part of our present existence?" Not only de Staël but Mary Wollstonecraft had interrupted her history of the French Revolution to invoke the ghosts who haunted the halls of Versailles.[50] Presenting this immanence became the task of the amateur, and was all the more important because in modern society—as Jameson put it— "the din of a city deafens the imagination to all such voices from the dead."[51] Immanence was complex, like Jameson's, or simpler, like the Stricklands', who reported that "as the anniversary of Edward VI's birth-night returns, the specter of Jane Seymour is seen to ascend those stairs [at Hampton Court], clad in flowing white garments, with a lighted lamp in her hand."[52] The better story was that powerful women remained as ghosts among the living.

Amateur history also reiterated and thus revived the wit of Old Regime women. De Genlis produced a series of court histories that described secret games, theatricals, and acts of frivolity, all of which came to be called "superficial."[53] Other histories of court life resound with striking stories, improbable tales, and the *bon mots* of many a high-society wit. Mary Berry presented tidbits from the salon of Madame du Deffand and from Empress Josephine's private life. Kavanagh described the women relatives of the duc d'Orléans (regent of Louis XV): his mother, who bragged about introducing herring omelets to the French court, who had "hands of

unrivalled ugliness," and who "wore a round close wig like that of a man";
his daughter, Mademoiselle de Chartres, who loved firing guns, setting off
fireworks, and bleeding the nuns in the convent she ran; and another
daughter, Mademoiselle de Valois, who brought her lover into her boudoir
through a secret "preserve closet." The regent called the petite duchesse
de Maine a "little wasp" (she had started the Order of the Honey Bees),
and his mother called her "the little dwarf." The duchess, though small,
beat her husband and smashed windows, mirrors, and crystal whenever
she was crossed.[54]

The inducement to amusement and mirth was omnipresent. Anaïs Bassanville chose to write about the history of French manners, of Neapolitan
life, and of eighteenth- and early nineteenth-century salons. During the
trial of Queen Caroline for adultery, she recounted, a nobleman known to
oppose the eccentric consort was forced by a sympathetic crowd to praise
her: "The poor lord . . . placed himself upright and superb on the running-
board of his carriage, and, waving his hat in the hair, shouted in a thunder-
ous voice, 'Yes, my friends, long live Queen Caroline, and may your wives
and daughters take after her!'"[55] History seemed full of amusing scenes,
even during the Terror. Having escaped to England early in the 1790s, the
princesse de Vaudemont asked her English hostess directions to the baths.
The hostess responded: "Take that street . . . walk straight ahead of you.
You will soon see a street that you don't take, right next to another that you
don't take either, a few more that you will go by, and then, after reaching a
certain point, you will find right there what you are looking for."[56] Even
Daniel Stern, who would write histories of republics and a monumental
account of the Revolution of 1848 in France, made the duchesse d'Orléans
the heroine of the February Days, in contrast to the ridiculous male leaders,
who were small and interested only in their own glory—all in all, a joke.
Stern used tropes that were aristocratic, too, favoring images like court
theatricals and witty remarks about her characters.

The jokes and anecdotes that propelled many histories of worthy
women not only made the Old Regime immanent—they undercut any
clear analytical trajectory that might have allowed a comparison between
the grandeur of queens and modernity's dependence on the denigration,
coercion, and impoverishment of the vast majority of women. For all that
queenship presented the "better story," it often ended up depicted with

just this kind of joking, precisely as a further buffer to accessing trauma. As Baudelaire explained at about the same time, laughter is itself a shock because it interrupts the rational progress of linguistic meaning and narrative.[57] In the case of amateur writing, the laughter and jokes stood in opposition to progressing toward the full meaning of the traumatic clash of past and present. Jokes, in a way, led nowhere, at the same time that they signaled a jolt in an account, repeating in an acceptable form a shocking moment outside meaning and signaling to us as readers today the force of trauma.

Amateurs' diversionary circuit around trauma underscores the doubling or split experience of trauma that commentators from Freud to Cathy Caruth have noted—a doubling that provides a further gloss on W. E. B. Du Bois's and Joan Kelly's ideas of "double vision." On the one hand, as experts on trauma write, the traumatized situation is one in which the subject is so deeply involved, or by which he or she is so firmly seized, as to be incapable of serving as a witness; it is impossible to think the unthinkable, and thus its history remains (as mentioned earlier) "yet to be told."[58] On the other hand, the traumatized person moves away from the event in order to be a survivor—and this has been noted for all degrees of trauma, from escaping a train collision (Freud's hypothetical example) to Freud's own experience of escaping the Nazis by leaving Austria for England. At the same time that one remains locked in a past experience, departure, escape, getting outside the event, experience, and condition take on narrative importance, and played a major part in amateur history.

Three characteristics of early nineteenth-century amateur writing—all of them signaling escape and survivorship—are particularly striking and remained so even into the age of high amateurism at the beginning of the twentieth century: the pronounced tendencies to write social history, cultural history, and history in the form of travel narrative. The exemplar or prototype in this was Germaine de Staël, but both her contemporaries and subsequent amateurs further developed these propensities, converting them into signatures of the amateur style. De Staël dramatized *On Germany* and *Corinne* as written amid foreign encounters, studying Germany explicitly in order to interpret German history and culture to non-Germans, drawing clear boundaries between national groups, and commenting as a foreigner in their midst. She laced all her work—these two, as well as

Considerations on the Principal Events of the French Revolution—with extensive descriptions of travel in coaches and walking. So did Anna Jameson's imitative history of Italy and its art; the best-selling *Diary of an Ennuyée* of the early 1820s; Julia Pardoe's *City of the Magyar; or, Hungary and Her Institutions,* as well as her *City of the Sultan* (both from the 1830s); and many of the writings of Johanna Schopenhauer, Ida Pfeiffer, and Ida Hahn Hahn. Amateur narrators and sometimes their protagonists crossed geographic borders that marked the physical limits of the state. The more important mental and cultural differences amateurs dissected to mark just how far from their own countries they had voyaged, how well they had escaped. Beaten and mentally abused by her husband, Hahn Hahn explained in her first book: "I travel in order to live."[59]

Such writings invoked the nation as an absence, something one had lost in one's travel and exile. They thus connected history and nationality differently from scientific narratives. Taking up residence in exile to earn a living or live less expensively, to find new material or a safe place from which to write, the amateur created the "better story." Olympe Audouard, who staged her history of the Ottoman Empire as beginning with a ship voyage necessitating some twenty trunks of clothing and materials, discovered in her travel histories of the empire and of the United States a far better story—one in which U.S. women were "immensely superior" to their men in character and talent, and in which Ottoman harem customs were at least equal to conditions in a French nuclear family. Lydia Maria Child was also an escapee, wandering New York in disguise looking for material, sending her white heroines into the Indian past, and introducing the story of an escapee from slavery.[60]

Amateurs were assiduous in writing the histories of other countries, mining these narratives especially for the ingredients of citizenship and sound political rule; but this was an area with ragged contours, and not necessarily a closed issue on the subject of women and virtue. Allart took up her history of Florence because the city-state had "great men in all fields; its people were perhaps the liveliest and wittiest of modern times; its civic life was very strong, . . . comparable to that of Athens and superior to all modern civism except England."[61] Daniel Stern—late in her life, after Napoleon III had overthrown the Second Republic—proceeded to write her *Histoire des commencements de la république aux Pays-Bas* (*History of the Beginnings of the Dutch Republic;* 1872) "in order to understand the sum of conditions that gave to [republican institutions] elsewhere, contrary to what we have [in France], solidity and viability."[62] Many histories that had a republican message were also detours around the site of the author's own trauma. The mirror reflecting the writer's own past and present provided too disturbing a picture, making her aphasic on this terrain.

Virtue and morality, the centerpiece of public debate and political discourse, thus formed the most disjointed part of historical discourse. Mercy Otis Warren traced the development of a republican sensibility before and during the revolutionary sacrifice, but she also castigated some of its leaders for abandoning virtuous ideals in favor of monarchical institutions and privileges. The idea that public life should display virtue formed the flip side to many of the theatricals and to much of the wit. Daniel Stern's *Essai sur la liberté* (*Essay on Liberty;* 1847) examined the status of liberty in modern French history; here, as in her later book *Histoire de la révolution de 1848 (History of the Revolution of 1848),* she deplored the corruption and frivolity of the upper classes. Stern judged the ruling elements culpable in their contempt for women and the proletariat, a corrupt attitude that called out for a more austere morality and rectitude. Her friend Allart, with whom she shared an intense political and literary correspondence, was always quick to criticize any slippages in Stern's thinking. Praising her general overview, she found nevertheless that Stern, in her novel *Nélida* (1845) and other writings, tilted toward presenting a dangerous public ethos. To Allart, the mention of austere public virtues invoked the kind of sexual propriety—"la moralité des boutiques," she once called it—so often used to censure women like themselves. The concept of virtue, she maintained, had to admit of passion. They both agreed that men monopolized the public sphere: "The academies, the newspapers—they praise one another, worship one another, and we haven't even a vote." But Allart always felt that Stern gave inadvertent ammunition to the enemy in her examples of virtue. Why did Stern cite the lives of Christian women, who were "without a doubt more beastly than Pascal," when she could invoke the "daughters of Sparta, the women orators of Athens"?[63] Here was a better story.

Amateurs openly questioned the postrevolutionary emphasis on the hero, great man, or male genius. The great man, Daniel Stern maintained, was "infinitely less important in epochs when the mass of people vegetated in ignorance and apathy. I don't hesitate to say that a man of genius, in our present civilization, would influence our destiny very little."[64] In her *Germany from 1760 to 1814,* Sarah Taylor Austin challenged the thrust of contemporary historical writing toward the scientific discussion of politics. Austin was deeply familiar with this nascent genre by virtue of her daughter's and her own important translations of Ranke's histories. Austin focused on what she called "German life" out of a civic position: "What does it signify, that in such an age, this or that country was the most powerful, this or that family enthroned, or in obscurity? What avail territorial divisions, military successes, or even political institutions and physical discoveries, if the heart of man is not at peace in his home; if he is enslaved by the tyranny of custom; . . . if a woman have no hold on any but the lower appetites or the despotic tempers of men." For Austin, all aspects of politics as well as "the great moral and intellectual revolutions are reflected by the incidents of social life, as from the thousand faces of a prism." In fact, a focus on social life was crucial to the mission of nineteenth-century history: "Such researches lead us to the very heart of the question, What *is* progress?"[65] Other writers, proceeding to analyze everything from sumptuary legislation to the founding of charitable institutions and churches, would make claims for the social.

The insider/male history written by both men of letters and professionals was based on the activities of great men and set in political and military narrative about them. The traumatized outsider escaped to study social life and artistic and intellectual achievement. Daniel Stern believed that one could read history in the social, which she defined as the condition of the lower classes and women; but she additionally saw women as an originary point for an alternative, cultural achievement. Speaking of Renaissance art, she wrote: "It was in the arms of his young mistresses, during the ecstasy of love, that the gentle Raphael dreamed up his Virgins."[66] Martha Lamb—in her *History of the City of New York* (1877), based on more than a dozen years of research—followed the line set up by the early amateurs, maintaining that her work would cover the European background to settlement ("wars and rumors of wars, its public characters and foreign relations"), but that she would concentrate on "the social thread, . . . the cable" which held "the multiplicity of [the city's] parts together."[67]

As Julia Kristeva suggests in her study of migrants and resident foreigners today, baffled outsiders and escapees need to get a grip on culture and to understand the important facts of social life in order to survive.[68] Indeed, amateur historians adduced cultural difference in minute detail. If one did not have political rights, one had to face the cultural community. Albertine Clément-Hémery, after exploring the art world in Paris during the Revolution and editing a woman's journal, spent the last years of her life writing the history of French local customs, avoiding "the long, fastidious, useless narratives" of battles, strategy, and rulers. "Destiny often depends on the customs of a people," she explained; and so informed, her histories described festivals, religious processions, diet and the cost of food, agricultural practices, charivaris, and the lore of local châteaus and their seigneurs.[69] The everyday life that one lived while in exile—that one had to deal with more deliberately as a stranger or escapee, whether at home or abroad—was also foregrounded in amateurs' comments on dress and appearance, the status of women, the comfort of accommodations, and standards of etiquette. The nation and its politics, in amateur history, became a more unthinkable presence than in other historical incarnations. Cultural and social history, while providing important survival information for those traumatized by the republican/liberal gendering of political and economic modernity, could simultaneously be a better story—again, one that told of women's influence and importance. To reiterate Austin's claim: "What does it signify, that in such an age, this or that country was the most powerful, this or that family enthroned, or in obscurity . . . ? The great moral and intellectual revolutions are reflected by the incidents of social life."

At the same time, social and cultural history worked through another source of trauma that has never really been explored in detail. Theories of trauma have sometimes focused on men's experience of pain, bleeding, disfigurement, and dismemberment in war. But there has been virtually no historical consideration of women's trauma from sexual, gynecological, and reproductive pain and painful bodily dysfunction as a result of childbirth—experiences which, as new studies show, were far different from and more crippling than their twentieth-century variants.[70] Cristina Belgiojoso was infected with syphilis by the age of eighteen by her profligate husband, and this dramatically exacerbated her epilepsy.[71] The rest of her life she spent on drugs ranging from belladonna to opium. At that time in history, pregnant women prepared themselves to die in childbirth—an outlook scarcely imaginable in the 1990s. Until the mid-nineteenth century, forceps and other instruments such as hooks inflicted more pain and injury than in subsequent years, when obstetric procedures gradually improved. The practices involved in slow labor, breech births, and other complications also added to the pain of childbirth. Sending children, especially prepubescent and adolescent girls, away during deliveries prevented them from being traumatized at too early an age by the agony of parturient and sometimes dying women. Grown women, in contrast, were expected to witness and assist in childbirth, further implicating them in trauma. Those who survived the experience of childbirth might endure disabling pain from mangled and misarranged internal organs. Moreover, we know little about ordinary gynecological pain in this period, which just preceded vast improvements in and increased knowledge of its treatment.

Pain has a profound relationship to cognition and narrative. According to Elaine Scarry, whose *Body in Pain* is mostly about men, the intense pain of torture makes details of rooms—and even the rooms themselves in which victims suffer—disappear, along with the victim's rational voice. In pain, as in no other human experience, the self has no extension but rather exists as its own object. The trauma of childbirth or of intense gynecological pain and frequent malfunctioning presents a similar situation: passing beyond or escaping this trauma would involve reinstalling the room, its details, and its contents in the sufferer's reality, and reextending the body to find objects. A few amateurs were able to depict the painful demise of such executed queens as Anne Boleyn and Katherine Howard; after all, this was a "better story" than the one that told of the legal coercion or sufferings of women in the more recent past. Yet the "reality effect" in women's social histories and in the lives of queens and notable women involved just this reobjectification of the universe—this posttraumatic escape into the details of rooms, clothing, jewelry, hairstyles, and other attributes of individual appearance.

Privileged Information

In the early postrevolutionary age, the medicalized body became a place from which one could produce knowledge; other "scientized" knowledges followed, in an array of disciplines.[72] The full-scale production of history as knowledge had not yet begun, however. Women amateurs did not participate in a professional, secular, and scientific approach to the dead. Instead, past deeds by great and insignificant alike, along with the fate of their bodies, remained effective for producing strong feelings of catharsis—not knowledge. In fact, the pursuit of the past was not part of the will to know. It was not a participation in and exercise of power but an overwhelming circuit, a journey, an emotional and mental praxis. By the time Anna Jameson came to publish her *Diary of an Ennuyée* in the 1820s, the languid travels of Corinne and her lover to view Italian history had metamorphosed into a young woman's anxious coach rides through Italy and France during which she scribbled their history. Frantic, haunted by memories, and transfixed by history, the heroine dies on the road as a result of the past's mortal influence.

History's immanence—its connection with trauma—was the unifying theme distinguishing amateur writing, with its repeated evocative stories, from professional history, which offered new discoveries of knowledge and a tamer narrative. Amateur accounts were often filtered through various disclaimers that are usually interpreted as stemming from female modesty. Holding off the publication of her monumental history, Mercy Otis Warren announced that even while writing it she had often thought "to throw by the pen in despair. I draw a veil over the woe-fraught scenes that have pierced my own heart."[73] Laure d'Abrantes, often beaten by her husband, warned people who read her six-volume history of the Napoleonic era that they might expect "a kind of irregularity in some of the accounts" because her memory often caused them to "vibrate" in an unruly manner. "So, no astonishment if sometimes I interrupt one account only to begin another."[74] Hesitation could appear in accounts of books that never got published: Stéphanie de Genlis, for instance, recalled in her memoirs the number of book manuscripts lost at various times in her life, in addition to numerous precious possessions such as her portraits and jewelry. Her actual work sounds like an elaborate alternation between savings and loss. On the one hand, she described the many ways in which she saved time by studying during her toilette, reading in a coach, or copying information and poetry between the time dinner was announced and the actual procession to the dining room. On the other hand, throughout her memoirs she marked her annoyance with rituals (such as court balls) and individuals who caused her to waste time.[75] Published writings expressed a sense that it was overwhelming for a woman to handle the mental work in intellectual production. In 1835 the prolific Valérie de Gasparin, in her very first book on the history of Italy, written as a travelogue, presented a narrator who attempts to suppress her emotions and maintain the stance of "ignorance" before great works of art, historic monuments, and other major sites; in this way, says the narrator, "a great deal in our own century touches me, without my letting the products of history exhaust my imagination."[76]

Confronting history was exhausting and menacing, not only because of its effect on the psyche but because the means for gathering crucial historical material were not in the least regular for these amateurs—or for anyone else, for that matter. Practices, methodology, and modern historicalmindedness were still in the making in this age of revolution and dramatic change, but amateur practices look especially polymorphous and unclear, demanding an unprogrammed ingenuity in the search for a very important past. One wintery night in 1814, Mary Berry returned unusually disappointed from a dinner at Madame de Staël's. Of the recently arrived guests from Geneva, "none of them know anything of their little republic but what they see in the English papers."[77] English newspapers were spare and unreliable in their accounts, and by Berry's standards were not a source on which to base political or other judgments. Rather, those coming from Geneva—eyewitnesses in high places—were the best informants, and thus Berry kept up a constant round of visits in London and to the countryside. She also traveled repeatedly to France, Italy, and Germany, ostensibly for her health, but she maintained an exhausting schedule of trips to monuments, sites of historic events, and the offices and palaces of the powerful. Her sweep was panoramic, comprising innovations in road construction, assessments of troops during military parades, new industrial procedures, and palace interiors of the highest leaders—all of which she used in her histories. By the 1830s Berry had seen much of western Europe and had developed connections with kings, queens, emperors, popes, princes, duchesses, and princesses, which helped her produce a two-volume work of comparative social history from the mid-seventeenth to the nineteenth century. Methods and message often intertwined for these irregulars, these expatriates, these foreigners in urgent quest of information.

Yet for them, personal access to the mighty was, ironically, one way to locate pertinent information and then gain entrée to collections of manuscripts. Lord Guildford, for instance, provided Mary Berry with valuable tips for locating material on Lady Rachel Russell, whose letters and writings Berry published as part of a biography. Guildford's letter mentioned seventeenth-century tracts he owned, Lord Bridgewater's collection held at Ashridge, the Somers Papers bought from Lord Lansdowne by the British Museum, papers held by Lord Chichester, the heirs of Lord Hardwicke, and so on.[78] With library holdings uneven, primary materials widely scattered, and access to repositories limited if not impossible for women, finding correct information was a test of resourcefulness in following webs of association and kin connections. Mademoiselle de Lézardière's *Théorie des lois politiques de la monarchie française* (*Theory of the Political Laws of the French Monarchy;* 1792) relied on books that she had bought and manuscripts that were sent to her from contacts around France.[79] Details of who was related to whom, who might own which books or manuscripts, made outsiders potential insiders to historical information, whereas social connections even at great distances permitted the broaching of historical questions and the initiation of contact that might lead to evidence. The commoners Agnes and Elizabeth Strickland gained access to French archival material through the good offices of minister and premier François Guizot, who indicated pertinent documents for their multivolume work on royal women of England and Normandy. Refused access to British state archives, they pulled all sorts of strings to gain admittance there, as well as to private archives and historical sites. Access developed neither from a civic identity that would give them rights to bureaucratic jobs as archivists or historians, nor from credentialing provided by university-taught skills or university-provided subsidies. Mastery of a certain amount of social and political detail as part of a contorted methodological indirection was essential before these writers could gather further information for their books. Official historical information was outside the purview of ordinary femininity, although these were not stereotypical women.

Privileged in one way or another (though without political rights, property of their own, or the ordinary right to information), women who gained entrée to powerful circles only after knowing the social and cultural details then learned of the workings of government and followed events up close. This allowed them to write histories. Mercy Otis Warren, whose husband and brother were leaders in the American Revolution, first produced propagandistic plays and journalism for the colonists' cause. Letters containing horrendous reports of bloodshed and devastation poured into her Massachusetts home. In 1805 she published *A History of the Rise, Progress, and Termination of the American Revolution,* based on her insider's knowledge and appraisal of that event. Thereafter she pursued a heated, even bitter correspondence with John Adams over the validity of her presentation of events.[80] More than half a century later, Daniel Stern's *History of the Revolution of 1848* relied on pamphlets, newspaper clippings, and first-hand accounts, but also on information gained in her own salon about how government decisions were made and what shaped policy. There was never full identity; rather, the accounts contained gaps and slippages because women were not insiders to truth the way statesmen such as Guizot and Adolphe Thiers were. The hodgepodge nature of their information—often quoted raw from letters, newspapers, and oral sources—made many such histories an obvious pastiche. Nor could these writers claim the citizen's secure and certain vantage point. "From the circumstances under which she has been compelled to make her references, it was impossible that she should be able to register the pages to which she has had references to refer," wrote Elizabeth Benger, referring to herself in the third person as she described her difficulties in working at the British Library.[81] But Benger's admission is oblique, even confusing: it seems unable to tell some disturbing situation that had actually prevented her from getting her page references, while it professes to describe historical truth. In the Stricklands' case, it is clear that women regularly faced problems getting to manuscripts; and once they did gain access, officials watched them more scrupulously than they did men, even commenting (as they did to the Stricklands) that unlike most foolish women, these could actually do intellectual work.

Traumatic narrative thus took shape methodologically in this relationship to historical information, and was further complicated by unpredictable torrents of material that might suddenly confront the writer. Charlotte Linsey wrote letter after letter to Mary Berry detailing the wrenching trial of Queen Caroline; and since the society lacked reliable newspapers, highly placed women in the royal family, including queens and princesses, depended on Berry to relay information in times of crisis such as the assassination of the duc de Berri. In a politically active family with highly placed friends like the Adamses, Mercy Otis Warren could not avoid the heartbreaking aspects of the American Revolution, as well as its "dry" factual details. Often quoting from letters that passed among her circle, she told of the "rapine, assassination, and robbery" accompanying revolutionary fighting. "The whole country," she wrote, citing Nathanael Greene's letter to the chevalier de la Luzerne, "is one continued scene of slaughter and blood."[82] Lydia Maria Child suddenly came face-to-face with the brutality of slavery when, through her connections with Amy Post, she became the editor of Linda Brent's life story.[83] These circuits and conduits resonated with important information that the amateur spread even farther, never in a position to tame it into specialized knowledge for a limited, professional readership but rather extending it outward.

Amateur knowledge was a web, a matted clump of amazingly disparate material which most of these writers worked to acquire within an environment that not only disparaged women's intellects but also contrived to impede any intellectual labor they aspired to do. Amateurs thus approached the past from an ambiguous position: at once politically, socially, and economically defined as "women," with all the despoliation that category entailed, yet living lives as money-generating writers and suffering marginalization from the culture of proper womanhood. Many had trouble getting basic information they needed to pursue their writing, to support themselves, and to access the past. This situation was at once symptomatic, symbolic, diagnostic, and therapeutic, perpetuating amateur history as an acting out of trauma even as the women pursued the wherewithal to write it. Each act of information gathering occurred from within a cocoon that resulted largely from women's inferiority, exclusion, and denigration, making the pursuit of that information all the more necessary and obsessive.

The Place of Cathartic History

The presentation of amateur writing as trauma has two endings. The most logical one argues for the importance of seeing amateur history in terms of trauma. Such a reading should help us revise histories of modernity and rethink an array of concepts, such as "culture" and "the social." It also enables us to speculate on amateur historical writings in the production of women's and then feminists' political imagination and motivation. And it shows the multiplicity of historical cognitions, sensations, and relationships to the past, a continuation of de Staël's practices and sensibility. In the amateur instance, important cognitions were based on trauma, fear, danger, and degradation—cognitions which, as feminist philosophers have already demonstrated in other contexts, provided reliable information.[84] These then hardened into a set of procedures, unwritten rules, and rituals for writing history.

Seeing amateurism as trauma helps us explore sexism's intersections with other trauma-inflicting acts. For example, an alternative "better story" for some amateurs would come to contain anti-Semitism, racism, and imperialist values as different circuits around one's own inferiority. When women's history emerged in the universities, it did so initially repeating the tropes of trauma by validating the importance of women worthies, social history, and cultural history. Within a few years, however, amateurs were vigorously disallowed as having anything useful to say on these topics (among the exceptions was Natalie Zemon Davis's early and continuing interest in the preprofessional woman historian).[85] Professionals came especially to disavow women worthies.

In so disavowing the historiographic past of amateurism, one takes a stand on the side of professionalism, which in its procedures, practices, methodology, writing, fantasies, and organization has built historical science out of gender by privileging male over female and by specifically contrasting male truth and female falsehood, male depth and female superficiality, significant male events and trivial female ones, male transcendence and female embodiment as part of professionalism's gains. Enforcement of this hierarchy was precisely the originary point of historiographic trauma for women, and one perpetuated not just in politics and the economy but in professionalization. Caution should be at a high level by this time, for we are left with an impasse for feminist professionals because of the way professionalism was built on defeating the amateur and feminizing the category. Thus, women historians must either denounce "woman" or denounce their own professional status—either of them a difficult choice.

The second ending points in a different direction: toward the unacknowledged cathartics and erotics in history that symptomatic reading addresses. Historical disciplining, practices, and erotics can be multiple: amateur women's writing was accomplished by an array of adulteresses, responsible wives, unwed mothers, adventurers, and assiduous, even obsessed writers, lighthearted and amusing but also virtuous and modest women. Trauma often produces "good girls," but this stance could also have worked an eroticization of traumatic historical practices analogous to men's eroticization of professional work. The queens and notable women of history could be pampered, beaten, or so perkily well-behaved that they reaped love and adulation. Such effects of amateur writing were irresistible to its practitioners and compulsively delicious to its readers.

Some male authors practiced a literary cathartics, too. Historians like Augustin Thierry (1795–1856) read and reread Scott, enthralled by his bloody and heroic narratives; and while Foucault explored the development of "knowledge," he was simultaneously interested in writers like Thierry who still experienced historic "rapture." Thomas Macaulay and Jules Michelet came to write in similarly heroic and florid ways, though both Michelet and Thierry spent long hours culling sources, and Thierry explicitly saw himself as bringing "science" to the study of France's past. But it was the "blood" of the past shed by ordinary members of society that equally motivated Thierry, as he led his own charge against idealistic pictures of England's slowly evolving constitution and its rational past. A scholarship student from Blois, Thierry supported himself under the Restoration by writing historical articles and books on the Norman Conquest, the history of France, and other topics. Thierry's hatred for "the odious and ridiculous aping" of English institutions led him to further inquiry into English history. One day, while reading Hume's *History of England,* a flash of insight struck him: "All of this dates from a conquest; there is a conquest behind it all." Crippled by locomotor ataxia and eventually blind, Thierry proceeded to talk about the blood and gore behind English parliamentarism, not only the violence of early tribes but that of the Norman Conquest, up to that of Cromwell and further, when the troops of Monk returned Charles II to the throne. From then on, Thierry's histories aimed at showing readers the sanguinary side of history, whether that of England or of France, as the bourgeois bearers of civilization—the artisans and merchants—struggled against the warrior classes and others of rude and savage disposition. Pillage, rape, booty, enslavement—history was about "*conquest and subjection; masters and slaves.*"[86] Yet this cathartics did not circuit trauma, but rather moved to confront it. There was an overt rapture in this writing before the full triumph of science.

Concepts of trauma, rapture, erotics, and cathartics allow us to use amateurism to interrogate our practices (their violent suppression of other historical accounts, for instance). One can similarly use professionalism as a point of entry into amateur cognition, uncovering its extremely interesting nature. By contrast, a dismissal of the amateur sustains the deeply gendered and Westernized nature of professionalized historical truth, knowledge, and institutional power. The failure to deal with this alterity leaves masculinity (defined not in terms of actual "men" but as gender privilege and as the capacity for violently suppressing or devaluing other voices) still ascendant in the profession. Amateurism shows us the constitution of a "minority" tradition, one destined to remain minor because of the closing off of legitimacy not only in the economy but in writing.[87] Although some theorists would see the potential for resistance in the carnivalesque aspects of amateur writing—say, its laughter and its excesses of useless detail—and would stress the political importance of the hopefulness that such writing generated, the enduring strength of the amateur's inferiority is what needs emphasis at this point. By mid-century, there was no amateur woman who was being called a genius as de Staël had been, but the ranks of "brilliant" male historians were swelling. Moreover, it remains almost impossible to talk about the oppression of women by men in any way that does not seem minor, amateurish, overemotional, and uncritical. Given this situation, amateurism must be held in a permanent place of alterity, with respect to the professionalization of history and even to the rise of women's history in the twentieth century.

What Is a Historian?   3

"What is an author?" the philosopher Michel Foucault asked some two decades ago, and although this question has fascinated literary theorists, it has barely interested historians, who are more absorbed by wrestling with issues of "truth" and "objectivity."[1] The accomplishments of scientific history are unquestioningly attributed to great historians, technically expert and visionary practitioners who soar beyond the passions and interests of ordinary people in ways that allow them to produce compelling if not always perfect history. Studies of one or two great historians per generation often serve to make up historiography, but while we examine the fortunes of modern history we rarely consider the shape of historiography itself and what it has meant to the profession to have its achievements contained in the biographies of a handful of great authors. What is the use to which these biographies are put, and how have these lives of great historians fortified the founding claims of objectivity? Why has the story of the scholar who wrestles to free his talent from the bias and banality of the quotidian been so central an ingredient of professionalization, yet so little explored? In this connection, "What is an author?" would indeed be a useful question for historians to ask, especially regarding their various nineteenth-century heroes.

The question of the "historian" becomes more pressing when considered in light of the way in which certain figures and the topic of the nation-state are seen as central to all accounts of nineteenth-century historical work. Female amateurs, with their ardent readership, disappear from historiography; far from informing history, they seem to clot it. Social and cultural history, especially when addressing women's concerns and issues of everyday life, come to have little value. No matter how much cachet social history may have from time to time, politics and the men who write about it are the "meat and potatoes" of great history. However, when seen as produced by intellectual and cultural forces that laced historiography with gender, the biographies of the great male historians—those who wrote about politics—help explain how we have come to exalt the male historian and devalue or even erase women's historical work.

The towering figures of modern historiography, by many accounts, have childhood experiences only incidentally, attend schools where they may study alongside other fledgling practitioners, often take a wife and have children (known but dimly to future generations), and then proceed to write important histories, usually from university positions or while holding important posts as public figures. Each of these institutions, however—including family, school, friendship, and marriage—was a locus of historical writing, a place where the historian was in fact "produced" as an exemplar for historiography and where politics acquired its gloss. Seen as separate from history—a separate sphere, in fact—the household was often a place where historians wrote their first serious works, using tools and gazing at artifacts that are more frequently associated with leisure rather than toil. Sex (rarely associated with the founding practices of modern historical writing) and children (the result of sex) were also in the orbit of historical work. Yet most historiography sees the narrative of everyday life, the narrative of family, childhood, sex, and marriage, as irrelevant to great historical writing and to the recasting of the discipline in the nineteenth century. To the contrary, this chapter argues that household, sex, and marriage have contributed key crucial material for gendering historiography by providing standards for the important and the unimportant, the brilliant and the derivative.

The Adolescent Road to Historical Science

Historical narrative and its values took shape in the conditions of nineteenth-century boyhood. John Lothrop Motley, age ten in 1824, wrote to his parents from boarding school outside Boston: "I want to see you very much. I suppose you remember that it is my turn to come home on Saturday next? This is Thursday, the day on which we speak. I was third best . . . My nose has bled very often lately, but I believe it will not bleed much more. I have had a pain in my side once or twice."[2] Motley's schooltime preparation for becoming a historian involved intensive training in languages, accompanied by his own growing thirst for reading, a thirst unwittingly fostered by a school where linguistic drill, math, and some science filled the curriculum. "In the morning, from half-past five to seven, I study French," he wrote his mother a year later. "After breakfast I study Spanish, from nine to half past ten, when we go out and stay about ten or fifteen minutes; and when we come in, I study Greek until twelve, when we are dismissed; and in the afternoon I study Cicero and recite to Dr. Beck, a German."[3] Motley asked his father for books, complaining about the lack of reading material; when a reading room finally did materialize at the school, it still failed to satisfy his cravings. No one contributed books, and the few newspapers were "a hundred years old" and all mutilated within an hour of being deposited. "Reading is not to be thought of, as there are no books in school."[4]

Motley went on to become a major U.S. historian of Europe, as well as an ambassador, but his education, one that was common for most important male historians of the nineteenth century, raises questions about its pertinence to the momentous changes occurring in historical writing and training. The first experience for many boys was despair at being wrenched from home, and their letters expressed a pathetic longing for family members and family rituals. "My dear Mamma," thirteen-year-old Thomas Macaulay wrote from school in 1813, "I do not remember being ever more gloomy in my life than when I first left Clapham."[5] In his letters, Macaulay counted the days till vacation, begged his parents to let him return for his birthday, and bombarded his mother with his memories of their happy walks and talks together. Sharing accommodations with forty other boys, the shy and quiet William Lecky, at school in the 1850s, disliked the size of his school—its very unhomelike atmosphere.[6] Young students not only wrote to their parents but sent off touching notes to brothers, sisters, aunts, uncles, and grandparents. Leopold von Ranke, Frederic Maitland, Henry Adams—innumerable historical authors sent heartfelt letters back to the domestic sphere, recounting their deprivation and loneliness. "Each evening, in the notebook where I entered my expenditures," remembered Ernest Lavisse, minister of public instruction and editor of a twelve-volume history of the world, "I counted, 'Only so many days left 'til vaca- tion'—and the last days seemed very long."[7]

School stood in marked contrast to the domestic sphere. "When the door of the *collège* shut, I was stupefied, and time did nothing but augment my sense of being a prisoner," Edgar Quinet wrote about entering board- ing school at the age of twelve.[8] For him, the sense of imprisonment stemmed from the difference between the school's rhythms and values and those of the home. He loved keeping a little garden, harvesting wheat and baking the flour into pastries, and roaming wild. But the most striking aspect of his confinement in boarding school was "the coldness toward one's own family that one was supposed to show in front of other students. One would incur merciless ridicule by embracing one's relatives effusively before witnesses."[9] There were respites from school's antidomestic values. Macaulay's greatest vacation delight was making plum and apple pies; his father, however, feared the boy's irrepressible "love of domesticity."[10] Carsten Niebuhr, whose son Barthold spent less of his youth learning at school than most historians, also worried that his son's "attachment to home was excessive."[11]

School rituals for the most part emphasized differences between the boy's world of study and the domestic world of family. Quinet, who made his first Communion later than usual, after he had entered boarding school, was keenly aware that the Catholic religion he was adopting diverged profoundly from the tolerant spirituality of his mother. Although raised a Lutheran, she had taken him to Mass regularly and exposed him to a wide variety of religious practices, but Quinet's religious instruction in boarding school made him fear that the priest would force a choice between the Holy Mother Church and his biological mother, and he knew that the Church considered her damned. Happy at being confirmed, "my only anguish was the absence of my mother."[12] Impersonal religious practices replaced do- mestic and village ones, and the "mother tongue" was swallowed up in the classical curriculum based mostly on Latin and Greek.

Epistolary longings for home and recollections of childhood pleasures were accompanied or soon superseded by accounts of studies, as nondo- mestic, nonfamilial concerns came to reshape each boy's identity. Typi- cally, boys wrote home about—and long remembered—their daily sched- ule of language and math drills, as well as the various books from which they learned grammar. "For composition Bland's Verses and, I think, Ellis's Exercises, which were manuals, from which we were led on through Kerchever Arnold's books and Kenrich's exercises for three or four years," recalled historian William Stubbs of his schooling in 1839. "The regular Grammar was the Eton Latin Grammar and the Charterhouse Greek Grammar, supplemented by some laborious and very useful MS. commentaries of the Head Master's composition."13 Schleswig-born historian of education Friedrich Paulsen remembered his first years in primary school, in the 1850s, as comprising the study of math, German, science, and geography. "In the German lessons we had to do syntactic exercises, distinguishing between subject and predicate or between principal and subordinate clauses." In 1861, in preparation for secondary school, his curriculum changed, beginning for the first six months with exclusive study of Latin. "To Latin were added—almost at one and the same time—Greek, Hebrew, French, English, and Danish. Mathematics and history were also included, and every four weeks I had to write a German essay. A whole library of dictionaries, grammars, and text editions had to be acquired, . . . [but] Latin always remained the most important subject."14 His account was not so different from that of Macaulay in 1813: "Before breakfast we say our Latin Exercises and Greek grammar which we prepare overnight and do two or three sums. Breakfast being over we study Euclid and Greek till one o'clock dine at two and learn Cicero and Horace," and so on.15

Thus, the training of these soon-to-be historians was not in history but in languages—so much so, that drills in language and in a different kind of formal system (math) absorbed almost all his school program. Lavisse's six years preparing for university were spent "writing Greek and Latin prose, Greek and Latin translations, Latin and French speeches, Latin and French essays, [and] Latin poetry."16 Leopold von Ranke attended Schulpforta in Saxony, a school known for perpetuating the kind of classical and other linguistic training first made important during the Renaissance. "I believe," he later remembered of his five years there (1809–1814), "that I read both the *Iliad* and the *Odyssey* through three times."17 He even sent letters home to his parents in Latin.18 Ranke, like other young German scholars, was required to do extensive language drill, but he also came to profit from philological studies as they were then revolutionizing the study of the classics. Inspired by Johann Winckelmann, Friedrich August Wolf, and scholars of antiquity in general, these drills aimed for textual translations that—through relentless pursuit of philological details—would be precise, accurate, and free of anachronisms.[19] In most cases, however, both newer and older methods of teaching languages gave low priority to the study of history, if it was considered at all. "History came into the school work only so far as necessary for understanding the classical texts, and then for the most part in a bare and dry fashion," reported Frederick Pollock.[20] In fact, students had no idea whether Julius Caesar preceded Virgil; or Homer, Plato; they only knew which was taught first in the curriculum. Lavisse wrote Latin speeches "for the most diverse characters. I gave Marsilio Ficino's funeral oration for Cosimo de' Medici, . . . and I let one of Seneca's slaves profit from the Saturnalia season to tell his master (a minister and courtier under Nero) some naked truths . . . [But] these were people I hardly knew, speaking on subjects about which I knew even less, for our teachers said little about these people or about Rome at the time of Scipio, or imperial Rome, or . . ."[21]

For the moment, then, history was an aside, a by-product or diversion in the study of the languages. It might enter the curriculum or the life of a boy because of the succession of wars and revolutions. The French Revolution, for example, moved the seventeen-year-old Barthold Niebuhr to start listing its major events. At Paulsen's school, one teacher of Greek and theology had a "great predilection for political harangues,"[22] and in the days of Bismarck's rising star students could easily induce him to speak more about current events. In the course of the school year, students everywhere debated pertinent topics and noted forthcoming debates on extracurricular political issues. "To day is a whole holiday," the thirteen-year-old Macaulay wrote home, "and I have employed it principally in taking notes for a speech [on] 'whether the Crusades were or were not beneficial to Europe.'"[23] When the debates were over, he commented: "I do not much like political subjects, for they make the boys rather too warm in defence of this or that Party." For Macaulay, such debates gave priority back to the home: "When some of the boys have their fathers in the house of commons, they fight for their father's party, right or wrong."[24] Other topics that the boys debated were the fall of Rome, the Peloponnesian Wars, and other major incidents found in Greek and Latin texts. In this case Macaulay was already constructing a hierarchy of right and wrong (objectivity and bias), with the family falling on the side of inferiority and error. Extraphilological debates evoked heated passions in the boys: "In the evening study hall, those who were 'strong in disputation' would go over their material, getting emotional, enfevered, the blood rushing to their cheeks, gesticulating, . . . their arms outstretched or raised."[25] But there was little historical knowledge informing this drive; most were animated by the competition for class ranking, or by the boyish experience of what their own disputes were like.

The main focus remained the "word"—the fervor with which it was pronounced, its intricate usages, and its grammatical constructions. Students wrote compositions of their own with the aim of duplicating the most sought-after *color latinus*. Paulsen remembered that the greatest excitement occurred when the teacher returned the corrected compositions. "To each of us he read out a list of mistakes, pointing out the worst blunders and also any mistakes of special interest, which gave him the opportunity to make instructive comments or witty remarks. If we had committed any grammatical blunders, we felt genuinely and deeply ashamed . . . [for having] offended against the logic and spirit of the language of the Romans."[26]

Accomplishments in classical languages were crucial because education involved being distinguished from other students through recitation and disputation, which were constantly ranked. Familial identity having been lost or discredited, a new persona took shape around what now mattered: "the grades in the record books, the weekly ranking of our compositions, our appearance on the honors list on prize day, when the general, the prefect, and the attorney-general sat on the platform in formal dress."[27] Ranking was often done on a daily basis: Motley, as we see in one of the letters he wrote as a ten-year-old, ranked third for that day's recitation. The English historian William Lecky, who hated the Cheltenham School he attended early in the 1850s, generally resisted the intense competition for prizes but nonetheless ranked tenth out of forty students tested to enter the University of Dublin; he also went on to become a magnificent orator. Despite Lecky's continual protests that he was "indifferent to college ambitions and competitions," he wrote to a friend after a debate in 1858: "This evening the Committee have made up the Oratory marks and I have got the Gold Medal, which is, I confess, very gratifying to me . . . My marking, they seem to think, is the highest which has been in the Society for some years. It is a fraction above what Plunket got last year."[28] Macaulay, like most other boys, wrote home at the onset of each examination period, informing his parents of his anxieties about competition from a particular student in the rankings, and then reporting on everyone's standing in every subject after the new class rankings had appeared. As Lavisse wrote, schoolmasters incited this psychically demanding competition: "I entered in my notebook my victories over Genaudet, Paul Grizot, and Sage; or, by the same token, my defeats."[29]

Many had initial difficulties not only with the constant quest for prizes and place, but also with the physical discipline and the mandated rough-housing. The latter constituted another side to the struggle for self-redefinition once the family had been left behind. Teachers struck or beat students as part of making them learn: "The discipline consisted in, first, a strong hand on the boys' heads, and a sharp cane on their hands," Stubbs recalled of primary school.[30] Paulsen, as a schoolboy, was struck sharply on the head with a pencil when his answers in Latin were slow in coming. Initially John Richard Green concentrated all his effort on avoiding beatings, but then one day he gave a wrong answer in class and received a thrashing. "I was simply stupefied,—for my father had never struck me." The ice once broken, he went to his regular punishments willingly, like all the rest.[31]

Frequent as pedagogical physicality was, the students' abuse of one other was equally common and usually more brutal. Macaulay silently endured beatings from a young bully, and told his parents only when the student had left the school for good. "I was generally beaten or taunted by him ten times a day. Though I was much too wise and perhaps a little too proud to let him perceive that I felt or heeded what he chose to do, yet I assure you my silence did not give consent. He is gone at last."[32] Lecky, although "horrified at the faces streaming with blood and men half insensible," was fascinated enough by the physical brutality of schools in his youth to produce accounts in his letters of student attacks on the police, one of which he dubbed "the Massacre of College Green."[33] In Germany, exactly at the moment when the conventions of scientific history were being established, this fighting continued on into university years in the form of dueling—a practice that was common and that seemed to absorb much student energy. "I have been here now about three weeks," the eighteen-year-old Motley wrote to his parents from Göttingen in 1832, "and during that time as many as forty [duels] have been fought *to my knowledge,* and I know of as many as one hundred and fifty more that are to take place directly." Motley characterized the duels as serious, though not usually deadly. "But the face is often most barbarously mangled, and indeed it is almost an impossibility to meet a student who has not at least one or two large scars in his visage."[34] A most important ritual of German student life was that of *Brüderschaft,* in which students adopted the familiar form of address *(Du),* drank a glass of wine together, linked arms, and kissed. This ceremony meant that the two would never fight a duel with each other.

The rituals of school life constituted an important indicator of values that differentiated high from low. Words in texts ranked above matters dealing with home and family. How one dealt with texts provided an important new identity to replace the domestic one. These textual moments were punctuated by physical pain and struggle, which also enacted not only a hierarchy between the word and the body but also between those who gave pain and those who received it. In examining schoolboy violence and its connection with abstract knowledge, Walter Ong has interpreted this phenomenon as unambiguously male, while Elaine Scarry has discussed bodily pain mostly in terms of an unproblematically male body. Yet histories of World War I, in describing the feminization of wounded soldiers, suggest that warfare and inflicting pain have highly gendered effects. Pain in violence and torture, Scarry maintains, makes one all body, nothing but an object of a superior's power. In so marking out the pained body as an inferior body—in coming to an understanding of the "weaker sex," we might say—the entire process of life in elite schools further delineated the masculine study of the word from the inferior feminine body.

A band of "brothers" whose adolescent combat and mastery of the classics united them and organized a worldview, educated young men, by the time they reached eighteen, had received a formation in the gendering of knowledge that distanced them from most young women. Carrying a Latin book in his pocket as a youth, Lavisse noted that foolish young women in church often asked to share his "missal." "One of them, a smiling, lisping girl from Touraine, said to me, 'I have a Lathin name—Hermione Vidi. Vidi meanzth I saw.'"[35] Niebuhr, barely eighteen, had utter contempt for a certain Madame de R.—"a miserable twaddler, shallow and insipid," who dared discuss with him whether the hand of God was more visible in nature or in the course of history. Upholding the latter position, Niebuhr claimed to get the best of her, and this he deduced from her gracious treatment of him over the next weeks. "[But] the honor that is my due can only be conferred on me by men, . . . for they have it in rich abundance to bestow . . . I will receive roses and myrtle from female hands, but no laurels; I only wish to plant them, and then be crowned by three or five men."[36] Twenty-one-year-old J. R. Green wanted a wife "who will never invade my study."[37]

These young men resented women who attempted to engage them on an intellectual terrain that, through their adolescent years, had been limited to a gendered competition and combat which valorized their own sex. By now they associated the keepers and subjects of knowledge with masculinity. Niebuhr had such a strict standard of gender order in intellectual matters that a visit to Westminster Abbey in 1798 both satisfied and appalled him. He "looked with gratitude" at "the busts of so many great men," but their ignoble company—"so many nameless and insignificant persons" whose tombs were graced by such "a quantity of nonsense"—sickened him. "One man writes a Hebrew inscription on the tomb of his daughter; on another, I think also belonging to a woman, there is an Abyssinian inscription."[38] Great men beside insignificant women, foreign languages (that he had mastered) assigned to commoners and the weaker sex, upset the ordering of knowledge constructed during adolescence. Young men's linguistic competition for academic honors had set standards for a common masculinity.

The forms and conventions of history merged with adolescent experiences of classical knowledge. Lecky's essay "Massacre of College Green" displays a nascent style in which the rhetoric used by classical writers to describe a battle or funerary scene coalesced with the collective and personal dramas of boarding school. Perhaps a more familiar account is Henry Adams' description of a snowball fight during the winter of 1850, in which students from Boston's Latin School faced some working-class opponents:

As night came on, the Latin School was steadily forced back to the Beacon Street Mall, where they could retreat no further without disbanding, and by that time only a small band was left, headed by two heroes, Savage and Marvin. A dark mass of figures could be seen below, making ready for the last rush, and rumor said that a swarm of blackguards from the slums, led by a grisly terror called Conky Daniels, with a club and a hideous reputation, was going to put an end to the Beacon Street cowards forever . . . The dark mass set up a shout, and rushed forward. The Beacon Street boys turned and fled up the steps, except Savage and Marvin and the few champions who would not run. The terrible Conky Daniels swaggered up, stopped a moment with his bodyguard to swear a few oaths at Marvin, and then swept on and chased the flyers, leaving the few boys untouched who stood the ground.[39]

Adams made the connection between the brutal customs of boyhood and the violence of history: "The boy Henry had passed through as much terror as though he were Turenne or Henri IV, and ten or twelve years afterwards, when these same boys were fighting and falling on all the battle-fields of Virginia and Maryland, he wondered whether their education on Boston Common had taught Savage and Marvin how to die."[40] Written late in his life, *The Education of Henry Adams* imposed conventions for writing history onto a childhood experience. But more important, the obverse also appears to be true: the terror the boy Henry felt on Boston Common and the lessons Marvin and Savage may also have learned there were the emotions later attributed to a Turenne or a Civil War soldier. Fighting as a constant and terror-inspiring part of adolescent life gendered youth's fledgling professional identity and provided the language for depicting a Turenne, a Henri IV, or a Civil War soldier.

Fights on the green and competition with classmates for prizes and place were the significant, heart-pounding moments of self-definition from which historical sensibility was constructed. The significant matters in school—what one wrote home about or recollected—were constantly transcribed in a kind of prewriting of history. William Stubbs, helping his chums cram madly for exams, kept a mock chronicle with himself as the abbot of a monastery, explaining, in this instance, that keeping early hours would promote good performance: "by ye ensample of ye holie saynctes which dydde rise and go to sleepe with ye sunrise: whilk habit (albeit it peradventure dydd arise from a wante or lacke of lyghte artifycialle) is greatly to be commended and verie desyrable to be restaured."[41] Letters presented certain kinds of information, which gradually banished domestic ritual and assigned merit to study, fighting, and ranking in the battle over languages. Something in this trilogy of significance recalls Ranke's maxim that history was not about "the quiet course of events alone or the noiseless progressive development of politics and legal relations"; rather, it concerned "clever politics, successful wars, and the force of powerful personalities."[42] "Ruse and deceit [were] used like defensive weapons," Lavisse wrote of the Lycée Charlemagne, "to win the battle of every minute."[43] A battle, we might add, to help a powerful hero triumph. Eliminating domestic events from letters and ultimately ridding epistolary and autobiographical accounts or behavior of too many familial and other personal emotions—as Quinet made clearest—was a major part of schooldays, but also of history. In boyhood descriptions of school practices, the stuff of "historical significance" had already emerged.

By the time these historians were nearing manhood, their lives had shifted from household matters and family routines to linguistic study in the classics and to the issues of war and politics. They pursued these topics in competition with one another, but also imbibed them as the subject matter of classical texts. Thus, it seems no accident that the premier historical writing of the nineteenth century would come to focus on finding objective truths in the words of state documents sequestered in closely guarded places like archives. Authentication, classification, dating, and other procedures had less to do with the feel of some universal past (as Lavisse complained) than with a kind of linguistic ritual that took place behind closed doors, among like-minded and similarly trained men. The thick walls of the boarding schools, so insistently invoked by Ranke a half-century later, prepared the temperament for cloistered archival study of the word, the sentence, the text—for objectification of political documents and the creation of a modern discipline of history. Though history employed already existing conventions, it performed a simulation of highly problematic, even troubled youthful workings of gender.

Young historians had rescripted the world during their school years, finding the most significant components to be knowledge of words, texts, struggles or wars, and the construction of powerful personalities.[44] Concomitantly they had identified characteristics, emotions, and subject positions associated with the inferiority of women, social life, and the home and that they would denounce as somehow contaminating the field of study. "I constantly become more and more estranged from the world in the ordinary sense of the word," the eighteen-year-old Niebuhr wrote his alarmed parents.[45] At age nineteen Hippolyte Taine claimed that, several years earlier, he had already become "master of myself; I had accustomed my body and soul to do my will. And thus I saved myself from those brutal passions that blind and stupefy man, and prevent his studying human destiny."[46] With personal passions and familial attachments pushed aside at the *lycée,* Taine had prepared himself for "la science," where he could "think a lot, discover many new things, contemplate and produce beautiful works." Besides this dispassionate study, Taine at age twenty had only one other goal: the companionship of like-minded, accomplished men, or what he called "love." In the world of disinterested contemplation, the perfect companion "is not a woman, but a man," he wrote to one of his high school competitors, whom he hoped to include in "the brotherly pursuit of truth."[47] The band of scholars that had become so hardened in the struggle for adolescent truth would remain intact to pursue "la science."

Objective scholarship had also been coded male through study of classical texts that imprinted an image of the hero-scholar on the adolescent mind. Boys who beat and bruised each other while they competed for prizes in their studies followed a junior version of the model found in Caesar or Cicero—a model of men who waged war and politics but who also wrote. Among the ancients, Niebuhr maintained, war, public office, and scholarship were gloriously combined in the life of a single man.[48] "From the particular direction of my mind and talents," he informed his parents, "I believe that nature has intended me for a literary man, an historian of ancient and modern times, a statesman, and perhaps a man of the world."[49] The experience of youth made up the professional credo, allowing Niebuhr to maintain the same comrades, pursue the same struggles, and keep up the scholarly study of texts that had showed him this route in the first place. At the same time men who chose this course or who later studied history could maintain the "objectivity" of such appraisals, for study was the higher, complex mental scrutiny that stood in opposition to the objectification in beatings, boyhood fights, and the brutal repression of a boy's domestic identity. Successfully producing the *color latinus* and the facts ended beatings and stabilized the adolescent's status, permitting him a new subjectivity. Objective study of the "word," repression of everything outside study in classical texts, brought both distinction and personal heroism. In the adolescent *agon* of boy versus master, boy versus boy, and boy versus the text—through the perpetual struggle against inferiority, the body, femininity—the adult historian painfully and passionately emerged. These tales of youth would be successfully reworked into historical science as distinguishing the winners from the beaten, the higher from the lower, and would become its foundational political narrative.[50]

Households and Great Historians

The twenty-one-year-old J. R. Green, who wanted a wife who would stay out of his study, nonetheless sought one "who can decipher my horrible scrawl and copy my manuscripts for the printer."[51] Green, who married Alice Stopford in 1877, was typical of those historians who needed household help to accomplish their numerous works.[52] Many wives of historians assiduously worked on their husband's projects, or even wrote books themselves. During the course of nineteenth-century professionalization and even into the late twentieth century, much historical writing and research was familial. Family members were researchers, copyists, collaborators, editors, proofreaders, and ghostwriters, and a great deal of writing took place at home.

François Guizot, who would serve as prime minister under the July Monarchy, earned his living in the 1820s and 1830s by teaching university courses and by writing, with full-time help from his first and second wives. At first, because Guizot's courses were irregular and even (in the 1820s) suspended as too liberal, the family survived only because of money brought in from their joint writing. Guizot and his first wife, Pauline Meulun Guizot, envisioned gathering large collections of documents, one on French history and another on England, so that she could do much of the compilation and copying. Although they eventually completed both collections, and published them along with histories of the two topics,

Pauline Guizot worried about the initial difficulties in getting a publishing commitment. "As you know, I wanted to find something which would give us a settled employment, and prove the foundation of a different sort of life than ours is now . . . It was to get over this difficulty that we thought of undertaking those two great works. They have both fallen through, and we soon shall have lost a year from the time when we had hoped to lay the first stone of the little fortune which we must build in one way or another."[53] Pauline Guizot wrote novels and pedagogical works, read books and took notes for François's articles, conducted the correspondence for his editorship of the *Revue Française,* helped her husband prepare his lectures, and finally edited the collection of documents on the English Revolution. The Guizot household was a literary workshop, and this continued after Pauline's death. Second wife Eliza Dillon Guizot also wrote. In the early 1830s, she sent to her husband the following outline of "their" work: "I am rewriting my chapter on the state of Gaul, and I shall have to write it a third time . . . I think that I shall be obliged to retouch the chapter on the Gallic wars." She was also preparing a review essay, which, when done, "we will put in your portfolio to use when the opportunity presents itself."[54]

Sister combinations such as the Stricklands were almost as common as female dynasties—for example, Sarah Taylor Austin, her daughter, and her granddaughter (Janet Ross), or Julia Cartwright and Cecilia Ady. François Guizot and his daughters, Pauline Guizot de Witt and Henriette Guizot de Witt, were another authorial team of history. Guizot prepared his daughters by writing them long letters not on everyday life but on such topics as their use of the comma. Equally pervasive were husband-wife collaborations, such as those of Alice Stopford Green and J. R. Green, Barbara Hammond and J. H. Hammond, Mary Ritter Beard and Charles Beard.[55] Despite the modern ethos of separate spheres for men and women, historical writing was implicated in domesticity, the family, and sexuality—all of which were rich in possibilities for authorial confusion and unprofessional influences.

As the demands for high-level scholarship and extensive research intensified, historians organized their households into efficient, complex systems. Max Müller noted, on a visit to the home of Eugène Burnouf, that the famed scholar had "four little daughters who were evidently helping him in collecting and alphabetically arranging a number of slips on which he had jotted down whatever had struck him as important in his reading during the day."[56] The historian Thomas Frederick Tout had his wife, sister-in-law, and other female relatives working for him. This joint authorship ensured that female relatives were the ones most familiar with the historian's work; consequently, they were the natural editors of his posthumous publications and his most knowledgeable biographers. Such publications were an essential stage in creating the persona of the autonomous historian: the stage in which the wife dismissed her own contribution.

Thus, in the periods of both nascent and mature professionalization, history had author-teams that worked in household workshops. Around this complexity arose conventions that formulated authorship as singular and male, as a public and extrafamilial undertaking. For instance, when a scholarly reviewer was assessing a work by a husband and wife, custom dictated attributing authorship to the man alone. The reviewer could do this, say, by talking about "Charles Beard's" *Rise of American Civilization* series and by noting "the assistance of his wife," and then proceeding as if Charles Beard were the sole author. The Beards' jointly written book *The American Spirit*, it was said, resembled "an encyclopedia of Charles Beard's reading for the past decade."[57] A compliment to the muse who had inspired the brilliant man indicated to a knowing readership that the wife's contribution had been negligible. These conventions veiled the complex authorship of many works.[58] An equally common convention comprised more explicit sneers at the pretensions of intellectual wives to any kind of accomplishment: Harriet Grote, who wrote several books—including the biography of her husband, George Grote, a historian of Greece—"seldom underrated her husband, and never herself," quipped Arnaldo Momigliano.[59]

Such work continued the process of distancing a higher, intellectual life from a domestic, affective one. Originating in the assiduous research of well-trained and self-abnegating historians, the best professional accounts contained their own positive truth because each author had put aside politics, class, gender, and other passions and interests, as well as concerns for literary drama, in order to achieve an autonomous, universally valid text. As history became professionalized, however, these claims to scientific impersonality were made into a discipline composed of such diverse ingredients as offices at home and work, research assistants, copyrights and royalties, translations, editions, editors, readers, and an academic hierarchy of flesh-and-blood human beings that reinforced professorial authority. While professional standards invoked impersonality, professionalism developed as an arena charged with human affect and fantasy. The scientifically minded French scholar Gabriel Monod confessed that a review of Ferdinand Gregorovius' biography of Lucrezia Borgia had "made my mouth water" for a "more intimate acquaintance with this 'loose, amiable'" woman[60] and he praised the rapturous Jules Michelet because he could "not escape the contagion of his enthusiasm, his hopes, and his youthful heart."[61] Reformers often had trouble avoiding not just sexual but familial terms, since they saw their new science as based on "principles," in the words of one, "that are transmitted from the fathers to the sons."[62] Initially envisioning their environment as a "workshop," they found the most important quality was "deference toward their masters."[63] Even into the mid-twentieth century, historical science could incite romantic expressions of masculine identity: "I study history," R. G. Collingwood wrote, "to learn what it is to be a man."[64]

Articulations of sexual excitement and emotional enthusiasm were rewritten into a complex historiographic script that depicted the great historian as someone struggling with the pettiness of everyday life and ultimately soaring beyond it to reach the realms of universal truth. Few historians have presented such a challenge to the task of rescripting as the passionate Jules Michelet, a perennial and exciting focus of historiographic attention. Yet Michelet's sexual and intellectual relationships with women, especially his second wife, have, ironically, for the past century facilitated depictions of him as a great author. They have shown the ways in which a driven man overcame a wide array of familial, marital, and other difficulties to pursue his obsession with history. In the process, for almost a century the portrait of Michelet's personal life—theoretically irrelevant to historiography—has served various intellectual schools, partisan politics, personal advancement, and a number of other causes. For all its specificity and intimate detail, the story may have a familiar ring.

Michelet's first wife, Pauline Rousseau, died in 1839, having given birth to two children and having been largely ignored by her husband as he made prodigious efforts to build an important career. Unlike the comparatively clean separation with Pauline in terms of work, Jules's second marriage, to Athénaïs Mialaret, was a complicated, literary experience. For one thing, Mialaret was already a studious woman who at the time of their first acquaintance, in 1848, was tutoring the children of Princess Cantacuzène in Vienna. Her relationship with Michelet began when she wrote him a letter requesting his moral advice, because her reading of his book *Du prêtre, de la femme, de la famille* (*On the Priest, the Wife, the Family*) had left her in need of guidance. They soon started writing to each other about the revolutionary politics of 1848, which she reported from Vienna and he from Paris. When Athénaïs first visited his apartment in the fall of that year, their interview took place in his study, and he reciprocated her visit by himself delivering a volume of his *Histoire de la révolution française* (*History of the French Revolution*) to her hotel. Their relationship thus began and progressed as a literary one, and it remained so throughout twenty-six years of marriage.

According to both their accounts, Athénaïs Michelet did research and reported on it, wrote sections of Jules's books, discussed projects and recorded details of their daily conversations on topics for books, and offered her judgments on the work that was published under his name. She wrote books of her own, one of them a story of her childhood. He drafted an unpublished manuscript, "Mémoires d'une jeune fille honnête" ("Memoirs of an Upright Young Woman"), about her young adulthood, After his death, she continued publishing: selections from his journal, a story of his youth, a posthumous edition of their love letters. During their years together, Jules kept a journal in which he recorded her personal feelings and many incidents in their work life.

Athénaïs was twenty-two at the time of their meeting; Jules, at fifty, was passionately attracted to her. But the marriage, despite his extreme sexual arousal, was consummated only with difficulty, after Jules had taken his young wife to consult with several physicians. These matters, too, were literary, for he recorded the course of the consultations in his letters and journal, noted her menstrual periods for more than two decades, and wrote about both their thwarted and their successful sexual relations. The literary quality of their common life constructed and even permitted Jules's final conquest of his wife. Before their marriage, he noted his growing desire, which was crushed on their wedding night: "All was refused me.

By her? No, her good little heart burned to make me happy."[65] On March 20, 1849, eight days after their marriage, Jules noted that the couple had done scholarly work together for the first time, but "physically, it's impossible to be less married."[66] This pattern continued for some time: work during the day, followed by "insoluble difficulties" at night.[67] Jules's reports spoke of increasing sexual despair, alternating with moments of "very tender abandon," "of certain sweet and kindly signs that . . . her poor young body, so suffering and charming, is nonetheless not insensitive to the breath of May." His accounts focused desire on Athénaïs' person and built an extraordinary, almost gothic literary drama of pursuit and escape.[68] "My love, very sweetly, received me for a moment in her bed."[69] Finally, on November 8, 1849, "in the morning, before my work," the couple had sex: "I penetrated her fully, . . . very hard as my doctor had indicated."[70]

Jules fashioned his journal into a sexual saga, and after this consummation his account of the marriage continued to charge domestic study and writing with sexual negotiation. Looking back over eight years of marriage and remembering their best sex, he picked a date in 1850, "near the end of the fourth volume of the *Révolution* [*Death of Danton's Wife*], a vivid, nervous emotion. She was moved also . . . and calmed this storm in an act of tender humility."[71] This was written in 1857, a year of particularly intense intellectual discussion surrounding composition of the book *L'Insecte* (*The Insect*) and a year in which Jules filled his journal with sexual detail. "After menstruation, extreme passion. I long to plunge myself into this fountain of life . . . She herself is burning, delectable, tasty."[72] These heady descriptions did not indicate very frequent intercourse (the couple had sex about every ten days), but it often occurred after reading and writing. Once, while Athénaïs cut flowers that she could study for their work, he read from the draft of *The Insect;* later, "she came to me like a little lamb and was very good."[73] Two days later, he described her reading another section, "and in an isolated alleyway, the second behind the grand canal, she showed me a great deal of friendship."[74] By this time, Jules had written more than once of their intertwined endeavors—sexual and intellectual—and of their intertwined personalities. In the ideal marriage, one he often claimed to have, each partner was constantly impregnated with the other, a transformation and movement in which "she, imbibing of him, is him while remaining herself."[75] He found himself absorbed in her, yet he tried to prevent that absorption from being complete. Writing gave him some sense of individuation, but he also struggled "to maintain a point apart from her where I can be strong."[76]

Jules further complicated his interpretation of their marriage by consistently referring to it as an incestuous one, in which he consciously played the role of father to her role of daughter. With Athénaïs virtually the same age as his own daughter Adèle, Jules wrote of her as "my child" even before they were married and continued to refer to her in that way thereafter. "*The most licit of incests.* Marriages of people unequal in age have a sweetness when the older resembles the father or mother of the younger and can thus be loved as such."[77] Even while noting his wife's orgasms, he referred to her as a little girl and spoke of her innocence: "All [her] pleasure . . . is true tenderness, affection, simultaneously conjugal and filial, and even more." And a few days later: "God forgive me for having been and for being so in love with a woman . . . and yet with a child. I was greedier and greedier for her sweet and wise words and for her virginal body; and the more I entered it, the more I left full of desire."[78] For her part, Athénaïs reportedly frolicked like a young colt, making saucy faces for Jules's paternal observation. Two layers of family relationships—father/daughter and husband/wife—enveloped these literary lives.

Thus, the collaboration of Jules and Athénaïs Michelet on such works of "natural" history as *L'Oiseau* (*The Bird;* 1856), *L'Insecte* (*The Insect;* 1857), *La Mer* (*The Sea;* 1861), *and La Montagne* (*The Mountain;* 1867) and on other writings was fraught with the ambiguities of domestic literary production.[79] Although *The Bird* was published under Jules's name, he himself broached the question of authorship, first by dedicating *The Bird* to Athénaïs as the product of "home and hearth, of our sweet nightly conversations."[80] That work, Jules explained, issued from domestic "hours of leisure, afternoon conversations, winter reading, summertime chats," and other joint efforts.[81] A reviewer in the *Moniteur*—not the only one to acknowledge the hint of collaboration—cited the work as having "the style of a superior man softened by the grace and delicate sensitivity of a woman."[82] Jules himself wrote to journalists suggesting its familial origins and asking them "to take this into account" in their reviews. The next year, he reported the authorship of *The Insect* somewhat differently to an Italian journalist; it was, he said, "in reality the work of my wife, but composed and edited by me."[83] Victor Hugo offered praise after receiving a complimentary copy of *The Insect:* "Your wife is in it, and I've sensed her passing in these subterranean corridors like a fairy, like a *luciole* guiding your genius with her ardent light."[84] In the wills he wrote in 1865 and 1872, Jules bequeathed Athénaïs the literary rights to his books and papers, not only because she had served as secretary, researcher, and proofreader, but because she had "written considerable sections of these books."[85]

When Jules died in 1874, his widow put aside some of the projects on which she had been working with special interest. She sorted out the papers that he himself had not destroyed, and used them as the basis for several books, including a summary of his youth, an abridged version of his journal, a history, a travel book, and a biography. Jules's son-in-law (a literary figure of some influence but slight reputation) and grandchildren contested his legacy in court. Athénaïs won, however, taking as her patron in these publishing endeavors Gabriel Monod—a friend of the family, a founder of the *Revue Historique,* and a pioneer in the development of scientific historical writing in France. Monod introduced selections from Michelet's work, wrote an appreciation of him in his book *Renan, Taine, Michelet* (which also paid tribute to Athénaïs' devotion to her husband's memory and to her continuation of his work), wrote a biography, and gave a course at the Collège de France on Jules's historical writing. Just before her death, Athénaïs gave Monod control over the disposition of many of her husband's papers. With that, her real troubles began.

From Monod to Lucien Febvre and beyond, attention to Jules Michelet swelled among prominent French intellectuals, but it was invariably accompanied by extraordinary invective toward Athénaïs—invective that has become ever more pronounced over the course of the twentieth century. Monod, who during Athénaïs' lifetime acknowledged her contribution to Jules's work ("faithful trustee of his ideas"),[86] and credited her with the publication of many posthumous papers, deftly changed course. Practitioner of a different, more scientific history, Monod attributed his choice of career to Jules, but "the feelings I have for him are not those of a disciple for a master whose doctrine one adopts."[87] Jules Michelet embodied a French historical spirit, "a sympathy for the untolled dead who were our ancestors,"[88] and as such served as the model historian of French nationalism, so deeply important to Monod's generation of scientific historians.[89] In fact, many scientifically oriented historians in this era of professionalization, though disavowing political interests and aiming to purge the political from their work, were unabashedly nationalistic, had friends in politics, or engaged in politics themselves, especially (but not only) during the Dreyfus Affair. As in the case of Monod, a commitment to the nation-state was an integral and formative part of the historical mind in this era,[90] but these scientific historians projected that patriotism back onto an earlier generation, conserving nationalism for history while divorcing it from scientific practice through frank discussions of patriotism and objective portraits of biased, dead historians.

Monod's first work on Michelet thus avoided a full discussion of the latter's method but touted the connection between patriotic sentiment and history. In 1905 Monod wrote *Jules Michelet: Etudes sur sa vie et ses oeuvres* (*Jules Michelet: Studies of His Life and Works*), which began sketching the outlines of the "historical Michelet"—one useful to the scientific aspirations of the profession. Invoking the study of history based on the scientific evaluation of documents, Monod published a few of the Michelet papers that had so recently fallen into his hands. The book opened by posing the question of authorship in Michelet's work, citing rumors that not he but his wife had actually written much of the material published under his name. Monod used the introduction to start defining what came from Jules and what came from Athénaïs in the work written during their marriage and in Jules's posthumous writings. He pointed to the liberties Athénaïs had taken in certain posthumous works and he affirmed Jules's genius in the strongest possible terms, but in general his judgment about her contribution was positive. In addition, the book published intimate parts of their journals, to show the complexities of their relationship and of Jules's relations with other members of his family. For all its measure, Monod's work was crucial to analyzing his authorship in "scientific terms," singling him out as the representative figure of Romantic historiography, and clearly delineating the contours of a unitary Michelet, the great historian. Chapters on two of Jules's children and material on his first wife enlarged public knowledge of his family circle, diminishing his second wife to one among many supportive actors. During these years, Monod also gave a course on Michelet at the Collège de France, and further augmented scholarship on Michelet by exhaustively examining the origins of his historical writing and establishing an interpretive precedent: Monod claimed that Michelet's most important work had been done during his first marriage and before the Revolution of 1848.[91]

Monod never definitively separated Jules from his wife. He neither ruptured the bond celebrated in Michelet's journal nor completely discredited the sense of fusion Athénaïs had promoted in handling posthumous publications. Other authors were bolder. In 1902 Daniel Halévy published a widely read article in the *Revue de Paris* on Michelet's second marriage—an article that asserted the utter worthlessness of Michelet's work after his dismissal from all his positions by Napoleon III (and by implication after his marriage).[92] But Halévy also explicitly attributed this failure to Athénaïs, who, he maintained, "suffered from spiritual frigidity" that contrasted sharply with Jules's "feverish mysticism and enthusiasm."[93] Distinct but also disturbed, she aimed for total and unnatural domination of her husband—"from the bedroom, because that was an essential step, to the worktable. It was the worktable she aspired to, and Michelet at first defended it, while she controlled the bed. For several months, the marriage was chaste. Finally Michelet gained control in bed, and, soon after, Athénaïs gained access to the worktable."[94] Halévy thus painted a chaotic, disordered domestic scene, from which he as historian could constantly rescue Jules's character, traced in bold, clear lines that further distinguished him from the surrounding cast of characters: not only were Jules and Athénaïs opposites, but her rule separated him, "the most miserable of modern men," from his family and friends.[95] Whereas Jules professed to have profited from the blurred authorship of domestic collaboration, subsequent biographers and editors rewrote the scenario as sexual inversion and misrule. The drastic revision of his script—one that portrayed a tender, erotic, and collaborative domestic life—was underway, perpetuating the hint of sexual secrets that motivated research, while allegedly clarifying authorship.

Thus dragged onto the historiographic stage, the widow served an important literary function by helping to set boundaries around the historical author and by acting as a double with whom the hero struggled in a classical agon of self-definition. Instead of being the dutiful daughter to a dominant father, Athénaïs became "one of those women who avariciously dispenses her sex," forcing Jules to wage a perpetual battle to get more of it.[96] In 1936 Anatole de Monzie, a lawyer and author who had successively been minister of public works, of finance, and of education, coined the term "abusive widow"—oddly enough, not for outrageously famous consorts like Catherine de Médici, who could be said to exemplify female "misrule," but for spouses of intellectuals. He accused these women of criminally meddling in the literary and artistic legacies of men like Claude Bernard, Leo Tolstoy, and Jules Michelet. Each woman either managed a dead husband's reputation, edited his work, or claimed an independent intellectual status for herself. Of all the offenders, Monzie took Athénaïs Mialaret-Michelet as "the model for these excessive, inopportune, and abusive widows."[97] He converted the Michelets' fraught sexualities (as reported in both their journals) into an evil repression by the wife, the result of which was to turn what Monzie viewed as Jules's innate puritanism into an obsession with women that ruined his historical sense. Monzie quoted George Sand's observation—that Michelet was "incapable of alluding to women without lifting their petticoats over their heads"[98]—and blamed this supposed incapability on Athénaïs' parsimonious control of the conjugal bed. Any weaknesses in Jules's writing resulted from her authority over sex, but also from her interference in his writing. A quote in Athénaïs' travel diary, in which she described exactly the food she apportioned to Jules, Monzie took as typical of her "accountant's mentality" ("vue comptable"). Widowed, however, and freed from his sanguine influence, she showed her true colors: when gathering quotes from his journals and letters, she "mixes this hash with passages from the *Hundred Years War,* stirs the whole thing, seasons it with oil and vinegar like a salad, then serves the dish to guests at the republican table with the appetizing title *Sur les chemins de l'Europe.*" This account contrasted Michelet's intellectual achievements with the domestic "hash" that the "widow-cook" (as Monzie called her) served up as history.[99] As another example of an "abusive consort," Monzie cited Jean-Jacques Rousseau's partner, Thérèse Levasseur. She continually interrupted Rousseau's learned discourses with questions about "the soup or the laundry," and he would make regal responses. "He would have ennobled a piece of cheese, had he spoken of it."[100] Sexuality and domestic detail were part of the wife's character; detachment and ennoblement, part of the authorial husband's.

And the disparity between the two grew greater when the discourse of separate spheres was put into service.

Monzie's and Halévy's characterizations seem harsh, even crude, but they were no more so than the portrait of the "abusive widow" solidified by the legendary intellectuals who next took up the project of confirming Michelet's stature and who further rescripted his life. Monzie, French minister of education in the 1920s, was a friend and mentor of Lucien Febvre, who was a student of Gabriel Monod, cofounder of the *Annales,* and Monzie's choice to edit the massive *Encyclopédie française*—a work designed to compete with Soviet and British encyclopedias by substituting a conceptual organization for the conventional alphabetical one. In 1946 Febvre published a sampling of Michelet's historical writing, an anthology whose introduction was lengthier than the material it presented. Febvre's *Michelet,* published in a series entitled "The Classics of Liberty," heralded the post–World War II era of freedom. "Why Michelet?" Febvre asked rhetorically. "His history is full of errors . . . [He's] a superpatriot, a liberal—a crybaby domesticated by a shrew."[101] Having endured immense deprivation in a family that struggled each day not for such luxuries as liberty but for daily bread, Michelet was the perfect symbol of all that the French had endured during the war. But he also represented "the France of twenty-five centuries . . . eternal France."[102] For Michelet embodied "history," or what Febvre saw (following Michelet) as the "successive victory of human liberty over the fatality of nature."[103] Under the Napoleonic Empire and the Restoration, censorship and political repression had prevented France from having any history at all. Then came the Revolution of 1830, when, according to Febvre, Michelet suddenly used the new freedom to start writing the first history in modern times. The deprived Parisian struggling to teach his students thus became the "Father of History."[104] In making Michelet relevant for "those who today have experienced Munich, the disasters of 1940, of 1942, of 1944,"[105] Febvre had willfully to discount the careful scholarship of his mentor Monod, whose detailed work had shown that Michelet's *Introduction à l'histoire universelle* (*Introduction to Universal History*) of 1830 had been the work of the preceding six years and that its preface had largely been written in the months preceding the summer of 1830[106]—that is, before the so-called era of freedom had begun. Constructing a usable author took precedence over scholarly accuracy, and Febvre would constantly refer to Michelet in his work, ultimately writing an article entitled "Comment Jules Michelet inventa la Renaissance" ("How Michelet Invented the Renaissance").

Taking command of the postwar project of publishing a scholarly edition of Michelet's papers and works, Febvre chose Paul Viallaneix and Claude Digeon as the editors, oversaw the project himself, and continued his great interest in Michelet. The volumes that have thus far appeared contain (among other things) Michelet's journal, his youthful writings, and the collaborative works with his wife. In all of them, the editors have included conspicuous attacks on any claims that Athénaïs had a substantive or even minor role in their authorship. They have proven this point in several ways, all of them accepted as part of the "scientific" method. First, manuscripts of *The Bird* (and other natural-history writings) were scrutinized for their handwriting. Anything in Jules's handwriting indicated to the editors his authorship; conversely, anything in Athénaïs' script indicated that she was *not* the author—that she was a "simple copyist." The editors allowed that she had done much preparatory work for *The Bird* (research, drafting outlines), but they undercut this single generous attribution by citing notes to indicate the "importance of [Jules's] personal work at documentation." Finally, the editors juxtaposed Athénaïs' copious first drafts with the final version of the book and judged that in contrast to her "verbosity," the final version was so "definitively" stamped with Michelet's "originality" that his wife's ideas, and thus any claims on behalf of her authorship, were completely eradicated. Thus, "'the collaboration' of Madame Michelet . . . ceases to be a problem."[107] Professing to be scientific, the editors saw Michelet's "creative spirit" firmly stamped on the work. "Her contribution to *The Bird* was effectively limited to the preparation." Transformed by his "vast design," her "childish book became an epic."[108] The editors constructed authorship on the basis of handwriting, and even then applied gendered standards to what that indicated. In no instance could they admit of substantive collaboration between husband and wife; rather, they cast the book as the product of a struggle between male and female in which male genius triumphed, giving the world another masterpiece.

Retelling Michelet's story, the editors dropped Monod's progressive but qualified disapproval of Athénaïs' authorship and instead constructed an utterly negative account of her "false" literary productions. Published after Jules's death, these included the editions of his youthful writings, excerpts from his journal, travel writings, and his love letters to Athénaïs. The scholarly edition (1959) of his *Ecrits de jeunesse* (*Writings from Youth*) opens with a description of the way in which this work inspires not only boys, who receive the book from their schoolmasters, but also older and more sophisticated youths, who see Michelet's friendships as analogous to the noble relationships depicted in the classical texts they study. But both groups of readers, if they went to the Michelet archives, would find that despite helpful lessons in the book, they had been betrayed and were (in the words of the editors) the "blissful dupes of a fraud."[109]

What is the nature of this fraud? Instead of revealing it and its perpetrator immediately, the editors keep readers in suspense by switching to the inspiring story of Michelet's life, which they represent as passed in a "mental fever" of preparing his various histories. Toward the end of his life, "considering his youthful writings a relic," Michelet began destroying them, along with many of his other papers. Although Jules describes the destruction in the first person singular, as his own doing, the editors add Athénaïs to the scene of destruction and provocatively ask: "To what extent did his young wife, gripped by a kind of retrospective jealousy, herself censor these vestiges of a passionate life in which she had not been queen?"[110] Besides suggesting that she, not he, had burned the papers, thus rewriting Michelet's own journal, the editors scorned her publication of selections from the various early writings in a lone book, *Ma jeunesse* (*My Youth*), as a travesty. Yet the editors themselves proceeded by gathering up what they admitted were random notes, mixed reading lists and observations, drafts, notes, and sketchy essays and making them into an integrated volume, to which they gave a similar title—*Ecrits de jeunesse*. Moreover, Michelet had expressly written that one section of his early writings "should never be published, but may be excerpted," a condition to which Athénaïs adhered far more faithfully than the twentieth-century editors,[111] who prided themselves on publishing everything.

Another volume of Michelet's writings, entitled *Journal* and prepared by the same editors, contains, according to their own admission, dispersed papers of different sorts, an intimate diary, various travel journals, and random notes from his course outlines assembled in chronological order. Even as the editors held Athénaïs in contempt for omitting vivid sexual detail, they saw to it that, in Michelet's jottings, notebooks, and other scraps of writing, paragraphs were made, spelling and punctuation corrected, and other "problems eliminated." "We didn't think that accuracy demanded us to respect those."[112] Thus the men who accused Athénaïs of eliminating phrases that failed to coincide with her values explained away the changes they themselves made wherever Michelet failed to meet their own, different criteria. The editors in fact created from fragments and assorted writings a "unique and complete" account, an integrated and whole Michelet separated from his perfidious wife. But this Michelet was the product of this particular edition of his works.[113]

The trope has remained powerful. For example, Roland Barthes's *Michelet lui-même* (published in English simply as *Michelet*) maintains that the widow "falsified Michelet's manuscripts, stupidly falsifying the themes—i.e., Michelet himself."[114] An exception to the prevailing view is Arthur Mitzman's recent study of Michelet, which has generously tried to absolve Athénaïs from many of these charges by explaining that she had no training as a scholar.[115] Moreover, as Mitzman points out and as his own work shows, this "abusive widow," even though she may have suppressed some sexually explicit material, still allowed so much to be published that Michelet's obsessions are more than amply documented. Mitzman also notes that the modern editors' version of Jules's love letters (a "sacred relic," the editors claim, canonizing Jules) omits Athénaïs', which she had included in the original edition. The omission often makes Jules's letters unintelligible. Mitzman continues to refer to the "false Michelet" created by his widow, but he acknowledges the interactive nature of the writings, at least the posthumous ones.

One might assume that feminist scholarship would support Mitzman's sympathetic treatment of a woman author, endorse appreciation of her work, and strive to establish at least a historically accurate contextualization of her accomplishments. However, this scholarship also runs the risk of replicating the historiographic problem of authorship—as would happen if, for instance, one argued that Athénaïs was a genius equal to her husband, or if one tried to carve her out as a distinct author. Devising some way of treating Athénaïs as a historian or author is not my intent. I broach the subject of her authorship only to suggest (along with Mitzman) its dialogic and collaborative qualities, to indicate the way in which she edited passages in the travel journals to describe women instead of men, and to note that a major part of the much-condemned editing of Jules's love letters involved omitting those letters in which he discussed her sexual and physiological state and the doctors' opinions of it.

The attacks on Athénaïs' authorship are interesting in themselves because, by using gender to create a historical author, they help define the historical field. To take another example: Michelet's editors wondered whether Athénaïs "reconciled her literary pretensions and her wifely love without asking herself if literary genius wasn't profoundly individual, if the most faithful writer doesn't find himself alone with his conscience and his talent when he writes, and if the first duty of fidelity toward his memory isn't to respect to the letter the work he has left behind."[116] Such statements remind us that the language of scholarship combines passages listing archival citations and professions of "respect to the letter" with emotionally or sexually loaded phrases. Hayden White has described the rhetorical style of scientific history as "genial" and "middle-brow," yet this history has simultaneously been highly charged, contentious, and loaded with gendered fantasy, passion, and outrage. The case of Michelet's widow shows all of these being deployed to establish the scientific confines of history, whose boundaries she so clearly challenged.[117]

The great author, created in so gendered a way, has served the authorial dilemmas of other historians. For example, Lucien Febvre's editorship of the new edition of Jules's work and his postwar devotion to and creation of the cult of Michelet covered ambiguities in his own authorship of the *Annales* and other works during the 1930s and World War II. Febvre cofounded the *Annales* with Marc Bloch, and their collaboration was never easy, as many historians point out. From the mid-1930s, funding for the *Encyclopédie française* enabled Febvre to employ an assistant, Lucie Varga, a young Austrian historian and regular contributor to the *Annales* with whom he became romantically involved. Febvre—whose wife, Suzanne Dognon Febvre, was also a scholar— relied on Varga for research, and her detailed commentaries on newly published works allowed him to produce book reviews quickly. By the late 1930s, his romantic relationship posed a threat to his marriage and career; Varga lost her job, and never found another in the field of history.[118] Another dilemma emerged under the Occupation, when, as Natalie Davis has pointed out, Febvre and Bloch were at odds over whether the cover of the journal should carry Bloch's name (which was Jewish). To Bloch's insistence that they resist the Nazis' anti-Semitic policies, Febvre responded, "So what if there's only one name on the cover? It's the enterprise that counts."[119] Davis illuminates the difficulties of authorship during the Occupation, citing the many alternatives, compromises, and resistances that were possible. Febvre chose neither to collaborate openly nor to resist openly, but rather took a middle way that would allow him to continue to appear an important historical author. Michelet's authorship having been firmly established in the gendered historiographic discourse of the preceding decades, Febvre consolidated his own by incanting the ritualized attacks on the abusive widow and by overseeing a project that, among other things, would strive to destroy her claims to authorship.

Establishing the bounds of history and the nature of authorial identity for generations of subsequent historians, the saga of Jules and Athénaïs Michelet may even have opened onto questions of French identity and the shape of its history. Twentieth-century France was particularly tried by issues of nationalism, gender, and history. While Monod and Halévy were outlining a story of female misrule in the Michelet household, the falling birthrate, the feminist movement, and the "new woman" had already raised questions of gender and provoked fears of the declining virility of French men. Since their defeat in the Franco-Prussian War of 1870–1871, the French had faced a world turned upside-down by defeat, reparation, and annexation. Only after 1920, however, did the discourse of the "abusive widow" take full and effective shape, as France struggled with its hundreds of thousands of war widows and with a gender order troubled by the effects of war and economic depression. Those men who returned from the war were often deeply disturbed; others found that their wives had abandoned them, and a confident feminist movement demanded rights equal to those of men. Misrule—the "decline of the Third Republic," as most historians of France would have it—led to the defeat in 1940 and to lingering malaise after World War II. The "abusive widow" offered a timely explanation, in which her stupidity, inferiority, and frigidity symbolized an inversion of all that French intellectuals took as their defining characteristics.[120]

If, as Hayden White suggests, factual storytelling or narrativity "moralizes reality," then Michelet scholarship (and this account has merely touched on a few highlights) had a direct relationship to the political reality of French history. Michelet's biography as a historian recapitulated the story of postrevolutionary France, using gender as its trope. Before 1848, Michelet engaged in heroic struggles for greatness as a historian, muting other attachments; but that revolutionary year was a watershed for him, just as it was for France—entrancing him, even enslaving him to an "illegitimate" ruler. Michelet continued to be productive, even opening new avenues of research, but his "enslavement" was continually wearing. Michelet died in 1874, and with the advent of a republicanism born of military defeat came French decline, as well as the abuse of his writings, an erosion of his genius. But the interwar period launched his rebirth, as well as that of history and of France, culminating in the triumph of scientism, planning, technocracy, and the professions that would rehabilitate France as they rehabilitated Michelet's reputation. Narrating Michelet—an enormous project of the postwar French Academy—moralized the story of France, using gender to mark out where science ended and error began. Though France was destitute economically and defeated militarily, its tradition of individual genius would help it survive.

These conclusions about Michelet and the history of modern France are speculative, and secondary to my real concern: the relationship between gender and historiography, between authorship and objectivity, between the state and the household as important historical topics. Recently, Lionel Gossman has proposed a "middle ground" between claims that history corresponds to reality (or objectivity) and claims that history may be relative or arbitrary ("decisionism").[121] Instead of saying that history is commensurable with reality, Gossman suggests that good historical accounts have some degree of commensurability among themselves, while in place of arbitrariness, decisionism, or relativity, he invokes "the ability to change one's mind for good reason."[122] In trying to apply these hypotheses to the case of Michelet's widow, I find myself in agreement with the objective conclusions about her scholarly inadequacy; that is, in all good faith I could also write a commensurable account about her inadequacy as a historical writer. In addition, the changing evaluations of Michelet as author make perfectly good sense, allowing both commensurability and relativity their day. But Gossman's criteria still fail to account for the repetitious attention to someone so insignificant as Athénaïs Michelet. Only exploring the ways in which gender is constitutive of history can do that.

Michelet, like most central figures in historiography, has been useful to individual careers not so much for the way he provides a nationalist refuge to those, like Febvre, who may have unconsciously worried about their own decisions during the tortured time of war and holocaust, but for the way he has helped construct the individual fantasy life of the scientific historian entranced by achievements of great historians. Wrapped in the mantle of science and impartiality, the saga in which Michelet was mutilated by his widow and rescued by heroic researchers is a melodrama whose psychological dimensions we should begin attending to, if only to achieve a better understanding of the world of history. Like most professionals, Febvre, the surviving cofounder of the *Annales*—so deeply indebted to Michelet's work on mountains and seas, to the sense of the local in Michelet's travel journals, and to the complicated relationship between historical actors and their environments on which Michelet pondered—fantasized unique and singular authors as the forefathers of and contributors to his new school of history, and he worked to script it that way, as had many before him. The category "author," as Foucault proposed, has helped organize the discipline around the classification of historical writing and the development of other critical procedures that the invocation of a single author facilitates, allowing for such genealogies of influence and parentage to arise.

"What is a historian?" we ask, altering Foucault's query. Until now, a historian has been the embodiment of universal truth, who, constructed from bits of psychological detail and out of the purifying trials dealt by the contingencies of daily life, human passion, and devouring women, emerges as a genderless genius with a name that radiates extraordinary power. It is time to begin thinking about the ways in which this authorial presence has in fact been gendered as masculine, and how it comes into being through repetitive pairings of a male "original" with a female "copy(ist)" or "falsifier" or "fake." In the nineteenth century, the process of creating the high and the low was part of educational practice, as well as of adult work. Although beatings have stopped in school, the agon of the winner and loser figures in our visual and historical culture. In historiography itself the great historian, coupled with his absent, inferior, unoriginal partner, remains the ever-present touchstone for misogynistic, scientific standards.[123]

The Practices of Scientific History | 4

Since the nineteenth century, claims that history is scientific have rested not only on its presumed objectivity but on the actual work performed in the pursuit of truth. "Every 'historical fact,'" the historian Michel de Certeau wrote, "results from a *praxis* . . . It results from procedures which have allowed a mode of comprehension to be articulated as a discourse of facts."[1] This formulation mirrors what historians of science have found: that intense and detailed activity necessarily precedes the production of scientific facts. Likewise, historical innovators in the nineteenth century were quick to claim that scientific truth about the past was grounded in a rigidly followed set of practices—foremost among them seminar training and archival research. These practices stimulated extraordinary excitement in the West, so much so that young men traveled thousands of miles to participate in seminars and—before the blessings of central heating, rapid travel, and a range of technological aids—to work assiduously in archives. These two activities were as foundational to and influential in the profession as were ideals of truth and objectivity. They captured the imagination of young men and allowed them to develop historical prowess and to exercise their individual judgment according to a set of rules learned in the course of this schooling and work. On the one hand, the new procedures associated with professionalization and scientific history produced skilled men with common ways of behaving—a brotherhood, a republic, a peer group. On the other, they yielded distinctive ways of imagining field-specific tasks, including highly gendered fantasies of historical work, that enticed people into and shaped the profession.

The fact that "objective" historical work has displayed powerful signs of gender, sex, and masculinity will perhaps not surprise people. But gendered descriptions of work were not merely signs of bias, momentary lapses in objective standards, or some other shortcoming for which our judgment should correct. The formation of a practicing collectivity of historians and their many metaphorical and emotional descriptions of scientific practices were inextricably intertwined with historiographic breakthroughs, accompanying them and facilitating the adoption of a scientific method. Mary Hesse, a philosopher of science, has demonstrated the ways in which natural scientists rely on metaphors ("waves," "packets," "elevators," "big bangs") as predicates that help explain and even contribute to the makeup of an explanandum. Thus, for Hesse, metaphor is central to the progress of knowledge in the sciences.[2] Gender was constitutive of procedures in scientific history, and the complex uses of gender were pivotal to scientific advance. At the same time, the unacknowledged connection between historical rationality and gender has had consequences, notably the development of the profession as an overwhelmingly male enterprise.

Historians have been slow to acknowledge the influence exercised in the profession by seminars and archival research, preferring to believe that scholars are molded by ideals. Yet these two practices worked what Bruno Latour has called (in the case of the scientific laboratory) "a reversal of fortunes" for the proponents of a professional, university-based discipline.[3] As the amateur case shows, history took many forms, venues, and valences before the advent of the seminar and other professional practices. Even in higher education, universities and academies staged the dissemination of historical knowledge like spectacles. Well into the second half of the nineteenth century, huge audiences—often said to be composed largely of society women—competed for seats at these lectures. "All the world might come," reported one American attending a course at the Collège de France, "and the audience, varying with each lecture, was composed of women, travellers, and old men, of whom many chose this opportunity for their afternoon nap." Only "here and there was a young man seen."[4]

Though amateurism flourished, by the end of the century the seminar and archival research had worked a reversal of fortunes by gaining ascendancy over other historical practices, setting the standards for historical writing as the investigation of politics and becoming the criteria for success within a powerful profession. This occurred especially within the seminar; but even amateurs did archival work, and some had received seminar training. Like most other professions in the modern period, history developed a sharper institutional profile by training historians in a distinct methodology, endowing them with a body of knowledge and credentialing them.

The ascent of scientific history through the growing power of its practices had gender implications, too. Seminars and archives were spaces reserved mostly for professional men, and it is in this context that the professional work of historical science can be seen as enmeshed in the development of masculinity in the nineteenth century. Discussions of the rise of intellectual disciplines in modern times have identified mastery, domination, and other characterological attributes as integral to professionalization, and have mostly classified them as bourgeois or middle-class traits.[5] Yet enough evidence exists to suggest that part of the appeal of these new practices was the way in which they proposed a masculine identity worthy of and equal to the arduous quest for objectivity. Disciplined by the seminar to become venturesome "citizens," young professionals set out for the archives, where they hoped to break open the gates of the documentary "harem," save the "fairy princesses" residing there, and find truth in the process.

The Historical Seminar

Prior to 1900, the historical seminar was a fledgling institution of such international magnetism that from great distances young men sent passionate letters home to anxious parents about their experiences in such a group. University professors wrote reports about it and circulated them widely, and university officials and even ministers of education sought to gain control over it. This new site of historical learning originated sometime between 1825 and 1831, when Leopold von Ranke invited a handful of students to work with him weekly in his home.[6] Interest spread across Europe and to the United States. According to the enthusiastic Herbert Baxter Adams of Johns Hopkins University, seminars functioned like "laboratories where books are treated like mineralogical specimens, passed about from hand to hand, examined, and tested."[7] As Ephraim Emerton of Harvard put it, the seminar was essential to "illustrate and enforce this truth": that history "has a scientific method."[8] Even a century later, Walter Prescott Webb, in his presidential address to the Mississippi Valley Historical Association, could rhapsodize about the historical seminar as an expeditionary adventure to an "unknown country," in which the professor was the leading trailblazer and the students "a crew of axe-men, observers, hunters and scouts, front, flank and rear."[9] The founding generations of the profession of history believed that instituting the historical seminar would transform knowledge. And later generations would gain almost their entire professional training in seminar work while finding their most important evidence in archives.

For all the invocations of Ranke's written works, his books have long been superseded by other scholarship and are rarely read; his seminar, however, continues to generate powerful cultural influence.[10] Begun as "historical exercises" *(exercitationes historicae)*, Ranke's seminar brought selected young men to his home for close scrutiny of documents. There, according to Wilhelm von Giesebrecht, his students were initiated into the processes of Ranke's "workshop" as they watched in wonder at displays of his scholarly virtuosity and erudition. They were also amused by Ranke's "jubilation" at exposing a forgery or someone else's mistaken scholarly move.[11] The earnest atmosphere in the seminar contrasted markedly with the antagonistic lecture scene, where Ranke and Friedrich von Raumer, "in defiance of each other, choose to lecture at the same time."[12] Others conjured up Ranke as a ludicrous lecturer—a characterization that was perhaps more legend than history. Wrote Andrew Dickson White, who was Ranke's student in the 1850s: "He had a habit of becoming so absorbed in his subject as to slide down in his chair, hold his finger up toward the ceiling, and then, with his eye fastened on the tip of it, to go mumbling through a kind of rhapsody, which most of my German fellow-students confessed they could not understand. It was a comical sight."[13] On a research trip in the 1840s, Ranke was accused by former student Jacob Burckhardt of exuding an air of intrigue in hopes of suggesting that some secret diplomatic mission lay behind his trips to archives.[14] But in the seminar (according to most former students), Ranke's true intelligence and character were fully revealed.[15]

As the seminar method in history evolved from the closely related philological seminar of the late eighteenth century, professors amassed documents for students to investigate, bringing original manuscripts or printed compilations of documents into class.[16] In Julius Weizsäcker's seminar on German history at Göttingen, held exceptionally at the university on one occasion because of an illness in his home, the professor arrived with his servant in tow, "a solid German woman of a certain age, who carried in her bare arms a huge rush basket" filled with volumes of the *Monumenta Germaniae Historica.*[17] Professors usually assigned topics for the students to investigate using original sources, but in some seminars students felt free to choose topics that most interested them.[18] What mattered most was that students learn "uniquely and by themselves the application of correct methods of historical inquiry."[19]Each member of the seminar presented his findings on his topic, and then perhaps faced a critic designated to respond to his investigatory methods, with the teacher himself providing necessary corrections and emendations. The professor reportedly also helped the group work collectively on batches of documents concerning a particular issue or time period.

Professionals claimed that the search for historical truth in the seminar gave birth to a new community based on an agreement to find the authentic or real past. It was a *"Gesellschaft,"* reported Emerton of Harvard, "a society, a club, presided over by a professor, but composed, not of subject students, but of members."[20] Within this community, the rules of etiquette, largely set by women in ordinary social interchange, fell by the wayside in the search for historical truth contained in documents.[21] Theodor Mommsen, an alumnus of Ranke's seminar, and Johann Gustav Droysen each refused to let a visiting Belgian scholar attend their seminars because "the criticism was so severe, so merciless, that it would have been impossible to admit a stranger."[22] Colleagues in seminars formed a defined collectivity that within several decades of Ranke's first "historical exercises" had developed its own identity. Seminar members in Germany gathered after each meeting in history clubs and associations, which adopted fixed rules and rituals and were devoted to the furtherance of historical study. Seminar members often collaborated on publications, giving rise to many reports on the "cooperative" method that document-based history and its specialized techniques ultimately generated. The fruits of Ranke's seminars were published as the *Jahrbücher des deutschen Reiches unter dem Sächsischen Hause* (*Yearbooks of the German Empire under the Saxon Dynasty*), while those of Droysen appeared as *Hallesche Abhandlungen zur neueren Geschichte* (*Halle Studies in Modern History*).

Seminars proliferated—especially when Ranke's students began setting up their own—and became pilgrimage sites for increasing numbers of young men from foreign countries. Germany had already been attracting foreign intellectuals concerned with the progress of secular and scientific philosophy, but by the middle of the nineteenth century some young men were concentrating more narrowly on the scientific practices that occurred only in history seminars.[23] They dreamed in advance of attending; even as late as 1887, the young Andrew Little of Oxford exulted in a letter to his mother at actually participating in Ludwig Weiland's seminar in Göttingen, after he had "looked forward to [it] as a vague possibility for two years."[24] For apprentice scholars, the need to participate stemmed from the seminar's ability to give historical science a force and focus that it had not had before. Future leaders in the consolidation of professional history—scholars such as Herbert Baxter Adams of the United States and Gabriel Monod of France—had all done seminar work, and indeed gained their prominence from having done it.

But how exactly did the seminar fire the move toward scientific history? For one thing, the seminar fixed the serious training in history in a single location: the professor's study at home or, somewhat later, the university seminar room, which unlike the public lecture hall displayed a kind of power by localizing the entirety of historic human experience under the eyes of a small and self-contained community. Occasionally the seminar room was likened to the paternalistic "workshop in which the experienced master teaches his young apprentices the deft use of the tools of the trade."[25] Whereas the public lecture was open to all, the seminar set the conditions for historical engagement, restricting it to a small place where entry was gained by invitation only. In middle-class homes, the man's study was often the most lavish room in the house, and for many it exuded an air of traditional male command and domination.[26] Manuscripts were laid out on a large central table or two, so that the stuff of past politics and the state was gathered where students and teacher could jointly scrutinize its meaning.

As the history seminar became institutionalized and state-supported, its venue began shifting to the university. At the Ecole Pratique des Hautes Etudes, founded late in the Second Empire with the aim of upgrading French higher education through scientific methods, Gabriel Monod's seminar started in his Paris apartment but then moved to two small rooms at the Sorbonne. These rooms, according to one quite unscientific description, had "something intimate about them which gave a certain charm to the lessons. It was a tiny, adorable spot."[27] This atmosphere of intimacy was enhanced by the contrast with the huge lectures halls (where orators like Heinrich von Treitschke enthralled as many as 700 students). Doors, desks, and cabinets were often locked, and access was restricted to those showing special talent for or commitment to historical research. Ernest Lavisse set boundaries to historical training by locking his classroom door.[28]

The seminar room itself bounded the community of historians, giving it order and definition. Early observers of the seminar took pains to describe the procedures in each one, and especially its physical features—how documents, books, newspapers, tables, chairs, desks, and other furnishings were arranged. Oral descriptions and accounts in letters, however, soon gave way to state-financed visits and official reports. The oft-quoted and translated Belgian historian Paul Frédéricq, whose lengthy studies of European seminars in the 1870s and 1880s included detailed accounts of seminar rooms, proved extremely helpful to other scholars trying to institute the proper atmosphere, the right procedures, and adequate bibliographic holdings. Charles Seignobos, attending a seminar in Leipzig, reported on the books in the room and added that it "seemed to us unworthy of both so great a university and so flourishing a seminar."[29]

Herbert Baxter Adams of Johns Hopkins University was the person who made the most lavish use both of this information and of personal experience in Germany, building on it to create and publish an actual blueprint for the perfect seminar room. His room included—in addition to the obligatory "Seminar Table with new books and current periodicals"—a horizontal-file chest for newspapers, another for maps, alcoves for various historical topics, revolving bookcases, desks for graduate students, a card catalogue, and a washroom. Adams prescribed the ways in which materials should move from one part of the room to another, from one desk to another, from one shelf to another, depending on the pertinence of a particular document to weekly seminar work. Other ingredients of the seminar room, though omitted from Adams' plan, included a red cover on the table, portraits of great historians gracing the walls, and a large banner proclaiming, "History Is Past Politics, and Politics Present History." Adams presented his utopian diagram so cogently that by the early 1880s European scholars had heard of it, and of his photographs of the Johns Hopkins seminar room, and had sought them out. William Stubbs of Oxford, for example, requested (via Daniel Coit Gilman) "the diagram, etc. of your historical laboratory."[30]

In all countries, proponents of seminars adopted a common, civic language to suggest that the character of a man was transformed and perfected through the new methods of historical study. Disdainful of aristocratic displays of inborn flair and brilliance, seminars produced scholars who were prepared for hard work, provided with technical competence, and skilled in critical thinking. The students in Henry Adams' experiment with the seminar method became an industrious and dauntless collectivity, transformed from gentlemen into professionals. "The boys," he noted, "worked like rabbits, and dug holes all over the field of archaic society; no difficulty stopped them; unknown languages yielded before their attack, and customary law became as familiar as the police court."[31] Seminar history would avoid the kind of superficial education offered in unreformed universities, where, as J. R. Green scornfully put it, any "gentleman" was said to be able to do history.[32]

Proponents of seminars articulated their values in terms that we could call middle class. In 1880, for example, Ernest Lavisse told candidates for the agrégation that a man trained in the close study of documents was a "useful man."[33] A seminar demanded, according to one professor, "manly work," and it differed markedly from both aristocratically patronized academies and the sociable salon, where eighteenth-century knowledge was debated. Sundered from the pretenses and posturings of Old Regime knowledge and conspicuously based on work, the seminar allowed—as in the case of Ranke—the forthright (or "transparent"), autonomous, and middle-class self to come into being. The seminar of Georg Waitz, according to a student in the 1860s, operated according to Waitz's own values: "integrity and candor, . . . an impartiality which made him worry less about his reputation than about the progress of science, the absence of parti pris, of any fanaticism, of all mischievous vanity."[34] Professional history depended on research skill and work, rather than on the vanity-driven rhetorical tricks of drums-and-trumpets narrative.

The nineteenth-century seminar promoted in miniature the interactive public sphere, forming a masculine marketplace of knowledge where many traditional hierarchies—estate, age, status—were leveled in the presence of expertise. In Waitz's seminar, another scholar observed, "whenever a student made an original observation, Waitz would exclaim that he himself had learned something on a topic he thought exhausted, and, pulling a small silver pencil from his pocket, he would note it in the margin of his copy."[35] Dealing in demonstrable truth, seminar participants created a true community where male virtue operated, as each person performed on behalf of the collectivity. On the one hand, their work made them autonomous; on the other, they surrendered individuality for a common brotherhood of professional practitioners. Their shared commitment to textual analysis and archival work made them "a grand republic of workers," as Stubbs put it in 1867;[36] the notorious jealousies of earlier practitioners came to an end. Yet maintaining the republic required great effort. Students, like those of Mommsen, were subjected to severe personal tests whenever the seminar community saw the slightest error or laziness creeping into their work. The communal norms of the seminar experience became the basis for a proliferation of fraternal history associations and history clubs. In Germany the seminar was regularly followed by a meal in a restaurant or pub, and the seminar propagated a range of subsidiary collective institutions wherever it came to dominate historical work.

The seminar's ability to generate an extraordinary array of coordinate clubs, associations, and other programs further established it as the center of the professional historical community. Duplicating the operations of the hardworking middle-class entrepreneur, the history seminar promoted an expanding market for historical goods, all of them stamped with the seminar's imprimatur. The seminar's offspring attained almost imperialist proportions. Herbert Baxter Adams, for example, posted a huge map of the United States, to which he affixed markers noting the places where his former seminar members were introducing modern historical methods. He called these sites his "colonies." "So I am a Margrave, am I?" a former student wrote Adams from Berkeley, California. "Here then the Margrave sends in his report of his dealings with the Huns and Slavs."[37] Making forays into uncivilized reaches himself, Adams traveled throughout Virginia, Wisconsin, and other states, gathering information about regional historical societies and urging his former students to build local power bases for seminar-type history.

More important, the historical seminar came to provide an imperative for transforming the entire system of teaching history in the Western world, bringing the system within the orbit of seminar-trained historians. Part of this imperative had to do merely with expanding the amount of and respect for historical subject matter, because in most countries history was little valued or taught. In Germany and the United States, study of the classics without historical context or content dominated the secondary-school curriculum. At the Lycée Charlemagne in Paris, young men composed Greek and Latin declamations for historical figures without knowing that Greece and Rome were different civilizations. "I thought the author who was taught at the beginning level was the one who came first in time . . . I knew nothing of the history of France."[38] When Johns Hopkins opened, there was no undergraduate teaching of history until a graduate fellow from the seminar introduced it. Herbert Adams worked to found the American Historical Association in the 1880s as a showpiece for seminar research, not the reverse, and the association almost immediately set up the famous "Committee of Seven" to draw up a national program for the reform of historical curricula in the schools. But the United States was far from an isolated instance of the expansionist nature of the historical seminar, fast becoming the center from which historical standards emanated. As Ernest Lavisse announced to an assembly of graduate students, the reforms in historical training that were then being implemented in Paris "will one day be felt in the humblest primary school of the humblest village."[39]

Although international travel by professionalizing historians occurred during extraordinarily tense, nationalistic times, and although historians were quick to draw comparisons about pedagogy and research, the acceptance of the seminar transnationally had the effect of making historical methods appear transcendent and universal, removed from the political, religious, and epistemological quarrels of the century. Located in a professor's personal office or in a particular seminar room, the seminar nonetheless acquired an international status that made personal, marked, and national space vanish in the name of a common methodological truth that yielded the past. The seminar thus led scholars to forget the conditions of history's production, particularly the gendered, middle-class, and civic imaginings that inspired historical science. In this way the seminar spiritualized and universalized the undertaking, purifying it of such contingencies as politics, economic interests, and personality. It was, as one scholar noted, "a silent, reasonable world, where the only action is thought, and thought is free from fear."[40]

Seminar devotees were always ready, however, to invoke the "manliness" of the seminar and its commitment to "manly work." For Gabriel Monod, the seminar professors were the general staff and the members were the army, while Lavisse saw the entire enterprise as an army doing battle against outmoded educational practices.[41] According to Monod's pupil Gabriel Hanotaux, who studied at the Ecole des Chartes (the premier French school for training in archival methods) early in the 1870s, seminar training had "a kind of male beauty."[42] For Emerton, "the name 'Seminarium' denotes the fertilizing power of the historical 'Gesellschaft.'"[43] A British historian described the seminar as "a bed in which to *sow* the seeds of intellectual effort."[44] More than a century after the seminar was founded, Walter Prescott Webb poured forth a stream of associations with male fecundity: the word "seminar" came "from French and Latin *seminalis,* French *semen,* again pertaining to or consisting of seed, source, first principle, germinal, originative."[45] The seminar rejected the femininity of the public lecture or salon. Though scholars might attend the latter, the seminar had replaced it as the focal point of their republic of letters. In the United States, where higher education for women was proceeding at a rapid rate, Charles Kendall Adams first introduced the seminar at the coeducational University of Michigan in 1870–1871. But even he had only a "polite toleration" for women students, and was quoted as saying that "of course the young women could not do seminary [i.e., seminar] work."[46]

A pioneer in expanding the seminar system, Droysen conflated the active manliness of the seminar man with history/time as a whole and posed it as the opposite of nature/space: "How is it, then, that amid the restless movement of things, human observation construes certain series of phenomena more according to their temporal side, and others more according to their spatial side, taking the former as History and the latter as Nature?"[47] The natural world was one of recurring cycles and repeating periods, that which sluggishly fills space, whereas the world of history was that of individuality, restless succession, and constant inquiry.[48] Droysen's comparison of the activity and initiative of scientific history with the passivity of female periodicity and nature merely replicated the terms that physicians used to delineate sex roles in nineteenth-century Europe and North America. Just as invocations of work, civic virtue, and transcendence were interwoven with specifics of scientific methodology, the inveterate use of gender hierarchies to characterize the scientific project molded historical practice out of the normative politics of the times.

To summarize: the seminar experience as a founding practice of scientific history was stimulating because it converged with the attractively progressive concept of male citizenship. There were certainly national differences in seminar development. In England, for example—though scholars flocked to seminars on the Continent, though professionals adopted republican language, and though scholars like F. W. Maitland tried to establish them—at Cambridge and Oxford the practice never displaced the perhaps parallel tutorial system.[49] But even in the monarchical German states, universities were noted for a certain efflorescence of republican principles, including academic freedom as part of modernization.[50] The transparent subject, the active and achieving scholar, a bounded community of historians cooperating like virtuous citizens: by the nineteenth century, all of these attributes of the seminar had also come to structure masculinity. From the beginning, the seminar member was considered a kind of participatory, universal citizen who was implicitly gendered male and whose autonomy was shored up by the excluded and dependent status of women—a view that was much like that of the citizen in republican-based theory.[51] The seminar was thus an extraordinarily powerful institution, producing "men" with specific disciplinary prerogatives and communal solidarity.

The republican paradigm in scholarship, as in politics, was nonetheless open to reform, resistance, and revolt. Its considerable power was never total, nor was its identity with expressions of national vitality and its congruence with male privilege seamless and consequently invisible.

Seminar work often provoked craven behavior, rituals of shaming, and mockery. At times insecurity, not success, could be read in the seminar's proliferation. Herbert Baxter Adams and Henry Adams directed their respective seminars to find the teutonic origins of U.S. institutions, an old cultural bias reinforced by their admiration for German power after the Franco-Prussian War. Monod, Lavisse, and others attributed the French defeat of 1870 to the lack of seminar and philological training for French historians, and although they promised a "manly" future for their trainees, the uninitiated were by implication feminized or unmanned.[52] These anxieties could provoke scholars to make prodigious efforts in order to emerge with the masculinity promised by the seminar; but some, like the seminar-trained Johann Jakob Bachofen, rejected the "Prussianization" of the historical field, with its attendant "smoke-filled rooms," "vain erudition and ostentation," and "bootlickers" of the new scientific masters. He resigned from the University of Basel and wrote the bizarre work *Das Mutterrecht*.[53] Jacob Burckhardt, similarly trained, refused the "call" to teach at Berlin; he turned, instead, to art history and to giving huge lectures on such topics as the history of cooking.[54] Out-and-out warfare (such as the Franco-Prussian conflict) inspired the spread of seminars; belligerent, destructive acts occurred in seminar rooms; and in the field at large, the coordinated ruination of some careers and the advance through the ranks of the more favored protégés shaped the profession.[55]

Some of the seminar's most avid followers introduced heterodox methods, again showing a potential suppleness in the seminar as a practice. Lucy Maynard Salmon, for example, was trained in the University of Michigan seminar and committed herself to archival research, introducing the seminar method at Vassar College. Salmon was remembered as an upstanding member of the Vassar community, stressing citizenship and courageous public behavior. But while adopting this republican stance, she ran her seminars in such an idiosyncratic way that, though held in high esteem, they were called "Miss Salmon's Laundry Lists." Instead of having her students study state documents, she "threw" onto the seminar table stacks of laundry lists, piles of train schedules, cookbooks, architectural designs for housing, and other artifacts of everyday life. Castigated by reviewers and scorned by publishers after her turn toward the history of the mundane, Salmon nonetheless showed that in the case of feminine intrusions (as in the case of nationalist passions) the doors of the seminar room could never be completely secured.[56]

Sex in the Archives

The seminar system produced, tested, and inspired the professional historian, incorporating the language of republicanism and masculine citizenship into scientific history and thus connecting historical innovation to the political imagination. The coordinate practice of archival research, however, was imagined differently. Early in his extraordinary career of incessant archival study, for example, Leopold von Ranke described documents sequestered in archives as "so many princesses, possibly beautiful, all under a curse and needing to be saved."[57] Ranke was hardly alone in depicting archives in such highly charged terms. For Léon de Laborde, head of the French national archives under the Second Empire, "A library is some*thing,* archives are some*one* . . . a someone who lives and breathes." Before professionalization, Laborde claimed, archives had been "raped" and "mutilated," their "arms and legs ripped apart," their "head" taken "cruelly" away from the body.[58] In order to anchor history's universal truth, professionalizers promoted a coordinate reliance on the methodical examination of state documents found in archives. This truth resulted from the common though expert hard work and skill of citizens in finding authentic documents. However, the archival quest that followed hard on the heels of seminar training often jettisoned the language of citizenship for that of love, melodrama, and even obsession.

From the beginning of the postrevolutionary era, archives and other repositories containing documentary and manuscript sources were sites of contest and intrigue, and thus anything but neutral spaces. During the revolutionary and Napoleonic periods in France, there were intense archival struggles, which raised the first hint of modern archival obsession. On July 29, 1789, the French National Assembly decreed the founding of an archive for its proceedings, and over the next decade a stream of legislation regulating French archival material poured from successive assemblies. When the Jacobins decreed the destruction of documents bearing the "least vestiges of the monuments of an abhorrent dynasty,"[59] they promoted archival drama. It seemed possible that the entire documentary past of France would go up in flames, along with titles, deeds, and other documents pertaining to agricultural property and services.

Thanks to the tireless efforts of the archivist Armand Gaston Camus, this did not happen; the Terror waned, and more moderate men came to power. But the saga of European archives in modern times had only begun. As Napoleon conquered Europe, he also confiscated its archives and gradually began to construct an enormous Palais des Archives on the Quai d'Orsay. The shell of this building was more than two meters high at the time the empire fell. Already vast quantities of archival material, including state and other papers, had been transported to Paris from Geneva, Belgium, Tuscany, Spain, the Netherlands, many German states, the papal states, and Piedmont. Napoleon's defeat refocused attention on archival material, specifically on the return of most of these papers, and it seemed to make high interest in archives permanent, as the dramas of nation-states and their archives were intertwined. Scholars like G. H. Pertz drove themselves to build published collections of documents, such as the *Monumenta Germaniae Historica,* as part of a quest for their national past. Sponsored by Baron von Stein, Pertz struggled to gain access to the papal archives, initially reviewing some 24,000 documents in 1822 and copying some 1,800.[60] Other scholars were now hot on the trail of collections, bribing archivists and politicians for their turn with this sequestered, "original," and "authentic" material. Bribes and political influence became paramount in gaining copies of documents. As procedures took on a more regular character, scholars from most European countries—often as an act of patriotism as much as an act of scholarship—published compilations of original state papers, especially from premodern times.[61]

Ranke became renowned for his forays into the archives. Educated in classical philology, he was so expert in comparing sources and sorting out competing accounts of an event that critical history was said to have begun with his *History of the Latin and Teutonic Nations* (1824), a book that earned him a post at Berlin. For four years (1827 to 1831) Ranke enjoyed a research leave, spent primarily in the archives of Vienna and various Italian states. He produced histories of the popes, of the Reformation, and of various European nations, and continued his research in European archives. Ranke used his famous seminar to disseminate his method of examining archival sources, thus making both practices pivotal to distinguishing scientific history undertaken by professional men from the dilettantish prattle of the salons, from lectures in universities and academies where men and women thronged to hear celebrated historians, and from Walter Scott's wildly popular historical novels.

The language of work authorized archival study; in contrast to the European aristocrat's Grand Tour (an extensive period of travel around Europe, considered part of a young man's education), such study was an arduous, joblike quest undertaken by expert citizens. Scholars subjected themselves to innumerable hardships and inconveniences in order to pursue scientific knowledge, traveling to libraries, archives, and other repositories as a professional requirement. Eugène Burnouf, ranging throughout England and the Continent in search of manuscripts in the 1830s, described in lurid detail the many indignities and sufferings he had to endure: sleepless nights in coaches, hard beds, "sad collections of meat and vegetables cooked in water," atrocious English food, "ugly clothes," "horrible dinner parties," homely wives of scholars.[62] These hardships notwithstanding, the commitment to historical practices inspired by German philology, which searched for original and authentic meanings based on strict rules for the use of evidence, spread across western Europe and the United States.

Scholars filled letters, memoirs, even their historical writing with intimate reflections on their travel to archives. Ranke described the beautiful maidens he met en route, the sensual poetry he read along the way, and the splendid apparel of society women he met in various capitals, thus revealing the additional attractions in archival work. Traveling to Prague, he saw "the hundred towers of the old city . . . In the museum, I found not only pictures but manuscripts." As the trip continued, he encountered an eighteen-year-old "lightly clad beauty," whom he had to "take under my cloak" because of the cold.[63] Trips to archives were imagined as feats of prowess, often taking place after mountain climbing in Switzerland or as part of extensive tramping from one county to another. James Froude claimed to have examined more than 100,000 manuscripts on the Continent and in England. The climbing, the tramping, and the great discoveries were reported back to scholars at home, arousing curiosity and creating imaginative intensity about research. "My dear Freeman," an ailing J. R. Green wrote to a colleague, "I wish I could have been with you on your northern campaign . . . [Such a trip would] drive me wild with delight."[64]

Archives revealed facts and evidence from which the historian impartially and rationally constructed a scientific account of past reality. But here is how Ranke, for instance, described his work in one repository: "Yesterday I had a sweet, magnificent fling with the object of my love, a beautiful Italian, and I hope that we produce a beautiful Roman-German prodigy. I rose at noon, completely exhausted."[65] He called another collection "absolutely a virgin. I long for the moment I have access to her, . . . whether she is pretty or not."[66] Throughout the century, other historians described archives in sensual or bodily terms, sometimes using more violent depictions. For Charles-Victor Langlois, French archives had been "mutilated" over the centuries, "the parts of the body . . . scattered across all of France and Europe: *corpus disjecta.*"[67] A young researcher avid to get into the foreign ministry archives in the 1870s was determined "to force open the doors and thrust past the keepers of the harem."[68]

Archives evoked this kind of imagery, and they also provided a place where scenarios of pollution and danger might be envisioned. To earlier scholars, archives had seemed like "Augean stables" in need of purification. Nineteenth-century historians had similar feelings. Archives were dusty and dark; light was the enemy of old documents, fading the ink, and extremes of temperature were also damaging. The French archives in the Soubise palace, it was claimed, were in utter chaos: cartons of documents littered the halls and stairways, ceilings were falling, and thefts and other irregularities frequently occurred. Not until the 1840s, when the palace was refurbished and expanded, did the situation improve.[69] In 1851, Heinrich von Sybel, examining the papers of the Committee of Public Safety, encountered "the dust of the year 1795."[70] In all archives, decay was everywhere: small animals gnawed at the documents, which were fouled with dead bugs, rodent excrement, worms, hairs, and nail clippings; old paper, vellum, and script were damaged by water, fumes, soot, extremes of temperature. Illegible writing, strange languages, shorthand, and secret codes all made archives places of mystery.

Moreover, the archives themselves were largely inaccessible. Readers, once they gained difficult entry, usually could see only a restricted number of documents, which were brought into conservators' offices or into some reading area. The Vatican Library not only lacked a catalogue but had 204 steps leading to its archival tower, with a further separation between the repository and the reading room.[71] But inaccessibility merely heightened the mystery of archives. Scholars like Ranke wrote excited letters to colleagues, friends, and family about the number of folios or cartons exposed to them each day. In 1848, revolutionaries brutally stormed and occupied the Vatican archives to discover its alleged secrets. Thus, descriptions of archival practices added a sense of forbidden knowledge and images of middle-class sexual prowess to the configuration of historical study as work and civic virtue.

The quest for original sources could be deeply troubled. Gabriel Hanotaux noted the effect of being "buried in the dust of my old parchments." In the 1870s he spent his youth working on Richelieu's papers, labor that resulted in a "sweet pain etched on my pale cheeks and weighing on my bowed back."[72] Others surpassed Hanotaux in evoking not just pain but morbidity. Writers often used the scholar's weddedness to documents and old books as a metaphor for disease and ill-health. George Eliot's *Middlemarch*, that towering novel of Victorian probity and balance, centered on a desiccated scholar whose work was fruitless and ultimately destructive. Sitting with his piles of folios, Casaubon showed "a melancholy absence of passion in his efforts at achievement, and a passionate resistance to the confession that he had achieved nothing." If his spirit had shriveled, his body was in no better shape: "Digestion was made difficult by the interference of citations, or by the rivalry of dialectical phrases ringing against each other in his brain."[73] Still other writers saw manuscript-based scholars as "dead from the waist down."[74] Historians, too, described their immersion in documents and old books in fraught terms. Attributing the onset of blindness to excessive study in libraries and repositories, Augustin Thierry imagined his scholarly frenzy as furthering a science that would benefit the nation: "I gave my country all that a soldier gives, mutilated, on the field of battle."[75] The death of the scholar Otfried Müller on a research trip to Greece was that of "a martyr in the land of his spirit, . . . a hero on his shield."[76]

Blinded by excess, Thierry depicted his actual research as a kind of delirium, an ecstasy. Theodor von Sickel described a moment in 1861 when Lord Acton, in impassioned search of a papal document, set out to burglarize the Vatican archives; he was taken into custody by Italian troops.[77] Autobiographical and other accounts of historical scholarship, as well as authors of fiction and nonfiction, hinted at the dangerous possibility that the pursuit of documents and rare books might contain elements of irrationality, madness, or perversion. Thinking of the scholars and collectors around him, the bibliophile and author Paul Lacroix Jacob exclaimed that "Paris is surely the paradise of madmen and bibliomaniacs."[78] From the 1830s on, writers staged the thirst for documents and books as a real and dangerous obsession. To take just the French case: in the 1830s alone, Charles Nodier and Gustave Flaubert were among many who produced notable stories about "bibliomania," which in the nineteenth century meant a crazed fixation on documents, manuscripts, and rare books that one wanted to observe, touch, or own at all cost—including death.[79] Some decades later, Jacob noted that a bibliomaniac would become faint at the sight of the greengrocer wrapping produce in a manuscript, and archivists in Marseilles reported in 1869 that obsessed Prussian scholars had been stealing documents for some two years.[80] In both cases, documents aroused such powerful emotions that strong men fainted and upright ones committed crimes. Thus, even as a scholar relied on documents like a scientist, his obsession with them could cause him to lose his wits—indeed might impair all those faculties necessary to distinguish true from false. An epistemological knot took shape: obsession blurred the lines between science and delusion, and could turn the rational words of the manuscript into a mere object of overwrought desire.

Tales of documentary obsession called into question the reliability of research, so central to the claims of professional scholarship. But why, given the pains that professionalizers took to distinguish their practices from those of earlier, religiously and philosophically motivated work, did they use the language of obsession to describe their own endeavor? Earlier scholars of history, in their descriptions of archival and manuscript work, had adopted a vocabulary that was actually useful to them—a language of love, obsession, and more particularly fetishism. The last involved strong emotional fixations on objects or parts of the body not normally evocative of such emotions. Powerful attachment to an object one believed to have magical power, as well as an overwrought commitment to some idea or ritual, also defined fetishism in the nineteenth century.

The language of obsession and fetishism had the same kind of currency among intellectuals as did the language of republicanism. It also provided a similar developmental impetus to historical science. Working its way into scholarly language, the concept of fetishism in particular was central to three middle-class preoccupations at the time: economic value, rational knowledge, and love. Marx would focus his attention on questions of fetishism and value in the concept of commodity fetishism. Other scholars not only adopted the language of love and obsession but focused their studies on the concept of fetishism, both to delineate boundaries between true and false knowledge and to score points against intellectual and cultural practices they did not like, thus cementing their claims to rationality. Early in the century, scholars, working with travel accounts and ethnographic material, built a complex picture of fetishism as an irrational commitment, usually by non-Western peoples, to ordinary items (such as a shell or a piece of fabric) believed to possess magical or divine properties.[81] This account of fetishism situated it in prescientific thinking, making it the opposite of modern rationalism. Beginning with Portuguese traders, then passing to Enlightenment *philosophes* and their accounts of African customs, the concept of fetishism became crucial to the process of constructing the value of such Western practices as trade and "rational thought." The seemingly bizarre value Africans attributed to objects seen as valueless to Western traders, and the fact that they attributed efficacious properties to these objects, helped define the term "fetish" as a symbol of African backwardness. As progressive interpretations of human history developed, "fetishism" was integrated into the historiography of religion and the nascent science of anthropology as an originating and primitive moment from which conceptions of the divine became progressively more enlightened.[82]

The concept of fetishism as derived from religious practice allowed scholars more emphatically to reject history based on totemic monuments and ruins, to avoid commonplace objects (rocks, feathers, and the like were the material of the fetish) in favor of hard-to-get documents, and to eschew the study of culture and society (the locus of fetishistic practice) for the more elevated, even transcendent reaches of the state. Scholarly journals used the language of the debased object to defeat practitioners of amateur and narrative history and their use of "rhetoric," characterizing such work as full of "tawdry trappings," "tinselled embroidery," and "allurements of style."[83] Good history was "unbedaubed with patriotic rouge, without stilts, buskins, tinsel, or bedizenment."[84]

In addition, the study of fetishism optimally allowed professional historians to confront epistemological problems involved in the study of documents. One of the foremost experts on fetishism, Alfred Maury, professor of history at the Collège de France and director of the French National Archives (1868–1888), addressed issues of knowledge and rational thought in the case of such image-producing experiences as overconcentration, dreams, hallucinations, and ecstatic trances.[85] From the stigmata of saints to the efficacious results of fetishistic worship, such deluded beliefs, Maury showed, stemmed from natural, explicable causes, ranging from immoderate consumption of coffee (in the case of some teenage convulsionaries who in 1857 professed to speak Latin) to an overly ascetic religious life (in the case of ecstatics and saints). Assigning transcendent meaning to ordinary objects, fetishism in particular was a lower form of human mental activity than intense scientific study. Several of Maury's books specifically considered the hallucinatory effects that "prolonged concentration [could have] on the nervous system": overconcentration on a thought or image or text could lead one to believe, for example, that an illusory occurrence was real or true. From concentrating too hard, one could find truth in false evidence or efficacy in a material object. This was precisely the problem of the fetish (as he outlined at length); but he unwittingly raised doubts about the truth that historians claimed to find in intense study of a document. In *La magie et l'astrologie dans l'Antiquité et au Moyen Age* (*Magic and Astrology in Antiquity and the Middle Ages;* 1860), Maury tried to find a way out of this problem. He took readers through a biographical morass of deluded ecstatics, then claimed reassuringly that in the case of delusion from overconcentration, "it is always women who predominate."[86]

Comforting as the study of fetishism could be to some, it ran up against a real difficulty in scientific work: intense study of documents could produce false or hotly contested results, and well-trained, well-meaning researchers could be deluded by their evidence. For example, an international controversy over the origins of the St. Bartholomew's Day Massacre erupted with particular virulence late in the 1870s and continued for decades thereafter, pitting careful researchers against one another. Reasoning from the existence or nonexistence of specific documents directly ordering the massacre yielded contradictory conclusions, and led some scholars like French archivist Henri Bordier to claim that the new methods were unsatisfactory: they could not deal with negative evidence, and they produced accounts that fixated on one particular document or series of documents to the exclusion of common sense and reason.[87]

The philosopher Michèle LeDoeuff has shown that when intellectuals reach the limits of explanation, need to "soften an aporia" (say, a philosophical problem or incompatibility), or work past a "blind spot," they often use an image that has already been validated by earlier scholars.[88] In the case of history, the problems of truth in archival research were softened by actually shifting to the metaphors of a less troublesome obsession than that involved in the scholarship on religious fetishism. That is, historians embraced the fetishistic imagery in the normative language of love and gender. One historian dismissed the question of delusion in archival work in this way: "How to avoid being seduced, intoxicated, and bewitched by the issues whose essence oozes from these leather bindings and heaped-up cartons."[89] These words eradicated delusion or fascination as an epistemological problem; instead, one moved through the thorny issues by expressly being swept up in love and seduction. One obviously *would* succumb, but this articulation of the normative papered over the philosophical difficulty. Using gender normalized and naturalized an epistemological impasse that studies of religious fetishism had attempted but had not always succeeded in resolving.

As novelists were adding a richly sexual component to fetishistic themes in their work—stories in which heroes became obsessively devoted to delicate feminine shoes, tiny gloved hands, fans, and other objects that stood for the totality of a living woman—so historians sheltered their commitment to documents in the lush safe-haven of sexually fetishistic or amorous metaphors. One caressed a rare book, wrote the historian Hanotaux, because it was "enveloped in skin, like a woman."[90] Expressions of fetishism as an attachment to an object that enabled sexual and not just religious feelings protected one from excessive attachment to archives—to their documents, dust, remnants of hair and offal—and thus gained in resonance. Ranke's characterization of his archival research as driven by "desire" and "lust" invoked the fundamental truth of sex, while his metaphors of princesses and virgins sheltered him in pure love. "Each discovery," Seignobos and Langlois exclaimed about finding untouched documents in a dusty archive, "induces rapture."[91]

The vocabulary of a diluted masochism and morbid descriptions of research (from the "attacks of paralysis" and "frequent vertigo" that Thierry experienced while working,[92] to the "sweet pain" etched on Hanotaux's "pale cheeks") hinted at the language of sexual dysfunction that also came to be connected with fetishism.[93] But here, too, the move from religious fetishism to sexual fetishism neutralized the threat that a madman's untruth might vitiate the results of historical science: "To love, one must suffer," the alienist Alfred Binet wrote in his 1887 study of fetishists.[94] Elements of suffering and torture that a man bravely endured became centerpieces of archival fantasies, in which the quest cruelly foregrounded masculine courage. Researchers dwelled on facing foul conditions and the pollution of death and femininity in their work. English historian William Lecky, who traveled extensively to small-town archives in France, Spain, and Italy searching for obscure manuscripts, noted a litany of hardships: at times the heat was so ferocious "it is scarcely possible to exist with one's clothes on; and the garrulity of French ladies, the ceaseless cracking of whips, barking of dogs, and other atrocious sounds make me perfectly miserable, especially as I am trying vainly to understand the theology of the Gnostics and the philosophy of Scotus Erigena."[95] Personal discomfort was accompanied by isolation, alienation, separation from friends. Ranke complained about the early hours, the scarcity and poor quality of documents, and the lack of letters and sociability; others described exhausting schedules for research trips, difficult relations with archivists, and other struggles. Heading for the archives, Ranke felt himself "no different from Hannibal."[96] There were metaphors of endurance, access, and control; scholars engaged in pitched battles for editorships of archival collections, and settled personal scores by working to deny their enemies admission to repositories.[97] In the fantastic, foundational metaphors of nineteenth-century researchers, the archives and their contents were indeed something against which one waged a "northern campaign." They were "so many princesses, possibly beautiful, . . . needing to be saved" at all cost. Invoking the image of the tortured and chivalrous knight, Lord Acton described history as "the heroic study of records."

The language of love was transcendent, and so was that of archival scholarship. Practices of fetishism were exhilarating—allowing its adherents to fantasize that they had surpassed the normal bounds of sexual pleasure, that they had overcome the messy facts of gender identity, or that they had eradicated distinctions between life and death. Simultaneously, the scientific study of inert documents, early historians theorized, would "awaken and stimulate a sensibility for reality."[98] Charles Seignobos explained the power of the fetishistic document thus: "A friend writes me, 'It's raining.' His letter is a material fact that allows me to prove the material fact of rain." Beyond this trivial information, however, one attended to the letter scrupulously, absorbing its import in order to enter "the exterior world of the past . . . [and] the thought of the author."[99] Ultimately, archival documents and their contents, as Wilhelm Humboldt put it, allowed the "fusion of the inquiring intellect and the object of the inquiry."[100] Overcoming the fundamental divide between life and death, the expert in the critical study of documents claimed to enter the mind of the dead. Michelet, after an alleged twenty years of daily archival work, professed to hear their moans, murmurs, and muffled cries.[101]

Historical scholars, like maniacs and fetishists who devoted themselves to their obsession, described a work experience far different from that of ordinary people. Fetishists spoke of soaring above the common herd by their assiduous veneration and appreciation of a manuscript's true value. "Happiness for me is not just pleasure; I have renounced it," wrote Hippolyte Taine to a friend. "My object is the good, or Being." He claimed kinship not with people of his own day but with men in the past, "Greek and ancient."[102] Other historians described stripping away the extraneous aspects of life, such as social engagements, pleasure trips, and amusements, to practice the higher devotion to documents. "I am predestined for solitude. Wherever I am, I will be alone," wrote Ranke, frequenter of salons and museums and companion of lovely young women.[103] Mandell Creighton, who added revelatory cultural material to the existing scholarship on the popes, wrote tirelessly to his fiancée about *Entsagung,* or renunciation. Creighton doubted the value of interacting with other humans when scholarly reality was so important,[104] and he hoped to lead a luminescent life distinct from the quotidian. Critical scholarship could be brutal, but its demands led to articulations of a heightened, elated sensibility that bespoke transcendence. The sensibility that soared to the farthest reaches of universality disdained ordinary interests and biases. The idealistic language of historical objectivity was strangely parallel the language of fetishistic love.

Regulations imposed by archives and libraries usually prohibited women, children, and uncredentialed men from entering, and these regulations furthered the possibilities for transcendence. Seminar rooms and men's studies at home served a similar function; they were often known as "closets" or "cabinets."[105] The closet, cabinet, or study was a site of contemplation beyond the reach of ordinary life, a space for men—but clearly threatened. Herbert Adams remarked proudly on the numerous keys to doors, desks, and cabinets in the Johns Hopkins seminar room. J. R. Green declared that any woman he might marry had to adhere to one restriction above all: she could not cross the threshold of his study. Furthermore, the closet or cabinet sheltered forbidden kinds of books, documents, artworks, and information (usually sexual) from any but men's eyes. On the one hand, the seminar room displayed republican health and manly vigor; on the other, it became a shrine to fetishistic documents and rare books.

Historical research constantly remade itself in metaphors of commitment to love objects. At the end of the nineteenth century, Lord Acton conceived the thirteen-volume *Cambridge Modern History* (1902–1911), a synthesis of modern findings designed to overcome the problem of mastering the great quantities of original research. Acton saw this synthesis as a timely one because "most of the official collections in Europe have been made public, and nearly all the evidence that will ever appear is accessible now." In other words, "the final stage in the conditions of historical learning" was at hand. Some one hundred writers, all of them well trained in scientific history, would be so objective in writing this complete history that "nothing shall reveal the country, the religion, or the party to which the writers belong."[106] Acton thus continued the perverse rhetoric of transcendence, but he was utterly unable to write a monograph himself, because (as Arnold Toynbee later said) he pursued the "will-o'-the-wisp of omniscience" before he could write—a mania that is yet another aspect of historical perversion.[107] Despite this, Acton became, for Toynbee and other later historians, emblematic of the superhuman erudition of the historian—a "miracle of learning," with "hundreds" of cardboard boxes of meticulously noted facts.[108] Dead historians whose work was no longer read, much less discussed, were invoked with emotional resonance as an authorizing and enabling image with magical powers. One had only to utter the name "Acton" and visions of his vast library, with its tens of thousands of books, documents, and manuscripts and its hundreds of boxes of note cards, would emerge to reinspire the tasks of scientific history. Historiography became a string of such names of lost love objects: names which lacked a meaningful "signified" but which served efficaciously—that is, fetishistically—to anchor young and old to scientific history's language of universal aspirations.

Scientific history in the nineteenth century staged the quest of middle-class men for competence and achievement, their will to professional power. The practices of professional history carved out a space where scientific history—that is, history as knowledge and as secular truth—could be written, judged, and promoted. The scientific seminar became the centerpiece of disciplinary power. In it, a "community" or "brotherhood" of true scholars took shape, archival findings were reverently displayed for scrutiny, and each fledgling professional showed his true mettle and received his credentialing. At the same time, archives became the richly imagined repositories of knowledge and the guarantors of truth around which the historical community reached a republican-style of consensus.

Today, the contradictions of the republican metaphor are as apparent as its enabling aspects, and nowhere is this more pertinent than in the professionalization of history. While competing drives for professional power often introduced distrust into the community of virtuous practitioners, the thirst for documents and its epistemological difficulties were often explained in the nineteenth-century vocabulary of fetishism, love, and heterosexual desire. Aiming to find a consensual truth, professionals in seminars and archives relied heavily on gender—a concept that at the time was riddled with hierarchy and dichotomy, and one that eliminated many people from consensus making. The enterprise was thus built on fissures, which were widened in the journals, associations, and other institutions that historical science generated. Ruthless or obsessive practices in the name of historical truth coexisted with articulations of community and rationality in the name of that same truth. Expressions of objectivity were often made in highly sexual metaphors—metaphors that appeared "natural" because modern ideology took sexual difference as natural. The practices of scientific history were simultaneously unifying and fragmenting, productive of democracy and redolent of hierarchy, committed to knowledge and dressed in fantasy.[109] An important point to stress, however, is that the contradictions within the field were quite productive. Scientific history was not just driven by the noble dream of objectivity; it was motivated by objectivity *and* the fantastical ingredients from which it was constructed. In the spaces left open by these contradictions and by the inescapable reliance on metaphor, innovators—or those who were merely different—could try to find new directions.

Men and Facts

5

A swelling output of historical writing based on professional principles resulted from the richly imagined work of seminars, archives, and households. In contrast to amateur work, this writing was said to be "scientific," and its political subject matter supposedly had significance far beyond that of any other history. In fact, the expansion of nation-states seemed to launch a new kind of writing about the past—a kind deemed scientific and political—and this development may look odd indeed from a certain perspective. History before professionalization, in comparison to the type that evolved in the nineteenth century, took a number of forms and comprised a wider field of human experience, a more varied source material, and a more complex epistemology. It could have an emotional valence or an erotic one, and could convey a sense of the past in all its memorialized immanence. If amateurism was being constructed as the "low," the extreme narrowing of subject-matter focus under professionalization and the "scientific" methodology of men in universities was part of the creation of the "high."

The concentration on national politics in professional and scientific accounts of the past has been explained as a natural development and one without gender import. As the unity of European religious belief fragmented and was replaced by the nation-state, historian Michel de Certeau wrote, history stepped in to give the new states a positive content, a knowledge of themselves that had previously been incomplete.[1] Others make the claim that scientific history had enriching potential for national identity. Anthropologist Benedict Anderson, for instance, has postulated that the nation-state came into being imaginatively through the medium of literature, which worked to create common bonds of information and stories among people who never saw one another. As modern nations developed their power in the eighteenth and nineteenth centuries, the increasing production of history by scholars and its eager reception by readers was a premier way to make the nation a reality in people's minds.[2] Philosopher Jürgen Habermas has posited the creation of a public sphere of opinion and knowledge that intersected with the growing political capacity of the state. History, no less than journalism and other institutions of social life, figured in this development of public discourse.[3] No matter how radically ongoing scholarship has modified some of these formulations, the primacy of politics stands, immediately making gender issues seem small—mere "slogans," as one historian put it, that intrude on this most authentic sphere of scholarship.

This scientific political history was new. It eschewed history's former role of bombastically praising dead monarchs and dynasties. It also increasingly avoided a moralistic or religious approach that strove to find sanctity, evil, or other ethical traits in the past. Empirically minded professional historians dismissed philosophical systems from which the past might be deduced, and excoriated their predecessors' romantic approach to history—an approach based on evoking emotional responses to all that was dead and gone. Plain writing, impartial judgment, and detailed factuality constituted the ingredients of scientific knowledge, which would drive modern political history. But the question remains: How did this focus on facts and on a knowledge of politics gender or regender historical writing, and how did the accrual of words like "reality" and "significance" serve a gendered motif? Moreover, in an ironic twist, political history came to serve as a sign of neutrality, whereas other subfields (for example, cultural and economic history in the late nineteenth century, and today's labor, ethnic, and gender history) were interpreted as being "political" and thus biased.

Political history's canonical place as objective, scientific knowledge has generated unsatisfactory explanations from eminent historians. Some claim that political history is dominant because political history of men formed the paradigm for Western historical writing as far back as the Greeks and Romans. But if professional history is only a repetition of old paradigms, in what way is it scientific and new? How did it come to be called "modern" from the mid-nineteenth century on, and why did young men become so excited about it? We should still be rejecting the heliocentric universe if science merely repeated its old paradigms. Others remark that, because men have always had power, they write about men and power politics to instruct one another in the ways of power politics. This answer has virtues but also limitations, especially those inherent in the very idea of a scientific history—one containing the universal truth of the past and thus beyond bias. Was this universal truth not also beyond the contingency of masculine prerogative? And if it were not, how had we come to believe—and why do so many of us still believe—in history's "universal" import, its truth, and its ability to convey knowledge? In other words, "politics" and "science" are not only terms that need exploring in and of themselves. More centrally, we must further scrutinize the force and import of their pairing, even as nations (to say nothing of political regimes) come and go and even as their incompatibility is from time to time announced (in the dictum that history is art, for example).

The coupling of science and politics is the quintessential installation of sexual difference at the core of professional history. The gendering of scientific history occurred, moreover, in a completely "natural" way, so that even today people will ask: "What has gender to do with historiography?" There is little more to say, some would claim, than that men are the historians. But how did that come about? Everyone said that historical science transcended all contingent categories, yet for many decades it appeared normal that those who practiced it professionally were mostly (and in some countries exclusively) men. The very naturalness of scientific political history belied the omnipresence of gender (history was about men only, and distinctly not about women) and its invisibility (history was about universal truth, not about men) in the nineteenth century. From the Age of Revolution onward, issues of class, gender, and race fueled politics, leading to the development of such mass movements as socialism, feminism, and anticolonialism. Yet historical science wrote its political narratives about a relatively small group of men of European descent, all the while appearing so genderless and—despite the pronounced gendering of society and the many contests over gender power—so real. This kind of history enraptured its practitioners through the "objective" depiction of past politics. What kind of magic could the rhetoric of facts perform, and why was it so entrancing?

The Science of Facts

History was professionalized in the nineteenth-century West as a science of facts and detail. Imaging themselves as scientists, historians founded a genre congruent with history on the basis of facticity, in contrast to the old-fashioned history based on chronicle, the evolution of spirit, and philosophical deduction. Early in the nineteenth century, Romantics had begun to analogize historical work and science. They valued the specificity involved in the amalgamation of history and science more highly than the abstract truths of Enlightenment philosophy. Emphasizing the retrieval of lost objects, the reappreciation of forgotten monuments, and the rediscovery of obscure sources of history (such as old documents), the Romantics saw in these material remnants of the past the foundation of history. Insofar as concrete materials, not mind or ideas, formed such a foundation, Friedrich Schlegel maintained, "there can be only one science: *physics,* for everything belongs to nature."[4] Late in the century the analogy gained power: "It must be made clear," wrote Ephraim Emerton of Harvard, "that the claim of history to rank among the sciences is founded in fact—the fact that it has a scientific method."[5] It has never been obvious why claiming this status and its attendant self-description was so attractive, especially because the invocation of the sciences constantly evolved and changed. Within the university (where professionalization was taking place), scientists still had less institutional power than theologians and classicists. Yet on the eve of professionalization, science was seen as congruent with history on the basis of shared facticity, and most professionalizers accepted this association.

The practices of the natural and physical sciences were already on their way to becoming highly gendered, tempting one to argue that the historian in his performance as scientist merely adopted a ready-made language and set of hierarchical values which helped construct his own masculinity and that of his subjects. Science was awash with active men observing, manipulating, dissecting, and finding the truth about women's bodies and the reproductive secrets of the universe. Some of the most dramatic discoveries of biology and zoology concerned ovulation and the menstrual cycle, while some of the most foundational beliefs in these fields focused on the impact of the uterus on women's mental capacity. Genetics concentrated on biological inheritance, thus on reproduction, while medicine itself evoked images of physicians experimenting in the many charity hospitals for unwed and poor mothers. Psychology's dramatic moments involved spectacular cases of murderesses where alienists debated the effects of menstruation, pregnancy, and the womb on women's ability to control their instincts, and equally spectacular depictions of psychiatrists dealing with hysterical female patients.[6]

Science had a capacity not only for portraying this relationship between male observer and female object, but also for projecting the gendered hierarchies of Western society onto the natural world. For example, "mammals" received this appellation during a time of intense debate over the female breast, even though the creatures classified under this rubric did not have mammae and even though other names like "the hairy ones" or "those with inverted ears" would have been more apt. Botanists, biologists, zoologists, and others scientifically described plants and animals in terms of human heterosexual frenzy, as these organisms produced seeds or developed eggs.[7] In other words, the language of science, just as historians began to make copious use of it, was already the language of gender and its hierarchies.

Professional history nonetheless had a gendered trajectory of its own, in which scientific analogies merely enabled history to develop. It was based in philological inquiry, which took a raw text and—by breaking down or analyzing and then recombining the elements in the text—produced a new, more accurate and knowledgeable exegesis or synthesis. When it came to reading texts and dealing with them critically, as the early modernizers of the field proposed, the analogy to chemistry was more pertinent. It was, to Schlegel's mind, nothing less than the "enthusiasm for chemical knowledge: for grammar is certainly only the philosophical of the universal art of dividing and joining."[8] As Ernest Renan later put it, one worked "on words and syllables, like a chemist in his laboratory."[9] And still later, Numa Fustel de Coulanges found the work of scientific analysis, "in history as in chemistry, a delicate operation . . . an attentive study of each detail to separate from the text all that one finds there."[10]

Philology influenced history as a discipline based on the minute, the detailed, the particular. Having developed its own methodology in the eighteenth century, philology isolated words, presented them as details and particulars within texts, and then explored their variety across time. Today the production of details and facts about individuals, institutions, and various aspects of the social order is central to modern epistemologies in the human sciences—medicine and criminology, for instance.[11] In a similar vein, the concern for "dividing"—that is, separating the detail or fact from the whole—was also central to the modern discipline of history. Modernizing historians made their relationship to facts a weapon against other genres and forms of historical writing. Philosophy and theology, Ranke wrote in the 1830s, submerged the individual and particular in the whole, the system, the totality. By contrast, history "turns sympathetically . . . to the particular . . . It hallows the phenomenal world."[12] Historical science differentiated itself from philosophical and theological brands of historical writing and from the arts by giving priority to research on facts and details.

The world of past experience, of course, was blanketed with particulars, an infinite field of them that women amateurs had endlessly described (or invented) in their wide-ranging histories. Professional history contrasted itself vis-à-vis the amateur relationship to facts in two ways. First, it professionalized the term "fact." The fact was not mere information that existed obviously or even naturally. Rather, its status depended on its discovery, scrutiny, and verification by the historian. In other words, it demanded his active input. As Ranke put it, "History is a science of collecting, finding, penetrating," and one that did not satisfy itself "simply in recording."[13] "Finding" as a disciplined act refused spontaneously to accept the past's initial appearance. "The fabric of events," wrote Wilhelm von Humboldt in his pioneering essay of 1821, "is spread out before [the historian] in seeming confusion."[14] The confusing appearance of historical information was only the point of departure, just as nature in its self-presentation was only the point of departure for science. "The historian, like the draftsman, will produce only caricatures," Humboldt maintained, "if he merely depicts the specific circumstances of an event by connecting them with each other as they seemingly present themselves."[15] The disciplining of the historian, along with the disciplining of historical confusion, was situated in the production, evaluation, and ordering of details, so that in their finished form they might serve as well-ordered facts.

Professional standards for historical work on facts relied on break-throughs in philology. Philological pioneers imagined their ultimate task as the creation and control of knowledge, "reproducing all that alien thought so that it becomes mine," as the great August Böckh wrote in his encyclopedia of philological method. Historians envisioned their work in a similarly productive and empowering way—work that differed from philology's while using its methods. Philologists had set new rules for verifying whether texts had been changed over time, and whether certain words had even been present in early versions of a literary work. A word or group of words and their arrangement in documents had a different status for historians, because words comprised not the important "facts" and "particulars" that historians sought but only their traces. The trace was the starting point leading to the fact, whereas the words themselves and the rich history of variations that would be produced around them satisfied philologists. Beginning with these traces or symbols found in the words in documents, historians worked backward through a series of "intermediary" signs until finally reaching a point at which they could construct a fact. "It is this series that one must reconstitute to ascertain to what extent the document is tied to a fact and can serve to understand it." Thus a fact took "a chain of essential operations in order to produce it."[16] While establishing history's difference from other disciplines, including some of the sciences, the complex work of tracing back from documents to produce facts depended on the historian's ingenuity, skill, training, and effort in a number of procedures—such as epigraphy, tracking down documents, and the like. These were all indicators of his disciplinary prowess. Additionally, by the time he brought forth or "produced" his facts, they had lost their originary luster in rhetorically splendid narratives, their own capacity to haunt or arouse.

Instead, facts had been reconstituted, authenticated, and qualified by the professional, who took pleasure in detail. Love of detail—filling books and letters—bound men together. For instance, Frederic Maitland and Henry Jackson corresponded at length over the letter "y" in a manuscript dating from 1285.[17] Simultaneously, the mastery of detail and the creation of facts produced manly competence and professional status, allowing one to measure oneself against another and thereby create an identity. "Bopp is completely beaten on the debate over *ao*," one scholar wrote home to his family. "In fifteen pages [of a manuscript he has just found], I have not seen a single *ao*."[18] In a much-publicized debate in 1887, Fustel de Coulanges accused Gabriel Monod of ignoring "the minute study of words and things, the patient accumulation of details, and that which one used to call the enumeration of facts." Monod, he claimed had been "seduced" by the "fashion" for large-scale comparisons.[19] "Le bon dieu est dans le détail" ("God is in the details") ultimately became a common credo for historians, in part because the capacity to survey even the smallest matter was a sign of infinite power. Here, too, Böckh had set the tone: "The task of philology is to dominate that which it has reproduced."[20] While the professional produced facts, the reputation for an accumulation of many well-constructed facts produced professional authority and distinguished one historian from another. Individuation, community, and top-ranked status in a professional hierarchy resulted from the use of historical operations to create facts.

The field of relevant facts ultimately detected by and known to the historian was always larger than could be processed in a narrative, and it was in this second regard that the professional also distinguished his love of detail from that of the amateur. Much of the past was irrelevant to history: real knowledge, wrote one advocate of philological and scientific study, "cannot be got from life."[21] Part of the historian's task lay in jettisoning most detail in favor of a small but important group of facts of higher value. Mastery of detail discriminated the more adept from the inferior historians, and, conversely, the ranking of detail itself created an additional space where the vocabulary of hierarchy informed historical science. Disciplinary standards measuring the relative importance of various details focused on their utility rather than their elegance, their status as "causes" rather than their own piquant or evocative qualities. The articulation of hierarchy and the establishment of standards for importance constructed professional expertise and power.

This articulation critically relied on gender to explain the process of discriminating among details. The task of historical science for the young Ernest Renan consisted in fundamentally dividing life in two parts: "One is vulgar and has nothing sacred, consisting in needs and pleasures of an inferior sort (everyday life, pleasure, wealth, etc.); the other is what one might call ideal, celestial, divine, disinterested, having for its object pure forms of truth, beauty, and moral perfection." Renan's division of the realm of the concrete into the everyday (associated with women) and the ideal (associated with men) had developed over the course of history's metamorphosis into historical science, and structured the imaginings of practices like seminars and archival research. But he explicitly saw the division between the nonhistorical and the historical as "the opposition between the *body* and the *spirit.*"[22] This antinomy of body (concerning women and everyday life) to spirit (indicating politics) generally resonated through the language of professionalization: Theodor Mommsen, for instance, believing strongly in the superiority of peoples federated into nations, contrasted the disunited Greeks unfavorably with the united Romans. "For the Greeks," he wrote, "everything is concrete, everything has a body; for the Romans, abstraction and its formulations alone engage their spirit."[23]

Such a division might seem to undermine the analogy of historical science to the natural sciences and other human sciences, because scientific method rested on observing physical bodies. Scrutinizing physical entities such as rocks, plants, and animals was crucial to the natural sciences, whereas census takers (an example of fledgling social scientists) counted bodies, observing their location in commercial, domestic, and industrial space. Both inner and outer aspects of bodies could serve the interests of science. For instance, a medical symptom might consist of an outward manifestation, from a rash or skin discoloration to gushing blood; it could also be an internal sensation of pain. Bleeding stemming from either a flesh wound or a more profound injury could be treated on the surface of the body.[24]

For historians, the first step in investigation did indeed occur in the realm of outward appearance. The initial focus was "the phenomenon itself, . . . its condition, its surroundings, chiefly for the reason that we would otherwise be incapable of knowing it."[25] The body metaphor helped organize these phenomena. Mommsen classified Roman laws, inscriptions, and other primary materials as part of a "body," an "organic unity," an "organism," whose "parts" he would analyze for "function." Such an analysis involved looking; it took a kind of observation practiced "solely

[by] the historian, whose eyesight is naturally keen and has been sharpened by study and practice."[26] Yet for all the emphasis on visible traces and surface detail, this surface or body of phenomena still had low status in the minds of Mommsen, Renan, and others. To stop at this surface, according to Humboldt, "would be to sacrifice the actual inner truth . . . for an outward, literal, and seeming truth."[27] One had to "plunge deeply" below, "dissect," or "penetrate" this surface or "physiological unity," this "physical world" and "organic life," as Humboldt and Ranke had it; it was only the treasure deep within that counted. Before the reign of science, as Renan saw it, great works were adjudged superficially, much as "we admire the beautiful shape of the human body." The scientific scholar of the future, however, would work "like the anatomist, who cuts through this sensual beauty to find beyond, in the secrets of its interior organization, beauty a thousand times superior." Abruptly changing his metaphors and cementing the superiority of inner to outer, Renan concluded: "A dissected cadaver is horrible in one sense, yet the eye of science discovers within it a world of marvels."[28] It was the bodily exterior that was horrible; deep within lay something higher. The raw material on which the historian worked was hierarchized as inferior to the universal truth that he would make it yield.

Thus far, little suggested the sex of this bodily exterior, which historians so constantly invoked as inferior to the spirit. As scientific history developed, however, professionals clothed "superficiality" and "surface appearances" in feminized language. Every suppression of error found on the surface of things meant suppressing confusion and unreason, which were increasingly defined as feminine, in the nineteenth-century language of science. But the sexing of the surface was more direct. As noted in Chapter 4, U.S. historian Richard Hildreth thought that superficial history was "tricked out in the gaudy tinsel of a meretricious rhetoric." For the sake of "our fathers and ourselves," the great characters in American history should be presented "unbedaubed with patriotic rouge, without stilts, buskins, tinsel, or bedizenment."[29] The *English Historical Review* launched its first issues with a promise not to offer its readers "allurements of style."[30] It praised works for their "utter want of tinsel embroidery" and their refusal to "adorn a tale."[31] Other scientific periodicals pointed to the "tawdry trappings" of more literary works.[32] In the nineteenth century, allurements, adornments, tawdry trappings, and tinsel embroidery formed the wherewithal of prostitution, of public women and their sexuality. Bad or superficial history, like the whore, was all decked out. "Clio is going to be just a gal-about-town," wrote one American university historian to a colleague, "on whom anybody with two bits worth of inclination in his pocket can lay claims."[33] It took work to sex the body in the nineteenth century, and this was accomplished not only by scientists but by professional historians.[34] Once they had sexed the body as female, historians set it in a hierarchical ordering to indicate how errors had been overcome, the enticements of literary flourishes refused, and even facts superseded. This was an integral and ongoing part of the development of history as a profession, and one that continued to be serviceable.[35]

In a coordinate gesture, the historian's own body disappeared, much like the body of a middle-class man was effaced by his black suit. In the work of science, claimed one historian, "the author is completely absent . . . It is intellectual work, not human work."[36] In general, only one physical part of the historian remained: the eye. The language of scientific history described historical methodology in terms of the historian's keen and well-trained eyesight, his powers of observation. Historical truth, wrote Humboldt, was "like the clouds that take shape for the eye only at a distance."[37] Historians trained themselves in the techniques of observation. Hippolyte Taine's determination to be scientific took him incessantly to the dissecting rooms and laboratories. The eyesight of the professional observer who scrutinized the feminized surface was compared to that of other viewers. For one thing, the historian's eye set his standards higher than those of "the common observer," who "constantly imbues this appearance with errors and half-truths."[38] His eye also distinguished him from those whose gaze might be lascivious, superstitious, or crude: "A miracle reported by a thousand Orientals is less probable than the observation of a single chemist."[39] The impressionable eye of the "savage," Renan believed, saw "a thousand things at once" without being able to prioritize; the result was a "sensual poem," "caprice," or wild metaphysical system—but not science.[40]

The eye of the trained historical observer was ostensibly untroubled by such confusion in the appearance of historical phenomena. Not participating in a bodily economy and thus not conflating the material and the immaterial, it fed information into the disembodied Cartesian *cogito* that needed, in the long run, not just to see the surface but to think its way toward the unseeable, invisible interior of historical truth.[41] Scientists in the early part of the century were distinguishing the eye and its connection to the brain as constituting a system distinct from other aspects of the body.[42] The eye was an unmoored, transparent lens operating cognitively outside the realm of the sensible (hence passionate, emotional, incorporative, and feminized) body. Specifically, it stood in polar opposition to the devouring eye-mouth of the feminine reader, whose compulsive reading fed erotic appetites.[43] The common image of the professional historian was of someone divorced from the body, as in the still-current image according to which one was "standing outside oneself" when examining evidence. As Humboldt claimed, the "realm of appearances [figured as the realm of the body] can only be understood from a point outside it."[44] The former was the realm of error, bias, and insufficient evidence from which one mentally plunged into the truthful, spiritual interior. The historian's self optimally lacked a physical register. In Fustel de Coulanges's canonical statement: "It is not I who speak, Gentlemen, but History who speaks through me."[45] Even in youth, fledgling historians developed the language of pure *cogito*. "I feel myself becoming a personification of Algebra, a living trigonometrical canon, a working table of Logarithms," one young scholar wrote his parents.[46] Subjecting the body to overwork, cold and damp, and the hardships of travel, the historical *cogito* could simultaneously claim, with some justification, "complete ignorance of real life."[47]

Through these moves, historical methodology articulated the femininity of the physical evidence that one looked at, in ways completely in accord with the general tendency of the modern period to sex the scientifically observed body as female. The methodology gendered history as well, since traits of the male historian recapitulated the general ideals of nineteenth-century manhood: self-regulation, transparency, authenticity, and a representation of universality; the need to accomplish hard work by following detailed procedures; and the priority of the calm, lucid, and disembodied mind beyond the realm of contingencies such as class, religion, race, or nationality. Historical language duplicated the language of a universalized masculinity—that is, a masculinity functioning beyond the realm of such contingencies as gender itself.

Professional history as the standard for "high" truth had major test cases distinguishing the significant from what should be left invisible, the spirit from the body, the male from the female. Confronting contingency and falsehood were necessary to mark out universal claims. In this regard, the case of Pope Joan loomed large in nineteenth-century professionalization. According to the narrative—repeated, rebutted, and refurbished over the centuries—Joan was renowned for her wisdom and was elected to the papacy in the middle of the ninth century. A woman of disputed origin, she went to Athens (or some other urban center) and became one of the most learned people of her day. For two years or so, she conscientiously performed all the duties of pope, but then, in a procession through the streets of Rome, she suddenly gave birth to a child. In so doing, Joan turned a religious display into a carnivalesque one, with cross-dressing and the grotesquery of childbirth right on the papal throne. As a result, she died on the spot (some said she was stoned to death, though Boccaccio's version maintains that she quietly and peacefully retired). From then on, popes received the symbols of office sitting on a pierced chair, so that the maleness of their genitals could be confirmed. Over the centuries, Catholic and Protestant historians, as well as popular culture, either reveled in this story or attempted to suppress it.

The phenomenon of Pope Joan piqued the historical imagination, but in the nineteenth century it became a virtual obsession. In the 1840s and 1850s, distinguished Dutch, German, French, and Italian historians all had much to say about her. Alfred Plummer of Trinity College, Oxford, called her story "monstrous" and "preposterous." Joan had transgressed the norms of credible knowledge, political power, and just about anything else one might think of. The newly opened archives of Europe expunged her from the record when, early in the 1860s, no less a historian than Ignaz von Döllinger, teacher of Lord Acton and definitely his superior when it came to publishing, took on the case once and for all.

Döllinger professed to know every archival source in Europe; no authentic written account of Pope Joan, he maintained, existed before the mid-twelfth century. She existed before then merely "in the mouth of the people," meaning well-intentioned but gullible clergy, monks, and other "guileless" folk. The props in her story lacked authenticity. For instance, the story that she had had a Greek education which impressed the Romans could hardly be true: by the ninth century, anybody who was anybody went to Paris. Then there was the problem of her name. Döllinger found that chroniclers gave her pre-papal name variously as Agnes, Gilberta, Gerberta, Joanna, Margaret, Isabel, Dorothy, and Jutta. Such textual inconsistency threw her very being into question. Her fate was just as inconsistently reported, and the details of how the people protected themselves thereafter from another woman pope were a travesty of historical logic. The pierced chair was not merely used to allow the crowd the chance to affirm for itself that the pope's genitals were male. For the serious and scientific Döllinger, authorities introduced the pierced chair into service only because of its "beautiful colour."[48] In sum, a woman of great learning and power could not have existed, because of universal standards like the beauty of a chair and the truth of writing.

Döllinger's account of Pope Joan was the first example in his book on forgeries and fables, and served as the gendered emblem for the progress of scientific history, conspicuously evoking femininity to repress it in the name of truth. Threatening the notion of history as male plenitude, Joan's story had many ingredients to make it so pivotal in defining the new scholarship. Far from being beyond politics, it served Döllinger's own cause of showing that the universal church could survive even in the face of inaccuracy and scandal. Fighting the secular power intrinsic to the new doctrine of papal infallibility, he was excommunicated in the 1870s. Yet the carnivalesque woman, who inverted the gendering of knowledge and power, was the sign of battle for him; by pushing her to the margins and then outside the canon, Döllinger, like other historians in the process of professionalization, made history universal by suppressing gender. Such stories as that of Pope Joan, and other piquant controversies such as that over the *droit du seigneur* (that is, the lord's right to have intercourse with any bride connected with his dominion), proved not just important to but constitutive of history. For one thing, they continued to channel libidinal energy into historical work providing brushes with dangerous outlaws and sexuality. Using women as the sign of both gender in its entirety (that is, both masculinity and femininity) and of all that was outside history, the new scholarship mimed the general Western world—a divided world in which an ideal and valuable history of the masculine "real" stood in opposition to a lesser, ahistorical sphere that was worth speaking about only as an example of error. The work of investigating the former was high-minded, legalistic, and noble; the work of suppressing the latter, in all its erroneous and superficial inferiority, often triggered fantasies of violence, mutilation, and passion.

Acting within these methodological parameters, historians claimed to discover the "real"—or, as Humboldt put it in his formative treatise, "what actually happened." Presenting past reality was scientific methodology's supreme, ungendered claim. From Humboldt on, however, some historians were aware of the problem of conveying reality via what could turn out to be a highly charged historical narrative, and they realized the damage it might do to the "real." The transition to narrative texts, as a means of conveying facts and the causes and inner connections unseen to the ordinary observer, did not occur without craft and manipulation. On the one hand, this demanded and created prowess, professional skill. But on the other, it entailed augmenting the seen with the unseen, with something beyond the given, beyond "reality." For instance, one used language, a medium cut loose from historical methodology itself, to materialize the immaterial. But language, "growing out of the fullness of the soul as it does, frequently lacks expressions which are free from all connotations."[49] The most intently scientific historians, like Fustel de Coulanges, tried to devise nonmetaphorical ways of writing—in his case, conspicuously without success.

Writing of what *actually* happened demanded productivity on the part of the historian: something had to be *added* to the bare events. "What do we say of those" (asked Renan), who, using a source, "merely copy or excerpt from it without any sense of what is essential and what accessory?"[50] Historical data could not just appear in its "raw" or "originary" state. The existence of an inner truth demanded its extrication, and addition to the traces of events or facts. "The truth of any event is predicated on the addition . . . of that invisible part of every fact, and it is this part, therefore, which the historian has to add."[51] From his trained position, the historian also saw causes and other invisible outcomes, which also were adduced for the account in question. Or, as Humboldt said, "it is this inner effect that history must always produce."[52] The scientific historical text added footnotes, appendixes, and other apparatus, making the historical "real" far more intense than and far different from what it originally was.

History was not just "what happened"; it was supplemental—"what *actually* happened."

The additional and supplemental constituted scientific representation of the past. They gave "reality" an artificial, excessive nature, situating scientific history in the realm not only of "hyperreality" but of paradox. Adding the many extras effected the representation of past reality as hyperreality, while it also constituted the historian's masculine and professional identity. The professional was not only transparently himself; he simultaneously knew more, saw more, and worked more. To arrive at the point of accessing and producing the real, the historian had abjured the masculine body, presenting his procedures as necessitating his own existence outside the physical or situated self—"independent in regard to oneself," as Fustel de Coulanges put it.[53] Often leading a complex personal life, the hardworking historian produced an identity that was also paradoxical, constituting himself simultaneously as vigorously productive and as a kind of absence. In the hands of these men, the past was similarly real and unreal.

The problems generated by the modern articulation of middle-class intellectual identity have engaged theorists from a variety of intellectual persuasions, who have explored these problems in terms of loss of self or of the body. For instance, the phenomenologist Maurice Merleau-Ponty offers a cogent critique of rationality, conceived as a process whereby one wills oneself out of the field of being to create an "object" that is totally distinct ontologically from the disembodied observer. Often made with the deepest humility, the claim of the historian to transcend life in general was, ultimately, a claim to extraordinary power and thus a way of constructing the "high." Laura Mulvey, a film theorist, sees the process wherein the splitting off of a bodiless self (in this case, that of the professional historian from the man) enables the individual to fashion an ideal, better self that stands in a complex relationship to a debased or inferior self. Such a split occurs in childhood, when the child gains a sense of identity and differentiates himself from the mother by seeing images that are simultaneously him and not-him. Like Mulvey, many philosophers and historians of science posit identity formation as similarly paradoxical or split. They attribute it to the discursive tradition of Western science, in which the disembodied *cogito* stands as markedly superior to the disenabling body.

Proceeding even further, Mulvey sees the better self as someone who is efficacious vis-à-vis the debased self, someone who can cause and do (in this case mentally), who thinks in terms of cause and effect, with the ideal self often acting upon and triumphing over the debased object (in this case the female surface of disaggregated detail, evidence, materiality) so as to fix the hold of the better self.[54] Nonetheless, the debased object—no matter how repressed or fantastic—remains a touchstone, a potency, which enables work to proceed.

These theories contribute to our understanding of the historian's articulation of self within the middle-class language of male identity in the nineteenth century. As part of a professional middle class, the historian figured his self as transparent, higher, better, and ultimately able to wield professional power so effectively as to reach a realm of universal truth. Better, higher, more disembodied, and thus less debased than women and people of other races, historians simultaneously imaged themselves as absent, empty, split, torn from their perceptual moorings in the body, and left to imagine a world beyond the language, instincts, and perceptions of everyday life. It was from this incredibly enabling but fraught realm of scientific language that history sprang forth as an identically paradoxical set of procedures. Scientific history was the articulation of a past reality that, paradoxically, was different from the historical given and "produced" by the work of historians. It was a history of a higher and more truthful reality than people had lived, so pure and invisible that no one but the trained historian could see. It was a history that jettisoned many physical details of the human past as unimportant, while affirming that what went on in the historian's dematerialized mind represented the "actual" reality. Historians' competition for footnotes, their struggle for virtuosity in finding causes and producing real "effects" and for devising fresh arguments, were part of an ongoing struggle "really" to produce reality by reaching deeper, past the inevitable feminine surface.[55] All of this was the work of facts.

The Facts of Politics

History as the "science" of facts solidified its position in tandem with the establishment of the modern nation-state. The linkage was both institutional and personal, professional and emotional. Historians gladly served their country in time of war, and many professionals had political or official identities; Jean Jaurès and Ernest Lavisse are two of numerous nineteenth-century French examples. Many historians—and not only zealots like Treitschke—were nationalists and patriots. It was "love of the Father-land," that motivated the historian Heinrich Böhmer: "'For people and fatherland': that is the motto of my life."[56] Moreover, it was common for professionals to serve political leaders as advisors and friends. Lord Acton spent his fondest moments with Gladstone, just as Arthur Schlesinger did with John F. Kennedy. While professing to occupy the highest, most disinterested reaches of truth, historians longed for—and still long for—political fame and influence. Some even achieved it: in the 1990s, François Furet has been called one of the three most powerful men in France. What is this seemingly paradoxical amalgamation of historical truth, defined as the sum of impartial facts, with an attendant fixation on so politicized an institution as the nation-state? And for our purposes, how does this amalgamation or "congealing"—this slide from facts to political value—connect with gender?[57]

Professionalizing historians wrote factual political history, imaged their work as an important contribution to civic virtue, and explicitly aligned themselves with the power of the nation-state. For more than a century, observers in a variety of fields emphatically connected science with citizen-ship, and factuality with the nation-state. "Disinterestedness" as a "mode of attention and concern," according to the earl of Shaftesbury, was a major condition of civic virtue.[58] "A republican government and science mutually promote and support each other," a Boston preacher sermonized late in the eighteenth century.[59] Professional historians felt no differently: "The power to stimulate national sentiment and moral strength lies in the historical-philosophical sciences," the historian Wilhelm Dilthey main-tained in the 1870s, as part of his plea for reorganizing the University of Strasbourg.[60] Although the connection between history and the nation-state is often invoked as an obvious one between history and men, logically the connection seems contradictory when writing the history of the nation-state and of men is seen as an apolitical undertaking. Even a historian's service to a partisan political leader fails to undermine his status as a truth-teller and scientist. In contrast, writing the history of women and minorities is usually discredited as partisan, "political."

History helped the postrevolutionary nation-state establish its identity. As Michel de Certeau suggested, history "permits a society to situate itself by giving it a past in language; and it thus opens up to [the society] its own space in the present."[61] By this account, historians perform a defining function for the nation-state, providing a story of the state's past that marks off and distinguishes the past as the neutral backdrop to the present state—a backdrop composed of mathematical time. Insofar as nations evolved in the modern period, history fundamentally enabled that evolution by continually creating narrative accounts of what had gone before, in order to give historical universality to a contingent, highly politicized institution. As each future became a present and then a historical past in the progressive time of historical science, history ensured "depth" and thus projected the nation's ongoing existence.

Having a past was indeed seen as the essence of a nation. Renan's "What Is a Nation?" (1882) argued against basing nations on visible markings such as race, ethnicity, and geographic boundaries. Like truth itself, the nation was "a spiritual principle"; it was "sacred," and rested on "a heroic past." The nation was "a large-scale solidarity, constituted by the feeling of the sacrifices one has made in the past . . . It presupposes a past."[62] Historical science did the major work, arguing over and searching incessantly for—among other issues—the ground or origins of the nation's existence (as did, for example, Herbert Baxter Adams and Fustel de Coulanges).[63] Jean-Luc Nancy has modernized this theory of history's efficacy as an essential act of "presencing" the community, or, in Benedict Anderson's phrase, "imagining" it, by showing citizens to one another even in the nation's most distant corners.[64] Like-minded nineteenth-century scientific historians testified to the defining role that history played in the formation of a nation. Scientific methods in history, wrote Augustin Thierry, provided the nation with a "history of everyone, written for everyone."[65] The wide-ranging political data found by professional historians in the French national archives comprised an "ossuary, enshrouded but living, that is France."[66] In this way, history served as one of the productive human sciences, generating discrete information, classificatory principles, and clusters of facts whose display created "real" images of the modern state for its citizens to read about. It helped the modern state unite people through a communal understanding of universally true historical facts and data, not through overt displays of dynastic might. It helped shape a modern, transparent legitimacy to replace a baroque one.

The story of the nation as it chronicled wars, revolutions, and the triumphs of great leaders became the center of narrative excitement. Just as the seminar focused and galvanized historical practice, so the nation-state fixed the written efforts of professionalizers, doing battle against cultural, social, and other varieties of historical thinking. Using official documents to answer looming questions about the state, large-scale institutions, and their rulers, professionally written history replaced local lore and culture, family sagas of dynasties and noble lines, and narratives in which God's will manifested itself in the past. Separating off the realm of appearance and prioritizing some aspects of knowledge above others entailed highlighting information about the nation-state, as we have seen, and repressing error and superficiality. It was Hegel who made the enduring formulation of these procedures when they were connected with the political history of European nations. Positing the preeminence of the state as the subject matter of history, and judging the detailed particulars of the state's history as very important manifestations of its evolution, Hegel derided Asian countries for having an immature history (because of their attenuated development) and African countries as having none. He pointedly scorned the history of either private life or the dynastic family as impermeable to modern analysis and narrative, for their interest was "confined to the family and the clan. The uniform course of events which such a condition implies is not a subject of serious remembrance." The historian's task was to suppress narratives based on these inferior subjects. "The community," Hegel maintained, "creates itself in what it represses and what is at the same time essential to it: womankind in general, its inner enemy. Womankind—the eternal irony of the community—alters by intrigue the universal purpose of government into a private end." This imperative, which subsumed the odious category of the local and familial under the still more odious feminine as the enemy of history, remained pertinent. Even in the mid-twentieth century, when Marc Bloch and Lucien Febvre had to some extent restored the local, Febvre emphasized that scientific history shunned the feminine above all: it refused to recount, he wrote, the romances of Mary Queen of Scots or to "throw light on the Chevalier d'Eon and her petticoats."[67]

In this repression lay some of the irresistible attraction of scientific, political history. The community or nation, like the procedures of history, was born of the creation of the high and the low enacted as a suppression of women (or Africans and Asians) in which truth and freedom entailed getting past female substantiality by incising or eliding it. The nation, like its history, was not materiality, which was feminine or local or clanlike, but rather an intangible universal that was arrived at in an exciting way. Michelet's achievement in his successive histories of France was not only a product of assiduous archival research; it was also said to rest on showing "the successive victory of human liberty over the totality of nature." The state—the culmination of the advance in human institutions—did not result from physical force, according to Fustel de Coulanges. Rather, it developed from the free play of spirituality, human consciousness, and morality—"the work of our mind."[68]

The disinterest of the citizen—that is, his freedom from attachments other than his civic ties—provided the vocabulary of both civic ideology and historical methodology. Thus, scientific history, wrote Fustel, "demands that the researcher be free," exercising "an absolute independence."[69] The discursive intertwining of historical science and the narration of the state lay at the heart of professionalization: "Above all, [history] should benefit the nation to which we belong and without which our studies would not even exist."[70] Methodology had already defined the realm of superficial narrative as feminine—as that which took "appearances for reality," in the words of Fustel de Coulanges. In terms of subject matter, the feminine was disqualified for its antipathy to the universal. Truth was where women were not—some invisible and free territory purged of error by historical work; purged of superficial, trivial, and extraneous detail; and thus purged, through a variety of procedures, of femininity. If methodologically historical truth lay in opposition to the feminine, in terms of subject matter (as historians from Hegel to Febvre put it) this realm of truth was the nation-state, where a congruent opposition to the feminine had been constructed in philosophy and in constitutional and positive law. The nation, like its history, lay in a realm of disembodied (one might say "empty") freedom, freedom defined as freedom from error—that is, femininity. Both nation and history were spiritual, like the historian, who was similarly operating in a disembodied realm, holding the feminine at bay beyond their borders. As Henri Berr put it, in his attempts to give more weight to generalization and synthesis in scientific history, France's "true grandeur is in its spirit."[71]

The nation's history operated in the free realm of time, posited from the scientific and Kantian revolutions forward as existing beyond all contingencies, including creed (that is, it was not God's time). It was a neutral, mathematical, unmarked time matching the transparency of both the citizen and professional historian and contrasting with the thick sluggishness of feminine space, as Droysen explained it.[72] Chronology, according to Ernst Bernheim, had served "since time immemorial as the eye of historical science."[73] In this regard, secular time was the transparent condition of possibility—the possibility of scientific history and that of the nation. At the moment of professionalization, the Western political imagination still contained localisms, ritual and household time, and aristocratic lore. It might also attach political rulership to a divinely ordained ordering of time and space. Historical science (like astronomical and geological science) evacuated such qualities from time, in order to make room for a new consensus about a transcendent, secular, serial time that was the same for everyone, yet outside household, family, church, and other competing senses of time.

Just as natural scientists produced a "deep time" in their studies of the universe, earth, and species, historical scientists produced this time for the nation-state by filling its emptiness with the historical facts of great national events and great men's lives. So situating the great individual in vacant seriality, scientific history textured time with the liberal ideal of the developmental man, whose perceptive powers grew incrementally, giving time a shape through narrating the individual unit of the nation: the autonomous male citizen. The emphasis on the individual "fact" as the primary ingredient of history congealed with the value given the individual man as its prime indicator, both of which were produced through complex methodology and hard work. In the hands of the scientist, leaders no longer served as a mere illustration of God's truth, but instead came to possess a deep individuality based on the "significance" of their accomplishments and character. The scientific historian adjudged this significance from the welter of details he surveyed, giving political time further weight.

The passage of historical time, signaled by the movement from one great (universal) individual man to the next, depended on distinguishing the reign of one man from another through detail. This differentiation, in turn, was indicated by showing how rivalries among men took shape and how one man conquered another. An individual character came into relief through comparisons with individuals who had gone before and others who would come after. For instance, Ranke wrote of Julius II: "Then came a pope who made it his object to assume a position directly opposed to that of the Borgias, but who pursued the same end, though he used different, and hence successful, means for his purpose."[74] As each differentiated himself from the others through political struggles, wars, great achievements, or momentous failures, narratives presented the classical agon in which character comes into being through complex contest with the "other." On the one hand, the prior or defeated figure in the agon was deftly feminized as the "weaker," the one surpassed or repressed. On the other, because the agon existed primarily among "the same"—that is, among male characters—the resulting narratives and analyses made the history of truth into an account of male identity which historians painstakingly established by ascertaining minute differences among men and by providing important information about men's lives as the repository of power and plenitude.[75]

Gender further weighted time as progressive, even when the historian was judging large-scale political institutions or entire epochs. Theodor Mommsen's multivolume collections of classical inscriptions and compendia of Roman law towered above all other works of scholarship for their detailed transcriptions, discussions of forgeries, and technical introductions to the material (in Latin). His work culminated in a nine-volume history of Rome, which situated the beginnings of the ancient world in the commonality of language and racial stock, then traced individuation through philology, until the Greeks and Romans came to represent opposite poles of historical development. According to Mommsen, the Greeks modeled such institutions as religion on the concrete—namely, nature: "For the Greeks, . . . everything has a body." This material cast to civilization had its most felicitous manifestation in artistic "fecundity," which "clothed" the Greeks' ideas and institutions. The Greeks excelled in things of the body—games, the theater, amusements. By contrast, the later Romans founded their identity upon abstraction and ideas—not on individual pleasures and the good life, but on the abstractions of patriarchal obedience, the law, and the state. Whereas the Greeks were thus blocked from unity by a particularist, embodied sensibility, the Romans, from their very awareness of abstraction, "gained a *fatherland,* a *patriotism* unknown in Greece. And it was also for that reason that, alone among ancient civilized peoples, the Romans, with a government founded on populist power, knew how to accomplish national unity and, by this unity, to surpass the ruins of Hellenism itself and arrive at world domination."[76] The progress of political history relied, yet again, on the work of gender, suggesting that political facts were laden with gender values: male importance versus female insignificance; superiority versus unworthiness; spiritual transcendence versus bodily materiality; the high versus the low; the winner versus the defeated.

We have always known that political history was laced with values, and never more so in the modern period, as scientific historians in the West acted zealously and in countless ways on behalf of their nations. Depending on whether a war had just been concluded, they might refuse to invite counterparts from other countries to international meetings or to collaborate in publishing. Many wrote books and essays justifying government policies such as the German annexation of Alsace-Lorraine in 1870–1871. But nationalist bias is one value for which it is always said we can correct. Belief in the superiority of one's country, once discovered by the discerning eye, succumbs, and then political history can be read as pure fact once more.

However, facts themselves—and indeed the very notion of political history—are so fundamentally constructed of gendered values that this correction may be difficult. Hailing politics and the factual story of the state, scientific historians saluted men's gender interests. As many historians and theorists have shown, the modern contractual nation involved an unfolding egalitarianism of political rights among men that depended on a concomitant legal and economic subordination of women. History retold this story by foregrounding and universalizing the facticity of the individual man (who was the basic component of the nation), then interpreting it as part of the progress of political entities as a whole.[77] Political history celebrated men's superior rights, actions, thoughts, and struggles, and their sacrifices to preserve that superiority in war—the final enactment of the hierarchy of winner over loser, victor over vanquished, male over female.

Although these values are often difficult to discern and dissect as part of facticity, analytic philosophers have depicted some ways of seeing how facts and values may be conjoined. "I owe the grocer money," is an example of fact and value tightly intertwined.[78] Such statements as Mommsen's—that the Romans were a united fatherland, while the Greeks were disunited; that the Romans were all abstraction, while the Greeks were all body—show this intertwining in the simplest historical formulations practiced by the most scrupulous of professionals. Scientific historians wrote political history in ways that make it hard to distinguish the border between fact and value, thus making assertions that history is "value-free" often quite persuasive.

Assertions of political history's apolitical, factual nature are held in place by various means. For example, seventeenth-century writing by French academicians (heavily supported by state and aristocratic patronage) worked to "cleanse" political traces from intellectual work, making the state appear more powerful, less interested.[79] Historians in the nineteenth century compared their work to that of chemists because of the "purification" their procedures worked, ridding state politics and state papers of their partisanship and giving them status as pure factuality or reality. Methodology removed traces of gender by pointing to itself and its production of facts, to its processes and scientific laws. Gesturing toward its own lawlike fairness, historical science purged itself and the narrative of the nation-state of any hint of gender hierarchy or other inegalitarian politics.

A second device was the professional consensus which grounded definitions of the past and of significant historical truth in decisions reached by a small group of men, but which made them appear to be agreed-upon by everyone. The shift from a heroic medieval perspective in both literature and art to realism in both the novel and painting was an essential ingredient in the privileging of "realism" generally. This new history of the real involved a spreading consensus over continuous (or chronological, serial) time packed with certain sequences of action, events, details, and effects, and over the invariable existence of meaning or abstraction that lay beneath surface differences.[80] The consensus further produced a set of procedures for holding this perspective in place through a distanced relationship allowing time and depth to operate for the observer. As with so-called realistic painting, written realism depends on consensus over practices, procedures, and principles. In history, this consensus operated to produce "realistic" accounts. To judge the state of mind of the author of a document, according to Seignobos, required judging the state of mind of the author's contemporaries, because "one assumes that similar states of mind will produce similar judgments."[81]

Through new rules for the perspective called "reality," or "factuality," realism in history depended on a community of verifiers who claimed to find this reality while they simultaneously produced it. "It is this knowledge of the standards for observation," wrote Seignobos, "that allows someone learned to accept unconditionally the observations of a colleague whose methods he knows, or similarly the observations of learned men across Europe."[82] Whether finding concordance in the use of a word, or agreement across precise historical accounts by well-trained contemporaries, historical science was tantamount to the group that practiced it. It was law and community, but one that included only males of European descent. Like the universal citizen, the most realistic work was "a plain, unvarnished narrative of facts," "original," "critical," "strenuous," "calm and temperate," "sturdy," full of "commonsense views," and "with a rigid abstinence from all excursions of the fancy."[83]

For the real to take shape, agreed-upon distancing procedures had to become the primary focal point.[84] Ranke, in the preface to his famous history of the popes *(Die römischen Päpste)*, described scientific historians as "lookers-on at a distance"—at so great a distance, in fact, that the topics "can now inspire us with no other interest than what results from the development of its history and its former influence."[85] He conspicuously situated himself at a distance from the universal church-state by successively invoking "Rome in the early years and the Middle Ages," "the first half of the sixteenth century," and then a "period of a revived church-temporal power"—all within the first three sentences of his book. His history, Ranke continued in his third sentence, critically depended on finding "certain materials hitherto unknown. My first duty is to give a general indication of these materials and their sources."[86] Between this universal church-state and the historian stood both time and source material, as procedures would stand between the historian and his nation. The depiction of political reality was the work of an imputed distance and separation, and the professional self contained within it the tools for distancing and distinguishing inside from outside: "A lucid and calm mind rarely takes its own conceptions for a perception," wrote Seignobos.[87] If the historian could stand outside his body to judge truth, this training made him the universal spectator or witness, able to describe the reality of institutions by splitting into someone who for long stretches of his life took up a position outside the scene, who both had and professed to lack a national identity.

Truth, factuality, and the general quest for knowledge about the nation-state and its heroes were increasingly seductive. Like the state itself, historians justified their exercise of power by claiming to stand for disinterested, high standards in which all had a stake and in which people should train themselves to participate. To ensure those standards, historical work entailed protecting boundaries, setting laws and rules, maintaining consensus, and working against threatening interlopers—the very procedures of politics as it came to be understood in the nineteenth century. The exercise of power through activities surrounding historical knowledge thus generated contradictory expressions. On the one hand, scientific historians spoke of being "passive" or "listening to reason speak within me" when faced with an array of facts to interpret.[88] On the other, many of the same people swung into soldierly action to justify their nation's wars and domestic policies, or to trounce women and people of other races presenting themselves either as practitioners or as subject matter.

At the time, none of this seemed contradictory, nor does it today, for the saturation of putatively neutral facticity with value involved precisely those values that were seen as natural and thus factual. Women, non-Europeans, amateurs, local events, and domestic life *were* inferior, superficial, less well-developed, less important. To catch this truth, one could indeed be "passive" and merely "listen to reason." However, to *protect* male plenitude—to narrate, elaborate, detail, enrich it—took prowess and vigilance. The scientific history of politics was fraught, inciting the profession's unacknowledged libidinal work, most recently imaged as male historians teetering "at the edge of the cliff."[89] Scientific historians wrote that they wanted to eliminate the cathartic side of history by turning it into a value-free knowledge based on facts. Professional knowledge nonetheless produced its own unacknowledged catharsis and erotics—those incited by structuring a factual history of politics out of so primal a value as gender.[90]

High Amateurism
and the Panoramic Past

6

Despite scorn from professionals, the themes of amateur writing—culture, social life, travel, and notable women—had worked themselves into a distinct literary genre by the last third of the nineteenth century. While scientific history flourished, writers like Julia Cartwright, Martha Lamb, Alice Morse Earle, and Ricarda Huch attracted an appreciative readership. Set in a deeply gendered society and shaped by the legislated inferiority of women, women's amateurism was, by this time, governed by fully developed conventions. Simultaneously, however, it provided an ever richer repeopling and refurbishing of the past. This was an age of "high amateurism," when the system of separate spheres reached one of its peaks. Middle-class domesticity, that container of womanhood, had attained its Victorian lushness, a comparatively luxurious standard of living enjoyed by the middle-classes in the Western world, thanks to an overlay of global plunder in the form of wealth, exotic goods, and artistic treasures. High amateurism surveyed this vast cultural and social domain, endowing the history of goods, works of art, and customs with a resonant symbolism, full of import and immanence.

Today this amateurism is usually seen as part of a late nineteenth-century cultural crisis, in some cases as a form of antimodernism. In the case of the United States, for instance, Earle's investigations of colonial household interiors and cultural traditions are viewed as part of a middle-class search for a colonial past that would stabilize Anglo-Saxon identity in the face of immigration and mass politics.[1] An accompanying sense of upper-class cultural malaise is thought to have generated women historians' copious studies of foreign cities and their art and architecture. No longer finding a place of grace in their home countries because of the rise of the masses, upper-class families pursued gentility in Florence or some other capital of aristocratic art.[2] Amateurism, it is claimed, was the late nineteenth-century refuge of a declining elite, although sometimes the attention to material objects is understood as part of an equally ignoble attention to consumption. In this single-minded reading, women devolve from virtuous republican mothers to avid consumers of culture and high-priced knickknacks.

A parallel reading sees some of these writers as colonial travelers and imperialists, exoticizing colonized peoples and worrying about European decline. Recent interpretations unmask the imperialist agenda in the work of feminist writers and reformers.[3] These evaluations usually take men's and women's writing as being all of a piece, yet unwittingly enhance gender disparities by selecting a few women writers as representing a smarmier imperialism, a more vapid antimodernism. Thus, conquerors like Louis Hubert Lyautey or nostalgic aesthetes like Jules and Edmond de Goncourt are seen as vigorous, honest, and accomplished, exemplifying the best of a bad genre, while women represent the worst. According to these interpretations, women authors, in the guise of feminism, made their claims on the backs of colonized peoples, fostering racist values from the comfort of the parasitic middle-class home. At least the male imperialist risked his life in the cause of his racism. Similarly, women historians of domesticity lacked the exquisite discernment of real tastemakers like the Goncourts, and thus fail even to appear in histories of consumption.[4] Their popularity is held up to show the pervasiveness of social, moral, and intellectual decline, to signal the effeminacy of thought in the fin-de-siècle West, and especially to foreground the rise of "mass culture."

In fact, the symbolizing work of amateur writing did not wane but only intensified during this time, resisting the onslaught of misogyny. Ironically, a burgeoning feminist literature made women's inequality even more visible, while the continued outpouring of popular misogynistic writings, such as those of Pierre Joseph Proudhon, further stressed women's innate inferiority and worthlessness for anything but breeding. This putative inferiority was being scientifically proclaimed in the works of Darwin, as well as in the writings of biologists, physiologists, and zoologists. These scientific dicta passed into the new social sciences, which produced numerous studies of the poor and especially of poor working women and prostitutes. The vivid representation of these people as impoverished and immoral embellished avant-garde fields like economics, authorizing such work as politically vital.[5] The studious amateur did her own writing in the context of these provocative, even terrifying scientific depictions of a degraded womanhood.

Women's amateurism was itself opening powerful new lines of inquiry and feeling the effect of new influences. For one thing, amateurism now rested on complicated methodological work that demanded regular travel by railroad and boat. These requirements changed the perceptual and stylistic weight of writing, yielding panoramic depictions of the past more like those of the photographer than of the footnote-burdened professional. For another thing, two innovative fields of study—feminist histories and investigations of working women's lives—absorbed a new group of writers. The former announced the unequal treatment of women in the past and charted the rise of the women's movement. Many of these feminist amateurs were connected with the women's movement or progressive reform clubs, both of which flourished at the end of the nineteenth century—even as activist women were jeered, jostled, arrested, brutalized, and beaten for their public demonstrations.[6]

Over this vast panorama, amateurs began placing an abstract statistical grid, especially in the form of surveys of how lower-class women worked and lived in contemporary and past times. The rise of professional history was ultimately compatible with these subfields of amateurism, to the extent that both relied on acquiring precise information. Feminist and reformminded amateurs believed that positivist study of a wide social field could contribute to progressive social policy, even to a better future for women. The influence of positivism on these historians might be said to have fractured amateurism, allowing some of their writing to look women's condition in the face.[7] Such a fracturing also provided their history with "modernist" characteristics: an array of intensely meaningful cultural signs and symbols, such as one finds later in the more self-conscious surrealist style of art; and a mathematical, gridlike, even nonrepresentational or abstract reckoning of the past.

Women's high amateurism occurred at that crucial moment for the development of the culture industry when color advertising, early films, photography, and pulp journalism appeared. If the culture industry was involved in disseminating images of the gazed-upon woman as the receptacle for a whole variety of fantasies, the historical panorama of womanhood and of all its accoutrements was available mostly through these amateur writings. Historical understandings of queens and how they lived, of women's religious faith, of salon women, of consumers and intriguers were all set in a dense cultural and social environment of abundant goods and bit-part players. The colliding historical fantasies—those of amateurs and of consumer-culture makers—may have joined together to produce a more general modernist mindset.

High Amateurism

Historical science constructed itself around assertions of its immunity to influences outside its own methodology and political subject matter. In contrast, amateurism stretched across genres, methodologies, and topics, producing a virtual panorama of literary possibilities. Many women demonstrated an acute sense of history, while they also enacted exile by working the disciplinary divides, crossing over a range of them and fusing the conventions of increasingly distinct genres. These writers may be seen in a variety of ways: as transgressors, expatriates, representatives of an increasingly outmoded literariness, or simply misguided writers. Or, in the context of a total literary production increasingly segmented by disciplines, they may be taken as producers of the closest approximation to the progressively outdated whole—those who covered a wider spectrum than the professionals.

By the end of the century, amateurs had reached the heights of polymathic writing, drawing on archives from various countries, commuting immense distances to see historical material, working in multiple languages, and using travel experiences, art, philosophy, and statistical data to produce their wide-ranging oeuvres. Almost all of them produced at least one work of historical fiction. Mary Louise Booth, an American, wrote the first comprehensive history of the City of New York, edited *Harper's Bazaar,* translated the works of Pascal, Cousin, Laboulaye, Agénor Gasparin, Henri Martin, and many others, and worked as a reporter for the *New York Times.* Amateurs wrote in virtually every genre.

160

Janet Ross, granddaughter of Sarah Taylor Austin, did translations from the Italian, composed travel literature, published political, architectural, and family histories, compiled the letters of her amateur-historian mother and grandmother, and even produced a collection of Tuscan recipes. An expatriate who lived in Florence and mined many of its archives, she was in close contact with other writers, such as Vernon Lee and Bernard Berenson. The German amateur Ricarda Huch, who was somewhat younger than Ross and one of the first European women to receive a doctorate in history, wrote poetry, essays, novels, and histories from outside academe. Like amateurism in general, her work remains hard to classify: her history of the Thirty Years War and her biography of Garibaldi are shelved in libraries under fiction.

Editing family papers, publishing local histories, short stories, historical essays, and biographies of famous women, and writing historical fiction consumed the prodigious energies of hundreds of amateurs in Europe and North America. By the end of the nineteenth century, there were thousands of such writers and historical activists, who worked to establish local history museums and archives. The impetus behind such historymindedness, which seemed in many cases to be motivated by the need for money, was actually polymorphous, including Confederate and regional patriotism, genealogical impulses, graphomania, reformist zeal, and feminism. Jessie White Mario, who wrote a history of Italian unification and biographies of Garibaldi and Mazzini, also published studies conducive to social improvement, such as *Il sistema penitenziario et il domicilio coatto in Italia, Le opere pie e l'infanticidio legale,* and *La miseria in Napoli.* During these years, professionalism was increasingly well-defined by the routines of university life, research in archives, political subject matter, participation in professional associations, and functional importance to the state and citizenship. In contrast, amateurism practiced by women was characterized as disorderly and relatively useless in terms of actual historical worth, as professionalism increasingly discredited its motives, conventions, and authors in professional journals.

Amateurs were immersed in their predecessors' work and eccentricities. The commonplace book of Egyptologist and novelist Amelia B. Edwards showed her to be steeped not only in the classics but in the writings of Anna Jameson, the Stricklands, Janet Ross, and others. Edwards regaled readers with amateur lore, especially about people whose "eccentricities of dress were proverbial."[8] In social terms, amateurism remained a place for unconventional lives that were, like writing itself, acted out on the boundaries of middle-class respectability. The widowed editor and author Martha Lamb attracted ardent suitors, although being in her sixties she felt that new relationships were not for her. Frances Pattison, an amateur historian of culture and art, decked herself out in seductive clothing, smoked French cigarettes, and, in the opinion of at least one young man, conveyed a distinct sense of "feminine fastness."[9] She lived apart from her scholar husband, Mark Pattison, for long stretches of time. Ricarda Huch as a teenager had a love affair with her brother-in-law, which not surprisingly estranged her from her sister. In her mid-forties Ricarda left her own husband and daughter to marry this man, and then fairly soon thereafter left him in turn.[10] More shocking perhaps was Vernon Lee, who sent mothers scurrying to hide their daughters from seduction whenever that notorious and charming lesbian announced a visit.[11] Her writing, according to Henry James, had "too great an implication of sexual motives." To his brother, William, he wrote "a word of warning . . . She's a tiger cat."[12] Close, not altogether decorous relationships existed among the amateurs: in her old age, Mary Robinson, who had been married to James Darmesteter (a scholar of Near Eastern cultures) and Emile Duclaux (head of the Pasteur Institut), reminisced to Vernon Lee of their early years in London as "new women" and struggling writers—of "our meagre, happy gruel suppers, . . . the nights I slept so securely in your arms."[13] Vernon Lee suffered a mental collapse on Robinson's first marriage.

Any sort of personal detail, from their appearance to their emotional lives, might turn up to trouble these women's reputations; but they were especially unconventional by middle-class standards because intense work utterly engaged them, supported them, and often kept their families going. In her seventies, Mary Robinson spent six to seven hours daily writing for pay at her desk. To accomplish this, along with the necessary research, she kept people "at bay except just one day a week, which one must, so to speak, throw to the wolves."[14] Needing money for charitable and other reasons, Vernon Lee inquired about publishing in France, where books sold better. When Théodore Benzton (Thérèse Blanc) asked her to collaborate on a book, Lee refused: "Unfortunately writing for me is in large part a question of money; consequently I cannot collaborate."[15] By her mid-fifties she had an annual income from family money of close to 600 pounds, so the excuse of money may have been a ploy—but a very credible one to other strapped amateurs. Julia Cartwright kept envious track of the huge sums Mrs. Humphrey Ward received for her novels, and when some of her own writing was made into a song for which she was paid, "it made me hunt through all my papers of odd scraps" to see if something else might be "turned to cash."[16] By the mid-1890s she had earned enough from her popular histories to send her daughter, the future professor Cecilia Ady, to boarding school and to Oxford. Earning money meant full-time intellectual work, along with full-time responsibilities in the middle-class and lower-middle-class household. Even a single woman like the Dutch historian Johanna Naber, whose parents made her tend the household while her brothers went to school and university, had to keep house in her later years for an older brother while writing her many histories.[17] American Alice Morse Earle, supposedly so middle class, was actually under great pressure as a result of her husband's failing fortunes; she wrote late into the night after she had put her children to bed, and she changed publishers if a royalty payment was late or if she could negotiate better terms. In the 1920s Canadian-born Constance Lindsay Skinner, author of two volumes in the *Chronicles of America* series published by Yale University Press, was so desperate for funds that she briefly considered accepting one of the marriage proposals she had received. Skinner drastically rewrote Herbert Boulton's volume for the series, and produced essays, short stories, historical novels, and other fiction, but constantly borrowed to keep herself alive.[18]

Writing entailed arduous and unladylike work. Matilde Serao—Italian journalist, chronicler of everyday poverty in Naples (*Il ventre di Napoli*, 1884), and sole support of her parents until their deaths—captured the scramble and struggle of the woman writer: "I write everywhere and about everything with a singleminded audacity. I win my position in a frenzy of pushing and elbowing."[19] The writer who publicly portrayed herself as the most hardworking and disadvantaged was Margaret Oliphant, who claimed to be lacking in talent and who characterized her approximately 300 articles and 100 volumes of history and fiction as "entirely a matter of daily labour."[20] Even as she pursued a strenuous career, her life was torn by repeated loss: two infants, her young husband, a daughter in childhood, her sons in early manhood. Having published her first novels as a teenager, she turned to writing in earnest to support her dying husband while they lived in Italy, and thereafter herself and her slowly decreasing family. Misfortune—for which she took much of the blame—haunted her as she traveled from England to Scotland, Italy, and France.

Oliphant explained herself in terms that social analysts were then using to describe the working-class mother—that is, as a drudge who was probably responsible for her children's deaths. "Mary Howitt . . . frightened me very much, I remember, by telling me of many babies whom she had lost through some defective valve in the heart, which she said was somehow connected with too much mental work on the part of the mother,—a foolish thing, I should think, yet the same thing occurred twice in myself."[21] Blamed as bad housewives, bad mothers, even child murderers, amateurs showed themselves as anything but professional writers. As scientists now had it, women's work was murderous—not just that of poor women, but the intellectual work of middle-class women as well. Thus, the role of amateur entailed an essential plasticity that played itself out in the multiple poses amateurs struck, from Janet Ross's wild abandon as a rider of Arabian ponies to that of the long-suffering and self-punishing Margaret Oliphant.

As science came to image women's mental work as homicidal, an increasingly prominent pose was that of the perfect heterosexual and monogamous partner-in-amateurism. Thus, alongside the sister-sister, mother-daughter, father-daughter, and other authorial combinations was companionate amateurism, in which husband and wife appeared as coauthors and even declared themselves equal partners in historical writing. Barbara and J. L. Hammond were the most popular of these early teams, publishing their book *The Village Labourer* in 1911; Will and Ariel Durant appeared several decades later.[22] Monogamous heterosexual coauthorship provided the woman author a kind of protective coloring to ward off some of the worst traumas of amateurism, since monogamy in general was said to shield women from the inequities of marketplace, politics, public life, and citizenship. It did not mean a lighter workload: Barbara Hammond's ill-health (necessitating removal of her ovaries) and the availability of a research assistant only temporarily curtailed her heavy archival and writing schedule.[23] There were other pitfalls: the woman might disappear altogether into her husband's persona, with the authorial voice in the most successful cases being seen as male. Reviewers, for instance, generally appraised the Beards' coauthored works as if they had been written by Charles alone.

Many amateurs did not achieve what one might call a "normal" persona, however. Some of the more florid ones imaged themselves and their work as bizarre. On a trip to procure letters for a biography, the young widow Oliphant retired to her room to make her way through a stack of documents in "diabolical handwriting." "The deep darkness and silence of a winter night in the country closed down upon me . . . The bed in my room was a gloomy creation, with dark-red moreen curtains, afterwards, as I found, called . . . 'a field to bury strangers in.' I had a pair of candles, which burned out, and a fire, which got low."[24] Cold marble floors, dying fires, and the mysteries of train travel textured Oliphant's autobiography, while neurotics, decadents, the insane, and the fantastic engaged French historian Arvède Barine.[25]

Some of the most active amateurs continued to mark out their generic and social liminality by publishing anonymously and pseudonymously. Violet Paget took the name Vernon Lee, although she also published early work anonymously. Some ventured forth in an array of guises. Charlotte Carmichael Stopes used the pseudonyms Lutea Reseda, C. Graham, Ursa Major, and Audi Alteram Partem. Although Ricarda Huch occasionally published under the name of her brother-in-law and lover Richard Huch, she generally used her own name. Louise-Cécile Vincens wrote prolifically under the name Arvède Barine, and Augustine Bulteau used the pseudonyms Femina, Toche, and Jacque [sic] Vontade.

Amateurs articulated liminality that worked to mark out the boundaries, spaces, and locations of femininity. That aspect of trauma based on the better story was now institutionalized in the publishing industry, which established series about the great cultural centers of the past and others such as *Famous Women* (published by Roberts Brothers, Boston) and *Eminent Women* (William Allen, London) about the accomplishments, loyalties, and misfortunes of female achievers. Although these series contained the standard lists of queens and women worthies, newcomers like the Countess of Albany, George Sand, Mercy Otis Warren, and other eighteenth- and nineteenth-century figures were introduced alongside Germaine de Staël and Elizabeth I.[26] The African-American novelist and essayist Pauline Hopkins wrote two series of historical articles entitled "Famous Men of the Negro Race" and "Famous Women of the Negro Race" for *Colored American Magazine.*[27] Repetition and ritual continued to result in numbness: "For years past neither praise nor blame has quickened my pulse ten beats that I am aware of," Oliphant wrote. "This insensibility saves me some pain, but it also must lose me a great deal of pleasure."[28] However, others were beginning to find a different value in repetition and ritual—namely, their inherent force.

The most prominent ritualized repetition occurred in the many cultural and social histories *cum* travelogues, especially those of Italian cities. Clara Erskine Clement's book *The Queen of the Adriatic; or, Venice, Medieval and Modern* (1893) focused, in its first six chapters, on the story of Barbarossa in Venice (for which the Piazza San Marco and the water served as a mnemonic device), on the competition between the gondola and the vaporetto, the doges, the Crusades, popular festivals, and the development of the Council of Ten. All of these chapters devote a great deal of attention to water travel. The chapter on Barbarossa (Frederick I) begins with a steamship voyage from Trieste to Venice, and contains a long section on Venetian boats. The next is given over entirely to the competition between the gondola and the vaporetto, but also digresses to wider discussions of travel. The movement of boats dominates the first half of the narrative, taking contemporary voyagers as well as historic travelers on trips that afford entry into history. Modernist literature, developing at the time, also used water imagery, but did so differently, portraying tension. For Clement, sailing from Trieste, "every poetic and artistic sense is filled to overflowing." At the end of her history of this city, she wrote: "You shut your eyes . . . [and] almost feel the motion of the gondola as you sweep around a curve, and a new and fascinating vista reveals itself."[29] Water tranquilized, thus facilitating and stimulating the spatial envisioning of history.

Within the panorama, detail remained luminescent, baroque, opaque. Descriptions of fabric, drapery, gardens, and works of art filled these volumes, organizing the space of the past. In and of themselves, minute depictions had importance; for example, the life of Isabella d'Este, as portrayed by Julia Cartwright, consisted of the details of her artistic purchases. The detail did not lead to a higher, transcendent truth, because it remained relentlessly physical. Beatrice d'Este, furious at discovering that her husband's mistress was living in their castle, "refused to wear a certain vest of woven gold which her husband had given her, if Madonna Cecilia ever appeared in a similar one, which it seems was also Lodovico's present."[30] The discovery of un-published archival sources and the development of better modes of travel and networks of researchers allowed amateurs to produce more and fuller details of everyday life and culture. Julia Cartwright rejoiced:

> During the last twenty years the patient researches of successive students in the archives of Northern Italian cities have been richly rewarded . . . We see now, more clearly than ever before, what manner of men and women these Estes and Gonzagas, these Sforzas and Viscontis, were. We gain fresh insight into their characters and aims, their secret motives and private wishes. We see them in their daily occupations and amusements, at their work and at their play. We follow them from the battlefield and council chamber, from the chase and tournament, to the privacy of domestic life and the inti-mate scenes of the family circle.

Typically, Renaissance history had depicted "bloodshed and strife," "low standards of morals," and "crimes and vices."[31] In the details of the quotidian, including artworks, home furnishings, needlework, and every-day customs, lay a set of elements that composed the Renaissance. By the end of the nineteenth century, it took an abundance of material details, drawn in generous physicality, to submerge both the historical and con-temporary evidence of these crimes and vices. Readers compiled entire libraries of Renaissance urban history and biographies that repeopled the universe, filled it anew with objects and artifacts, and thus created a believable panoramic and a resonant surface of the past that they could pose against the crimes and vices of other accounts.

Amateurs also focused intently on the local past in telling their medie-val, Renaissance, or more modern histories. Many participated in large collections of "city" history: Virginia Wales Johnson, Elizabeth Robbins Pennell, Laura Ragg, and Clara Erskine Clement (later Clara Erskine Waters) were among these. Louise Guiraud and Adine Riom developed regional and local specialties that focused on archeology, folklore, genealogy, and linguistics, developing into what Vernon Lee called the *"genius loci."* The most persistent and successful of local historians were women in the U.S. South, who engaged in an effort, as one put it, to see "the wrongs of history righted."[32] These women supported the development of local archives, the erection of statues to heroines like Virginia Dare, the interviewing of veterans and other denizens of the Confederacy and the Old South, and the conduct of historical societies. They published pamphlets and books and contributed to periodicals like the *Confederate Veteran,* but devoted equal effort to a visual re-creation of the homes, families, mores, architecture, furniture, statuary, and artwork of the past.[33]

Intense literary wandering through the precise details of society and culture, which was connected from time to time in the narrative to the most important eras and events, complicated high amateur writing by comparison to the singleminded and linear political focus of the professionals. Digressions on paintings and poetry, attention to the small events of everyday life, and even failure to reproduce the "big event" in toto—the functioning of these conventions has remained elusive even to those few critics who have bothered to take them seriously. For instance, Ricarda Huch's historical vignettes utterly baffled reviewers, who, if they had any insight at all, saw these stories as part of the "charm" of women's amateurism.[34] Huch's two-volume account of Italian unification, which was loosely centered on the figure of Garibaldi, shifted rapidly from individual to individual, allotting three or four pages each to Crispi, Victor Emmanuel, Cavour, Ugo Bassi, Mazzini, and other great and minor actors. The defeated and the victorious alike presented their innermost feelings about Italy and were shown contemplating action. They quarreled and plotted against one another, and the plots were so numerous that murders, affronts, and successful intrigues kept the pace brisk, if uncentered and nonlinear. It was the less significant actors that were puzzling: the Baroness Sant'Anna, Fra Giovanni Pantaleo and his pupils, Captain Carini, Giorgio Menotti (a friend of Garibaldi's son), the Count and Countess Castroforte, the parsimonious mother superior of an orphanage, and any number of anonymous monks, society ladies, and children. Huch detailed the story of the widow La Giovannara—an unknown, a historical nobody—who kept an inn in Naples and cared for her pet monkey, all the while proclaiming her faith that unification would be accomplished.[35]

When the subject was a woman, the heroine herself—that is, the big story—often dissolved in these details and collapsed into accounts of other, more glorious lives. Julia Cartwright's *Sacharissa*, the biography of Dorothy Sidney, Countess of Sunderland, had more about Philip Sidney (the author of *Arcadia*), Sacharissa's brother Algernon Sidney, her first husband, Henry Duke of Sunderland, and many other figures than it did about the purported protagonist. Cartwright provided the most vivid depictions of her only through the images of poets, artists, and essayists such as Edward Waller and Antoine Van Dyck, who celebrated her beauty. In more than three hundred pages, Dorothy Sidney appeared only briefly—to be married, be widowed, raise a son, remarry, and give birth to another son, the sporadic narration of these events perhaps accounting for 10 percent of the book, if that. Instead of the self breaking out to narrative autonomy, the bulk of this engaging and best-selling history involved the many people in Sacharissa's orbit (and beyond) and their connections to the momentous events of seventeenth-century England. The political events were displaced onto the social, the social was displaced onto the familial, and the female biography drowned in all of these. Dorothy appeared in the book as an obedient, virtuous, and entirely appropriate woman protagonist who had no legitimate narrative, as would the victim of social or any other kind of abuse. Everything from legal codes to definitions of personhood and citizenship prescribed such a disappearance, and amateur writers worked the ensuing trauma into a historical tale.[36]

The panorama made possible by new forms of modern transport, so important to the amateur quest for heterogeneous material and often so traumatic to their users, also worked this kind of disappearance of the foreground and thus coincided with amateur historical depiction.[37] Amateurs operated in worlds of multiple shock, however—in the world of industrialization and that of gender. Thus, even as large foreground characters and incidents were dispersed, amateur works offered an intense visualization of the past, differing both from full panoramization (which often omitted the small detail) and from the scrutiny of the document (which was supposed to eradicate sensory and emotional reactions). The historical world was reborn in a rich perceptual frame, where one saw, heard, smelled, touched, and indeed felt the medieval city resonating through multiple senses. The writer evoked the physical experience of travel to the castles, châteaus, urban mansions, and country homes of great queens and notable women. While amateurs continued their detailed descriptions of women's fancy work, furniture, sculpture, jewelry, and other works of art, increasingly their books carried many pictures (some, in fact, were quite lavishly illustrated), further stimulating the imagination and senses to grasp this better world. Amateur history also provided a social panorama far fuller than the one earlier works had presented. It included images of popular participation in Renaissance festivals, the guildsman pursuing his craft, the woman innkeeper, and other types of women plying their trade or serving as faithful sisters, wives, and mothers. Set in such a pictorial frame, each of these was seen by professional critics as trivial, especially when operating within or posed against the linear importance of modern history.

Vernon Lee, however, began explicitly to fashion travel and visualization into a thoroughgoing and coherent critique of professional history that would justify amateurism. Calling herself an aestheticist, Lee saw history in terms of the changing perspectives offered by travel: "Like a real landscape it [history] may also be seen from different points of view, and under different lights; then, as you stand, the features of the scene will group themselves—this ridge will disappear behind that, this valley will open out before you, that other will be closed." Making these observations early in the 1880s, she adhered to the specular trope of the professionals, but her interpretation differed from theirs in significant ways. For one thing, the professional's trained, individual eye connected along the brain circuitry to find a firm, spiritual, or transcendent truth that did not figure in her discussions. Instead, Lee advocated a wide-ranging sensory process that allowed for multiple perspectives and for the dramatic consequences of that multiplicity—for example, the big mountain would disappear. Her perspectival method proceeded onto fresh ground when it invoked Impressionist painting.[38] These painters, she noted, had jettisoned the "realistic" drawing of life in favor of less precise depictions or "effects . . . at a given moment." Those professional historians who tried to depict the world in a universal way rendered reality "as it never is at all." This translated historically to mean that "the past, to the people who were in it, was not a . . . marvellous diagram constructed on the principle of getting at the actual qualities of things by analysis . . . but a series of constantly varied perspectives."[39] Thus, Lee derided history that stemmed from "the scalpel and the microscope,"[40] and historical writing that was "a mere onslaught of archivists and documentary criticism, . . . abusiveness, . . . [and] the attempt to make opponents grotesque."[41]

The ways of the voyager were posed against those of the archival researcher, not only procedurally but also in narrative. Since published work was increasingly part of a segmented market, Lee warned Bernard Berenson against the pitfalls of ignoring the "question of literary exposition" and thus of merging a scientific with a more popular style. "The mind is utterly *dérouté* and knows not which attitude to assume"—the former style, portraying difficult issues, or the latter, "producing an effect of ease and pleasantness."[42] This jarring merger of perspective contrasted with the crafted but no less complex perspectival emplotment that shaped much of Lee's historical oeuvre and punctuated the amateur project. She enacted this by employing attractive framing devices. Her chapter on the music scene in eighteenth-century Italy begins by taking readers on a walk through the streets of Bologna, ushering them into its Philharmonic Academy, and showing them the portraits of great musicians guarding the door to the Academy's archives. Amid the letters and musical scores in the archives, the narrator finds Charles Burney's account of Italian music, and it is through his travels that cultural history proceeds. As they travel with Burney, readers are interrupted by other accounts, gleaned from letters, music reportage of the day, and additional travelers' records. The tour comes to an end with the narrator's departure from the archives.

Easing the voyage for others and producing "aesthetic enjoyment" resulted from a stern amateur discipline, itself the outcome of "knowing *what not to do*."[43] The avoidance of all obstacles, arguing, and untoward sights made amateur history a soothing, orderly panorama that deliberately set itself against the distortions of historical science. Most amateurs agreed not only that the local, tangible, social, and cultural realms contained reality, but that this reality conveyed kinetic as well as mental impressions. The most palatable of these should be conveyed to the reader, whose responses would also be mental and kinetic. This appeal to the kinetic separated the authoritative scientific narrative voice, which wanted to convince, from the unauthorized narrative one, whose bold statements would automatically produce disbelief because they were constructed as "low."[44] Thus, the amateur expanded cognition to include aesthetic, emotional, and kinetic registers,

constructing these within a historical knowledge that was—and remains—beyond the horizons of the professional. As a result, this amateur
cognition formed a distinct historical language, similar to that of the discredited articulations of victims and the traumatized. It had a syntax of its
own. Whereas a certain group appreciated its force, found it credible, and
hungered to read it, professionals did not.[45] Tension, fear, joy, pleasure, and
other unvoiced sentiments, which we recognize today as conveyors of
knowledge, constituted the language of the disbelieved.

In this endeavor, amateur histories destabilized themselves, sometimes
producing moments of intense shock, when the traumatic and painful went
too far. Ricarda Huch's *History of the Thirty Years War* flows with
women's blood; it is filled with scenes of violence against them, committed
by them, and carried out by both sides. In various works, Vernon Lee
would unexpectedly reveal "the foulness of adultery, . . . which must strike
almost like a handful of mud in the face"; she described a wife's first
experience of her royal husband's "bestial and unquiet drunkard's sleep,
which kept her awake in disgust and terror."[46] Occasionally the members
of the Men's and Women's Club in London—against the male leadership's
wishes—would conduct research on the history of venereal disease, por-
nography, and sexual relations among the Greeks or among the Swiss
during the Reformation. The club's projects, such as the various studies of
prostitution it carried out, occasionally led to unpleasant associations; as
Lina Eckenstein put it in a letter to fellow club member Karl Pearson, the
studies "remind us that in past centuries, just as now, the treatment of one
class of women reflects on the other."[47] Encountering grim truths, however, was one of the hazards amateurs faced as they worked with the
inescapable findings produced with the tools of the new scientific history.

Working Women and the Social Science of the "Real"

In the second half of the nineteenth century, amateur history began coming in contact with a variety of reform movements, such as feminism,
programs to improve conditions for the poor, and anti-imperialist or nationalist causes. For example, Alice Stopford Green (the widow of J. R.
Green) joined with friends such as Emily Hobhouse to attack imperialism
and with likeminded citizens to promote Home Rule for Ireland. Her

histories of Ireland, which aimed at showing a vibrant but law-abiding past, were criticized by one professional for intimating that the Irish lived "in a perpetual state of exaltation."[48] Though professionals were free to speak passionately on behalf of causes without damaging their reputations (J. R. Seeley could argue for British imperialism and Treitschke could boldly advance German nationalism), such was not the case with amateurs, whose reform-minded politics further undermined the limited accept-ability of the conventional amateur voice.

After the revolutionary period, the burgeoning social sciences, espe-cially political economy, made working-class women a central figure in their analyses. Around them swirled the drama of wages, consumption, and prices, often told in terms of dead or starving children, women's penchant for spending their wages on ribbons and lace instead of on food, and degraded family life passed in filthy, bare hovels. In England the parliamentary inquiries in the early nineteenth century focused on the condition of women working in mines; thereafter, political economists, such as Paul Leroy-Beaulieu in France, followed Michelet's flamboyant lead by highlighting the sordid situation of women who worked. Since the 1980s, historians have pointed out the stereotypical and truncated discus-sions of women's work (they were all "seamstresses"), the descriptions of sparse household furnishings (a stool, a table, a cupboard), and the con-ventionally excessive metaphors of blood and luxury goods that charac-terized most of these writings. Scenes of dying children, frail mothers, and filth provided the emotional capital that made social science work. Once again, fantasies of the low marked out and propelled interest in the high.[49]

Gradually, women writers came to investigate these social conditions. Among the first in Germany was Bettina von Arnim, whose *Armenbuch* (*Book of the Poor*) was one of three hundred such works to appear before 1848, but the only one written by a woman.[50] It took several more decades for a larger number of women to take up this problematic subject matter. On the one hand, the material on poor women presented only an additional gloss on the picture of degradation and inferiority. Other ingredients of the depiction—bloodshed, out-of-wedlock childbearing, love of baubles and lace—furthered women's association with the carnivalesque, transgressive, and abnormal world that had come increasingly to differentiate the world of powerless women from that of powerful men. On the other hand, the subject of poor women offered an opportunity that some women writers and researchers were beginning to welcome. Through the eyes of researchers, poor women testified to appalling conditions that were not of their own making.

In 1931, introducing a fifty-year study of working-class women's lives, Virginia Woolf claimed that middle-class researchers on their own had "little knowledge of what it pleases them to call 'reality.'"[51] Amateur historians had contrived a subject matter and literary style that involved the carnivalesque, the spatial, the pleasant, and ultimately the powerless. Professional historians, in contrast, hailed their own work as the study of the real, factual, detailed, powerful, and important, because it used archival material and chronicled the rise of the nation-state. In general, however, they did not study poor or ordinary people, since they did not study women. As Social Darwinism and the imperial agenda advanced in the West, and as working-class movements loomed larger politically, motherhood was declared important to the health of a nation's citizenry and thus crucial to its survival.[52] Simultaneously, married women gradually won the right to retain their wages and in many instances to own property independent of their husbands. Although law codes continued to guarantee male supremacy in the family, there was some improvement in women's legal position. Political reality acquired a different shape, but one for which there was as yet no well-developed historical vocabulary.

The summons to the "real" meant that scientifically minded women left much of their traditional practice behind. Many flocked to the new societies for the study of social science, announcing the importance of their "perspective" on women's labor and other issues. One American enthusiast for this kind of study was Caroline Dall, who in 1860 published a study of women's work. "In Physics," she wrote, "no scientific observations are reliable, so long as they proceed from one quarter alone: many observers must report, and their observations must be compared, before we can have a trustworthy result. So it is in Social Science."[53] In the 1860s and 1870s in Germany, Lina Morgenstern began a network of schools for "household science"; somewhat later, in France, Augusta Moll-Weiss established similar institutions. The aim was to teach bourgeois women household skills, but also a precise vocabulary of classification and order in household procedures. Moll-Weiss attacked the foolish pretensions of the bourgeois home, with its recipes for pâté of hare *en gelée* or for mousseline of herring roe; traditionalists, in turn, attacked her ways as "inelegant" and tantamount to a dangerous and irreverent "trespassing" on the family. Moll-Weiss nonetheless continued to teach the nutritional aspects of food (albumen, vitamins). As late as 1930, Alice Salomon in *Das Familienleben in der Gegenwart* (*Family Life Today*) deplored the general tendency toward immunizing the household to scientific knowledge among women of all classes.[54] In a major hermeneutical breakthrough, the household was being reconfigured as a place for classification where everything from kin networks to food could be talked about in new ways. Researchers saw an end to the silence, negativity, and powerlessness that science had attributed to everyday life.

Like most amateur work, chronicling workers' lives entailed collecting myriad data, in this case an array of physical evidence such as the contours of neighborhoods, statistics, and even testimony from the poor women themselves. Caroline Dall, in comparing the work of social scientists to that of physicists,[55] was—like Vernon Lee—widening the field of vision, contesting the point from which men had dominated observation. From the late nineteenth century on, researchers entered the home and factory to obtain knowledge and to urge working women to speak and write, about their lives in the present and about their families' lives as far back as oral tradition could take them. In this endeavor to transform the poverty of the home into a powerful scientific presentation of social facts (both past and present), hundreds of studies appeared that were supposed to present the reality of poor and working women. Among these books were *Married Women's Work* (1915), by Clementina Black; *Le travail à domicile: Ses misères, ses dangers, les moyens d'y remédier* (*Household Labor: Its Miseries, Its Dangers, and the Ways to Alleviate Them*; 1914), by Gabrielle Duchêne; and *Das Leben der jungen Fabrikmädchen in München: Die soziale und wirtschaftliche Lage ihrer Familie, ihr Berufsleben und ihre persönlichen Verhältnisse* (*The Life of the Young Factory Girl in Munich: The Social and Economic Situation of Her Family, Her Worklife, and Her Personal Relationships;* 1911), by Rosa Kempf. In Italy, Maria Pasolini wrote for the *Giornale degli Economisti* and produced an account of the peasants of Ravenna. In Vienna, Marianne Pollack produced numerous studies, such as *Frauenleben von gestern und heute* (*Lives of Women, Today and Yesterday;* 1928), and Käthe Leichter published, among many other books, *Frauenarbeit und*

Arbeiterinnenschutz in Österreich (*Women's Work and Protections for Working Women in Austria;* 1927).[56] Other researchers included Magdalen Pember Reeves, Margaret Llewelyn Davies, Margery Spring Rice, Caroline Milhaud, Marie-Louise Rochebilliard, Odette Laguerre, Rose Otto, Käthe Schirmacher, Marie Bernays, and Marie Baum. These studies were often sponsored by newly formed collectives, such as the Fabian Women's Group, the Section d'Etudes Féminines of the Musée Social, and the Deutsche Akademie für soziale und pädagogische Frauenarbeit.[57]

Social investigators and historians produced an accounting of women's lives, including the amount that families spent for food, methods of food allocation, fertility rates, infant mortality, household income, size of living space, hours spent in different household tasks, hours that different family members spent with each other and in different tasks. Other topics were length and severity of illnesses, household budgets in general, income from different household members, sleeping arrangements, numbers and descriptions of kitchen utensils, appliances, furniture and dishes, information about other kin, and statistics on migration. In this way, a scientific portrait of poor women took shape—one in which there was little place either for reticence or for the charity worker's moral judgment. These were replaced by classificatory speech and writing, which transformed the sentiment of family life into scientific analysis. Explaining the need for researchers, Alice Salomon and Marie Baum claimed that "often a stranger can gain a substantially deeper understanding of the relations between family members."[58]

These historians and researchers were rescuers, saviors, deliverers. Moreover, investigators could root out randomness and elicit accurate reporting, guarding it from error. In preparation for Magdalen Pember Reeves's study *Round About a Pound a Week*, the Fabian Women's Committee selected a neighborhood near an infant-health center, and then chose, as participants, pregnant women with a weekly family income of 18 to 30 shillings. To forestall random observations, "it was found to be necessary, in order to secure the success of the investigation, to inaugurate a system of accurate accounts. In no case were these accounts already in being, and it was therefore the task of the [representatives of the Fabian Society] to teach each woman in turn."[59] These researchers were thus not only rescuers, but teachers. It took work to produce the observable experience: Reeves's report makes it clear that there was much resistance to directed writing. The

176

housewives of Lambeth rebelled, forgot, and forced the researchers to impose requirements. Or sometimes they were illiterate or too old. "The older women, and those who had had no reason to use a pencil after leaving school, had completely lost the power of connecting knowledge which might be in their minds with marks made by their hands on a piece of paper."[60]

An absence of physical goods diluted but did not destroy the spatialization of life that had characterized amateur portrayals of women's experience. This stab at science pruned many of the carnivalesque excesses of other amateurs, political economists, and journalists. The concerted effort to build a picture of poverty and to describe women's plight went some distance toward confronting the sources and effects of women's inferior condition. Alice Clark described the deterioration of competence and skill in household matters that had begun in the seventeenth century, while Caroline Milhaud charted the conditions of women homeworkers (nonpayment of wages, long periods without money).[61] Both placed women in an era of devolution, not progress. Yet the full picture of women's condition was still wanting, for what was actually happening remained only inferential. Looking at some of these studies today, we see that for several centuries in the West respectable working-class women and often their children were fairly consistently starved by a system that allocated food and other resources mostly to grown men. Laboring incessantly and ingeniously—this much was clear—to enable at least some members of their families to survive, poor women themselves lacked medical care, adequate food, housing, heat, and clothing. Ventriloquistic narratives—in which historians and other social scientists spoke of women's condition through studies of the working class—still did not yield direct statements about women's harsh and violence-filled lives, or about the political and legal privileging of men that enforced their inferiority. Although ventriloquism made these articulations possible, because amateurs adopted the accepted role of rescuer, teacher, and improver, the scientific voice when applied by women still amounted to euphemism and, oddly enough, a perpetuation of the "better story"—but a story suddenly riveted to what it called "the real."

Speaking as improvers and translators of working women's experience, amateur historians employed conventions of class and gender hierarchy, while they opened the door to a science of "reality" where women strove to replace the barrage of heady "metaphorical" depictions. One surprising concomitant of their endeavor was the historical and autobiographical writing that working-class women began to pursue. Women like Elena Elek, Adelheid Popp, Louise Delétang, and Jeanne Bouvier produced autobiographies, memoirs, and histories distinguished by accounts of relentless misery. Adelheid Popp, an Austrian and a Social Democrat, wrote that whereas most people remembered their youth with longing, "I face the recollection of my childhood with other feelings. I knew no point of brightness, no ray of sunshine, nothing of a comfortable home in which motherly love guided my childhood."[62] Popp followed funeral cortèges to collect charity from mourners, while in Budapest Elek begged regularly as a child to support herself.[63] Parents were often absent, negligent, or abusive, and fathers were the worst offenders—as investigators and poor women never failed to point out. Popp's father returned home drunk one Christmas eve and destroyed the only Christmas tree she had ever had. "I can't remember his ever saying a word to me, and I never spoke a word to him."[64]

Working women emphasized that conversation and words were not initially part of their lives. Dwelling on early silence, their writings indicate the interlaced presence of the middle-class amateur. Jeanne Bouvier, born in the mid-nineteenth century, recorded in detail some fifty years after the fact her budget as a young seamstress: "My expenses went as follows: bouillon and beef, .50 francs; wine, .20 francs; bread, .15 francs . . . My weekly expenses for food were 8.40 francs, which made, with linens and lodging, 15.15 francs."[65] These strict accountings and the chronicle of misery could hardly have been aimed at a working-class audience familiar with such details. Instead, they acknowledge a preverbal condition and a coming-to-writing in the social scientific field, authorized by the ventriloquism of the amateur researcher. In the case of Jeanne Bouvier's budget, neither Caroline Milhaud nor Magdalen Pember Reeves could have asked for more.

Jeanne Bouvier emerged to become a full-fledged historian in her seventies, when Georges Renard, professor of history at the Collège de France, asked her to contribute a volume on the *lingère* (seamstress) to his multivolume *Bibliothèque Sociale des Métiers*. Bouvier presented her trajectory from worker to writer as guided by the middle-class rescuer. She had found syndicalism and renown while working as a seamstress, when a client with connections to the feminist paper *La Fronde* had encouraged her to activism. Fighting the male leadership of the unions on moral and feminist grounds, Bouvier became prominent among a certain Parisian set, and this made her proud of her achievements. Of her burgeoning historical renown, she noted: "I am the only worker who was called on [to write]." She maintained a fierce independence, refusing help from academicians. "When my manuscript is ready, I'll bring it to you. If there are changes to be made, I will make them. I want to put my book together the way I think it should be."[66]

As her first historical work grew in size, Bouvier marveled at its length. Contemporary authors have criticized Bouvier for touting her own writing—have smirked, for example, that her histories sold in minuscule numbers.[67] Yet Bouvier offered another narrative: the tale of the amateur self, as a worker who took pride in her métier. Oblivious to any traps down the road, Bouvier recounted at the end of her autobiography an ongoing correspondence with Franklin Roosevelt, then president of the United States, about the declining quality of paper and its certain improvement if surplus cotton were used in paper manufacture rather than burned. "Scholarly writing and archives—precious sources of history—are threatened with destruction in the near future." Handling a letter of Charles VII written in 1491 had brought Bouvier to this appreciation of the durability that fiber gave to paper.[68] History for her had become a craft—a skilled process, predicated on good materials, which resulted in a durable product that the worker could take pride in.

The working woman remained a privileged subject for women historians, her status growing with the feminist movement of the late 1960s. She gave a sense that it was possible to confront historical "reality," and, interpreted as someone without words of her own, she filled the requirements of middle-class feminist ventriloquism. The "real" could be accessed through the working woman, who was meant to be degraded and inferior without opening onto the unspeakable situation of the researcher's own middle-class degradation. Those, like Bouvier, who attempted to write their own history undermined that agenda and were sometimes rebuked for it. Yet the dialogue of historical writing had added new voices, making it more polyvocal than ever.

The Indignant Amateur

In the second half of the nineteenth century, writers began producing a serious kind of history set in the chronological frame of politics and explicitly connected with the rise of the women's movement. This history was written by amateurs, usually activists who were participants in the movement itself. In 1871 Paulina Wright Davis, activist, publisher, and founder and editor of the feminist journal *Una*, wrote *A History of the National Women's Rights Movement, for Twenty Years*. A decade later, Elizabeth Cady Stanton and Susan B. Anthony collaborated with Matilda Joselyn Gage in a multivolume work entitled *History of Woman Suffrage* (1881), which was expanded with the help of another suffragist, Ida Husted Harper. The British suffragist Charlotte Carmichael Stopes, a prodigious writer and an honorary fellow of the Royal Society of Literature, published articles and gave talks on aspects of the women's movement and their access to higher education. Seeking to show that women's suffrage had a constitutional basis, she wrote *British Freewomen: Their Historical Privilege*.[69] In 1902 Helen Blackburn, editor of the *Englishwomen's Review*, published "the standard work" on British feminism: *Women's Suffrage: A Record of the Movement in the British Isles*. In 1929, a granddaughter to the movement, Ray Strachey, published *The Cause*, a detailed account of the nineteenth-century activists' work. Caroline Dall, Luise Büchner, and Florence Buckstaff also worked in an overtly feminist historical mode; Büchner simultaneously exercised feminist and reformist leadership by starting projects to help working women.[70] After a long discussion of dower law in the Middle Ages, Buckstaff declared it a "curious fact" that unequal provisions for women should be "still the rule eight centuries later in a large number of the laws of a race which has no prouder name for itself than Anglo-Saxon."[71] In the Netherlands, Johanna Naber also compiled documents from the women's movement of the nineteenth century. Biographies of individual leaders such as Susan B. Anthony and Antoinette Brown Blackwell followed.

The first chapters of the massive *History of Woman Suffrage* open with a cursory treatment of the London Anti-Slavery Conference of 1840 (at which women were not allowed to speak and had to watch the proceedings from a distance, behind a curtain), the Seneca Falls Convention of 1848, and the first meeting of Susan B. Anthony and Elizabeth Cady Stanton. The major events begin only after 1850, as this team and other actors turn away from their focus on abolitionism and toward women's rights. Documentation for the book consists of newspaper articles, speeches, interviews with participants, congressional and other legislative records, and legal documents. Spending intensive time researching and writing, Anthony and Stanton were virtually captive to the work. The five thousand pages of the *History of Woman Suffrage* abound in detail, direct quotation, and eyewitness accounts.

Yet for all that, the book does not provide a historical analysis of women's situation; it does not close the door on narrative trauma, but instead shows signs of its persistence. The prefatory material alludes to unfair treatment of women in the past, particularly the fact that women were denied equal political rights of citizenship in the aftermath of the American Revolution, and the full rights to property that men enjoyed. For lack of education, the preface maintains, women and their children have had to submit to male doctors, resulting in high mortality. They pay taxes but receive few benefits, since the money goes to support schools and other institutions reserved for men. In general, however, the history tells the better story because it soon switches to charting the movement's development rather than chronicling or analyzing the historical experience of women. *Woman under Monasticism,* by amateur philologist and historian Lina Eckenstein, inverts this strategy by alluding briefly to women's inferior position in the early modern and modern periods, and recounting the better story of monastic women who wielded power. A feminist influenced by the work of Bachofen, Eckenstein presented papers to the Men's and Women's Club and did historical research for pay. She thought it important not to focus on bad times but to give examples of how, despite oppression under Germanic "fatherlaw," women had made good.[72] Thus, both of these important feminist histories remain heroic narratives of escape from conditions, not chronicles of the conditions themselves.

A pastiche and jumble of documents, the *History of Woman Suffrage* fails to smooth over the rough edges to construct a seamless narrative. Despite its cascade of documentation, the work falters at narrative because the authors stake their credibility on adducing evidence, not integrating it. They add feminism to the amateur practice of trying to create a believable authorial voice through excessive data. Feminism, however, ensures that they remain outside the community of believable historians even though their work treats a major political event and takes place on the hustings and in the courts and legislatures of the local, state, and federal governments.

Since the prefatory remarks attack male government, educational institutions, and legal codes, the ensuing account is already contaminated by its lack of commitment to the terms of the nation-state. The preface, moreover, fails to replicate the genial rhetoric that the professionals employ in their narratives. Nonetheless, feminist histories moved beyond the carnivalesque, humorous, and traumatic tropes of earlier amateurism. This history has become indignant, yet confounds itself by making the professionals look more reasonable, agreeable, and thus universally true because free from partisanship.

The *History of Woman Suffrage,* many amateur cultural histories, and social scientific studies crammed primary material into their texts. Letters, newspaper clippings, long excerpts from personal journals, and samples of household accounts comprised these works. They testified to a drive that ultimately metamorphosed into an amateur impulse to establish women's archives; eventually, there were many such collectors and collections. Women's archival activism involved very different people—for example, Aletta Jacob, a Dutch physician and feminist whose collection of writings about women constitutes the basis of the Gerritsen Collection; Marguerite Durand, a French feminist and publisher who gave her name to an important women's library in Paris (which includes the archival collections of several women); Johanna Naber, Willemign Posthumus–van der Goot, and Rosa Manus, Dutch historians who in 1935 founded the International Archive for the Women's Movement in the Netherlands;[73] and the historian Mary Beard, who worked tirelessly and unsuccessfully to establish a women's archive in the United States.[74] Although a few archival collections ultimately found homes in large universities or were scantily funded by governments, women's archives had a diasporic relationship to the official archival enterprise of the nineteenth century.[75] In the case of state archives—which encompassed private and governmental papers, as well as artifacts such as coins, seals, and works of art—by the end of the nineteenth century these were not only well-funded and professionally staffed, but centralized and regulated. Papers about women survived in various places—the attics of suffragists, flea markets, dank basements, local libraries, crumbling châteaus, government repositories—with very little concern for their preservation, in contrast to the attention given to highly prized, primary documents about men.

Although the archival quest concerned middle-class feminists, it also enthralled some distinctly working-class types. One of the most striking was Marie-Louise Bouglé (1883–1936), a typist who worked part time as a restaurant cashier in order to get free meals. Economizing in every way, including wearing a single skirt for eight years, Bouglé worked her two jobs, opened a small women's library two nights a week, and devoted the rest of her time to hunting for documents. "How many times I fainted, exhausted by work and fatigue and promising each time to take better care of myself!"[76] In 1933 Bouglé married, and ceased to work on anything but her library and archive. After her early death in 1936, her husband, André Mariani, preserved the collections until they ultimately passed to the City Library of Paris. When I was a graduate student in the 1970s, her rich collections were known of only by rumor, totally uncatalogued, and said to be the legacy of two *men* with the surname Bouglé; they were barely accessible until the appearance of a typescript inventory in the 1990s. On the basis of such maniacal, focused work, subject to equally pointed neglect, and in the context of a degraded amateurism, women's archives took shape.

By the end of the nineteenth century, women's amateurism had created a thickly painted historical surface of everyday life, material culture, working women's lives, and, to a lesser extent, women's activism. It showed an array of social types, a multiplicity of sites for historical study, and an expansive assortment of material from which historical narrative could be constructed. On the one hand, in an age when the scientific and historical "laboratory" provided a focus for disciplinary power, amateurism's wide and unruly range worked to contrary effect: it was a category bursting its bounds and swamped in various impulses and movements. On the other hand, the amateur panorama, so sweeping in its minuscule depictions, provided the basis for changes in professional history. So hyperprofessional a historian as Charles Langlois came to see poetry and fiction as source material, interpreting them as literally as he would have a royal manuscript. Others would swoop down on everyday life, scorning those who confined their efforts to high politics. Amateur studies of convents and women's work would provide the entry point for many women professionals, who by the late nineteenth century were gradually increasing in number.

Amateurism was thus the intellectual avant-garde of a general historical project to reach the past. It marked out the psychic hotpoints where memory work was at its most active, and did this in so transgressive a way, crossing borders and disciplinary divides, as to provide safe passage for those professionals who started to venture a bit further themselves. Amateurism also spewed forth detailed pastiches of symptoms and symbols for psychological, aesthetic, and other treatments of the past that would take shape in psychoanalysis and other disciplines. The dreamwork and modernism of historical science in the early twentieth century were prefigured in the increasingly lush amateur bricolage of goods, objects, and topography. Amateur adventurism continued to spark the professional psyche in an alternation between fantastic escapes to new lands and a disciplined returns to practices and procedures. In the retreat to disciplined mastery lay the gendering of history, for it entailed an assertion of the amateur's inferiority to the male professional.

Amateur history in those days was what people read in trains or on board ship—the forerunner of what was read in even faster kinds of travel, restoring the details to a life that had been stripped of them and traumatized out of them by modernity and gender. No one, it has been said, went to Italy without a copy of Julia Cartwright's histories. Amateur history was simultaneously pillaged from without and disrupted from within, but it maintained its hold because of the special perspective of its broad yet detailed vistas in a time of disorienting social and economic change. "Life is like a panorama, and we the spectators for whose amusement it is played off," commented Amelia Edwards, an avid reader, author, and traveler. "Scenes, events, people seem to pass before us as upon a canvas, while we fancy that we are standing still—and it is not till the music comes suddenly to an end that we find it is we who have been moving all the time, that we have passed through life."[77] Amateurism was producing the modernist sensibility.

Women Professionals

A Third Sex?

7

At about the time professional history became a career possibility for women, psychologists and homosexuals began creating a modern sensitivity to the possibility of there being a "third sex." The term pertained to sexual preference, but its definition also covered cross-gender behavioral characteristics, personality types, and ways of thinking. Crossover characteristics depended in the first place on clear boundaries between the sexes—boundaries that the powerful ideas and institutions of separate spheres had established. One then transgressed those to amass sufficient behavioral detail to establish oneself as a member of the third sex. An ostensibly "female" member of this group might tend toward virility, having a career and shunning motherhood. In the effort to situate professional women historians who began their careers late in the nineteenth century, it has seemed plausible to hypothesize that they might indeed have degendered themselves, as in fact many feared that career women were doing at the time.

This hypothesis, along with the problematic status of women worthies, makes the emplotment of the work and careers of these early professionals difficult. Because they have been ignored by virtually all historiography, including many feminist works, one might say they need to be restored to historiography, their achievements fully charted, their absence carefully explained. Yet they themselves turned out to be highly perplexing. Some, like Margaret Judson, were prim in the extreme, almost asexual, and appeared to deny that they ever received unfair treatment. They lose their appeal because they seemed to lack courage, keeping silent about the bad conditions they suffered, not witnessing. Judson even told young colleagues in the early 1970s not to be so outspoken, so feminist.[1] They were "spinsters," who lived for the most part in women's ghettos in academe. One could celebrate these women's communities, although this would simultaneously mean celebrating their confinement, degradation, and limited opportunity. Then there were the "bad girls," who were perhaps more appealing—flamboyant and somewhat outrageous, piquing the libidos of their male colleagues, and thus living somewhat longer in academic memory. When they did appear in historiography, they were made sparkling, even erotic and amateurish, but in the long run they were often judged to be so whimsically original and so wanting in traditional scholarship as to offer little of lasting value to the profession. They seemed merely to reverse the opposing terms assigned to femininity: nice girl or bad, Mary or Eve, good wife or harlot.

The gender characteristics of women professionals were more blurred than this dichotomy suggests, however, and their identities were less neatly defined. For instance, only a handful of these women did women's duty by having children, nor were any fully integrated into a traditional domestic culture. If we can accept that male historians were part of the reproduction of middle-class masculinity, in what relationship did professional women and their work stand to women's (and men's) gender definition? In searching for answers, one faces dilemmas, such as posing "mature" professional women against "inferior" amateurs and thus perpetuating trauma. Or one might find that the history of women professionals does not work in the ways one hoped it would and may even be distasteful. The professional personae of early women scholars may be so troubling as to block a satisfactory reading. Dominick LaCapra has recently pointed to the possibilities of working with the libidinal, the traumatic, and the repressed and incorporating them into historical accounts—a suggestion that can advance this chapter's analytic project.[2] And LaCapra's notion allows an additional hypothesis: it is no accident that the history of women's professional scholarship been repressed for so long.

Another seemingly intractable problem concerns writing about important women—writing that can always make a "better story" as a substitute for an analysis of the issues. Moreover, writing about important women has been dismissed by some of the major feminist theorists of our day for any number of good reasons. It is "compensatory" or "celebratory," a naive "herstory" instead of the more sophisticated work of gender or social history. People poke occasional fun at "great men" history and historiography, but such accounts nonetheless anchor narratives of the past. The accomplished woman is devalued these days in an ongoing process that advances the arguments against her, including claims that she is a manifestation of trauma.

Early professional historians—invisible, devalued, paradoxical, or bizarre—have thus been conflated with the "low" of scientific history, and have been so almost from the beginning. "The very word ['science'] was a fetish," wrote the historian W. Stull Holt of the climate in the early days of professionalization. As a result, he concluded, "such monstrosities developed as 'library science' and 'domestic science.'"[3] Holt alluded in his list of monstrosities to science's production of professional women historians, lured by visions of competence, citizenship, and jobs in the academy. Scholars like R. H. Tawney and Marc Bloch were hostile to such women.[4] This "monstrous" status draws attention once more to the incredibly anomalous situation of women in professional history at the end of the nineteenth century. How was it possible, given the gendered fantasies, language, and practices shaping the field for women, even to consider professional historical work? Excluded from the military, from citizenship, and even from receiving university degrees in many places, how could they normally enter a profession built for men? Indeed, in some cases antagonism toward women doing history became increasingly explicit, and, despite the language of meritocracy, doors closed as well as opened. Treitschke announced that only over his dead body would a woman cross the threshold of his classroom.

Epistemologically, too, the deck seemed stacked against women's professional accomplishment. The historian, like the scientist, had after years of training rid himself of emotion, intuition, and partiality in order to attain a state of mind devoted totally to truth. Kant and Hegel, the philosophers on whom most historians relied for their orientation (if only in a derivative way), had spent long sections of their work describing such unwanted subjective states as feminine. To Kant's mind, only men could operate morally according to the principle of the categorical imperative, and only they could fully bring innate reason to bear on what was outside the understanding—that is, nature—and thus develop knowledge. Kant placed women's activities in the realm of nurture, emotion, sensibility, and culture. A plateau in this divide came with Hegel, whose dialectic bifurcated the world into a subject and an object sharply opposed to each other: master and slave, male and female, two mutually antagonistic parties. The sovereign male subject struggled for mastery, knowledge, and control of the feminized object. For historians, this objective reality was found in archives, facts, and the data of their craft. Where did the woman professional position herself in so gendered a portrayal of scientific work?

Assuming the Professional Role

The woman professional worked like a man to train herself as a disembodied observer, a disciplined member of the scientific community, a transcendent purveyor of historical truth. Beginning late in the 1860s, when universities in the United States and Great Britain began accepting women for professional training, women students attended seminars, lectures, and tutorials in history and did independent research in archives, libraries, and other repositories of historical material. The first woman to receive a doctorate in history in the United States was Kate Ernest Levi, who earned her degree from the University of Wisconsin in 1893.[5] Although women could study at Oxford and Cambridge after 1869, they did not receive degrees at these two universities until after World Wars I and II, respectively. Women at the University of London received degrees from 1878 on.[6] In the United States, professionally trained historians who found jobs in academe most often found them at women's colleges, while the women's colleges of Cambridge and Oxford also hired them. A notable cluster of them worked in economic history at the London School of Economics, with Lilian Knowles holding the first professorship in economic history there.[7] Finally, despite the fact that publishing was not crucial to professional advancement in the period before World War II, women academics wrote in a variety of fields, including classical, economic, medieval, social and cultural history.

For all the access to training, the opportunity of these women to serve as unmarked scholars—unmarked, that is, by professional conventions—was much less than men's. The examples that follow are not meant to be indications of discrimination; rather, they are markers that show the impossibility of transcendence or disembodied observation. They are signs of the complicated way in which the feminine professional was produced. For one thing, families of limited means, like the parents of Helen Maud Cam, might not send their daughters to school but would instead teach them at home. "As we grew older," Cam reported, "we reached the limits of [my mother's] knowledge of grammar and syntax. She would say: 'I know that's wrong, but I don't know why.'"[8] By the time women entered the university, the disapproval of their intellectual education that had developed after the French and American revolutions had evolved into the well-established "scientific truth" that study undermined their physical and emotional health. The work of Patrick Geddes and J. Arthur Thomson in Britain and of Dr. Edward Clarke at Harvard stated that intellectual work would ruin women's ability to reproduce and nurture. According to Herbert Spencer and other social scientists, women's abstinence from intellectual activity as part of a sexual division of labor was the highest stage of evolution.[9] As fertility rates declined at the end of the nineteenth century and as important Western powers worried about the general "fitness" of their populations, women's intellectual work was seen as especially problematic, dangerous, and even unpatriotic.[10] After World War I, fears that women's intellectual activity was "destructive to health and brain" intensified.[11]

Professional women historians, in contrast to other middle-class women and most amateurs, were not married. Their "spinster" state was increasingly noticed as the twentieth century advanced. Whereas professional male historians used a middle-class, heterosexed rhetoric of work and breadwinning in connection with their scholarship, and whereas they enlisted the efforts of a team of helpmates to research, edit, and write their history, such benefits did not exist to enhance professional women's situation. Marriage and heterosexual partnership were virtually foreclosed to them, despite the normative language of heterosexuality that infused historical work. They knew that taking an academic job or even pursuing an academic degree meant renunciation of family life. The majority taught and wrote without authorial or domestic support, a lack that enhanced their singularity in the academic world. Although a tiny number was married, the marriages of such outstanding women as Eileen Power (late in her forties) and Lilian Knowles were and still are often remarked upon.

Marriage undid the autonomy so central to the construction of the citizen-scientist. More than one professional—the Cambridge classicist Jane Ellen Harrison, for instance—acknowledged refusing proposals because of the inferior position she would immediately assume on marriage.[12] Knowles was unique in having a professional career *and* a child.

In general, what the unmarried professional historian benefited from was the personal companionship of another professional woman—Eleanor Lodge with Janet Spens at Westfield College; Lucy Maynard Salmon with Adelaide Underhill at Vassar; Katharine Coman and Katharine Lee Bates, who lived together in what was called a "Wellesley marriage."[13] The dozens of female couples among historians functioned in the context of new womanhood and the "surplus-women" phenomenon. Growing numbers of women in many Western countries stayed unmarried, and lived together independent of their families as couples or in large boarding houses, clubs, and apartments for women.[14] In all-women communities, such as many of the women's colleges were, homosociability reached new intensity and exclusivity. Some women scholars were able to rely on their partners, mothers, and sisters for research, note-taking, proofreading, and other editorial aid. Eileen Power, who was elected secretary of the Economic History Society in the 1920s, enlisted her aunt, Bertha Clegg, to take minutes at meetings and persuaded the organization to pay Clegg a small stipend. But generally, women's authorship and professional personae were more singular and less well-paid than men's, although women professionals who had dependent relatives were no less financially responsible than their male peers. Power's *Medieval Nunneries* was readied for press by a woman friend, and her widower, Michael Postan, claimed to have initiated or actually written most of her works.[15]

Women's intellectual work was thus not only set in a context of transparency, middle-class expertise, and republican community but also situated—perhaps more powerfully—within a problematic, inferior femininity. Although some men could use, with reference to women professionals, the rhetoric of professional collegiality, university membership, and collaborators in research and scholarship, other men could not envision them in these terms. Undergraduates from one end of Europe to another periodically rioted and aimed violence against women in universities. In Spain, women students were stoned; and at Newnham College at Cambridge

University, male students stormed the gates in protest. Professors employed their own form of "disciplining," a counterdiscursive but effective envisioning of the woman professional. "I have never felt so bitter in my life," Eileen Power wrote in 1921 on hearing that Cambridge dons had voted once more against women's receiving degrees and being members of the university."[16] Foreign women who studied in Germany found themselves treated exceptionally in one way or another. Edith Hamilton, who studied philology in Leipzig and Munich in 1895 and 1896, put it this way: "To be American was, of course, to be uneducated, and, if a woman, incapable of really acquiring education." While German women were prohibited from classrooms entirely, Hamilton had to join those foreign women who, although admitted, were cordoned off on the stage next to the professor. At Cambridge, "some lecturers made great play of seating the women separately and addressing themselves solely to the 'gentlemen.'"[17] From U.S. professors who maintained that "of course women could not do seminar work," to Oxbridge dons who actively worked to keep them from getting degrees, taking classes, and passing exams, scientific history marked out women as different—less worthy, less competent, and dangerous if intellectual. Women scholars were not even part of a second sex; they were a third sex.

Many people tried to keep women from getting jobs, but in general such opponents didn't have to work hard. Men were envisioned as members of the brotherhood, as scholars and colleagues; women, as something other. The result further marked women historians as unsuitable for the academy. Frances Collier, author of *The Family Economy of the Working Classes in the Cotton Industry, 1784–1833*, held an advanced degree from the University of Manchester but could find work there only as a department secretary. Despite a growing list of distinguished scientific publications Eleanora Carus-Wilson (1897–1977) had to work at governmental and private social-work jobs; she was hired to a full-time position at the London School of Economics only in 1946. In the United States, many women who held doctorates in history, such as Helen Sumner Woodbury, went into governmental and other research because, as one put it, "the authorities prefer male to female professors."[18] Jane Ellen Harrison tried to get professorships many times, but always failed. The appointment of one rival, Ernest Gardner, particularly annoyed her because he stood for all that she despised in the academic world: "dullness and conventionality, and hatred of ideas."[19]

Local historical societies, libraries, archives, and scholarly journals also hired women scholars, who were seen as less suitable to a university career than men were. Julia de Lacy Mann at first got a job as secretary to a historian, and later became involved in the editing of the *Economic History Review*, newly founded at Cambridge. The Ecole des Chartes in Paris, which trained professional historians, archivists, and librarians, admitted women in 1906. Within twenty years, two had graduated at the top of their class and gone on to archival careers. "Even while regretting that woman does not keep to the role nature assigned her," director Marcel Prou wrote, "one cannot deny that women are suited for scientific studies." In fact, if women had to pursue a career, he concluded, archival work "was most congenial to the role of mother and homemaker."[20] Archives and other repositories had been gradually feminized during the nineteenth century; and in the twentieth, archivists themselves became known as "history's handmaidens."[21]

During World War I, English dons tried to rid the universities of women faculty altogether, and one proposal involved conscripting all university women into a "domestic service" army. In the academic world, the war could help restabilize gender by making ambiguously female dons "women" again. But these dons had indeed crossed the line of the feminine. There were "quite useful people who could never put a garment together," Ada Elizabeth Levett of Westfield College protested, and who were already making major contributions to the war effort. Furthermore, she asked, what right had educational institutions to set such policies?[22] The profession was constructed as democratic and open to talent; yet men were better, higher, and more intelligent, while women scholars were automatically domestic.

By these lights, one could pay women scholars of equal or better accomplishment than men a far lower salary, because while equal or better they were also inferior and worth less. Before World War I, the much-touted Lilian Knowles was paid far less than her male peers, even as she reached the professorial level.[23] In Canada, in 1929, Sylvia Thrupp could get only an instructorship at the University of British Columbia, though she was beginning to publish widely admired works. Meanwhile, men were taken into the tenure-track ranks, promoted, and given almost double her salary, despite their lack of publications all along the way. Like amateurs, professional women needed to make money: they were autonomous and, like men, needed to support themselves and their families—usually parents and siblings. However, in the libidinal logic that had informed the profession since its inception, they were also situated in the fantasy world that menaced the masculine world of history, and that triggered research but did not undertake it.

The profession remained just as confusingly gendered after World War I as it had been in the prewar years. It accorded more women in Germany and Austria doctorates; and in the United States some women did graduate work at elite schools like Harvard, often sent there by their teachers in the women's colleges.[24] According to Margaret Judson, who attended Harvard in the 1920s, most male professors at Harvard "never seemed to regard their women students as inferior or as not worthy of their best teaching." Until the 1950s, Samuel Eliot Morison walked across Massachusetts Avenue to give a separate lecture for the Radcliffe students in his American history course. The "only hater of scholarly women" that Judson personally encountered at Harvard was Roger Merriman: he would never let women into his classes, and would not teach courses at Radcliffe. But she had to take Renaissance and Reformation as a field, and despite Merriman's reputation she was obliged to consult him. She thus went to his office: "Half opening the door and seeing a woman outside, he kept one foot firmly planted beside the door, and quickly slammed it in my face, only taking time to say, 'I never have anything to do with women.'" Merriman refused to serve as her examiner, and the department found a substitute. Women had to leave Widener Library at six in the evening and could not go into Harvard's law library. Much later, Judson did get permission to use the Harvard law library, but "only if I entered by the *back* door." In 1931–1932, when she was at the library at Lincoln's Inn (a school of common law in London), many scholars from various parts of the empire, particularly India, all of them men, filled the reading room. Only she had to sit at a table with a librarian on each side. "Why? I can only guess that the male librarians in that masculine sanctuary wondered why a woman should be interested in manuscripts."[25]

When Judson served on search committees and other professional bodies, she had to eat alone while men dined at the Harvard Club or some other all-male institution. She thus missed information and received a more limited view of the issues being considered. By the late 1920s, however, she could count herself lucky even to have a job. Although women were earning degrees or keeping men supplied with students by doing advanced coursework in many universities, their prospects for university employment were grim. A doctorate, "when saddled with the wrong sex," as Canadian historian Hilda Neatby put it, helped not at all in the 1930s. George Wrong of the University of Toronto, who backed women's equality in the profession, tried to maneuver around the fact that everyone "preferred to appoint a man" by sending his best women students to the United States or England.[26]

By the 1920s, these scholars formed not only visible, individual targets within the profession—colleagues that men worked to keep out of meetings or made decisions against—but also a visible cohort of accomplished women professionals. Their own performance was thus both invisible (like that of the normally competent scholar) and highly marked. The president of Vassar could feel permitted to reprimand the nationally known Lucy Maynard Salmon for wearing a type of culotte when she rode her bicycle to class. Jane Ellen Harrison is still described by the color of her clothing: she loved greens and blues. Wives, it is reported, found her necklines too low and her behavior too flirtatious. Men were expected to smoke, but she was not supposed to (although she did). For those reasons, and perhaps because she loved to tango, many acquaintances would not invite her to social events. Even to her best friends, Harrison appeared bold and experimental in her behavior. "If you ever let me come again," she wrote her friends Mary and Gilbert Murray in 1903, "I promise and vow not to—eat a cocaine lozenge." In the 1920s and 1930s, it was noted that Eileen Power spent many of her evenings dancing in London clubs and "making eyes at the men." Eulogies to Knowles and Power worked to feminize and sexualize them. Knowles was known for her "startling hats, unshrinking self-confidence, and a mother whose garden contained most excellent strawberries."[27] Many a story was spread about Power's femininity, but usually to corroborate her personal qualities as "radiant" and "an enchanting creature." She was memorialized in comments and vignettes (concocted by men) that referred to her "long earrings of exactly the right shape and color" and gave other descriptions of her dress.[28] The "matronly" Helen

Maud Cam, in contrast, worked in the Bodleian Library at Oxford "looking like a broody hen in a nesting box, placid and comfortable, but ready to peck if the occasion demanded. Some of her best articles must have been hatched there."[29] In order to become a professional writer, Virginia Woolf commented, "I had to kill the angel of the house." Many professional women historians seem or were seen to have done likewise.

At the same time, other women professionals appeared as distinctly asexual, prim models of sobriety and diligence. Men often adduced this primness as the reason these women should not be allowed to attend professional functions, such as smokers and dinners: men would just not be comfortable if they could not smoke, drink, or talk frankly.[30] In making these decisions, men were similarly acting out gender and its hierarchies, adding a new aspect to their persona: whether they would socialize with women, teach them history, or help them acquire advanced degrees. Frederic Maitland was known for his support of Mary Bateson. "We may find another editor [of the *Cambridge Medieval History*]," he wrote on her death at the age of forty-one, "but not another Miss Bateson. I can hardly believe that she has gone."[31] Gustav Schmoller would accept women students, whereas Treitschke would not; Langlois was known for teaching women students, but would assign them only "women's topics" to research. Even young male newcomers to a department would feel confident enough to attack female students and senior scholars in order to undermine their connections to professional history. The story of a male assistant professor's attempt to unseat Lucy Maynard Salmon as chair of the Vassar history department is legendary there. It took Salmon's full mobilization of alumnae, trustees, faculty, and students to keep the effort from succeeding.[32] Madeleine Wallin, a member of the history faculty at Smith College until her marriage in the 1890s, wrote acerbically about a new colleague, Charles Hazen, who thought the uncle of an undergraduate was a "brute" for wanting "a pretty girl like her" to take a course in the history of politics. She quickly sensed Hazen's dislike for women of "trained intellect" and soon left the profession.[33] The sum of this information was important for women to have. It constituted the gendering of the professional road map, laying out dangers they had to memorize, learn to navigate, and prepare for. Yet because the rhetoric of scientific history was at once egalitarian and hierarchical, there was often no telling what might happen.

Excluded from male homosociability and networks in the profession, and often from heterosociability if they worked in mixed environments, cohorts of women professionals in their respective countries increasingly identified themselves as men identified them—that is, as different and distinct. They formed groups, such as the Berkshire Conference of Women Historians, that stamped a further special identity on professional women historians. Yet others gained an identity from breaking rules: Caroline Ware, for example, admitted to attending all-male smokers and being treated with the utmost respect. From whatever vantage point, they lived a crossover life. Often they associated with a wide range of amateurs and valued their work. Even as she admired Frederic Maitland, Helen Maud Cam wrote many an appreciation of historical novelists, and an entire book on the genre. Jane Ellen Harrison associated with lusty amateurs like Alice Stopford Green but hated more professional women educators like Miss Beale; and Eileen Power was a great friend to the Hammonds. Ambiguity entered the interpretation of these women's sexual identity. Eileen Power was thought by some to be a lesbian, and was sometimes approached as one. Jane Ellen Harrison was flirtatious with women as well as men, and was especially conscious of women's beauty. A promoter of Isadora Duncan, she read Greek poetry aloud as Duncan danced.[34]

In the end, it becomes unclear how to align these women straightforwardly with conventional categories. Consider Anna J. Cooper, the first African-American woman to obtain a doctorate in history (1925). "The whips and stings of prejudice," she wrote, "whether of color or sex, find me neither too calloused to suffer, nor too ignorant to know what is due me."[35] Born a slave in 1858, Cooper struggled to receive a classical education and vigorously protested the obstacles that the African-American community placed in the way of women's education. "A boy, however meager his equipment and shallow his pretensions, had only to declare a floating intention to study theology, and he could get all the support, encouragement, and stimulus he needed, be absolved from work and invested beforehand with all the dignity of his far away office. While a self-supporting girl had to struggle on by teaching in the summer and working after school hours to keep up with her board bills, and actually fight her way against positive discouragements to the higher education."[36]

With B.A. and M.A. degrees from Oberlin College, Cooper taught Latin at Dunbar High School in Washington, D.C., until her retirement in 1930. Her goal, however, was a doctorate, initially denied her because of political struggles in her school and because of Columbia University's residence requirements. Outside the academic network, her contacts were black-community leaders and other activists. Only in her sixties did Cooper receive her doctorate from the Sorbonne, with a thesis entitled "The Attitude of France toward Slavery during the Revolution." She had already published a volume of essays, *A Voice from the South,* and books on the life and work of Charlotte Forten Grimké. Credentialed as a professional after many decades of determined struggle and work outside the university, Cooper, like many other professional women, amalgamated various types of writing, intellectual experiences, and arduous breadwinning activity, making her hard to categorize. The professional woman was an imprecise entity, a paradox, a blur.

Professional Work

The paradigms of professional historical work consisted of a focus on politics in scholarship, a methodology stressing a disembodied, well-trained observer, and a set of practices based on scrutinizing state documents and displaying the resulting historical writing for the adjudication of a community of experts. These universally accepted practices were expressed in terms of gender dimorphism: a valued and important male sphere of activity that generated history existed alongside a historically negligible female and familial sphere. Moreover, practitioners were described in terms of a middle-class community of male experts whose special understanding of and training in historical science were inaccessible to the less able—meaning women in the West, and non-Western people as a whole. But this science was simultaneously seen as universal, as available to all, as unmarked and ungendered. Scholarship was thus the conduit away from a degraded femininity toward the higher universal. "I *am* glad to know," one of these women pioneers wrote to me, "that your focus is on women's *scholarship* rather than on women writing about women's history."[37]

From their entry into the academy, professional women followed the road to the same universally true scholarship that men valued. Americans made the obligatory trips to Germany and France to learn the techniques of philology, seminar criticism, and archival research. British women made the same pilgrimages—Eleanor Lodge and Eileen Power, for instance—studying at the Ecole des Chartes in Paris. Once established in universities and women's colleges, these historians devoted as much time as possible to archival research. For Lucy Maynard Salmon, this entailed going to the Continent regularly; Margaret Judson made several sabbatical and summer trips to England; Violet Barbour spent every summer in archives in the Netherlands.[38] Mary Bateson, Caroline Skeel, Eleanor Lodge, Ada Elizabeth Levett, Maude Violet Clarke, Eileen Power, and Helen Cam were others who made extensive use of records in monasteries and local archives.[39] Advances in women's professional training also interested them, and they produced articles on women's scholarly opportunities in universities across Europe and the United States.[40] More in keeping with professional goals, they published philologically expert, densely referenced editions of institutional records and manuscripts, produced in an expository style congenial to experts. Bateson, a fellow of Newnham College, received the ultimate eulogy when Maitland praised her for never having stooped to write anything for the general reader.[41]

These professionals imagined their work in socially responsible, civic terms, and one important locus of community was the women's college. During the late nineteenth century, men's colleges were rapidly evolving away from the idea of a semimonastic population of scholars and students, but many women's colleges still worked on this kind of model. Women scholars often lived in the college's confines, taking on a fully academic persona. Whereas the vast majority of their male peers had wives and families and lived in individual houses, women historians had no immediate, heterosexual family life and had a tighter connection to the institutions of collegiate life. Occasionally a woman would rebel, but the rebellion amounted to a variation in the assertion of the autonomous, civic self. Lucy Maynard Salmon rejected living in Vassar College housing in favor of taking a trolley from Poughkeepsie to the campus. "I am a member of a community," she maintained, claiming disdain for the isolation of the typical intellectual and for domestic life as mimed by college dormitories.[42]

The strenuous effort by feminists and other activists to gain access to higher education provided a partial context for women's scholarship. An imperfect public and private world would be made better by the training of women's minds, many believed. Westfield College at the University of London had been started partly with the aim of providing improved training for missionaries, while women's colleges at Cambridge University were to be a wedge in the modernization of curricula in the men's colleges.[43] The language of citizenship, mass politics, and social responsibility that accompanied the admittance of women to higher education led many of them to articulate their work in terms of reform. In addition to her scholarship, Jane Ellen Harrison wrote on suffrage. Ada Elizabeth Levett gave lectures and wrote popular pieces on university women and World War I, on prostitution, on university women and religion, and on women in the postwar world. Caroline Skeel left lecture notes on women in the English Civil War and on women preachers. The committed Labourite Helen Maud Cam lectured on the woman suffrage movement in England, on Susan Warner's *The Wide Wide World,* and on social conditions in the United States. In the United States, where the reform movements strongly affected colleges like Wellesley, faculty and students were among the most committed reformers, working on behalf of settlement houses, suffrage, and pacifism and producing amateur-style writings about many of these causes.[44] Cultural historian Caroline Ware remembered learning at Vassar that historical knowledge was the "prelude to responsible social action." Lucy Maynard Salmon would reprimand students for dropping the slightest bit of trash: littering was a dereliction of civic responsibility.[45]

Women's professionalism was thus generated within an extraordinarily wide compass that included the vocabulary, scholarly trajectory, sense of time, and many other impulses of both male professionals and women amateurs. Some wrote the most traditional of scientific political narratives, often favoring legal and constitutional history of the medieval and early modern periods.[46] Others ventured far afield at an early date, showing their virtuosity by professionalizing the amateur impulse in a move toward economic and social history. These fields, more than any others, were used to show women's professional expertise. Lucy Maynard Salmon, for example, had begun with an award-winning book on the appointing powers of the presidency; her second major work was a statistical and qualitative study of domestic service. Nellie Neilson, the first woman president of the

American Historical Association and professor of history at Mount Ho-
lyoke College, published her *Economic Conditions on the Manors of Ramsey
Abbey* in 1899. Scholars of the next generation continued to show interest
in medieval economic history. While Bertha Putnam showed that records
of justices of the peace were rich sources of information on everyday
economic life in the Middle Ages, and Ada Elizabeth Levett continued
work on the economic contours of rural life in the Middle Ages, Eileen
Power moved into areas like wool production and trade.[47]

Power's predecessor at the London School of Economics, Lilian
Knowles, trained both amateurs and professionals in economic history,
while her own work centered on the economic history of early modern,
modern, and imperial Britain. At Wellesley College, Katharine Coman
wrote *The Industrial History of the United States* (1905), a richly illustrated
statistical work, and *Economic Beginnings of the Far West* (1912). A variety
of impulses promoted such histories. "Instead of the enthralling clash of
hero and villain," wrote Mabel C. Buer in an economic and demographic
history of the Industrial Revolution that she dedicated to Knowles, "we
have presented the drab blunderings of ordinary men and women. But the
gray is only gray at a distant and imperfect view," she continued, reflecting
the amateur's panoramic and perspectival vision. "More closely seen, it is
a queer, jumbled pattern of sharply contrasted colours."[48]

Accompanying the economic pattern of this work was its local orientation. Caroline Skeel of Westfield College wrote a book on the cattle trade,
as well as a two-volume study of local government in the Marches of Wales
in the sixteenth and seventeenth centuries. Eleanor Lodge, who also liked
economic history and who trained several important women economic
historians, wrote studies of Gascony, edited the account book of a Kentish
estate, and composed a study of the French communal movement for the
Cambridge Medieval History. Helen Cam wrote about great men in the legal
world and great scholars of legal history, often including rich economic
data. Many women historians came from families of the country clergy;
since they lacked funds, research, for them, was about "finding things
under your feet."[49] Thus, although archival research was crucial, professionals employed amateur methods. To give one example, Caroline Skeel's
manuscript notes for her books and articles reveal that she used not only
traditional economic data, but also travelers' accounts, interviews with

aged residents of various localities, and letters from local informants about customs, terms, and practices.[50]

Professionals abjured scholarship on the woman worthy in favor of economic and social data about women that the amateurs were also working hard to develop. After Power returned from France to England, for example, she dropped the thesis on Queen Isabella that Langlois had assigned her. Since the beginning, however, avoiding the woman worthy had served as a hallmark of the most distinguished, professional scholarship. Affirming scientific history's values as situated in gender hierarchy, outright denigration of the woman worthy as an important topic has periodically fueled women's professionalism and effectively served their quest for institutional power. This rerouting took two paths. On one, these newly scientific women committed themselves to the profession by writing biographies of men. In Britain, Beatrice Lees of Oxford University's Lady Margaret Hall wrote about Alfred the Great and about biographical writing in general; Kate Norgate, who straddled the amateur and professional worlds by writing for the *Dictionary of National Biography* and assisting Oxford dons in their research, editing, and writing, produced her own studies of John Lackland, Henry III, and Richard the Lion Heart; Cecilia Ady (daughter of the amateur historian Julia Cartwright) wrote on Lorenzo de' Medici and Pius II and received a *Festschrift* in her honor. Mary Williams, a professor at Goucher College in Maryland and an adamant promoter of women's rights in the profession, published surveys of Latin American politics and diplomacy, as well as a biography: *Dom Pedro the Magnanimous, Second Emperor of Brazil* (1937). These subjects of study—powerful, at times vulnerable men—continued the historical project of showing male mastery, self-sufficiency, and accomplishment in the face of great odds. Because the studies were compelling narratives of male identity, they underscored the female professional's ambiguous position.

Despite ignoring the chance to professionalize scholarship on the worthy woman, many but by no means all of the first few generations of professionals used the opportunities in social and economic history to continue in one way or another exploring women's collective past. For most, the inspiration was part of an acknowledged feminist commitment. According to T. F. Tout, ardent suffragist Mary Bateson had a "tendency to dissipate her energy in public agitation on the platform or in the press."[51] Convinced by her first mentor, Mandell Creighton, that her scholarship was more important than her feminism, she became an avid researcher, specializing in editions of texts and local records. She also wrote a pioneering study of double monasteries, some of which were controlled not by the men but by the women, who heard men's confessions and had the power to excommunicate.[52] She pointed out misogyny in the church: Saint Columban, according to her account, was a "woman hater." Despite "scanty, scrappy, and disjointed" evidence, Bateson maintained that double monasteries could be found throughout a large part of Europe and that individual houses had long lives, the tenor of her article suggesting the potential of the newly integrated British university.

In the next generation of Cambridge women, Eileen Power's *Medieval English Nunneries, circa 1275 to 1535* (1922) was a model of professional scholarship, resting on archiepiscopal and episcopal registers, account rolls of individual houses, petitions, inventories, cartularies, and physical plans of the houses. Power stopped Eckenstein's line of speculation about mother-right among the pre-Christians, pagan rituals and their relationship to Mariolatry, and issues of feminine spirituality. Instead, she focused on the wealth of detail that was in such archival sources as monastic account books, bishops' registers, and wills. The result was a dense account of the social origins of nuns, the institutional structure of the nunneries, the everyday activities of their inhabitants, wealth and money-making activities, and disciplinary and economic problems. Some of the detail looked positively amateurish in its superficiality: several pages describing the dogs, monkeys, squirrels, rabbits, and other animals the nuns kept as pets; rich depictions of food eaten at every meal in different nunneries; schedules of meals, gardening sessions, prayers, reading, and a wealth of other activities; running accounts of trivial squabbles among prioresses and the nuns concerning clothing, furniture, food, tasks, visitors, and general conduct. *Medieval English Nunneries* constituted an unromantic, well-documented revisionist study. Most nuns, it showed, were aristocratic; they fought over who would be prioress, or simply agreed that the richest among them would become head; nunneries were in large part a "dumping ground" for the surplus, unwanted, deformed, mentally impaired, illegitimate daughters of the upper classes; in England, except during the Anglo-Saxon period, they were neither educational nor intellectual centers, and they never produced a Hildegarde of Bingen or an Elisabeth of Schoenau; many English nuns during those centuries were as bawdy, worldly, tavern-haunting, and sexually active as their male counterparts in monasteries.[53] The feminist Power found the aristocratic nun as "real" as the working-class woman, and then some.

Power's strategy yielded a kind of carnivalesque scholarship. There were so many types of fish and other fine food, so many silver belts, ribbons, silks, furs, and gold jewelry, so many instances of whining, intrigue, and drunken carousing that church authorities had constantly to intervene in nunnery life. Revisionism was rampant in Power's work. She showed that nuns and monks alike—aristocratic, and usually scrupulous about their noble prerogatives and luxuries—exercised their right to a variety of carnal pleasures. This practice went against the higher commitment to the spiritual life and vows of chastity. Such women as left husband and children to take the veil must have been moved by a very strong vocation for religion, or else by excessive weariness. She made the option vivid: some women may have found married life odious, "a licking of honey off thorns" (40). Nuns were not universally high-minded: the typical abbess was neither devout nor committed to building a great institution to the glory of God; she was ordinary, and like others she sought "escape sometimes from that common life, which is so trying to the temper" (94). Power portrayed nuns sleeping through services, failing to attend altogether, or bringing their hounds, monkeys, and birds with them to make the time pass more agreeably. More generally, they devised formulas for abbreviating the offices. "They left out syllables at the beginning and end of words; they omitted the *dipsalma* or *pausacio* between two verses . . .; they skipped sentences; they mumbled and slurred over [them]" (292). Indeed, the most serious result was a kind of medieval anomie that plagued congregations: "*accidia,* that dread disease, half ennui and half melancholia" (293, 294–297). "For the strain was a double one; to monotony was added the complete lack of privacy, the wear and tear of communal life; not only always doing the same thing at the same time, but always doing it in company with a number of other people" (297).

Power wrenched a normative feminine piety from the history of women, making their religious vocation "pre-eminently a respectable career" (29) and explaining their sexual activity in convents as "comprehensible." In

Power's writing, a complex prototype of the woman professional as a third sex came into being: "The initial difficulty of the celibate ideal need not be laboured," she commented, referring to nuns' turn from chastity to profligacy (436). Jane Ellen Harrison also attacked theology (and covertly women's characteristic religiosity) in much of her work: "God and reason are contradictory terms," she maintained. These two historians, as well as many of their colleagues, portrayed a femininity that was at odds with the devout femininity of the middle-class ideal: "All theology is but a thinly veiled rationalism, a net of illusive clarity cast over life and its realities." Yet the profession's commitment to hyperrationalism fell short, too: "intellect" should be "the servant, not the lord, of life."[54] History, properly practiced, undermined gender.

An interlacing of sexuality, the rational, and the irrational characterized the work of women professionals. "Have you read William James's 'Gifford lectures?'" Harrison asked her friends Mary and Gilbert Murray. "The mysticism and drunkenness parts delight me, and the 'revelation under anaesthetics' experiences are my very own."[55] Harrison's sense of the intellect's workings could follow the paradigm of vision, only it depended on newer technology than medical procedures. The great work, she maintained, "casts, as it were, a great searchlight into dark places . . . Things unseen before or insignificant shine out in luminous projection . . . New tracks open out before us."[56] Harrison saw the drunken, subconscious, Dionysian workings of even the professional self. Drawing conclusions in scholarly work had a wide physical range: "a sudden sense of warmth, an uprush of emotion, often a hot blush, and sometimes tears in the eyes." Intellectual work was "a process so sensuous and emotional."[57]

The blurring of categories became quite pronounced in Harrison's writing, as well as in the presentation of her professional self; but its import seems to have escaped most people, except perhaps Virginia Woolf. Woolf's character Orlando, who was both or many sexes, was said to include a good deal of Harrison. Further blurring occurred in Harrison's book *Themis,* which undermined the idea of the agon as involving real heroes in the ancient world struggling for individuality. Instead, Harrison proposed, the agon was an aspect of the earliest fertility rituals, which regularly began with a contest enacting a mythical struggle. Only later did interpreters come to see, in the repetition of agonistic rituals in early plays, the struggles of actual individuals. The hero was not, she maintained, "a real actual man, [but] only an ancestor invented to express the unity of a group."[58] Given that the entire movement of realistic history followed the agonistic pattern, one could have extrapolated that historians had patterned their realism on fertility rites—that, far from surrendering myth for truth, history merely perpetuated a derivative myth. Although Harrison's writings had enormous influence among some male classicists, other scientific historians read Harrison's iconoclastic, erudite work as feeble, inferior, unprofessional: "The book on the whole will appeal rather to the easy-going amateur than to the trained expert."[59] Women scholars were seen as undermining professionalism, as they tried to rework gender.

Harrison's study of fertility rites and matriarchal myth as the originary point for later Olympian religion similarly confused standard interpretations and practices. Her commitment to Darwinism, so popular among many scientific historians at the time, might be said to mitigate her finding's transgressive potential: the movement from fertility rite to principled creed could be seen as consistent with a progressive, upward movement from matriarchy to patriarchy. Although Harrison more than hinted at the aptness of such an interpretation, she simultaneously found Olympianism, like succeeding theologies in general, more oppressive than chthonic rituals. Theology encoded into law what was merely group belief, creating dogma out of primitive practices that expressed joy, fear, and other emotions. In the opening pages of *Themis,* adhering to recent theories in psychology, Harrison insisted that both the conscious and the unconscious were fundamental, and although she associated the conscious with masculinity and theology, she had already connected the emotional and unconscious firmly to the intellect. Finally, Harrison opened the way to bringing "truth" back down to earth, demystifying it and associating it with power and group practice. Most people, she maintained, say, "I think, therefore I act; modern scientific psychology says, I act (or *re*act to outside stimulus), and so I come to think."[60] The turn to materialism and psychology would slowly come to guide more members of the history profession. To some extent paralleling the profession's impulses, Harrison claimed to find an "origin" or foundation for religion in the body's creation of rituals from its own sensations. But when elites suppressed this bodily activism in favor of religious and philosophical dogma, history took a wrong turn that had multiple repercussions, foremost among them the suppression of women.

Scientific history was advancing and changing at the hands of these professionals. Armed with formidable training, Lucy Maynard Salmon moved away from her initial focus on political history—apparent, for example, in her prize-winning *History of the Appointing Power of the President* (1886)—toward the wide investigatory field she would mine thereafter. Her study of domestic service, a mixture of history, economics, and sociology, used surveys administered and answered by Vassar students and alumnae.[61] These questionnaires asked for economic data about pay and hours, as well as for information about the likes and dislikes of domestic servants. Salmon prefaced her analysis of the data with an extensive history of domestic employment. But her picture of such employment was far from conclusive. Some domestic workers hated their job: "I would give up housework if I could find another position that would enable me to advance"; "I did not realize what I was doing until too late." Others loved it: "There is no healthier work for women," or "I have more comforts than in other work." Thus, unlike reformers, Salmon found that wages were not the only factor in attracting people to domestic employment or driving them from it. "That which decides the question is not always the economic advantage, not always the personal treatment, but the subtile thing the woman calls *life*. 'Wages, hours, health, and morals' may all weigh in the scale in favor of domestic service, but *life* outweighs them all." Although Salmon marshaled a great deal of meticulous detail and used it as skillfully as any amateur or professional, her work received harsh criticism for its low subject matter; the enterprise was "unworthy of her," a reviewer for *The Nation* declared.[62] Domestic workers were an appropriate subject for amateurs, but not yet for prize-winning professionals.

Salmon was part of a cohort of scholars who expressed frustration with the limiting of sources to government documents and who began following the amateur road of social, cultural, and statistical description. The range of sources was being widened by the new fields of anthropology and archeology. As a classicist, Jane Ellen Harrison had at her disposal an expanding array of pottery, art, inscriptions, literary texts, and archeological evidence. Before entering the university, she had used this range of material in composing lectures for popular audiences in London. At Cambridge, where she was the first woman allowed to lecture in university buildings, she used it to develop an interpretation of the origin of religious ritual: religion began as practice and as part of everyday exigencies, she claimed, not as a high-falutin' theological theory that only subsequently acquired a ritual shape. Thanks to the prestige of classical studies, her eccentric work was published. Lucy Maynard Salmon, however, not only constructed new theories but taught the uses of a virtually unlimited, even low kind of source material. Railroad schedules, laundry lists, trash piles, kitchen appliances, the position of trees, and the condition of buildings in urban spaces conveyed critical historical information.[63] Salmon tried to add prestige by citing the civic content of these data: "Sanitation is recorded in our garbage can, municipal improvement in our disused cistern . . . Economic theory lifts up its head in the single tax on land."[64]

Salmon taught her new methods to eager undergraduates, and so thoroughly converted the Vassar history department to seminar teaching that until recently the lecture method was hardly used there. To do history, she lectured at the opening of the school year, "the first essential quality it seems to me is *enthusiasm*"—not "gush" or "sentiment," but "that which the old Greeks meant by *enthusiasm,* the very god within us."[65] Though she also advocated patience and industry, few important people supported the pedagogy and practice of her maturity. Her program greatly dismayed the Vassar administration. When the college first hired Salmon in 1887, it had no history department or history curriculum. Trained in modern methods, she moved quickly to institutionalize them in bibliographic work, library research, criticism of sources, and the exploration of heterogeneous historical artifacts and documents. Her enterprise included a constant concern with raising money for library acquisitions. Having overheard students discuss the preparation of a lengthy bibliography for Salmon's course, Vassar's president, James Monroe Taylor, wrote her a letter of complaint. The young women had not been at all "critical" of the assignment; but he personally wondered, "What possible value can there be to the average student in such extended bibliography of books they have not and do not read?"[66] Taylor went on leave the following year, apparently directing that in his absence the history department be divided into U.S. and European history sections, and that a young male professor be put at the head of the more prestigious European section. The reason, reported "unofficially," was that the administration wanted the young man to have more responsibility and felt that the "fact side of history" needed more emphasis.[67]

The implementation of Salmon's version of scientific history was thus incredibly fraught. Even in the sanctuary of Vassar, there was opposition, struggle, and trauma over so gendered a questioning of expertise. Salmon softened or displaced the import of what she was doing by fictionalizing her moves, and never more so than in the essay "History in a Backyard," which explained her expansion of historical material in amateurish terms. The author presents herself sitting on her porch, frustrated because she cannot get to European archives that summer. In this bounded, cozy, and properly domestic setting, she discovers that everything she can see in her backyard provides a wealth of sources—just as valuable as archival ones—for writing history. There are the fences, the garage, the laundry line and pulley, electric wires. Though her purview is more restricted than that of the amateur historian *cum* voyager, her eyes travel domestic space as she herself would travel such spaces—virtually outdoor museums. Salmon was a pioneer in converting such methods into science.[68]

"We do not feel your 'History in a Backyard' has enough specific gravity for the *Yale Review*," an assistant editor wrote Salmon, throwing science back in her face.[69] The larger world of scientific scholarship was just as hostile to her work, rejecting her articles on sinks and bedding, and relegating many of them to Vassar College publications. Salmon knew from the beginning that she was anomalous: "Gaining admission to the salon . . . does not prevent the work of an amateur from being 'skyed,' and *Domestic Service* was hung above the line."[70] *The Chatauquan*, the *Boston Cooking School Magazine*, and *The Craftsman* carried her most innovative work, thus lumping her with the amateurs. Only after her death did a group of alumnae pay to have the most offensive essays gathered in two volumes, *Historical Material* and *Why History Is Rewritten*, and published by Oxford University Press. Salmon was defensive, apologetic for the reactions the academy had to her. She appended an "Apologia" to *Progress in the Household* (1906), a collection of essays on such topics as domestic employment, domestic science, and the ethics and economics of domestic work. She presented herself as a "poacher" on economics and a "wanderer" from history, but also as someone who, along with her college-educated students, was making a contribution that would "serve to atone for both voluntary and involuntary neglect of matrimony."[71] While she spun her domestic historical fantasies still further, she went more than a quarter-century without producing a monograph. Her two books *The Newspaper and the Historian* and *The Newspaper and Authority* (1923) begin, respectively: "*Peccavi* should be the opening word of many prefaces" and "*Mea apologia* may well be the opening words of the preface of a second work dealing with the press."[72] In her old age, Salmon was playing the part of good girl while she worked to reshape the role.

Other historians employed amateurish irony, constantly undermining established truths. After describing a several-year ruckus ensuing from the election of an abbess at medieval Elstow, Eileen Power commented: "Here was a pretty state of affairs in the home of buxomness and peace."[73] Jane Ellen Harrison challenged the idea that, after she undermined former interpretations of Greek religion, the subsequent Greek heroes would provide "facts at last, simple, historical facts." Outlining the story of Cecrops, the oldest of these heroes and the first king of Athens, she proceeded to detail the record of his accomplishments, but at the end found problems with the "factuality" of Cecrops in his representation: "In this unblemished career there is one blot, one skeleton in the well-furnished cupboard . . . Cecrops the hero-king, the author of all these social reforms, Cecrops the humane, the benevolent, has a serpent's tail."[74]

The professional scholarship of women and their presence in the academy provided them with greater exposure to men's fantasies—sometimes curdling those fantasies, as well. If the foundational images of the profession had included sequestered virgins and beautiful princesses, someone like Salmon showed a different picture of womanhood: at kitchen sinks, in domestic employment, and working to professionalize the history of the household. In contrast, Eileen Power fed those fantasies, not only with her "enchanting" self but with her stories of coquettish, promiscuous nuns. Scientific men waxed rhapsodic: "Eileen Power—would that I could hope ever again to come under her friendly lash," wrote G. G. Coulton in his autobiography.[75] Jane Ellen Harrison invoked primitive fertility rituals and their mythical female guardian: the pre-phallic mother, Themis. Studying the sexual, the passionate, the prerational and emotional, she made them an explicit part of historical work and gathered many proposals of marriage from academic men. Neither these women nor their work undid the hierarchies of gender operating in the profession; rather, they changed the mix, ratcheted up the intensity, and increased the number of sexual and prerational topics, tropes, and illusions. The profession came to seem imperiled by confusion and cacophony.

The work of Mikhail Bakhtin has provided a series of critics the theoretical wherewithal to discuss the ability of the low (in this case, the sexual, cultural, emotional, and domestic) to mock the high (the intellectual, spiritual, and political). To some extent, outbursts of the low are said to contest the power of authorities. All societies, the argument goes, are ordered and governed around a sense of the higher and the lower. In the modern West, these hierarchies elevate the spirit, men, the state, and "European" ethnicities, which govern what are said to be the lower realms—namely, the body, women, the household, and non-"European" groups. According to recent scholars of the carnival and other popular demonstrations, those out of power—by deliberately flaunting the body and other aspects of the lower—can disrupt and question hierarchy, to the point of providing the inspiration for overthrowing certain standards of order or even political power itself. Naysayers, however, point out that the entire order of the lower is implicated in the higher, that the very idea of the carnivalesque is an integral part of social order, functioning as its authorized safety valve.[76]

The women professionals whose works have served as examples in this chapter took many of the ingredients of the carnivalesque—which were also the ingredients of middle-class male professional fantasies—and subjected them to scientific scrutiny. Harrison explored the fantastic mother's relationship to depictions of male heroism, finding the latter a fictional displacement of the former and dripping with the psychologically primitive. Her analyses of snakes and other symbols were graphic and sexually suggestive, thus making fantastic sexuality an explicit focus of scholarship. Likewise, Salmon began by converting another object of fantasy—the servant—into an object of science. If those in power in the West have often appropriated the socially marginal—women, servants, darker races—to perform as their cultural and sexual symbols, Salmon was involved in the process of blocking their availability. Bateson's and Power's studies of abbesses and wealthy nuns did the same work, bringing religious women from the world of the fantastic into the scientific. Finally, Salmon studied "lower" details (beds, sinks, fences, and other common objects) in a way that challenged the much-vaunted status of government documents as a higher historical source.

Some professionals reveled in the disciplinary power this expansion of historical work suggested. In her Ewart Lecture of 1916, Ada Elizabeth Levett argued for "a stricter method, more rigidly exact in its collection of evidence." She cited her female contemporaries at Oxford as examples of this new excellence and, invoking an old Saxon source, urged that no detail be neglected, "not even a mouse-trap, nor even, what is less, a peg for a harp."[77] Others, like Salmon, looked forward to the historicization of everyday life and its potential for a more useful civicmindedness: "In every study except history the teacher seeks to make the important and normal clear at any cost." The result was that history, as it was usually taught, failed to "meet our daily needs."[78] A wider variety of sources was the building block of autonomy. No longer would researchers or well-trained citizens be coerced into relying on "Mommsen the authority"; rather, they could go to a "source" for original information, around which they, like the citizen, could develop their critical skills.[79]

These were prodigious women—prodigiously prim, hardworking, experimental, committed, and confident in facing the adventure of women's scholarship. At the same time, they further muddied the epistemological waters, bringing to historical science the concerns and even some of the wide-ranging methodological practices of amateurs. Their presence disturbed the finely equilibrated rhetoric of objectivity and gender that had propelled professionalization from the mid-nineteenth century on. They did not upset history's gendering, but added new elements, notably actual women practitioners and women's topics. Professional women were often likened to amateurs: they were remunerated like women and they introduced amateur topics. Consequently, the profession's gendered language could be mustered, or its objective language used in hyperbolic form. Opportunities for exaggeration, reversals, confusion, blurring, contradiction, disorientation, and disorder became more frequent in historical writing, practices, and institutions. As this new and odd group of professionals pieced together a work culture, not surprisingly a sense of menace activated some of the most distinguished historians of the early twentieth century. The presence of this third group—professional women historians whose "womanhood" could never be overlooked, despite history's claims to universalism—marked the eruption of historical "modernity," propelling the profession to its recent and no less gendered incarnations.

Modernism, Relativism, and Everyday Life   8

On the eve of World War I, the profession looked different. Not only had women entered its ranks but new generations of scientifically trained men were disputing and even overturning some of the founding paradigms of historical science. Among historians, an overlay of new concerns complicated the republican imagery, the quest for detail and facts, the transcendent truth, and the language of love that had inspired the first generations of scientific practitioners. The agon of individual historians that we call "historiography" assumed its modern shape as Ranke and his cohort came under intense fire from new generations of scholars for using limited sources and addressing a small range of subjects. Even political history lost a bit of its luster. While some pushed the quest for detail to extremes (the scholar Philippe Tamizey de Larroque used at least 500 footnotes per article), others during the fin-de-siècle questioned the traditional commitment to research and scientific standards. From 1890 until World War II, the profession seemed to pull in multiple directions, moved less by consensus than by controversy, as belief in a historical "grand narrative" weakened.[1]

Historiographers have characterized this questioning and extreme revisionism—which affected history, in addition to other fields of intellectual and artistic endeavor—as a "modernist impulse," if not full-fledged "modernism." In the social sciences, "modernism" is said to include an understanding that subjectivity and the perceptual situation of the scientist play an important role in analyses. Modernism can also, and paradoxically, consist of a hyperscientific faith in technology and in humans' ability to understand rationally just about anything—not just political processes.

213

According to this Faustian belief, scholars in command of scientific methodologies could grasp everything from the psyche to everyday life. Other Faustian aspects of modernism involve paring away still more excess, to reach an exquisite, unifying truth—a truth that might nonetheless signify primal tides of historical movement. Professional historians began viewing the details of social, economic, and cultural life as precisely that primal undercurrent, somehow even deeper than politics. "Beneath the constitutional forms and ideas, beneath political issues," wrote the young Frederick Jackson Turner in a notebook of the mid-1890s, "run the great ocean currents of economic and social life, shaping and reshaping political forms to the changes of this great sea, which changes continuously."[2] Turner would polish up this rough notation, forging his "frontier thesis" from it.

Modernism is seen as a set of ideas contained in historical writing. Like historical practices themselves, these modernist moves have rarely, if ever, been examined for signs of gender, though we have already encountered some of these themes in the work of amateurs. The priority of the social had appeared in the work of Martha Lamb and Sarah Taylor Austin, to name just two, and everyday life was a staple of these histories. Water imagery infused amateur writing as well, leading to a concern for perspective well before the fin-de-siècle. Both the amateur embrace of tropes associated with historical modernism, and the intense revisionism of historical science's founding paradigms in a modernist direction, suggest unexplored terrain for the pursuit of gender. Did the modernist impulse in historical science refashion gender, making it more or less central to the profession? Alternatively, did gender give rise to historical modernism and perhaps reshape the men who practiced it?

In this pursuit, literary critics have shown the way, with their acute analyses of the feminine and its use as a powerful symbol by modernists, whether they portrayed the sexuality of the "modern woman" or refigured themselves in avant-garde terms that included the decadence, enervation, and sensuality of the whore or houri. Some modernists in the arts also portrayed women's consumerism, appetites, and hysteria, using them as a foil for the brisk hyperrationality of men. At the same time, hypermasculinity was emphasized by other members of the avant-garde in the form of perversion and diverse manifestations of excess, designed to distinguish these artists from the newly enfranchised masses. Cultural modernism, critics have shown, was multifaceted and polyvalent, perhaps also providing a screen or model for the production of a regendered scientific self.[3]

Complex modernism entered historical science not just as idea but as practice, and as a reimaging of the historian's self. Those were the days when concepts like relativism gained currency—concepts that ultimately opened the floodgates to a history of the trivial and the everyday, of minorities and women. It is claimed that at this modernist moment, scientific truth and historical values first became attenuated, with a permanent loss of professional fiber. In fact, evidence shows a more complicated movement, in which each questioning of the profession's practices was answered with new ways to express the historian's muscularity and rigor. The fin-de-siècle ratcheted up the pressures on white men. And in history, the response was a modernism that incorporated the low, the everyday, the feminine, the aesthetic, the statistical, and much much more.

Modernity and the Historian's Self

After more than a decade of archival work, Benedetto Croce recalled that by the mid-1890s, "my sense of revolt and of inner alienation from these 'sound studies' had reached its climax."[4] "Wearied of filling my mind with lifeless and disconnected facts," Croce yearned to "break through the narrow and trivial limits" of research and "rise to the heights" by doing a different kind of history.[5] Henri Berr described the library where he had set out to work as "embalmed in mauve lilacs . . . The fragrance intoxicated me."[6] Languor, suffocation, emptiness, an inability to concentrate, and a rising disgust with the human race troubled the historian's mission. Many were tempted by a flight from facts into philosophy, synthesis, theory, and other more unitary ways of accessing truth.

Behind the arduous work of producing facts, historians sensed a loss of wholeness. By the 1930s, R. G. Collingwood was describing his sensibility as fragmented: "There was a first R. G. Collingwood, who knew . . . that 'theory' and 'practice,' being mutually dependent, must both alike suffer frustration if segregated . . . There was a second R. G. C., who in the habits of his daily life . . . [lived] as a professional thinker whose college gate symbolized his aloofness from the affairs of practical life." The third

Collingwood was a "man of action," a would-be Karl Marx.[7] Modernizing scholars like Paul Lacombe divided humanity into "general man," "temporary man," and "individual man," as the ground for historical categorization. Many identified themselves as scientists and reiterated their faith in history as "science, nothing more nothing less," as J. B. Bury put it in 1903. Yet some in the profession, and others who straddled the professional-amateur divide, saw theirs as a more complex task, one fragmented into the scientific work of the researcher, the literary art of narrator, and the judgmental activity of the philosopher. G. M. Trevelyan, for instance, saw himself as necessarily all three.[8]

The language of malaise and fragmentation, an overstimulating urban life, and a simultaneous dullness associated with incipient mass society constructed many a historian's self and became part of a general (and contested) revamping of the profession's vocabulary and practices. Henri Berr, one of those who devoted his life to revising historical practice in France in the late nineteenth and early twentieth centuries, spun out several novelistic memoirs of the intellectual's life around 1890, when materialism, the lures of sexuality, and the uncontrolled desires of the new woman served as "a veil stretched between our eyes and the view of infinity."[9]

These challenges, this fragmentation and malaise, worked to send the historian's self soaring: "It is we, in this universe, who are gods," Berr wrote.[10] The old kind of historian produced a history that "groped around . . . Or it is satisfied with more or less vague procedures."[11] The new history needed supermen. Historians saw scientific progress, as well as individual spirit, impeded by the forces of materialism, the proliferation of artistic achievements rooted in money, and the acclaim given to banal and easily comprehensible work. Berr, who inspired historians like Marc Bloch and Lucien Febvre and revitalized the profession in France, wrote prolifically about feminized, decaying elites devoted to fleshly pleasures.[12] Influenced by Nietzsche's depiction of the *Übermensch*, vigorous new historians performed as supermen with inordinate capacities, reaching to encompass an ever-broadening field of data. Karl Lamprecht, whose drive to reconceptualize historical science as a search for the psychosocial contours of an era put him at the center of controversy, found his promethean deployment of facts and prodigious writing greeted with paeans to his physical achievements: Georg Waitz wrote in "true astonishment at your energy," while Julius Weizsäcker called one new volume of Lamprecht's German history "new testimony to your enormous energy."[13] The eccentric Henry Adams, who vacillated between amateur and professional personae, pushed his rhetoric heavenward in *Mont-Saint-Michel and Chartres,* which spoke of "soaring spires" and described Gothic architecture as "flinging its passion against the sky."

The single trajectory of the eye-brain between detail and transcendent truth, which had seemed so natural in the early days of professionalization, was now branded the "lifeless" work of "scissors-and-paste men," causing a visible rupture in the consensual values of historical science.[14] Foregrounding detail and truth, historians simultaneously saw their disconnectedness as alternating with godlikeness, the debased and lifeless sensibility forming a counterpoint to the superhuman.[15] Although sometimes drawn to a rhetoric of languid femininity, younger historians found the old professional persona irrelevant in a rapidly changing world. Even Ranke was feminized in comparison to these new heroes: he was "plums and no suet . . . all garnish, but no beef. He is a great historical decorator, . . . always in pumps and kid gloves."[16]

"Our situation is so novel," wrote James Harvey Robinson. To him, the verities about history's usefulness to the state, once a major claim, also seemed doubtful. It was possible that Napoleon might have learned something from reading Caesar, Robinson maintained, but "it is quite certain that Admiral Togo would have derived no useful hints from Nelson's tactics at Alexandria or Trafalgar."[17] In this regard, however, male historians differed very little from their contemporaries in other elite fields, who sensed rupture and unprecedented change vis-à-vis the past. Admiral Togo, after all, had smashed Russia's fleet at Port Arthur in 1904 and its Baltic fleet at Tsushima in 1905, signaling the decline of the West. The appearance of professional women historians, a declining birthrate, awareness of a variety of male sexualities, successful colonial challenges to Western hegemony, spreading consumerism, and other social changes called the ascendancy of professionals into question, sending their claims into the stratosphere (or the abyss) and forcing them to reappraise history and rescue it with newer tactics. It was no longer a time, some historians charged, when "the brain dominates the senses."[18]

In this situation, historians were expanding history's reach, absorbing the terrain of the amateurs and even expressing aspects of a feminine sensibility, and modernizing the scientific image by intensifying the old demands for factuality, data, and transcendence. Regrouping addressed the challenges of modern times, and historians leveled a charge against the "isolating" results of old-fashioned professional erudition, which necessitated long hours alone.[19] Henri Berr proposed a new kind of history, one based on the extra effort of generalizing or synthesis. Erudition was a base, but "it does not suffice" as it once "claimed to suffice."[20] The historian had to integrate sociology, psychology, and economics, and even see himself as an artist as well as a scientist.[21] The historian's imagination, something more innate and less susceptible to democratic formation, took center stage as the consensus building of the seminar came to be seen as vitiated by research, isolating men and pitting them against one another ("Men have seen themselves as isolated, disunited, and rivals for too long," wrote the much-admired Berr)[22] in the face of new rivals: the masses, the women, the colonized. "The democratization of university knowledge in England only makes for vulgarization," Berr noted, whereas true expansion of the university would consist in the "dissemination" of "the highest truths by an elite."[23] Images of cathedrals and an elite priesthood abounded in historical work, and historical knowledge was equated with exquisite light filtering through a cathedral window, unaccessible in its full aesthetic resonance to any but the specially gifted and well trained. With the rise of modernism, the old historical self, shaped within a republican brotherhood, was replaced by a self that functioned as part of an avant-garde.

In this respect, historians were borrowing yet other visions of male ascendancy and plenitude: those being created by writers, visual artists, musicians, and other intellectuals. For example, in *Concerning the Spiritual in Art* (1911) Wassily Kandinsky described the realm of artistic spirit as a triangle, moving ever higher because of "one man, and only one," whose struggle at the triangle's apex drew the entire form ever upward. Resisting the temptations of material gain and mass popularity, the "solitary visionary" raised the "spiritual triangle, slowly but surely, with irresistible strength . . . onwards and upwards." The movement was also horizontal and territorial: one of Kandinsky's prototypes was the young Picasso, who "leaps boldly and is found continually by his bewildered crowd of followers standing at a point very different from that at which they last saw him." Thus, the image of multiple spatial vantage points, heroically occupied, accompanied the artist-hero's trajectory, his movement away from earth. Those below were "dragged slowly higher," as the powerful visionary "boldly attacks those pillars which men have set up," until finally "the whole universe is shaken." In the midst of this cosmic trembling, the triangle moves "still higher" because the solitary artist's strength produced this incredibly difficult ascent through space on behalf of the weak.[24] This was heady stuff, and historians began characterizing their procedures as similarly inspired, as well as rigorously scientific. In tandem, these two personae would allow the attainment of an exquisite truth—a magnificently formalist light.

Using the modernist metaphors of artistic movements such as purism, historians soared to the heights of "synthesis," and leaped across fields of knowledge like Picasso. Though professing a weariness with archival tedium, they nonetheless extended the historical purview to include more aspects of cultural, mundane, everyday life—another concern of modernism. The focus on political facts had been used against the powerful tide of amateur history, against its interest in civilization, culture, and households. Scientific historians, even in the earlier days of documentary fervor, saw scholarly attention to the lower classes as fruitless, in terms of both narrative and the advancement of scholarship: "The laws of society originate in the higher classes; when they reach the lower, all sorts of incongruities take place," Guizot wrote to his wife, who did most of the work collecting and assembling their compilations of manuscripts.[25] After the revolutions of 1848, somewhat more attention was given to the laboring classes. Wilhelm Heinrich Riehl soon thereafter produced *Die bürgerliche Gesellschaft* (*Civil Society;* 1851), *Land und Leute* (*Land and People;* 1853), and *Die Familie* (*The Family;* 1855).[26] Gustav Freytag produced highly lauded studies of the German people. And by 1897 Karl Weinhold had published the scholarly work *Deutsche Frauen in dem Mittelalter* (*German Women in the Middle Ages*), suggesting that women might come under scrutiny, too.

The most modern science—Darwinism, genetics, and germ theory —provided the language with which to image these newcomers from "the people." Herbert Baxter Adams, for example, had a mania for discovering the migrating "germs" of Teutonic institutions. Others saw in the lower classes and women the taint of genetic inferiority. The invisibility of this genetic taint, which lay hidden within individuals, families, and nations, increased the demands on the scientist, who could not simply dissect like a biologist but whose inner eye needed expanded powers to penetrate both the surface and interior realms. Bury called for "microscopic research." However, a new historical X-ray vision, a characteristic of scientific and artistic "naturalism" and of the elitist superman, was taking shape, allowing historians to grasp invisible, underlying forces that made things happen—the "'*mal du siècle*' that has passed from generation to generation."[27] By the early twentieth century, this X-ray vision permitted historians like Lamprecht to see the hidden psychosocial contours of collective mentalities.

Historians historicized the expanding citizenry, carrier of political subjectivity and rights, by claiming as the century opened that everyone had a narrative, a history, and that it was crucial to investigate these. Republican imagery added an elitist overlay, and critics sensed the reach of a self-proclaimed aristocracy: "Heretics have been excommunicated," G. M. Trevelyan charged, "by the priests of an established church." Instead of eradicating the special self of professional historians and converting them into equal members of a mass brotherhood, the expanded pool of detail enhanced their prowess and made them even better. "There is a great need for the enormous accumulations of classified and isolated traditional data produced by the unceasing mills of naturalistic criticism," wrote Lamprecht. "It is necessary that we employ some means of mechanical combination of the parts of the huge world of facts which knowledge alone can supply—that we employ certain forms of criticism to classify the mass of material and thereby control it."[28] As historians came to investigate the material bases of past societies (and not just their politics), the demand for detail widened to include not just facts of the state but those concerned (in the words of James Harvey Robinson) with "our tools, our instruments, a watch, a ship, a gun," and the myriad needs, movements, uses, inventions, aspirations, institutions surrounding and generated by those tools.[29] The description of one pioneer in economic history illustrates this profusion: "It was not by hundreds but by thousands and tens of thousands that, in the course of his thirty years of labor, François

Simiand . . . effected his calculations, made tables for his figures, and drew graphs."[30]

The detail involved in tracking down and counting the new mass of historical subjects became a measure of the real, as well as a measure of the superhuman power of the economic or social historian. "This is to be done under the direction of an authoritative and constructive mind, and not without the aid of the imagination. How else is the control of such vast amounts of material possible? . . . They must be grouped according to a system which does not overlook the universal course of things, and which makes the whole more intelligible."[31] Detail proliferated, becoming more minute and more extensive, while the skill needed for classification (called "pragmatics" or "synthesis" or "the universal") mounted. The rise of economic and social history was accomplished under the coordinate signs of heightened mastery over the masses and their factuality, and a more probabilistic and imperfect universal truth.

By the 1920s the influence of Einstein's thought was apparent among the historical vanguard, further vitiating history's claims to a single certainty. Historians across Europe and North America jumped on the bandwagon of "perspective" and "relativity." Charles Beard epitomized this tendency in his "thundering" presidential address at the meeting of the American Historical Association in 1933: in the writing of history, he declared, one must see "its appropriate relativity"—must realize that it was nothing more than "contemporary thought about the past."[32] Simultaneously, professionals resisted the competition and influence of amateur writing by criticizing its "reckless disregard of perspective."[33] Ten years later, *Apologie pour l'histoire; ou, Métier d'historien* (*Apology for History; or, The Historian's Craft*)—which Marc Bloch wrote in hiding, without notes and based solely on his prodigious capacity—showed that the historian had more identities than ever: by the early 1940s, those left over from the nineteenth century (pathologist, biologist, geologist, artisan) had been supplanted by explorer, staff member, policeman, criminal lawyer, cross-examiner, and Einsteinian.[34] Not just the ever-swelling range of human subjects but, increasingly, the historian's prodigious self represented male plenitude.

"Every historical book worthy of the name ought to include a chapter entitled 'How Can I Know What I Am About to Say?'" Bloch wrote.

"Even the lay reader would experience real intellectual pleasure in examining these 'confessions,' . . . with [their] successes and reverses."[35] In this call for some account of the historian's self, Bloch reiterated a common credo of the Cartesian *cogito*. Ranke had believed that it was the historian's "duty" to account for his self and its work, to represent the relationship as the condition of truth; and so he sporadically produced an autobiographical manuscript. At the same time as Bloch, yet in different circumstances, Friedrich Meinecke undertook to note down "the development of his self" in relation to historical work.[36] Despite the announced irrelevance of the self (except as an object to be stripped of contingency), historical writing became increasingly saturated with autobiographical and self-producing gestures. It was this self that resolved many of the contradictory claims in the scientific past. Historical science announced the past's finitude and self-sufficiency, even while proclaiming its infinite expanse and lack of original intelligibility. As these claims clashed more loudly and fragmented the "grand narrative," the story of the pure, self-policing, and prodigious *cogito* of the professional avant-garde gave twentieth-century historiography its libidinal force. Wherever changes in the field threatened the certainty of men's plenitude in history, the "dominant fiction" of men's importance was recouped in the excitement generated by the impressiveness of the historian's self, as told in the new "grand narrative" of historiography.

Modernism had further to go. Croce invoked language, common sense, and syntax as the loci of historical meaning and the conditions of historical possibility. Croce's focus on these elements in his idea of the aesthetic's powerful relationship to history echoed the general modernist impulse to emphasize formalist aspects of cultural work. Croce thus resembled other modernists who charted history's turn toward aesthetic imagery—another amateur trait whose absorption into professionalism ironically furthered history's gendered claims. Historians of art have connected modernism to a concern with surface, montages of heterogeneous materials and objects, the invocation of psychic (not spiritual) interiority through surface, and the undermining of realistic depth perspective. In this period historians, too, refocused their sense of surface and depth.

It had become clear, Robinson allowed, that human history went back not just the 3,000–5,000 years for which there were records, but an additional 300,000 years or more, for which no records existed. If we imagined history "as a vast lake into whose rather turbid depths we eagerly peer," we would barely penetrate the surface. "We can have no clear and adequate notion of anything happening more than an inch—indeed scarce more than half an inch—below the surface."[37] According to Robinson, historians were condemned to superficiality, and many made the most of the opportunity. The desire to stretch across wider reaches of the historical surface was never more intense than in the period 1880–1930, for it was then that historians began massively to gather statistics, use the new tools of economics and sociology, and embrace geography.

With their initial focus on the surface, historians found evidence piling up helter-skelter before their eyes in a confusing montage. "Civilization today is pure chaos. The [Universal] Exposition, let's admit it, has shown it to our eyes—a chaos of ideas and a chaos of institutions."[38] But unlike mid-nineteenth century practitioners, they now went, so to speak, with the flow. History could indeed be a pastiche of anything, a montage, a discontinuity: "The jury, the drama, the Gatling gun, the papacy, the letter *S*, the doctrine of *stare decisis*." According to Robinson, "the historian may elect to describe a Roman villa or a primitive steam engine, or contrast the theology of Luther with that of Thomas Aquinas; he can trace the origin of Gothic architecture or of the Egyptian calendar, portray the infatuation of Henry VIII for Anne Boleyn, or Bismarck's attitude toward the socialists, or the hatchets of neolithic man."[39] Far from occluding depth, however, historical montage may actually heighten one's sense of it. Examining the work of Jackson Pollock and other abstract expressionists, the art historian T. J. Clark has noted that their particular kind of highly worked, discontinuous surfaces provided an invitation to an even deeper interiority. Gaps in surface space offered places where the eye and mind could wander; similarly, graphs and tables suggested all that lay behind them, drawing the virtuoso into the crevices and the unseen but libidinally sensed depths. Historical modernism opened opportunities for a more virtuoso male performance and a heightened fascination with the historian's own interiority.

One of many instances of opening up the interior by focusing expressly on a surface aesthetic came in the eccentric yet continually discussed work of Henry Adams, who hovered between amateur and professional even when serving as president of the American Historical Association. The back-and-forth movement in and out of the profession that generated so much excitement around male historians such as Adams, Beard, and Trevelyan was characteristic of the splitting—and thus libidinally exciting—historian's self of the time. Adams' status as avant-garde can be argued on the basis of his unswerving disdain for the bourgeois guild-mentality of the professionals, and for his complete emotional investment in the exotic. Traveling to Japan, Tahiti, Cuba, and many other parts of Asia and Latin America, Adams the discriminating consumer bought great quantities of art, bric-a-brac, clothing, and textiles. Meanwhile, he sustained an adulterous passion and worshiped young girls, including his nieces, with whom he regularly traveled throughout Europe.[40] Themes of incest, exotica, and avant-garde goods evoke modernism.

It was as a trip with a young niece that Adams imaged his descriptions in *Mont-Saint-Michel and Chartres,* a work initially printed privately and distributed only to an elite group of readers, including the artist Augustus Saint-Gaudens and the writer Henry James.[41] Adams was an assiduous researcher, using archives wherever he traveled and consulting other documents from out-of-the-way repositories. But he was nonetheless a Belle Epoque aesthete in his lavish use of "woman" as a modernist theme or trope, especially in his focus on the Virgin Mary. Mary, to whom the cathedrals of the Middle Ages were dedicated, "was absolute; she could be stern; she was not above being angry; but she was still a woman, who loved grace, beauty, ornament—her toilette, robes, jewels" (94). Modernists figured women as cruel; and according to Adams, Chartres and indeed every cathedral in twelfth- and thirteenth-century France were built to satisfy this commanding, exigent, and selfish mistress and her taste for light in her buildings. "[The architects] converted their walls into windows, raised their vaults, diminished their piers, until their churches could no longer stand" (102). Mary's passionate personality served as the source of the medieval aesthetic of surface, in which cathedrals no longer derived from theological principles (104). Flying buttresses and soaring spires took shape not according to architectural, mechanical, or even theological law but according to "ludic aestheticism."[42] In the process, Adams' history of life in medieval France became driven by the emotions of the ordinary people who worked to build those massive structures. The thousands of stone carriers did their work penitently, united in their endurance of physical torture, sobbing and sighing in the felt presence of their heavenly dominatrix, their female dictator.

The historical libido, like most other kinds, is an unruly place. Scripting the age of cathedrals as perverse, highly aestheticized, and ruled by the whip of a phallic queen, Adams relinquished his grip on serial time, as one would when under the reign of libidinal forces. *Mont-Saint-Michel and Chartres* refused to stay anchored in historical time. Adams noted that cathedrals solicited investment like railroads; they were Mary's dollhouses, much like his niece's; or expressions of energy, like a coal-pit, a world's fair. Scholars, architects, and clergymen across the centuries chipped in to measure, sanctify, and explicate the cathedral for early twentieth-century tourists like Adams and his niece (as he continually reminded her). Thus, the time of the libido, though equated with dynamo and entropy, finally moved *Mont-Saint-Michel and Chartres* from the peak of fervor, when spires soared, to the exhaustion and depletion of the twentieth century. Having experienced it all as a modern aesthete, Adams repeatedly called himself an old fossil.

Everything was permissible in the expansion of the historical libido that modernism provoked. Adams reveled in "my historical indifference to everything but facts, and my delight at studying what is . . . debased and degraded."[43] He saw his travels to Asia, the South Sea Islands, Latin America, and other parts of the world as revealing the "virile" world of primitive sexuality. Recording nude bathing and other rites with his Kodak camera, Adams sought out the "force" that the exercise of such energy entailed, using his exotic and sexually driven ocean travels to image history. Installed in the National Archives with his own copyist, working tirelessly in the Bibliothèque Nationale or in England so that there would not even be "gleanings" for any other researcher, Adams acted out another version of the frantic and polymorphous world of historical modernity.[44]

The travel writing of amateurs, imperialist energy, the wanderings of people like Adams, and the development of geography as a scientific field also propelled history along its modernist trajectory. At the turn of the century, historians such as Lamprecht admired the way trained geographers like Friedrich Ratzel and Paul Vidal de la Blache vied with international explorers and local savants for control of the field, gaining university posts and creating academic departments. Although historians fiercely debated geography's claims and its importance to history, some increasingly incorporated geographic perspectives.

Two notable and enduringly influential examples were Lucien Febvre and Marc Bloch, among the first contributors to Henri Berr's series on the "regions" of France. Their early works showed geography as expanding the potential of the surface.[45] Bloch's *Caractères originaux de l'histoire rurale française* (*Basic Characteristics of French Rural History;* 1931) was but the longest of his many discussions of geographic material, all tending to promote its incorporation into history. He reminded Febvre of their common aim to make the *Annales* a "mouthpiece" for the good that geography could do history. Bloch reviewed geographic scholarship, proposed standards for atlases and maps, and began adding geographic terms such as "stratum," "substratum," and "morphology" to his liberal use of the older scientific conventions ("dissection," "anatomy," "physiology"). Although scornful of academic disputes focused narrowly on the precise determination of political, regional, and other boundaries, Bloch nonetheless advocated aerial photography as a technology that could show geographic boundaries and borders more accurately.[46] Within those boundaries, one probed to find "man in society" or social reality itself.

Adding geography to history was certainly not the work of Bloch alone, nor was it by far his major accomplishment. It marked, nonetheless, a renewed attention to surface—this time the geographic surface that began, in Bloch's case, with borders shown in aerial photos. Geographically inspired historians considered soil type, rivers, river settlements, climate, and other factors that came to be called the *habitus*—a habitus quite distinct from the idea of a home. Distinguishing themselves from geographers, however, they scorned those who tended to stop at borders and ignore the depths, the "substratum," "human studies," "man in society," and "reality." "A 'landscape of civilization' is only, after all, the expression of a society which, with '*un élan vital,*' shapes and reshapes it." What mattered was "the physiology of the living animal." But the "physiology" was no longer the sure truth of several generations earlier, produced by the hardworking researcher. Truth was now based on infinitely more physical, surface details—those that were accessible to the tourist, traveler, and everyman, and that were learned and classified by the mapmaking historical scholar. The expanded surface made finding truth more "complex" and "probabilistic." Thus, attention to that stable entity, the historian's self, intensified so that the scientific vantage point could be controlled.

A new concern with surface—aesthetic or geographic—contributed to redefining historical methodology, practice, and narrative as "modernist." These and many other changes in the field created a climate in which male practitioners could experiment by drawing on the rich pool of possibilities proposed by amateurs, women professionals, and experts in new academic and economic fields. Discipline, Michel Foucault proposed, can be enacted only after the full *tableau vivant* has been laid out. In the case of history, the rich potentiality of the past revealed itself in amateur writing, for those involved in the scientific "will to know." Only then could science do its work of dissecting, classifying, and synthesizing; but like Impressionist painters challenged to differentiate themselves from the mere photographer, historians once again had to do more, be better. Challenged and enabled by the amateur's panoramic historical realism, based on travel, research, and documents, scientific historians became "artistes," aesthetes, and thus modernists as well.

Yet this dependence did not automatically entail equality or even acceptance for either amateur or professional women. "Unless we get more history and less flatulence into our management," Henry Adams commented on Lucy Maynard Salmon's AHA committee membership, "we shall not get far towards omniscience except in . . . female story-telling."[47] The connoisseurship of the disinterested male observer, the reconceptualization of history as the historian's "thought," the expansion of legitimate subject matter to the everyday, and the turn toward "synthesis" re-created modernist history as an enhanced story of male identity, leaving the field open to the same gendered paradigms that remain intact today. Not that some women weren't allowed to soar, too: Eileen Power was distinguished, it was repeatedly said, by combining "the graces of the butterfly with the sober industry of the bee."[48] Tiny creatures, they did not ascend too high. As the dominant fiction of Western male plenitude was undermined by the presence of women in the academy, by the challenges to Western intellectual hegemony from other regions of the globe, and by differing analyses and cognitive programs from the masses, the perspectival privilege of Western men was reanchored in a polymorphous modernism. This inflated modernist self, endowed with muscular, cognitive claims and staking out a vast territory for control by an elite, enabled historical science to move in fresh directions, all the while preserving its traditional hierarchies and protecting gendered power.

Gendered Boundaries to Women's Modernism

Thus, amid the chaos and confusion between the fin-de-siècle and World War II, there was opportunity, change, and (paradoxically) stability, in all of which women historians played a significant role. On the one hand, in the half-century between 1890 and 1940 they constituted a hinge swinging between amateur and professional versions of the past, sometimes translating amateur work into a bit more professionalized and thus palatable language. The water- and travel-imagery in amateur work, along with women's generally destabilizing presence as practitioners, provided a range of images that blurred rules and perspective just enough to usher in modernist questioning and to provide tempting images—for instance, of a languishing researcher overcome by the fragrance of lilacs.

On the other hand, however, women's writing and practices marked out borders, limits, dead ends. Their presence signaled dangers and thus mobilized a normative, albeit heightened, masculinity which permeated elites of all Western societies in that age of total war. They set trajectories and terms, indicating where the circuit of innovation stopped. Like de Staël, historians such as Power, Salmon, Harrison, and the extremely ambivalent Mary Beard merit a central position among scholars for their innovative work in social, domestic, and other aspects of women's history. They are quintessential models and institution builders—founding journals, encouraging the organization of archives—and they are hardworking researchers. Working with data and detail, they often wrote the homosocial story, of men as well as women, but with reversals that marked out the female positioning of the low versus the high.

Yet these amateur and professional women authors, writing in the heyday of modernism, merit an alternate reading as writers often marking limits to their science. Lucy Maynard Salmon, for instance, wrote many pieces that can be interpreted as forming the bounds of historical modernism. Her books *The Newspaper and the Historian* and *The Newspaper and*

Authority (published in 1923, when she was seventy) asked what happens to facts when they pass through a journalistic medium. Her interpretive tool did not consist of narrating the rise of the newspaper or describing its virtues as a purveyor of information; rather, it was the idea of "refraction." Watching the newspaper gather facts from multiple points in society and then rebroadcast them as pictures of daily life, Salmon worked her own refraction on the newspaper by breaking it down. Editors, correspondents, illustrators, advertisers, critics, feature writers, interviewers, interviewees—such were a few of the many refractors she listed, in subjecting journalism's pure image to scrutiny. The book fragmented and dismantled that unitary entity called the newspaper, and created a modernist canvas spread with splotches of information. The table of contents of only one of the volumes contained more than a thousand clusters or subdivisions, ranging from the human to the vegetable and mineral aspects of the press. Here is a sample of the narrative:

> Plate service is furnished in the form of metal plates that can be cut into pieces and as much or as little used as may be desired; ready-print service furnishes sheets printed on one side, on two or more pages, by or through the distributing organization, the remaining pages being printed in the office of the paper receiving the service. Plate service does not carry advertising, but ready-print service carries advertising and derives its greatest revenues therefrom, the newspapers receiving nothing from it. In 1912, it was estimated that 16,000 newspapers in America received either plate service or ready-print service, and that these newspapers were read by 60,000,000.

This sort of writing resembles a cubist canvas—a canvas without the possibility of depth. It is a list of disembodied facts.

Salmon's "History in a Backyard" likewise summoned modernist themes, describing the mental confinement of a researcher stuck at home for the summer. As the researcher's eye surveyed the backyard, it spotted objects such as the fence that marked the boundaries between adjacent properties. The essay painted a canvas of the backyard, then allowed the mind to wander along the surface of the image, slip into memory cracks, and find associations that created a certain amount of depth. In Salmon's essay, the modernist project advanced along a trajectory of material objects that carried a lesson about history's localization and its existence in the commodities of everyday life. Insofar as modernism concerned a newfound interest in commodities and the commercial in general, Salmon's writing pointed specifically to it by alluding to archival research in a commercial way: "Did not three months of acquisition in Europe leave one rich, while nine months of constant depletion of mental capital at home left one bankrupt?" Finally, Salmon's short essay carried with it the exoticism of Henry Adams, in the prodding friend who "put Aladdin's lamp in our hands and opened up before our eyes as large an undiscovered world as could be found in seven kingdoms." In this regard, Salmon's essay was a pivotal work, swiveling between the amateur and the modernist professional and blurring the distinctions between the historical and the everyday.

With opportunity, however, came dead ends and blind alleys, for where there is a possibility of depth there is often a simultaneous occlusion of "meaning." Some of Salmon's writings were illustrated with pictures of her own kitchen. She wrote an infamous yet serious "Ode to the Kitchen Sink," which—more experimental than her essay—outrageously blocked access to the possibility of historical analysis. While such an affront to the historian's self in some way mimed the portrait of the historian as languishing artist, it also pointed to the kitchen, a place without the possibility of either depth or ascent. In the kitchen, Salmon found archival treasures such as cookbooks, and with all the absorption of a Proust she summoned and categorized the recipes. Many were based on place-names and travel:

> Lady Baltimore cake, Philadelphia ice cream, Irving Park cake, Bangor pudding, Berkshire muffins, Boston brown bread, Saratoga chips, and Maryland chicken . . . Parker House rolls, Waldorf salad, Delmonico cream . . . Vienna coffee, Yorkshire pudding, Nuremburg cakes, Banbury tarts, Bavarian cream, Irish stew, Scotch broth, English muffins, Hamburg steak . . . macaroni, spaghetti, sauerkraut, frankfurters, chili con carne, tamales, Devonshire cream, Neufchâtel cheese, chop suey, Brussels sprouts.

This passage conveys a monomania that both separated her from, and connected her to, amateur writers on material culture like Alice Morse Earle, as well as professionals.

Other recipes showed family ties and those of friendship: "Aunt Hannah's loaf cake, Cousin Lizzie's waffles, Grandmother's cookies, Grandma Lyman's marble cake, Sister Sally's quince jelly, Mother's raspberry vinegar." Salmon also suggested that the housewife was no mere drudge but aspired to poetry in her recipes: "birds on canapés, bird's-nest pudding, floating islands, apples in bloom, shadow potatoes, cheese aigrettes, apple snow, snowballs, gossamer gingerbread, fairy gingerbread, aurora sauce."[49]

The housewife's poetic images pointed to a naggingly ahistorical limitation in Salmon's oeuvre, not only in her piece on cookbooks but in her ode to the kitchen and her notecards for an unfinished manuscript on the hand-held paper fan. The power of such imagery, Gaston Bachelard has suggested, lies in its ability to use the commonplace spaces and objects of life to provoke evocations, reverberations, and echoes rather than to generate discussions of cause and effect. Although Salmon's writings sought to uncover the household as a place for scientific historical treatment, they also moved in the opposite direction of poetry, using description to create images that resonated in the reader's psyche.[50]

Salmon's lists, her stacks of notecards on the history of the fan, each with an isolated sentence, her repetitive lines of recipe-names, her pages enumerating single facts about the newspaper: these could be seen as analogous to the arrows, isolated lines, and grids in modernist paintings. The repetition and stark lack of meaning capture one's attention; but, like the graphs and statistics compiled by women social scientists and the numerous women economic historians, they call attention to the unsaid. "What about all these household artifacts?" one wants to ask. But instead of an analysis or story, Salmon's account of the household remained a series of disconnected images, lacking a historical narrative, perhaps because history was not about locations of trauma but about sites of power. Although psychoanalysis might weave similar objects and images into scientific narratives, and indeed thrive on manipulating them in the name of "cure," professional history could not. Trained as a historian, Salmon could only point repetitively to this domestic space.[51] In general so unconventional, Salmon has been lost to historiography and analysis by working the terrain at history's borders. Despite attempts today to focus on literariness and to articulate history's seams and shared boundaries with litera-ture and other fields, no one has yet done what Salmon did in her modern-ist pointing to domestic space. And a good deal of this bizarre work cannot be subjected to the profession's critical eye.

American author Mary Beard worked in similarly irreconcilable ways, using lists and poetics. Her histories of women ranged from chronicles of their accomplishments in municipal government to descriptions of "woman as force in history" (a phrase that serves as the title for one of her books). She used copious data to write a revisionist history, striving to undermine the feminist emphasis on a modern movement that fought women's oppression and lack of opportunity. Beard added women's and cultural history to the surveys of United States history that she wrote with her husband, Charles; according to many estimates, these texts contain more women's history than any others of their type, even by the standards of the late 1990s. She was thus a pioneer, a foremother, and an example to hundreds of women in the profession as women's history took shape in the 1970s—the quintessential better story. Her progressive views, like those of her husband, made history more socially aware and democratic. As they saw it, all kinds of history—economic, political, and cultural—were sub-sumed in the synthetic term "civilization."

Beard, however, also occluded "meaning" and "depth," the sine qua non even of modernism. For although people invoked (and still invoke) the aesthetic, narrative, or "living" aspects at the heart of history, no one did so in the ways that Beard practiced in her works. In one of her histories, instead of narrating or analyzing women's activities, she substituted blank verse, creating a text that was also linear and listlike—"Steinian," in a word:

> exotic entertainers firing young blood, circus performers, swan and
>   nose divers, rodeo strategists, parachutists, and high kickers
> domestic amusers with babies, one baby this year, another next,
>   possibly one free year, then twins, one's own, one's employers
>   pushing carts, scolding, chattering, spanking, laughing,
>   wheedling, nursing, bottling, with nice babies, lovely babies,
>   cross babies, sick babies, babies learning to walk and babies that
>   won't walk, anyway babies

dog fanciers and tenders
actresses putting new wine into old bottles to tempt the uninitiated
    and excite the jaded
hostesses promoting trade, letters and philosophy, marrying off
    their sons and daughters, allaying tedium[52]

Eileen Power's *Medieval People,* and to a lesser extent her *Medieval Nunneries,* share these listlike qualities. Based on the premise that history was made in kitchens, the former book reveled in the low and preconceptual, the world whose contours Harrison had explored more systematically: formulas for eradicating stains, removing fleas, and delousing; lists of food that the burgher, nun, or peasant might eat; copious excerpts from the love letters of a Calais wool trader; the daily gossip of a peasant woman; the goods Marco Polo saw during his extensive wanderings; the varied pets of nuns, abbesses, and noblewomen. The thick imagistic surface, which was meant to snare the reader, undid the extensive scholarship that informed it, leaving no high to correct the low, no depth to redeem the surface.

Ricarda Huch proposed that it was the imagistic quality of a historical fact which mattered, the resonance that would strike readers enough to grab their intellect and emotions. With the factual being used as domination, the fantastic in history was an important means of keeping this source of oppression under control.[53] Eileen Power worked this same terrain in her early books and radio presentations, aiming outright for the common reader and young children. A world traveler, she alluded to the superiority of far-flung empires by enumerating their customs, goods, and cosmopolitan households—a technique she used in her book *Medieval People.* It might seem surprising that Power afterward turned full-tilt toward statistical, graphlike economic history and away from the blind alleys to which this style of writing led; but graphs had their own modernism, a different sort of imagery.

Whereas Power tried to make her early work palatable to the professional and general reader alike, Beard warned academics about the kind of history she was writing: "This book may appear weird and unsymmetrical to the masters with a profounder sense of system."[54] Her scheme involved assaulting the hallowed foundations of the profession. In *America through*

Women's Eyes, she suggested that this hallowed tradition could be recounted differently. When it was, the usual topics and the expected orderliness of past orthodoxy failed to appear. Beard showed Lucy Laney teaching Latin verbs to black children, while Southern women fought against lynching. She let Sarah Orne Jewett tell how much late nineteenth-century America reminded her of Rome before its fall. Meanwhile, Marietta Holley laughed at that most male institution—the horse race, complete with its feminine accessories. Through list after list of topics, seen through "women's eyes," the great American dream had a perverse twist. In an essay entitled "The Great Fact-Finding Farce," discussing the statistics, inquiries, governmental commissions, and research groups that came up with the facts about poverty, coal industries, and family life, Lillian Symes showed that these sources presented numerous untruths covering the "big lie" about American society. She declared that facts were ruthless and dehumanizing, even as men were searching out more of them. Each individual had a separate set of facts, to use as protection against other facts that threatened his or her self-interest. "Over written history the gods of chance and chaos have evidently presided," Beard concluded.[55]

Beard explored a territory that few have entered since. She laughed, for example, at science:

> I want to thank that little band
> Of atoms whose persistency
> In following a pattern planned
> Results in my identity.[56]

Although committed to women's archives, she utterly derided science, feminism, war, politics, and other sacred articles of professionalized history and a subsequently professionalized women's history. Indeed, she coedited an anthology of women's humor that included farcical vignettes of women's visits to World War I battlefields—and she published it in 1934, in the depths of the global Depression. Of little scientific or modernist use to anyone, this example of bad taste has not been adopted by the academy.

Yet Beard became a foremother, whose work was seen as part of the early anthropological impulse that did so much to open up women's history. Decrying feminists who said there was nothing to write about except famous women because women were generally oppressed, she wrote that U.S. history began "with the very Indians," with women priestesses—in fact, with every woman who ever succeeded in giving voice to some "expression."[57] An early multiculturalist? Perhaps, although amateurs from the early nineteenth century had already written about women in Africa, Asia, and other non-Western regions.[58] Yet Beard also noted the interest that fascists took in women, discussing what she saw as their appreciation of women's "force" and contrasting it with Enlightenment and post-Enlightenment devaluation of the feminine.

In fact, Beard was at once progressive and distasteful, innovative and repulsively iconoclastic. So extreme was her modernism that she was able to admire both the new character "Wonder Woman" and women fascists, with no discrimination whatsoever. Her modernist use of the word "force" uncoupled it from the moralizing that usually accompanied discussions of science, relativity, and (later) multiculturalism.[59] Beard grouped together, in one disturbing mix, fascist women, quarreling women, beauty contestants, and the Neolithic sower-gatherer who "lifted her low-browed male companion above the wild beasts that he hunted with stone and club and devoured in the raw."[60] She had read Croce, Karl Heussi, and others innovators, bringing them to her husband's attention. But whereas he adapted them to the innovative conventions of the day, so that the U.S. profession as a whole was initiated into a more or less agreeable language of "relativity" and "perspective," she did not. While Charles wrote in lock-step cadences to advance his clear, intelligible revisionist theses, Mary Beard took seriously the observation that "everything seems to depend upon the historian—his locus in time and space, the mere detail of birth, affiliations of class, and the predilections of sheer uncritical emotions."[61] Other women writers invoked science at the time: Maude Violet Clarke lectured on the "kinetic stage" of historical science and on the importance of drawing on "subliminal activities."[62] But this was acceptable, usable, indicating that historical science had depth. In Beard's case, acknowledging that the universe was riddled with individual force, that *everyone* had a history, and that facts were perspectival led to work that often was unusably flat.[63] She was repetitively iconoclastic and boldly lacking in scruples.

Jane Ellen Harrison's Nietzschean approach to the primitive pushed at the edges of intelligibility, but in a different, more explicitly sexual way.

As mentioned earlier, her *Themis* undermined the status of the Olympian gods when it found that there had been older, more primal religions based on instinctual rituals springing from the body. Drawing on the findings of anthropologists and theories of collective religious life, she described initiation rituals:

> So vital, so crucial is the change, that the savage exhausts his imagination and his ingenuity in his emphasis on death and new birth. It is not enough to be killed; you must be torn to pieces or burnt to ashes. Above all, you must utterly forget your past life. The precautions taken to secure this completeness of death and resurrection and consequent oblivion are sometimes disgusting enough. Murder is carefully counterfeited with the help of bladders of blood and the like . . . Not only does the boy forget his own name that in this his social baptism he may receive a new one, but he does not know his own mother, he has forgotten how to speak and can only stammer, he cannot even swallow, he has to be artificially fed.[64]

Although part of this passage suggests the description of women hysterics in the nineteenth century, Harrison, in *Themis*, actually thought her way back to an age when the self was but a series of rituals, counterfeit deeds, and disguises. This epoch preceded that of classical Greece, when subject-object differentiation and transcendence allowed for the projection of a god or gods distinct from the self, before the days when gods were perceived as representing something higher and better. Instead, life was lived within a social and naturalistic milieu where the power of nature and social value (Themis) determined what may only roughly be called a human condition.

Professing not to value "savagery," Harrison had nonetheless come close to entering it intellectually. More important, she had worked her way back philologically and iconographically to a world before depth, transcendence, body-mind opposition, and the humanistic self. From the most primal of social-natural phenomena—namely, birth—developed an array of expressions including mother-child figurations in ritual and iconography. Here, too, in the proliferation of birthing rites (including counterfeit ones), was the "birth of tragedy." Harrison was suggesting something normatively iconoclastic, claiming that patriarchy, theology, transcendence, the individual, and other attributes of civilization derived from this prior origin. What was unthinkable, however, was her exploration (thick but ultimately unsatisfying because unintelligible to the modern scientist) of the primacy of matrilineal birth, the body without selfhood, the eating of raw flesh as a means of imbibing cosmic power, and human expression in the form of "tragedy" that did not have an aesthetic or moralizing message. Rather, drama began and ended in the body, with no modern cognitive or aesthetic valence.

Modernism had vitalistic overtones from the beginning, but these always operated within the context of the intelligible—unlike Harrison's work, which departed from it. Especially after World War I, women historians, along with male professionals, rejected the "lifeless" history of preceding generations somewhat the way contemporary historians are calling for a return to "narrative." For men, fulfilling the summons to "life" usually meant (and still often means) making greater use of colorful anecdotes, lush adjectives, thumping verbs, and character sketches. Yet more extreme interpretations of "life" existed alongside these humanistic ones. The experiences of the body before its submission to Western ideas of the transcendent "self," and the development of a cohesive society based on group rituals of the body, are subjects that historians have begun to approach with some semblance of Harrison's modernism.

Historical modernism reached full flower early in the twentieth century, when women and men inhabited the profession together, albeit on consistently unequal terms. An occasion for changing paradigms, an opportunity for the professional persona to metamorphose, and a moment when the subject matter of scientific history broadened, modernism opened the professional study of the past to issues of probability, aesthetics, and perspective. Identities were sometimes differently expressed, and the performance of the professional role was no longer so unitary, so relentlessly part of a brotherhood. A Maitland could mentor a Bateson, and this remained possible, if not prevalent, until the Depression and World War II, when women were pushed out of the profession to restore men's prerogatives in the workplace, according to the general view that men had a right to jobs whereas women did not.

Movement and countermovement: the play of the Western male professional identity was as fraught as any other, and never more so than under the menace of feminism, global resistance movements, and socialism. As a result of the more flexible, complex, and powerful self that invisibly re-armed professional supermen and installed their own agon alongside that of historical characters, modernism heightened the gendered profile of historical science. Despite vast changes and new opportunities in the profession, there remains within today's most sophisticated historical para-digms and practices a modern and modernist legacy—that is, a pervasive recourse to the fascinating self of the male historian, as *the* authority on the past. Given the varied contours, blurring, and inconsistencies of modern-ism, historians are most comfortable when they are fitting history's many conundrums into the lush, masculine contest of a more traditional histori-ography—a historiography of opposition and struggle over an immense, seductive array of topics. With the historical tableau so inhabited by the masses, women, children, and non-Western races, male plenitude is best asserted in historiographic, not historical, form.

For instance, David Hollinger's appealing essay on modernism, "The Knower and the Artificer," portrays less the difficulties of epistemology, form, and narrative than the styles of authorial intellect, one type of modernist ("the knower") being prototypically a scientist, the other ("the artificer") being a more promethean, Romantic author.[65] Hollinger builds his typology by posing authors like Marx and Mill against Eliot and Joyce, and charting the way they thought, wrote, and interpreted intellectual activity. According to this typology, the quintessential historical and his-toriographic narrative works by propelling masculine identity through the agonistic time of realist, modernist, or even postmodernist evolution.

At the center of historical explanation, the towering and seductive male authorial subject rules as a pioneer, a member of an avant-garde, a dazzling virtuoso—and all the more so, given the way "truth" and "universalism" have dissolved in the course of the twentieth century. Although the rest of the historical field may be crowded with heterogeneous characters, histo-riography is not.[66] The historian of historiography, which is virtually all male, seldom shares the stage with a woman; rather, he is fortified by epigones admiring his laws and making him a "star," fraternal clusters who think of contesting them, and still others who will analyze the agon in terms of historical movement through serial or even postmodern time. Whether produced by his facts, the range of his historiographic reach, or his flights of theory, this imposing construct of male subjectivity (albeit with new demands for public performance and new calls to meet the challenge of powerful women, themselves increasingly cast as phallic maternal rivals) continues to function as the centerpiece for an increasingly difficult historical epistemology. No matter what the changes from realism to modernism or modernism to postmodernism, from claims of truth to claims of explanation, masculinity continues to function as it did in the nineteenth century: as part of a flight, a deepening, a broadening in which the historian ascends, reaches, incises, and conquers to surpass himself and all others. He creates more, a supplement, an extra, beyond what others have done—but does it transcendentally, invisibly, so that while we see powerful historians as men, we also see only truth, pure intelligence, and compelling explanation. The profession's unacknowledged libidinal work—the social ideology that draws us to value male plenitude, power, and self-presentation—is but rarely glimpsed in the mirror of history.

Some women have challenged professional values outright, calling unspoken male privilege and higher esteem to account. For instance, Mary Alice Williams, of Goucher College, caustically described the program of the 1919 meeting of the American Historical Association: "Not a woman's name appears upon it; and yet you know and I know that there are at least a dozen women in the country who could present papers equal if not superior to those given by some of the 'two-for-a-penny' men who are listed. Most of the influential men of the A.H.A. stand tight, shoulder to shoulder, with both fore-feet in the trough."[67] This was one of those incidents of contestation and reversal, part of the modernist moment when the underside of the mirror appeared as surface and when women like Williams imagined that things could be different.

But lack of attention to the array of hierarchical dynamics is the more general rule, in a profession that talks in terms of transcendent truth. Feminist scholars in such disciplines as literature even imagine that recourse to history would be a liberating way of resolving their own intradisciplinary debates, while minority and women historians think that they need only work harder for the truth to appear. Although the play of gender—that is, of fantasies of male plenitude and female inferiority—allows breakthroughs, and although the libidinal work of the profession is there for all of us to reshape in one way or another, lack of attention to its existence exacts costs, sometimes heavy ones. We inhabit a gendered profession, one in which the higher status of the male historian and his topics—considered the loci of universal value—fosters much bad "acting out" of this obviously fraught role; yet the more sophisticated stage of "working through," which accompanies issues of power, abuse, and trauma, is never reached.[68] The play of gender, race, and ethnicity could and does enrich scholarship. It would be salutary for all if the price of such contributions were lowered—if we acknowledged the dialogical, multiple, and charged nature of writing the past.

Notes / Index

Notes

INTRODUCTION

1. My discussion of gender is informed throughout by Joan Scott, *Gender and the Politics of History* (New York: Columbia University Press, 1988).
2. Lawrence Stone, "Only Women," *New York Review of Books* 32 (April 11, 1985), 21, enthusiastically set rules for the new field.
3. Peter Novick, *That Noble Dream: The "Objectivity Question" and the American Historical Profession* (Cambridge: Cambridge University Press, 1988).
4. For a summary of this position, see Rodolphe Gasché, *The Tain of the Mirror: Derrida and the Philosophy of Reflection* (Cambridge, Mass.: Harvard University Press, 1986), 13–34. Many scholars employ the topos: e.g., François Hartog, *The Mirror of Herodotus: The Representation of the Other in the Writing of History*, trans. Janet Lloyd (Berkeley: University of California Press, 1988).
5. J. P. Kenyon, *The History Men: The Historical Profession in England since the Renaissance* (London: Weidenfeld and Nicolson, 1983).
6. Jack H. Hexter, Review of Mary Beard, *Woman as Force in History*, in *New York Times Book Review*, March 17, 1946, 5. I am grateful to Judith Zinsser for this reference.
7. See especially Susan McClary, *Feminine Endings: Music, Gender, and Sexuality* (Minneapolis: University of Minnesota Press, 1991); and Susan McClary, "Narrative Agendas in 'Absolute' Music: Identity and Difference in Brahms's Third Symphony," *Musicology and Difference: Gender and Sexuality in Musical Scholarship,* ed. Ruth A. Solie (Berkeley: University of California, 1993), 326–344.
8. Londa Schiebinger, *The Mind Has No Sex: Women in the Origins of Modern Science* (Cambridge, Mass.: Harvard University Press, 1989); idem, *Nature's Body: Gender in the Making of Modern Science* (Boston: Beacon, 1993).
9. Michèle Le Doeuff, *The Philosophical Imaginary*, trans. Colin Gordon (London: Athlone, 1989); and idem, *Hipparchia's Choice: An Essay Concerning Women, Philosophy, etc.*, trans. Trista Selous (Oxford: Blackwell, 1991).
10. Andrea Nye, *Words of Power: A Feminist Reading of the History of Logic* (New York: Routledge, 1990).

11. Jean-Paul Sartre, *L'être et le néant* (Paris: Gallimard, 1943), 700–701, quoted in Le Doeuff, *Hipparchia's Choice,* 80–81.

12. Maurice Merleau-Ponty, *The Visible and the Invisible,* ed. Claude Lefort, trans. Alphonso Lingis (Evanston, Ill.: Northwestern University Press, 1968), 52–56, 69–71, 193.

13. Deirdre Bair, *Simone de Beauvoir: A Biography* (New York: Summit, 1990), passim. Bair's biography of de Beauvoir in no way glorifies her but rather shows her decline into a pathetic slavery to Sartre, during which she wrote for him, found him sexual partners, and procured him illegal drugs. Le Doeuff makes many similar observations. These points are reevaluated in Toril Moi, *Simone de Beauvoir: The Making of an Intellectual Woman* (Oxford: Blackwell, 1994).

14. Because this book began as a study of women exclusively, I have gathered information on hundreds of women whose names do not appear here. I would be happy to share it with anyone interested in pursuing these historians.

15. Neither Philippa Levine nor Rosemary Jann considers women. See their excellent studies of amateurism and antiquarianism: Philippa Levine, *The Amateur and the Professional: Antiquarians, Historians and Archeologists in Victorian England, 1838–1886* (Cambridge: Cambridge University Press, 1986); and Rosemary Jann, *The Art and Science of Victorian History* (Columbus: Ohio State University Press, 1985).

16. These questions are complicated by etymology. The term "amateur" in English gained its greatest currency beginning in the early nineteenth century, when the "amateur" was a connoisseur of something (say, the pineapple) and thus very knowledgeable about it or was someone who practiced one of the arts (though not for money), while the professional had corporate rather than national interests, or a religious rather than a lay identity. As the term developed, the professional became someone who did not write for the general public, while the amateur woman often depended on the public for her livelihood.

17. The interpretation of trauma informing this analysis comes from Laura S. Brown, "Not Outside the Range: One Feminist Perspective on Psychic Trauma," *American Imago,* 48 (1991), 119–133. According to Brown, psychiatrists have claimed that women cannot be classified as traumatized because incest, rape, and general abuse of women is so much a part of everyday life that they should be used to it. Men's experiences (of war, for example) are "outside the range" of normal experience and thus "real," "legitimate" trauma. Brown locates racial minorities and women as being inside the range of trauma because of their consistent abuse in the society. On some early nineteenth-century historical/ethnographic writings by African-American men, see Mia Bay, *The White Image in the Black Mind, 1830–1925* (New York: Oxford University Press, forthcoming), ch. 2. These works are sparse, their authors ephemeral and hard to trace.

18. For examples of the way in which trauma is connected with history and historical events, see Michael S. Roth, *The Ironist's Cage: Memory, Trauma, and the Con-*

struction of History (New York: Columbia University Press, 1995); Dominick LaCapra, *Representing the Holocaust: History, Memory, Trauma* (Ithaca: Cornell University Press, 1994).

19. Hayden White, *The Content of the Form: Narrative Discourse and Historical Representation* (Baltimore: Johns Hopkins University Press, 1987), 89.

20. LaCapra, *Representing the Holocaust,* esp. 1–17.

21. The discussion draws from Peter Stallybrass and Allon White, *The Politics and Poetics of Transgression* (Ithaca: Cornell University Press, 1986).

22. Elaine Scarry, *The Body in Pain* (New York: Oxford University Press, 1985); Walter Ong, *Fighting for Life: Contest, Sexuality, and Consciousness* (Ithaca: Cornell University Press, 1981).

23. For a sample of work addressing new ideas of evidence and objectivity in the sciences and other disciplines, see Allan Megill, ed., *Rethinking Objectivity* (Durham, N.C.: Duke University Press, 1994). Monographic studies include Lorraine Daston, *Classical Probability in the Enlightenment* (Princeton: Princeton University Press, 1988); Steven Shapin, *The Social History of Truth: Civility and Science in Seventeenth Century England* (Chicago: University of Chicago Press, 1994); Bruno Latour, *Laboratory Life: The Construction of Scientific Facts* (Princeton: Princeton University Press, 1986); Bruno Latour, *The Pasteurization of France,* trans. Alan Sheridan (Cambridge, Mass.: Harvard University Press, 1988); Elizabeth Lunbeck, *The Psychiatric Persuasion: Knowledge, Gender, and Power in Modern America* (Princeton: Princeton University Press, 1994); Andrew Pickering, *The Mangle of Practice: Time, Agency, and Science* (Chicago: University of Chicago Press, 1995). These studies were antedated by the work of Gaston Bachelard, Robert Merton, and, more recently, Mary Hesse.

24. Mary Hesse, *Revolutions and Reconstructions in the Philosophy of Science* (Bloomington: Indiana University Press, 1980), esp. xvi–xx, 111–124.

25. Rita Felski, *The Gender of Modernity* (Cambridge, Mass.: Harvard University Press, 1995); Marianne DeKoven, *Rich and Strange: Gender, History, Modernism* (Princeton: Princeton University Press, 1991).

26. Natalie Zemon Davis, "History's Two Bodies," *American Historical Review,* 93 (February 1988), 1–30, is one model.

1 THE NARCOTIC ROAD TO THE PAST

1. See Joan Wallach Scott, "Women in History: The Modern Period," *Past and Present,* 101 (1983), 141–157.

2. In particular, see Simone Balayé, *Madame de Staël: Lumières et liberté* (Paris: Klincksieck, 1979); Simone Balayé, *Madame de Staël: Ecrire, lutter, vivre* (Geneva: Librairie Droz, 1994); Gretchen Rous Besser, *Germaine de Staël Revisited* (New York: Twayne, 1994); Madelyn Gutwirth, Avriel Goldberger, and Karyna Szmurlo, eds., *Germaine de Staël: Crossing the Borders* (New Brunswick, N.J.:

Rutgers University Press, 1991); John C. Isbell, *The Birth of European Romanticism: Truth and Propaganda in Staël's "De l'Allemagne," 1810–1813* (Cambridge: Cambridge University Press, 1994). For contrast, see Margaret Higonnet, "Suicide," in Gutwirth et al., *Germaine de Staël,* 69–81.

3. See, for instance, Christopher Herold, *Mistress to an Age: A Life of Madame de Staël* (Indianapolis: Charter Books, 1958), which focuses on sexual promiscuity.

4. The literature on the idea of genius is enormous: for a summary, see the articles on genius by Giorgio Tonelli, Rudolf Wittkower, and Edward Lowinsky in Philip Wiener, ed., *Dictionary of the History of Ideas,* 5 vols. (New York: Charles Scribner's Sons, 1973) II, 293–326. For the French context, see Kineret S. Jaffe, "The Concept of Genius: Its Changing Role in Eighteenth-Century French Aesthetics," *Journal of the History of Ideas,* 41 (1980), 579–599; and Nedd Willard, *Le génie et la folie au dix-huitième siècle* (Paris: Presses Universitaires de France, 1963). For the German context, which was also part of Germaine de Staël's intellectual horizons, see Wendelin Schmidt-Dengler, *Genius: Zur Wirkungsgeschichte antiker Mythologeme in der Goethezeit* (Munich: C. H. Becker, 1978). For a more contemporary exploration of genius' modern meanings, see John Briggs, *Fire in the Crucible: The Alchemy of Creative Genius* (New York: St. Martin's, 1988).

5. Nineteenth-century biographies of de Staël by women were legion, written in almost all Western countries. In addition, *Corinne* provided a model for numerous fictional writings, beginning with Anna Jameson's *Diary of an Ennuyée* (London: H. Colburn, 1822).

6. On this point, see Michael Polowetsky, *A Bond Never Broken: The Relations between Napoleon and the Authors of France* (Rutherford, N.J.: Fairleigh Dickinson University Press, 1993). For a running account of Napoleon's increasing hatred and persecution of de Staël, see Ghislain de Diesbach, *Madame de Staël* (Paris: Perrin, 1983); or Paul Gautier, *Madame de Staël et Napoléon* (Paris: Plon, 1903).

7. Lydia Maria Child, *The History of the Condition of Women in Various Ages and Nations,* 2 vols. (Boston, J. Allen: 1835), II, 157.

8. Ellen Moers, *Literary Women* (Garden City, N.Y.: Anchor Books, 1977), 263.

9. For a critique of women professionals' attachment to the Enlightenment project, see Jane Flax, *Thinking Fragments: Psychoanalysis, Feminism and Postmodernism in the Contemporary West* (Berkeley: University of California Press, 1990); and idem, *Disputed Subjects: Essays on Psychoanalysis, Politics and Philosophy* (London: Routledge, 1993).

10. See, for example, Nina Baym, *American Women Writers and the Work of History* (New Brunswick, N.J.: Rutgers University Press, 1995). This interpretation is based on the concept of "republican motherhood," as historians of women (Linda Kerber, Claire Moses, and Karen Offen, for example) in the 1980s came to describe it for France and the United States of the postrevolutionary period. The idea of republican motherhood is then seen as the bias in and inspiration for women historians' writing.

11. See especially Michel Foucault, *The Birth of the Clinic: An Archaeology of Medical Perception*, trans. Alan Sheridan (New York: Pantheon, 1973); Michel Foucault, *Discipline and Punish: The Birth of the Prison*, trans. Alan Sheridan (New York: Vintage, 1979).

12. For the varied German training of historians prior to professionalization, see Horst Walter Blanke and Dirk Fleischer, *Theoretiker der deutschen Aufklärungshistorie* (Stuttgart: Frommann-Holzboog, 1990), II, 771–811; for France, Donald R. Kelley, *Historians and the Law in Post Revolutionary France* (Princeton: Princeton University Press, 1984); for the United States, John Higham, *History: Professional Scholarship in the United States* (Baltimore: Johns Hopkins University Press, 1965), 6–25, 150–157. On scholarly work at Göttingen in the eighteenth century, see, for instance, Hans Erich Vödeker, Georg G. Iggers, Jonathan B. Knudsen, and Peter H. Reill, eds., *Aufklärung und Geschichte: Studien zur deutschen Geschichtswissenschaft im 18. Jahrhundert* (Göttingen: Max-Planck-Institut für Geschichte, 1986); and for early modern French research, one example is Blandine Barret-Kriegel, *Les historiens et la monarchie*, 4 vols. (Paris: Presses Universitaires de France, 1988).

13. The following works as a whole give some idea of the range of historical production in the West during de Staël's lifetime: June K. Burton, *Napoleon and Clio: Historical Writing, Teaching, and Thinking during the First Empire* (Durham, N.C.: Duke University Press, 1979); Charles Rearick, *Beyond the Enlightenment: Historians and Folklore in Nineteenth-Century France* (Bloomington: University of Indiana Press, 1974); Roland Mortier, *La poétique des ruines en France: Ses origines, ses variations, de la Renaissance à Victor Hugo* (Geneva: Droz, 1974); Stanley Mellon, *The Political Uses of History: A Study of Historians in the French Restoration* (Stanford: Stanford University Press, 1958); Laurence Goldstein, *Ruins and Empire: The Evolution of a Theme in Augustan and Romantic Literature* (Pittsburgh: University of Pittsburgh Press, 1977); Anne F. Janowitz, *England's Ruins: Poetic Purpose and the National Landscape* (Cambridge: Blackwell, 1990); Peter H. Reill, *The German Enlightenment and the Rise of Historicism* (Berkeley: University of California Press, 1975); Karl Hammer and Jürgen Voss, eds., *Historische Forschung im 18. Jahrhundert* (Bonn: Rohrscheid, 1976); Edward Fueter, *Geschichte der neueren Historiographie* (Berlin: R. Oldenberg, 1936); Theodore Ziolkowski, *German Romanticism and Its Institutions* (Princeton: Princeton University Press, 1990); Suzanne Marchand, *Down from Olympus: Archeology and Philhellenism in Germany, 1750–1970* (Princeton: Princeton University Press, 1996); Nina Baym, *American Women Writers and the Work of History* (New Brunswick: Rutgers University Press, 1995); Bonnie G. Smith, "Women's Contribution to Modern Historiography in Great Britain, France, and the United States, 1750–1940," *American Historical Review*, 89 (June 1984), 709–732; Michael Warner, *Letters of the Republic* (Cambridge, Mass.: Harvard University Press, 1990).

On the various origins and training of historians in the West prior to professionalization, see Horst Walter Blanke and Dirk Fleischer, *Theoretiker der deutschen Aufklärungshistorie* (Stuttgart: Frommann-Holzboog, 1990), II, 771–811; Donald R. Kelley, *Historians and the Law in Post Revolutionary France* (Princeton: Princeton University Press, 1984); Higham, *History*, 6–25, 150–157. On the beginnings of modern scholarly work in the eighteenth century, see, for instance, Bödeker et al., *Aufklärung und Geschichte;* and Barret-Kriegel, *Les historiens et la monarchie.*

14. Burton, *Napoleon and Clio.*

15. Information on de Staël and drugs can be found in Christopher Herold, *Mistress to an Age: A Life of Madame de Staël* (Indianapolis: Charter Books, 1958); and Diesbach, *Madame de Staël,* which also mentions visits with Humphrey Davy, experimenter with opium and chemist. Memoirs of the period also note her regular, even massive use of drugs.

16. See Marie-Claire Vallois, *Fictions féminines: Mme de Staël et les voix de la Sibylle* (Saratoga, Calif.: Anma Libri, 1987); and Marie-Claire Vallois, "Old Idols, New Subject: Germaine de Staël and Romanticism," in Gutwirth et al., *Germaine de Staël,* 82–100. Vallois cites de Staël as operating in the world of the uncanny—that is, the world of such irreconcilable elements as male and female. Recently historians of World War I have noted the phenomenon of the uncanny in connection with the irreconcilable, unspeakably horrible trauma of wartime loss, disfigurement, and hysteria which manifests itself in the appearance of ghosts and other apparitions. See, for example, Paul Fussell, *The Great War and Modern Memory* (London: Oxford University Press, 1975); Susan K. Kent, *Making Peace: The Reconstruction of Gender in Interwar Britain* (Princeton: Princeton University Press, 1993), ch. 5; Robert Whalen, *Bitter Wounds: German Victims of the Great War, 1914–1939* (Ithaca: Cornell University Press, 1984); Antoine Prost, *In the Wake of War: "Les Anciens Combattants" and French Society, 1914–1939,* trans. Helen McPhail (Providence, R.I.: Berg, 1992); Joanna Bourke, *Dismembering the Male: Men's Bodies, Britain and the Great War* (Chicago: University of Chicago Press, 1996). For a thorough theorizing of the uncanny and post–World War I trauma, see Roxanne Panchasi, "Reconstructions: Prosthetics and the Rehabilitation of the Male Body in World War I France," *Differences,* 7 (Fall 1995), 109–140.

17. Further citations from Germaine de Staël, *Corinne, or Italy,* trans. Avriel H. Goldberger (New Brunswick: Rutgers University Press, 1987), will appear simply with page numbers following the quotation.

18. Quoted in Molly Lefebure, "Consolations in Opium: The Expanding Universe of Coleridge, Humphrey Davy and 'The Recluse,'" *Wordsworth Circle,* 17, no. 2 (Spring 1986), 58.

19. Ibid., 54.

20. The most helpful general works on opium use in this period are Althea Hayter, *Opium and the Romantic Imagination* (Berkeley: University of California Press, 1970); and Virginia Berridge, *Opium and the People: Opiate Use in Nineteenth-Century England* (New Haven: Yale University Press, 1987). See, additionally, Jordan

Goodman, "Excitantia: Or, How Enlightenment Europe Took to Soft Drugs," in Jordan Goodman et al., eds., *Consuming Habits: Drugs in History and Anthropology* (London: Routledge, 1995), 126–147. This article is also influenced by Laurence A. Rickels, *Aberrations of Mourning: Writing on German Crypts* (Detroit: Wayne State University Press, 1988); and Avital Ronell, *Crack Wars: Literature, Addiction, Mania* (Lincoln: University of Nebraska Press, 1992).

21. See especially Dena Goodman, *The Republic of Letters: A Cultural History of the French Enlightenment* (Ithaca: Cornell University Press, 1994); Daniel Gordon, *Citizens without Sovereignty: Equality and Sociability in French Thought, 1670–1789* (Princeton: Princeton University Press, 1994); and Adam Potkay, *The Fate of Eloquence in the Age of Hume* (Ithaca: Cornell University Press, 1994).

22. Germaine de Staël, *De la littérature* (Paris: Flammarion, 1991), I, 46.

23. Humphrey Davy, Notebook 20a, quoted in Lefebure, "Consolations in Opium," 54.

24. On republican rhetoric and values, especially that of transparency and lack of theatricality, see, among many works: Jean Starobinski, *Jean-Jacques Rousseau: La transparence et l'obstacle* (Paris: Gallimard, 1975); J. G. A. Pocock, *The Machiavellian Moment: Florentine Political Thought and the Atlantic Republican Tradition* (Princeton: Princeton University Press, 1975); Lynn Hunt, *Politics, Culture, and Class in the French Revolution* (Berkeley: University of California Press, 1984). De Staël's frequent production of and participation in theatrical pieces in her home is well known.

25. On the host of associations in *Corinne*, see, for the particular example of Sappho, Joan DeJean, *Fictions of Sappho, 1546–1937* (Chicago: University of Chicago Press, 1989); and idem, "Portrait of the Artist as Sappho," in Gutwirth et al., *Germaine de Staël*, 122–140.

26. Germaine de Staël, *Oeuvres complètes* (Paris: Treuttel et Würtz, 1820), XIII, 110; XII, 354; XIII, 136; XII, 347.

27. Martin Heidegger, *Being and Time*, trans. John Macquarrie and Edward Robinson (New York: Harper, 1962), 195.

28. Benedict Anderson's *Imagined Communities* (New York: Verso, 1991), also places the modern nation in the realm of the imaginary or transparent by focusing on readership. While this interpretation has been monumentally important in a variety of ways, there remained theories of the nation, like theories of citizenship (in this case de Staël's), that were embodied.

29. For historical and bibliographic background to hermeneutical thought see Robert S. Leventhal, *The Disciplines of Interpretation: Lessing, Herder, Schlegel, and Hermeneutics in Germany, 1750–1800* (Berlin: Walter de Gruyter, 1994). Joachim Wach, *Das Verstehen: Grundzüge einer Geschichte der hermeneutischen Theorie im 19. Jahrhundert* (Tübingen: Mohr, 1926–1933); Hans-Georg Gadamer and Gottfried Boehm, eds., *Seminar: Philosophische Hermeneutik* (Frankfurt: Suhrkamp, 1976); Kurt Mueller-Zollmer, ed., *The Hermeneutics Reader* (Oxford: Blackwell, 1986); Gayle L. Orniston and Alan E. Schrift, eds., *The Hermeneutic Tradition from Ast*

to Ricoeur (Albany: State University of New York Press, 1990); Manfred Frank, *Das individuelle Allgemeine: Textstrukturierung und Textinterpretation nach Schleiermacher* (Frankfurt: Suhrkamp, 1985).

30. For the sake of clarity, this essay omits the struggle for generic definition that occurred in de Staël's writing and that intensified the hermeneutical quest in her work. For some background on the topic of literary indeterminacy, see Thomas DiPiero, *Dangerous Truths and Criminal Passions: The Evolution of the French Novel, 1569–1871* (Stanford: Stanford University Press, 1992)); Suzanne Gearhart, *The Open Boundary of History and Fiction* (Princeton: Princeton University Press, 1984); Lionel Gossman, *Between History and Literature* (Cambridge, Mass.: Harvard University Press, 1990). De Staël's writing, as well as the increasing numbers of women who took to producing history during the age of revolution in particular, shows an instability or contest over any gendering of that still-indeterminate entity called history. For a different opinion on this point, however, see Carla Hesse, "Revolutionary Histories: The Literary Politics of Louise de Keralio (1758–1822)," in Barbara B. Diefendorf and Carla Hesse, eds., *Culture and Identity in Early Modern Europe, 1500–1800: Essays in Honor of Natalie Zemon Davis* (Ann Arbor: University of Michigan Press, 1993), 250.

31. On the concept of abjection, see Julia Kristeva, *Powers of Horror: An Essay on Abjection,* trans. Leon Roudiez (New York: Columbia University Press, 1982); John Fletcher and Andrew Benjamin, eds., *Abjection, Melancholia and Love: The Work of Julia Kristeva* (New York: Routledge, 1990). Judith Butler's *Bodies that Matter: On the Discursive Limits of Sex* (New York: Routledge, 1993), connects the idea of abjection to political exclusion. On abjection in *Corinne* put to different use, see Nancy Miller, *Subject to Change: Reading Feminist Writing* (New York: Columbia University Press, 1988), 182–191. Miller focuses on analyzing the gender of the gaze and its emplotment in rejection of Corinne's abjection.

32. On issues of trauma and mourning in relation variously to memory, writing, and drugs, see Sylvie Le Poulichet, *Toxicomanies et psychanalyse: Les narcoses du désir* (Paris: Presses Universitaires de France, 1987); Rickels, *Aberrations of Mourning;* Ronell, *Crack Wars;* Ian Hacking, *Rewriting the Soul: Multiple Personality and the Sciences of Memory* (Princeton: Princeton University Press, 1995).

33. For a discussion of poetic evocations and resonance versus science, see Gaston Bachelard, *Le poétique de l'espace* (Paris: Presses Universitaires de France, 1957).

34. For an important (and delightful) rendering of Necker's serious attentions to her salon, which would make it the prototypical site of the virtuous republic of letters, see Goodman, *Republic of Letters,* 79–84.

35. On the philosophical dimensions of the controversy over female literacy, see Geneviève Fraisse, *Reason's Muse: Sexual Difference and the Birth of Democracy,* trans. Jane Marie Todd (Chicago: University of Chicago Press, 1994).

36. Mary Wollstonecraft, *Maria, or the Wrongs of Woman* (New York: Norton, 1975), 108.

37. For a different interpretation of de Staël as exile, see Linda Orr, "Outspoken Women and the Rightful Daughter of the Revolution: Madame de Staël's *Considérations sur la Révolution Française*," in Sara E. Melzer and Leslie W. Rabine, eds., *Rebel Daughters: Women and the French Revolution* (New York: Oxford University Press, 1992), 128–130.

38. Quoted in Diesbach, *Madame de Staël*, 349–352.

39. De Staël, *Oeuvres*, XII, 255–256. The connection between the baroque and the foreigner appears in Julia Kristeva, *Strangers to Ourselves*, trans. Leon S. Roudiez (New York: Columbia University Press, 1991).

40. De Staël explicitly compared women and especially women intellectuals to "the Pariahs of India" in *De la littérature*, II, 158–167. See Flora Tristan, *Peregrinations of a Pariah, 1833–1834* (Boston: Beacon, 1987), originally published as *Les pérégrinations d'une pariah*, 2 vols. (Paris: A. Bertrand, 1838).

41. For one important, early imitation see Jameson, *Diary of an Ennuyée*, in which the heroine travels by coach through Italy, expounding on works of art and eventually dying.

42. For the advantages to thinking in terms of multiplicity when presenting or conceptualizing a self—one's own as well as an other's—see Judith Butler, *Gender Trouble: Feminism and the Subversion of Identity* (New York: Routledge, 1990); Diana Tietjens Meyers, *Subjection and Subjectivity: Psychoanalytic Feminism and Moral Philosophy* (New York: Routledge, 1994); Diana Tietjens Meyers, "The Family Romance: A Fin-de-Siècle Tragedy," in Hilde Lindemann Nelson, ed., *Feminism and Families* (New York: Routledge, 1997); and Naomi Scheman, *Engenderings: Constructions of Knowledge, Authority, and Privilege* (New York: Routledge, 1993). Meyers, in "The Family Romance," cautions that the "multiple self" or "multiplicity" espoused by philosophers, like other figurations, needs to be approached cautiously because of its current popularity in diagnoses of "multiple personality disorder," again associated with women.

43. De Staël, *De la littérature*, II, 150.

44. As if nothing had changed in twenty years, P. N. Furbank writes of *Corinne* that it "is marvelously, is inexpressibly, absurd . . . Her novels simply won't do." Furbank, "Call Me Madame," *New York Review of Books*, December 21, 1995, 64.

45. Homi K. Bhabha, *The Location of Culture* (London: Routledge, 1994), 123–138.

46. Hans-Georg Gadamer, *Truth and Method* (New York: Crossroad, 1982), 159.

47. For a brief summary of this point see Jean Grondin, *Sources of Hermeneutics* (Albany: State University of New York Press, 1995); and for a fuller account of universal misunderstanding of genius in de Staël's day, see the chapter on Schleiermacher in Jean Grondin, *Introduction to Philosophical Hermeneutics* (New Haven: Yale University Press, 1994).

48. "Mirza," trans. Françoise Massardier-Kenney, in Doris Y. Kadish and Françoise Massardier-Kenney, eds., *Translating Slavery: Gender and Sex in French Women's Writing, 1783–1823* (Kent, Ohio: Kent State University Press, 1994), 146–156.

49. I take my cue in this area from many sources, including the dialogue between Sharon Bell and Françoise Massardier-Kenney, "Black on White: Translation, Race, Class, and Power," in Kadish and Massardier-Kenney, *Translating Slavery*, 168–184; and Laura E. Donaldson, *Decolonizing Feminisms* (London: Routledge, 1993).

2 THE BIRTH OF THE AMATEUR

1. Neither the study by Rosemary Jann nor the one by Philippa Levine treats women. See Jann, *The Art and Science of Victorian History* (Columbus: Ohio State University Press, 1985); and Levine, *The Amateur and the Professional: Antiquarians, Historians, and Archeologists in Victorian England, 1838–1886* (Cambridge: Cambridge University Press, 1986). Charles Carbonell does give a brief description of some amateurs in the nineteenth century, in *Histoire et historiens: Une mutation idéologique des historiens français, 1865–1885* (Toulouse: Privat, 1976). Because this is an interpretive essay, I have had to omit most of the amateur women historians of this period, but I would be happy to communicate information about them with interested scholars.

2. See in particular Nina Baym, *American Women Writers and the Work of History, 1790–1860* (New Brunswick, N.J.: Rutgers University Press, 1995); Susan P. Conrad, *Perish the Thought: Intellectual Women in Romantic America, 1830–1860* (New York: Oxford University Press, 1976). Dorothy Mermin, *Godiva's Ride: Women of Letters in England, 1830–1880,* surveys a wide range of women's nonfiction writing. Mary Kelley, "Reading Women / Women Reading: The Making of Learned Women in Antebellum America," *Journal of American History,* 83 (September 1996), 401–424, emphasizes intellectual work as itself identity producing, an interpretation closer to the one offered here.

3. In addition to the works by Kent, Ronell, Rickels, and others cited in the previous chapter, this study of amateurism is explicitly informed by *American Imago,* 48, nos. 1 and 3, ed. Cathy Caruth (1991). See especially Laura Brown, "Not Outside the Range," *American Imago,* 48, no. 1 (1991): 119–133; and Kevin Newmark, "Traumatic Poetry: Charles Baudelaire and the Shock of Laughter," *American Imago,* 48, no. 3 (1991): 515–538. See also Dominick LaCapra, *Representing the Holocaust: History, Theory, Trauma* (Ithaca: Cornell University Press, 1994); and Cathy Caruth, *Unclaimed Experience: Trauma, Narrative, and History* (Baltimore: Johns Hopkins University Press, 1995).

4. See, for instance, Anna Clark, *Women's Silence, Men's Violence: Sexual Assault in England, 1770–1845* (London: Pandora, 1987); Sharon Block, "Coerced Sex in British North America, 1700–1820," Diss., Princeton University, 1995; Elizabeth Pleck, *Domestic Tyranny: The Making of American Social Policy against Family Violence, from Colonial Times to the Present* (New York: Oxford, 1987); Paula Giddings, *When and Where I Enter: The Impact of Black Women on Race and Sex*

(New York: Morrow, 1984); A. James Hammerton, *Cruelty and Companionship: Conflict in Nineteenth-Century Married Life* (London: Routledge, 1992). For the later nineteenth and early twentieth centuries see, for example, Linda Gordon, *Heroes of Their Own Lives: The Politics and History of Family Violence, Boston, 1880–1960* (New York: 1988); Karen Dubinsky, *Improper Advances: Rape and Heterosexual Conflict in Ontario, 1880–1929* (Chicago: University of Chicago Press, 1993); Ellen Ross, *Love and Toil: Motherhood in Outcast London, 1870–1918* (New York: Oxford University Press, 1993), 56–127.

Women also participated in some aspects of violence during these years. See, for instance, Carola Lipp, ed., *Schimpfende Weiber und patriotische Jungfrauen: Frauen im Vormärz und in der Revolution, 1848–1849* (Moos, Germany: Elster, 1986); Janet Polasky, "Women in Revolutionary Belgium: From Stone Throwers to Hearth Tenders," *History Workshop*, 21 (Spring 1986), 87–112; Darline Gay Levy, Harriet B. Applewhite, and Mary D. Johnson, eds., *Women in Revolutionary Paris, 1789–1795* (Urbana: University of Illinois Press, 1979); Barbara Clark Smith, "Food Rioters and the American Revolution," *William and Mary Quarterly*, 51 (January 1994): 3–38.

5. Victorine de Chastenay, *Mémoires de Madame de Chastenay, 1771–1815*, ed. Alphonse Roserot, 2 vols. (Paris: Plon, 1896), I, 128; Mercy Otis Warren, *History of the Rise, Progress and Termination of the American Revolution*, ed. Lester H. Cohen, 2 vols. (Indianapolis: Liberty, 1988; orig. pub. 1805), passim; Hannah Adams, *A Memoir of Miss Hannah Adams, Written by Herself, with Additional Notes by a Friend* (Boston: 1832), 22 (on her poverty in general, see 17–22).

6. Chastenay, *Mémoires*, II, 545. See also Bibliothèque Nationale, NaFr 11771–2: "Mémoires de Victorine de Chastenay." On Chastenay, see G. Laperouse, *Mme la comtesse de Chastenay* (Châtillon-sur-Seine, 1855).

7. Warren, *History*, I, xx–xxi. On Mercy Otis Warren, see Jeffrey H. Richards, *Mercy Otis Warren* (Boston: Twayne, 1995); Lester H. Cohen, "Mercy Otis Warren: The Politics of Language and the Aesthetics of Self," *American Quarterly*, 35 (Winter 1983), 481–498; Frederick Hollister Campbell, "Mrs. Warren's Revolution," Diss., University of Colorado at Boulder, 1993; Carolann O'Malley Davis, "Wherein Lies Personal Identity," Diss., University of New Hampshire, 1995; Pauline E. Schloesser, "A Feminist Interpretation of the American Founding," Diss., Indiana University, 1994; Theresa Freda Nicolay, "Transforming the Traditional," Diss., University of Rochester, 1993; Katherine Anthony, *First Lady of the Revolution: The Life of Mercy Otis Warren* (Garden City, N.Y.: Doubleday, 1958); Alice Brown, *Mercy Warren* (New York: Scribner's, 1896); Lester Cohen, "Explaining the Revolution: Ideology and Ethics in Mercy Otis Warren's Historical Theory," *William and Mary Quarterly*, 37 (1980), 200–218; Lawrence Friedman and Arthur H. Shefler, "Mercy Otis Warren and the Politics of Historical Nationalism," *New England Quarterly*, 47 (1975), 194–215; Maud Hutcheson, "Mercy Warren, 1728–1814," *William and Mary Quarterly*, 10 (1953), 378–402; Judith Markowitz,

"Radical and Feminist: Mercy Otis Warren and the Historiographers," *Peace and Change*, 4 (1977), 10–21; William R. Smith, *History as Argument: Three Patriot Historians of the American Revolution* (The Hague: Mouton, 1966); Joan Hoff-Wilson and Sharon Bollinger, "Mercy Otis Warren: Playwright, Poet, and Historian of the American Revolution," in J. R. Brink, ed., *Female Scholars: A Tradition of Learned Women before 1800* (St. Albans, Vt.: Eden Press, 1980), 161–182.

8. On Schopenhauer, see Ludger Lütkehaus, ed., *Die Schopenhauers: Der Familien-Briefwechsel von Adele, Arthur, Heinrich Floris und Johanna Schopenhauer* (Zurich: Haffmans, 1991); Gertrud Dworetzki, *Johanna Schopenhauer: Ein Charakterbild aus Goethes Zeiten* (Dusseldorf: Droste, 1987); Rüdiger Safranski, *Schopenhauer: The Wild Years of Philosophy*, trans. Ewald Osers (Cambridge, Mass.: Harvard University Press, 1990), 7–83 and passim; Laura Frost, *Johanna Schopenhauer: Ein Frauenleben* (Berlin: Schwetschke, 1905). See Johanna Schopenhauer, *Johann van Eyck und seine Nachfolger* (Frankfurt: H. Wilmans, 1822); idem, *Jugendlieben und Wanderbilder* (Braunschweig: G. Westermann, 1839); idem, *Ausflucht an den Rhein und dessen nächsten Umgebungen im Sommer des ersten friedlichen Jahres* (Leipzig: F. A. Brockhaus, 1818); idem, *Reise durch das südliche Frankreich bis Chamouny* (Vienna: Bay Kaulfuss und Krammer, 1836); and idem, *Reise durch England und Schottland* (Leipzig: F. A. Brockhaus, 1817); as well as her novels, historical novels, and collections of letters.

9. On Helen Maria Williams, see Gary Kelly, *Women, Writing, and Revolution, 1790–1827* (Oxford: Clarendon Press, 1993); Helen Maria Williams, *Letters from France*, ed. Janet Todd, 2 vols. (Delmar, N.Y.: Scholars' Facsimiles and Reprints, 1975; orig. pub. 1797); Helen Maria Williams, *Letters Written in France, 1790* (Oxford: Woodstock Books, 1989; orig. pub. 1792).

10. See Louise Keralio, *Histoire d'Elisabeth, reine d'Angleterre*, 4 vols. (Paris: Lagrange, 1786–1788); idem, ed., *Collection des meilleurs ouvrages français composés par des femmes*, 14 vols. (Paris, 1786–1788); idem, ed., *Journal d'Etat et du Citoyen* (newspaper, 1789); idem, ed., *Mercure National et Etranger* (newspaper, 1791); and idem, *Crimes des reines de France* (Paris: Lemoine, 1792). She also translated books by John Carr, Riguccio Galluzzi, John Howard, John Gregory, and Henry Swinburne. On François Robert, see L. Antheunis, *Le Conventionnel belge François Robert, 1763–1826, et sa femme Louise de Keralio, 1758–1822* (Wetleren: Bracke, 1955); Isabelle Bourdin, *Les sociétés populaires* (Paris: Recueil Sirey, 1937); Jules Michelet, *Women of the French Revolution* (Philadelphia: Baird, 1855); and Jack R. Censer, *Prelude to Power: The Parisian Radical Press, 1789–1791* (Baltimore: Johns Hopkins University Press, 1976). See also Carla Hesse, "Revolutionary Histories: The Literary Politics of Louise de Keralio (1758–1822)," in Diefendorf and Hesse, *Culture and Identity*, 250.

11. Beth Archer Brombert, *Cristina: Portraits of a Princess* (Chicago: University of Chicago Press, 1977); H. Remsen Whitehouse, *A Revolutionary Princess: Christina Belgiojoso-Trivulzo, Her Life and Times* (London: T. L. Unwin, 1906). Belgiojoso's

work includes: *Il 1848 a Milano e a Venezia, con uno scritto sulla condizione delle donne* (Milan: Feltrinelli, 1977; orig. pub. 1849); "On the Present Condition of Women and Their Future," *Nuova Antologica* 1 (January 1866); *Asie mineure et Syrie: Souvenirs de voyage* (Paris: Michel Lévy, 1858); *Essai sur la formation du dogme catholique,* 4 vols. (Paris: Jules Renouard, 1842–1843); *Histoire de la maison de Savoie* (Paris: Michel Lévy, 1860); *Osservazioni sullo stato attuale dell'Italia e sul suo avvenire* (Milan: F. Vallardi, 1868); *Premières notions de l'histoire à l'usage de l'enfance: Histoire romaine* (Paris: J. Renouard, 1850); *Scènes de la vie turque* (Paris: Michel Lévy, 1858); *Souvenirs dans l'exil* (Paris: Prost, 1850); *Emina: Récits turco-asiatiques* (Leipzig: W. Gerhard, 1856). She also translated Giovanni Battista Vico's *Scienza nuova* into French: *La science nouvelle* (Paris: J. Renouard, 1844).

12. Margaret Fuller, "*New York Daily Tribune* Dispatches," in Mary Kelley, ed., *The Portable Margaret Fuller* (New York: Penguin, 1994), 463–472.

13. For examples in the case of historic poetry, see Baym, *American Women Writers and the Work of History,* 67–91.

14. Reported in Narcisse Carré, *Nouveau code des femmes,* 2nd ed. (Paris: Roret, 1828), 37.

15. *L'Athénée des dames,* 1 (January 25, 1808), 4.

16. On the protests of Murray and other women in the United States, see Linda K. Kerber, *Women of the Republic: Intellect and Ideology in Revolutionary America* (Chapel Hill: University of North Carolina Press, 1980); Vena Bernadette Field, *Constantia: A Study of the Life and Works of Judith Sargent Murray* (Orono: University of Maine Press, 1931).

17. Agnes Strickland, *Lives of the Queens of England, from the Norman Conquest,* 16 vols. (London: Eveleigh Nash, 1905; orig. pub. 1843), V, 234. On the Stricklands, see Una Pope-Hennessy, *Agnes Strickland, Biographer of the Queens of England* (London: Chatto and Windus, 1940).

18. Mary Berry, "Journal," May 7, 1797, August 24, 1814, and March 16, 1822, in *The Berry Papers,* ed. Lewis Melville, 3 vols. (London: John Lane, 1914), I, 22, and III, 34, 332.

19. Quoted in Charles Capper, *Margaret Fuller: An American Romantic Life,* 2 vols. (New York: Oxford, 1992), I, 287–288.

20. On Jameson, see Clara Thomas, *Love and Work Enough: The Life of Anna Jameson* (Toronto: University of Toronto Press, 1967); Adele Holcomb, "Anna Jameson, 1794–1860: Sacred Art and Social Vision," in Claire Richter Sherman, ed., with Adele M. Holcomb, *Women as Interpreters of the Visual Arts* (Westport, Conn.: Greenwood, 1981), 93–122; Geraldine MacPherson, *Memoirs of the Life of Anna Jameson* (London: Longmans, Green, 1878).

21. Deborah Pickman Clifford, *Crusader for Freedom: A Life of Lydia Maria Child* (Boston: Beacon, 1992), passim.

22. On Allart, see Léon Séché, *Hortense Allart de Méritens dans ses rapports avec Chateaubriand, Béranger, Lammenais, G. Sand, Mme d'Agoult* (Paris: Mercure de

France, 1908); Charles-Augustin Sainte-Beuve, *Correspondance générale,* ed. Jean
Bonnerot, 23 vols. (Paris: Stock, 1935–); Prudence de Saman [Hortense Allart], *Les
enchantements de Prudence* (Paris: Michel Lévy, 1873). On d'Agoult, see Jacques
Vier, *La Comtesse d'Agoult et son temps,* 6 vols. (Paris: Armand Colin, 1955–1963);
and Dominique Desanti, *Daniel* (Paris: Stock, 1980). See also Whitney Walton,
"Writing the 1848 Revolution: Politics, Gender, and Feminism in the Works of
French Women of Letters," *French Historical Studies,* 18 (Fall 1994): 1001–1024.

23. Letter to Hermann Pückler-Muskau, June 5–6, 1832, quoted in Lotte Hamburger
and Joseph Hamburger, *Contemplating Adultery: The Secret Life of a Victorian
Woman* (New York: Fawcett Columbine, 1991), 120.

24. On their marriage, see Lotte Hamburger and Joseph Hamburger, *Troubled Lives:
John and Sarah Austin* (Toronto: University of Toronto Press, 1985). For a
sanitized version, see Janet Ross, *Three Generations of English Women* (London: T.
Fisher Unwin, 1893).

25. Letters to Hermann Pückler-Muskau, March 23–29, 1832, and July 1833, quoted
in Hamburger and Hamburger, *Contemplating Adultery,* 126. J. S. Mill accused
Austin of disloyalty during his love affair with Harriet Taylor and cut her off: see
F. A. Hayek, *John Stuart Mill and Harriet Taylor* (London: 1951).

26. De Saman [Allart], *Les enchantements de Prudence,* 250–251.

27. Letter to Marie d'Agoult, August 10, 1839, Bibliothèque Nationale, NAF 25185,
Fonds Correspondance de Marie d'Agoult, fol. 489.

28. Quoted in M. L. Clarke, *George Grote: A Biography* (London: Athlone, 1962), 66.

29. See Katherine Frank, *Lucie Duff Gordon: A Passage to Egypt* (London: Penguin,
1994), passim.

30. Quoted in Clifford, *Crusader for Freedom,* 2.

31. Letter to George Davis, quoted in Charles Capper, *Margaret Fuller: An American
Romantic Life,* 2 vols. (New York: Oxford, 1992), 289.

32. Daniel Stern [Marie d'Agoult], *Mes souvenirs, 1806—1833,* 3 vols. (Paris: Calmann-Lévy, 1877), I, 126.

33. De Saman [Allart], *Les enchantements de Prudence,* 266.

34. "Hypatia": Letter of Hortense Allart to Marie d'Agoult, undated, Bibliothèque
Nationale NAF 25285, Fond d'Agoult, fol. 152. Letter of Hortense Allart to Marie
d'Agoult, August 28, 1840, ibid., fol. 96.

35. François Buloz to his wife, letter quoted in Marie Pailleron, *François Buloz et ses
amis: Les écrivains du Second Empire* (Paris: Calmann-Lévy, 1919), 31–33.

36. This idea comes from Karen Ordahl Kupperman, "The Names of God," paper
presented at the Rutgers Center for Historical Analysis, October 1996. I would like
to thank Professor Kupperman for permission to use her analysis. On African
name-changing, see Jean Comaroff and John Comaroff, *Of Revelation and Revolution: Christianity, Colonialism, and Consciousness in South Africa* (Chicago: University of Chicago Press, 1991).

37. Journal of Evelina Metcalf, quoted in Capper, *Margaret Fuller*, 235.

38. Sarah Taylor Austin, *Germany from 1760 to 1814; or, Sketches of German Life from the Decay of the Empire to the Expulsion of the French* (London: Longman, 1854), 5.

39. Quoted in Clifford, *Crusader for Freedom*, 226.

40. Stern [d'Agoult], *Mes souvenirs*, I, viii.

41. De Saman [Allart], *Les enchantements de Prudence*, 291.

42. Ross, *Three Generations of English Women*, I, 199. Letter to Harriet Grote, October 25, 1843.

43. Strickland, *Lives of the Queens of England*, I, xiii.

44. On Fortunée Briquet, see Nicole Pellegrin, "Entre local et international—botanique, poésie et 'feminisme': Fortunée Briquet (Niort, 1789–1815)," in *Les apports de l'histoire des provinces et des régions à l'histoire nationale* (Versailles: UFUTA, 1994), 97–110; Louis-Hilaire Briquet, *Histoire de la ville de Niort*, 2 vols. (Niort: Robin, 1832), II, 52–58. Briquet's dictionary was dedicated to "the first consul."

45. Strickland, *Lives of the Queens of England*, I, xxxiv.

46. Julia Kavanagh, *Woman in France during the Eighteenth Century*, 2 vols. (London: Smith, Elder, 1850), passim; Dora d'Istria, *Les femmes en Orient*, 2 vols. (Zurich: Meyer & Zeller, 1859–1860), I, 91ff.

47. Anaïs Bassanville, *Les salons d'autrefois*, 4 vols. (Paris: P. Brunet, 1862–1866), I, 1.

48. Stern [d'Agoult], *Histoire de la révolution de 1848*, 46.

49. Richard Garnett, *Dictionary of National Biography* (London: Smith, Elder, 1892), XXIX, 232.

50. Mary Wollstonecraft, *An Historical and Moral View of the Origin and Progress of the French Revolution and the Effect It Has Produced* (London: J. Johnson, 1794), 161–164.

51. Anna Jameson, "The House of Titian," in Jameson, *Memoirs and Essays* (London: Richard Bentley, 1846), 9, 26, 66.

52. Strickland, *Lives of the Queens of England*, V, 31.

53. On court life, see Genlis' *Dictionnaire critique et raisonné des étiquettes de la cour, des usages des Français, depuis la mort de Louis XIII jusqu'à nos jours*, 2 vols. (Paris: 1818). Her productivity was massive and constant because, especially after the French Revolution, she needed money. See Gabriel Broglie, *Madame de Genlis* (Paris: Perrin, 1985)—the best modern work, although Genlis' memoirs remain a wonderful source.

54. Kavanagh, *Woman in France*, I, 36–63 passim.

55. Bassanville, *Les salons d'autrefois*, I, 32–33.

56. Ibid., 34.

57. Charles Baudelaire, "De l'essence du rire," as analyzed in Newmark, "Traumatic Poetry," 515–538.

58. Shoshana Felman and Dori Laub, *Testimony: Crises of Witnessing in Literature, Psychoanalysis, and History* (New York: London, 1992).

59. Ida Hahn Hahn, *Jenseits der Berge*, 2 vols. (Leipzig: 1840), I, 16. See Elke Frederiksen, "Der Blick in die Ferne: Zur Reiseliteratur von Frauen," in Hiltrud Gnüg and Renate Möhrmann, eds., *Frauen Literatur Geschichte: Schreibende Frauen vom Mittelalter bis zur Gegenwart* (Stuttgart: J. B. Metzler, 1985), 104–122.

60. Clifford, *Crusader for Freedom*, passim. Child's historical novel *Hobomok* (1824) is an example of such a history. Her introduction was to Harriet A. Jacobs, *Incidents in the Life of a Slave Girl* (1861).

61. De Saman [Allart], *Les enchantements de Prudence*, 238–239.

62. Daniel Stern [Marie d'Agoult], *Histoire des commencements de la république aux Pays-Bas 1581–1625* (Paris: Michel Lévy, 1872), 1.

63. Letter from Hortense Allart to Marie d'Agoult, February 12, 1842, in Bibliothèque Nationale, Fonds d'Agoult, Nouvelles acquisitions françaises 25185, fol. 104; letter from Hortense Allart to Marie d'Agoult, April 6, 1851, ibid., fol. 216; Hortense Allart to Marie d'Agoult, [1847], ibid., fol. 160.

64. Daniel Stern [Marie d'Agoult], *Lettres républicaines* (Paris, 1848).

65. Austin, *Germany from 1760 to 1814*, 6–7.

66. Stern [d'Agoult], *Mémoires*, II, 126.

67. Martha Lamb, *History of the City of New York: Its Origin, Rise, and Progress*, 2 vols. (New York: A. S. Barnes, 1877–1880), I, iii. See Susan Elizabeth Lyman, *Lady Historian: Martha J. Lamb* (Northampton, Mass.: Smith College Library, 1969).

68. Julia Kristeva, *Strangers to Ourselves*, trans. Leon Roudiez (New York: Columbia University Press, 1991).

69. Albertine Clément-Hémery, *Histoire des fêtes civiles et religieuses, usages anciens et modernes du département du Nord* (Paris: J. Albert Mercklein, 1834), 5. See idem, *Histoires des fêtes civiles et religieuses, usages anciens et modernes de la Flandre et d'un grand nombre de villes de France* (Avesnes: C. Viroux, 1845); idem, *Notices sur les communautés de femmes établies à Cambrai avant la Révolution* (Cambrai: S. Berthoud, 1826); idem, *Promenades dans l'arrondissement d'Avesnes* (Avesnes: C. Viroux, 1829). She had also written vigorously against proposals to ban women from learning to read and write; see idem, *Les femmes vengées de la sottise d'un philosophe du jour* (Paris: Mme Benoist, 1801). On her experience of the French Revolution, see idem, *Souvenirs de 1793 et 1794* (Cambrai: Lesne-Daloin, 1832).

70. Nina Gelbart, *The King's Midwife* (Berkeley: University of California Press, 1998), has been important in describing reproductive dysfunction and treatments in the eighteenth and early nineteenth centuries.

71. The work of Jill Harsin and others suggests that syphilis in middle-and upper-class women in the nineteenth century was widespread, little discussed, and poorly treated, if treated at all.

72. This is the point of Michel Foucault's book *Birth of the Clinic*.

73. Warren, *History of the Rise, Progress and Termination of the American Revolution*, I, xlii.

74. Laure d'Abrantes, *Souvenirs historiques*, 6 vols., 2nd ed. (Paris: Mame, 1835), I, 417. Note that her warning did not even come in the correct place: it was placed nearer the end than the beginning of the first volume.

75. Stéphanie-Félicité de Genlis, *Mémoires*, 10 vols. (Paris: Ladvocat, 1825)—for example, I, 241, 266, 285, 334, 359; II, 156, 275–276, 373; IV, 343.

76. Valérie de Gasparin, *Voyage d'une ignorante dans le midi de la France et l'Italie*, 2 vols. (Paris: Paulin, 1835), I, 202–203.

77. Mary Berry to the Countess of Hartwicke, January 17, 1814, in *Extracts from the Journals and Correspondence of Miss Berry*, ed. Theresa Lewis, 3 vols. (London: Longmans, Green, 1865), III, 2.

78. Letter from Lord Guildford to Mary Berry, January 27, 1818, ibid., III, 153.

79. Marie-Charlotte-Pauline-Robert de Lézardière's major work is her four-volume *Théorie des lois politiques de la monarchie française* (Paris: Nyon l'aîné et fils, 1791–1792). It was reprinted in 1844 under the sponsorship of Guizot, who had become an enthusiast of her work. For more information on Lézardière, see Elie Carcassonne, *Montesquieu et le problème de la constitution française au XVIIIe siècle* (Paris: Presse Universitaire de France, 1927); idem, ed., *Ecrits inédits de Mlle de Lézardière* (Paris: Presse Universitaire de France, 1927); Octave Demartial, ed., *Essai sur la Théorie des lois politiques de la monarchie française par Mademoiselle de Lézardière* (Poitiers: Dupré, 1864).

80. *Correspondence of John Adams and Mercy Otis Warren* (Boston: Massachusetts Historical Society, 1878).

81. Elizabeth Benger, *Memoirs of Elizabeth Stuart, Queen of Bohemia*, 2 vols. (London: Longman, Hurst, Rees, Orme and Brown, 1825), I, xiii.

82. Warren, *History*, II, 438.

83. On this story, see Harriet A. Jacobs [Linda Brent], *Incidents in the Life of a Slave Girl Written by Herself*, ed. Jean Fagan Yellin, previously edited by Lydia Maria Child (Cambridge, Mass.: Harvard University Press, 1987), xix–xxiv.

84. See, for instance, Alison M. Jaggar, "Love and Knowledge: Emotion in Feminist Epistemology," in Ann Garry and Marilyn Pearsall, eds., *Women, Knowledge, and Reality: Explorations in Feminist Philosophy* (Boston: Unwin Hyman, 1989), 129–156.

85. Natalie Zemon Davis, "Gender and Genre: Women as Historical Writers, 1400–1820," in Patricia Labalme, ed., *Beyond Their Sex: Learned Women of the European Past* (New York: New York University Press), 153–182.

86. Augustin Thierry, *Dix ans d'études historiques*, 6th ed. (Paris: Furne, 1851), 1–3.

87. Gilles Deleuze and Félix Guattari, *Kafka: Toward a Minor Literature*, trans. Dana Polan (Minneapolis: University of Minnesota Press, 1986), although not parallel, has been helpful on this point.

3 WHAT IS A HISTORIAN?

1. Michel Foucault, "Qu'es-ce que c'est l'auteur?" *Bulletin de la Société Française de Philosophie,* 64 (1969), 73–104. Among the recent works on truth in history, see Joyce Appleby, Lynn Hunt, and Margaret Jacob, *Telling the Truth about History* (New York: Norton, 1994); Robert F. Berkhofer, *Beyond the Great Story: History as Text and Discourse* (Cambridge, Mass.: Harvard University Press, 1995); F. A. Ankersmith and Hans Kellner, eds., *A New Philosophy of History* (Chicago: University of Chicago Press, 1995).

2. John Motley to his father, May 13, 1824, in *The Correspondence of John Lothrop Motley,* ed. George William Curtis, 2 vols. (New York: Harper and Brothers, 1889), I, 1.

3. John Motley to his mother, May 31, 1825, ibid., I, 5.

4. John Motley to his brother, July 26, 1829, ibid., I, 8.

5. Thomas Macaulay to Selina Mills Macaulay, February 3, 1813, in *The Letters of Thomas Babington Macaulay,* ed. Thomas Pinney (Cambridge: Cambridge University Press, 1974), I, 14.

6. *A Memoir of the Right Hon. William Edward Hartpole Lecky* (London: Longmans, Green, 1909), 8–9.

7. Ernest Lavisse, *Souvenirs* (Paris: Calmann-Lévy, 1988; orig. pub. 1912), 130.

8. Edgar Quinet, *Histoire de mes idées: Autobiographie,* ed. Simone Bernard-Griffiths (Paris: Flammarion, 1972; orig. pub. 1858), 121.

9. Ibid., 125.

10. John Clive, *Macaulay: The Shaping of the Historian* (New York: Knopf, 1973), 23–39.

11. *Life and Letters of Barthold George Niebuhr,* ed. Dora Hensler, 3 vols. (New York: Harper's, 1854), I, 24.

12. Quinet, *Histoire de mes idées,* 130.

13. *Letters of William Stubbs, Bishop of Oxford, 1821–1901,* ed. William Holden Hutton (London: Archibald Constable, 1904), 13.

14. Friedrich Paulsen, *An Autobiography,* trans. Theodor Lorenz (New York: Columbia University Press, 1938), 113–115, 130–131.

15. Thomas Macaulay to Selina Mills Macaulay, February 12, 1813, in Macaulay, *Letters,* I, 17.

16. Lavisse, *Souvenirs,* 212.

17. Leopold von Ranke, *Sur einigen Lebensgeschichte,* in Ranke, *Sämmtliche Werke,* ed. Alfred Dove (Leipzig: Duncker & Humblot, 1890), LIII–LIV, 21.

18. Eugen Guglia, *Leopold von Rankes Leben und Werke* (Leipzig: Grunow, 1893), 18.

19. Important studies of the changes in philology are Suzanne Marchand, *Down from Olympus: Archeology and Philhellenism in Germany, 1750–1970* (Princeton: Princeton University Press, 1996); Anthony Grafton, "Prolegomena to Friedrich August Wolf," in Grafton, *Defenders of the Text: The Traditions of Scholarship in an Age of Science, 1450–1800* (Cambridge, Mass.: Harvard University Press, 1991), 214–243.

20. Frederick Pollock, *For My Grandson* (London: John Murray, 1933), 20–25, quoted in C. H. S. Fifoot, *Frederic William Maitland: A Life* (Cambridge, Mass.: Harvard University Press, 1971), 21.

21. Lavisse, *Souvenirs*, 216.

22. Paulsen, *Autobiography*, 148.

23. Thomas Macaulay to Selina Mills Macaulay, March 17, 1813, in Macaulay, *Letters*, I, 22.

24. Thomas Macaulay to Zachary Macaulay, March 23, 1813, in Macaulay, *Letters*, I, 23.

25. Lavisse, *Souvenirs*, 216.

26. Paulsen, *Autobiography*, 152–153.

27. Lavisse, *Souvenirs*, 166.

28. William Lecky to Knightley Chetwode, June 16, 1859, in Lecky, *A Memoir*, 17.

29. Lavisse, *Souvenirs*, 166.

30. Stubbs, *Letters*, 10.

31. *Letters of John Richard Green*, ed. Leslie Stephen (London: Macmillan, 1901), 7.

32. Thomas Macaulay to Selina Mills Macaulay, January 31, 1815, in Macaulay, *Letters*, I, 57.

33. William Lecky to Knightley Chetwode, March 1858, in Lecky, *A Memoir*, 13.

34. John Motley to his mother, July 1, 1832, in Motley, *Letters*, I, 20–21.

35. Lavisse, *Souvenirs*, 213.

36. Barthold Niebuhr to his parents, September 7, 1794, in Niebuhr, *Life and Letters*, I, 44.

37. John Green to W. B. Dawkins, July 25, 1859, in *Letters of John Richard Green*, 31.

38. Barthold Niebuhr to Amelia Behrens (his fiancée), August 10, 1798, in Niebuhr, *Life and Letters*, 114–115.

39. Henry Adams, *The Education of Henry Adams* (New York: Random House, 1931; orig. pub. 1907), 41–42.

40. Ibid., 42.

41. Stubbs, *Letters*, 31.

42. Ranke, *Deutsche Geschichte*, quoted in Georg G. Iggers and Konrad von Moltke, "Introduction" to Leopold von Ranke, *The Theory and Practice of History*, ed. Georg G. Iggers and Konrad von Moltke, trans. Wilma A. Iggers and Konrad von Moltke (Indianapolis: Bobbs-Merrill, 1973), xxxix.

43. Lavisse, *Souvenirs*, 265.

44. Allan Megill has recently outlined the concept of objectivity as having cognitive, procedural, dialectical, and other discrete meanings that may even operate at odds with one another. Here I employ several of those meanings, rather than treating objectivity as a unitary concept. See Megill, *Rethinking Objectivity* (Durham, N.C.: Duke University Press, 1994), 1–20.

45. Barthold Niebuhr to his parents, November 15, 1794, in Niebuhr, *Life and Letters*, I, 47.

46. *Hippolyte Taine: Sa vie et sa correspondance,* 4 vols. (Paris: Hachette, 1902–1907), I, 24. This quotation is in the introduction to an unfinished manuscript entitled "La destinée humaine," which Taine wrote as a youth.

47. Hippolyte Taine to Prévost-Paradol, March 2, 1849, ibid., I, 51.

48. Barthold Niebuhr to Dora Hensler, September 6, 1797, in Niebuhr, *Life and Letters,* I, 84.

49. Barthold Niebuhr to his parents, November 7, 1794, ibid., I, 115.

50. The conclusions of this section are based on Walter Ong, *Fighting for Life: Contest, Sexuality, and Consciousness* (Ithaca: Cornell University Press, 1981); Walter Ong, *Literacy and Orality* (New York: Methuen, 1982); Megill, "Introduction," in Megill, ed., *Rethinking Objectivity,* 1–20; Johannes Fabian, "Language, History, and Anthropology," *Philosophy of the Social Sciences,* 1 (1971), 19–47; Martin Heidegger, *Being and Time,* trans. John Macquarrie and Edward Robinson (New York: Harper and Row, 1962); and such studies in the history of science as Mario Biagioli, "Scientific Revolution, Social Bricolage, and Etiquette," in Roy Porter and Mikulás Teich, eds., *The Scientific Revolution in National Context* (Cambridge: Cambridge University Press, 1992), 11–54.

51. John Green to W. B. Dawkins, July 25, 1859, in *Letters of John Richard Green,* 31.

52. R. B. McDowell, *Alice Stopford Green: A Passionate Historian* (Dublin: Allen Figgis, 1967); *Letters of John Richard Green,* passim.

53. Henriette Guizot de Witt, *Monsieur Guizot in Private Life, 1787–1874,* trans. M. C. M. Simpson (Boston: Estes and Lauriat, 1881), 76.

54. Ibid., 117–118.

55. On the comma, see François Guizot to Henriette Guizot, June 3, 1839, ibid., 187–190. On the Hammonds, see Stewart Weaver, *A Marriage in History: The Lives and Work of Barbara and J. H. Hammond* (Stanford: Stanford University Press, 1997). Primary material on Barbara Hammond is in the archives of Lady Margaret Hall, Oxford University. See also Anne Ridler, *A Victorian Postbag* (Oxford: Perpetua, 1988).

56. F. Max Müller, *My Autobiography: A Fragment* (London: Longmans, Green, 1901), 163.

57. For example, Bernard C. Borning, *The Political and Social Thought of Charles A. Beard* (Seattle: University of Washington Press, 1962); Richard Hofstadter, *The Progressive Historians* (New York: Knopf, 1968); Cushing Strout, *The Pragmatic Revolt in America: Carle Becker and Charles Beard* (New Haven: Yale University Press, 1958); Forrest McDonald, "Charles A. Beard," in Marcus Cunliffe and Robin W. Winks, eds., *Pastmasters* (New York: Harper and Row, 1969), 110–141; Howard K. Beale, ed., *Charles A. Beard* (Louisville: University of Kentucky Press, 1954); Marvin C. Swanson, ed., *Charles A. Beard* (Greencastle, Ind.: DePauw University, 1976).

58. Jack Stillinger, *Multiple Authorship and the Myth of Solitary Genius* (New York: Oxford, 1991), calls for a more complex view of authorship that would acknow-

ledge the work of editors, but his book tends to reinforce the view that men were geniuses whose editors and wives made no "substantive" contributions. For instance, although John Stuart Mill calls the "whole mode of thinking" in *On Liberty* his wife's, Stillinger says that scholars should really focus on Harriet's editorial role (ibid., 66) and stop worrying about whether she had ideas—she didn't, he implies. Ultimately, he describes her role as "the middle-aged Mill being spruced up by his wife for attractive autobiographical presentation" (ibid., 182).

Another fascinating recognition of authorial complexity comes in Lionel Gossman, *Towards a Rational Historiography* (Philadelphia: American Philosophical Society, 1989), which sympathetically describes the community of criticism absorbed into scholarly publications. Yet when speaking of a work by Stephen Toulmin and two other authors, Gossman (except for the first mention) cites it exclusively as Toulmin's, even referring to "his" thought, argument, thesis, and so on.

59. Arnaldo Momigliano, *George Grote and the Study of Greek History* (London: H. K. Lewis, 1952), 7.

60. Gabriel Monod to Gaston de Paris, August 6, 1874, in Bibliothèque Nationale, Manuscrit nouvelle acquisition française 24450, Fonds Gaston de Paris, fols. 131–132.

61. Gabriel Monod, *Renan, Taine, Michelet,* 5th ed. (Paris: Calmann-Lévy, n.d.), 178.

62. Victor Duruy, quoted in William R. Keylor, *Academy and Community: The Foundation of the French Historical Profession* (Cambridge, Mass.: Harvard University Press, 1975), 70.

63. Ernest Lavisse, quoted ibid., 70–71.

64. See Bonnie G. Smith, "Gender, Objectivity, and the Rise of Scientific History," in Wolfgang Natter, Theodore Schatzki, and John Paul Jones, eds., *Objectivity and Its Other* (New York: Guilford, 1995).

65. Jules Michelet, *Journal,* ed. Paul Viallaneix (Paris: Gallimard, 1962), II, 32.

66. Ibid., 34.

67. Ibid., 35.

68. Ibid., 37, 47.

69. Ibid., 73.

70. Ibid., 75. Jeanne Calo has attributed Athénaïs Michelet's prolonged virginity to vaginismus (an involuntary contraction of the vagina that made intercourse impossible); Halévy, Monzie, and Jules Michelet's editors (among others) attributed it to willful frigidity; and Michelet himself attributed it to various ailments and physical fragility. See Jeanne Calo, *La création de la femme chez Michelet* (Paris: Nizet, 1975).

71. Ibid., 326.

72. Ibid., 329.

73. Ibid., 330.

74. Ibid., 331.

75. Ibid.

76. Ibid., 127.

77. Ibid., 323.

78. Ibid., 343, 345.

79. On these works and their very important connection to Michelet's evolving conceptualization of historical issues, see Linda Orr, *Jules Michelet: Nature, History, and Language* (Ithaca: Cornell University Press, 1976).

80. Jules Michelet, *Oeuvres complètes,* ed. Paul Viallaneix (Paris: Flammarion, 1986), XVII, 45.

81. Ibid.

82. Ibid., 41.

83. Ibid., 279.

84. Ibid., 280.

85. Will composed in 1872, quoted ibid., 188.

86. Monod, *Renan, Taine, Michelet,* 289.

87. Ibid., 179.

88. Ibid., 178.

89. Keylor, *Academy and Community,* 43–44 and passim.

90. See Smith, "Gender, Objectivity, and the Rise of History."

91. Gabriel Monod, *La vie et la pensée de Jules Michelet, 1798–1852: Cours professé au Collège de France,* 2 vols. (Paris: Champion, 1923). This posthumous publication clearly influenced Arthur Mitzman's engaging psychological interpretation, which ends in 1854 even though Michelet lived two more decades, wrote abundantly, and produced works of natural history that would influence Lucien Febvre and other historians of the *Annales* school.

92. Daniel Halévy, "Le mariage de Michelet," *Revue de Paris,* 15, no. 9 (August 1902), 557–579.

93. Ibid., 577.

94. Daniel Halévy, *Jules Michelet* (Paris: Hachette, 1928), 133.

95. Halévy, "Le mariage de Michelet," 579.

96. Anatole de Monzie, *Les veuves abusives,* 6th ed. (Paris: Grasset, 1936), 105.

97. Ibid., 3.

98. Ibid., 111.

99. Ibid., 114, 118.

100. Ibid., 35.

101. Lucien Febvre, ed., *Michelet* (Geneva: Trois Collines, 1946), 11.

102. Ibid., 82–83.

103. Ibid., 58.

104. Ibid.

105. Ibid., 30.

106. Monod, *La vie et la pensée*, I, 185–187. Febvre surely knew Monod's careful scholarship on Michelet's work—scholarship demonstrating that the *Introduction à l'histoire universelle* had not been "écrits sur les pavés brulants . . . d'un incroyable élan, d'un vol rapide," as Michelet would claim forty years later.

107. Michelet, *Oeuvres complètes*, XVII, 187.

108. The quotes refer specifically to the editors' discussion of *The Bird*. See Michelet, *Oeuvres complètes*, XVII, 187–206.

109. Jules Michelet, *Ecrits de jeunesse*, ed. Paul Viallaneix, 5th ed. (Paris: Gallimard, 1959), 10.

110. Ibid., 17.

111. Ibid., 10.

112. Michelet, *Journal*, I, 31.

113. Those with further interest in the editors' relationship to Michelet might consult the introductions to his *Journal* and other work. Many of them rely on purple writing; the introduction to the *Journal's* second volume, for instance, is a dramatic imagining of Michelet's life with Athénaïs, written in the second person plural: "You leave without your companion. She is out of sorts today, 'a sick person, a wounded one,' like all women. You pass your friend Quinet's door without knocking. You haven't the heart to expound on the future of democracy. The sky is too pure, the light too warm. This September evening is given to you freely. It requires meditation." Michelet, *Journal*, II, xi.

114. Roland Barthes, *Michelet*, trans. Richard Howard (New York: Hill and Wang, 1987; orig. pub. 1954), 206.

115. Arthur Mitzman, *Michelet, Historian: Rebirth and Romanticism in Nineteenth-Century France* (New Haven: Yale University Press, 1990). Mitzman's two appendixes excusing Athénaïs provided the inspiration for this chapter.

116. Michelet, *Journal*, I, 25.

117. In this regard, readers can consult the way in which Peter Novick uses such words as "sexy," "hot," and "fashionable" to discredit certain groups of historians. See also Hayden White, *The Content of the Form: Narrative Discourse and Historical Representation* (Baltimore: Johns Hopkins University Press, 1987), 71.

118. See Peter Schöttler, *Lucie Varga: Les autorités invisible* (Paris: Cerf, 1991). Schöttler has done an extraordinary job discovering the details of Varga's obscure life and reprinting her essays and articles. He suggests Bloch's misogynistic attitude toward women intellectuals, but, more important, Bloch's distress at finding his collaboration with Febvre still further complicated by Varga's work. Schöttler was loath to reveal the extent of Varga and Febvre's relationship: "La vie scientifique et l'amour . . . are not considered pertinent in accounts of the life of a scholar." Nonetheless, Schöttler considered it necessary to reveal the romance because "its consequences were sufficiently determining that one could not keep it quiet without falsifying history" (57, n. 142). This ambiguous statement may refer to Varga's subsequent employment selling vacuum cleaners, then working

in an advertising agency, after which, under Vichy, her utter destitution kept her from getting the necessary medicine to treat her diabetes. She died in 1942 at the age of thirty-four.

Natalie Zemon Davis, "Women and the World of the *Annales*," *History Workshop Journal,* 33 (1992), 121–137, describes the contributions of Suzanne Dognon Febvre to Lucien Febvre's work, and considers the important part played by Paule Braudel in Fernand Braudel's work.

119. Lucien Febvre to Marc Bloch, 1941, quoted in Natalie Davis, "Rabelais among the Censors," *Representations,* 32 (Fall 1990), 5.

120. This part of my argument relies on Mary Louise Roberts, *Civilization without Sexes: Reconstructing Gender in Postwar France, 1917–1927* (Chicago: University of Chicago, 1994).

121. Lionel Gossman, *Towards a Rational Historiography* (Philadelphia: American Philosophical Society, 1989), 61–62.

122. Ibid., 62 and passim.

123. On this point, see R. Howard Bloch, "Medieval Misogyny," *Representations,* 20 (Fall 1987), 1–24.

4 THE PRACTICES OF SCIENTIFIC HISTORY

1. Michel de Certeau, *The Writing of History,* trans. Tom Conley (New York: Columbia University Press, 1988).

2. Mary Hesse, *Revolutions and Reconstructions in the Philosophy of Science* (Bloomington: Indiana University Press, 1980), xvi–xx, 111–124. Another important philosophical understanding of the role of metaphor comes from Donald Davidson, who maintains that metaphors are causal to the extent that they open the way to new knowledge by allowing people to approach conventional problems in new ways; see "What Metaphors Mean," in Donald Davidson, *Inquiries into Truth and Interpretation* (Oxford: Clarendon Press, 1984). For a comparative elaboration of both points of view, see Richard Rorty, *Objectivity, Relativism, and Truth* (Cambridge: Cambridge University Press, 1991), 162–172. I do not employ metaphor with the precision of analytic philosophers but accept the shared position of Davidson and Hesse that metaphor is not just decorative and that it is pertinent to cognition and knowledge.

3. My discussion has been influenced by Bruno Latour's studies of laboratory life, especially *The Pasteurization of France,* trans. Alan Sheridan and John Law (Cambridge, Mass.: Harvard University Press, 1988); and Latour, *Science in Action: How to Follow Scientists and Engineers through Society* (Cambridge, Mass.: Harvard University Press, 1987). Although many national studies of the professionalization of history and the rise of the social sciences have helped shape my argument, I do not consider national differences but instead focus on common institutional development. Readers who would like background on national de-

velopments should consult Dorothy Ross, *The Origins of American Social Science* (New York: Cambridge University Press, 1991); John Higham, *History: Professional Scholarship in the United States* (Baltimore: Johns Hopkins University Press, 1965); William Keylor, *Academy and Community: The Foundation of the French Historical Profession* (Cambridge, Mass.: Harvard University Press, 1975); Horst Walter Blanke, *Historiographiegeschichte als Historik* (Stuttgart: Frommann-Holzboog, 1991); T. W. Heyck, *The Transformation of Intellectual Life in Victorian England* (New York: St. Martin's, 1982); Philippa Levine, *The Amateur and the Professional: Antiquarians, Historians, and Archeologists in Victorian England, 1838–1886* (Cambridge: Cambridge University Press, 1986); the indispensable classic, G. P. Gooch, *History and Historians in the Nineteenth Century;* and Peter Novick, *That Noble Dream: The "Objectivity Questions" and the American Historical Profession* (New York: Cambridge University Press, 1988). The biographies, letters, and papers of individual historians have been indispensable to my study.

4. Ephraim Emerton, "The Practical Method in Higher Historical Instruction," in G. Stanley Hall, ed., *Methods of Teaching History,* (Boston: Ginn, Heath, 1885), 44. I am not trying to corroborate this or the many other reports that European lecture halls were lacking in vigorous young men, but the perception was widespread. Anne Martin-Fugier, *La vie élégante; ou, La formation de Tout-Paris, 1815–1848* (Paris: Fayard, 1990), provides copious evidence that this situation existed in France; Jacob Burckhardt at mid-century lectured to Basel society; and there are reports that English and German university lectures had numerous women in the audience. The lectures of Treitschke later in the century were often cited as an exception: each drew hundreds of young men eager to hear his militantly nationalistic brand of history. But the oft-reported perception that audiences were stocked with women and old men should count as having some meaning to observers.

5. See, for example, Burton Bledstein's characterization of Andrew Dickson White in *The Culture of Professionalism: The Middle Class and the Development of Higher Education in America* (New York: Norton, 1976). Notable exceptions to the tendency to overlook the development of masculinity in professionalization include Elizabeth Lunbeck, *The Psychiatric Persuasion: Knowledge, Gender, and Power in Modern America* (Princeton: Princeton University Press, 1994); and Barbara Melosh, *"The Physician's Hand": Work, Culture and Conflict in American Nursing* (Philadelphia: Temple University Press, 1982). The voluminous literature on professionalization comprises such helpful works as Andrew Abbott, *The System of Professions: An Essay on the Division of Expert Labor* (Chicago: University of Chicago Press, 1988); Charles E. McClelland, *The German Experience of Professionalization: Modern Learned Professions and Their Organization, from the Early Nineteenth Century to the Hitler Era* (Cambridge: Cambridge University Press, 1991); Geoffrey Cocks and Konrad Jarausch, eds., *German Professions,*

1800–1950 (New York: Oxford University Press, 1990); Werner Conze and Jürgen Kocka, eds., *Bildungsbürgertum im 19. Jahrhundert: Bildungssystem und Professionalisierung in internationalen Vergleichen* (Stuttgart: Klett-Cotta, 1985); Gerald Geison, ed., *Professions and the French State, 1700–1900* (Philadelphia: University of Pennsylvania Press, 1984); Harold Perkin, *The Rise of Professional Society in England since 1880* (London: Routledge, 1989).

6. My purpose is not to provide a general history of seminars before Ranke but rather to note the expanding influence of Ranke's seminar. Expert work on the philological seminar by William Clark ("On the Dialectical Origins of the Research Seminar," *History of Science,* 27 [1989], 111–154) charts the way in which the state-sponsored philology seminars in German universities developed from four early modern educational institutions: professorial chairs, private courses or *collegia,* pedagogical seminaries, and private societies. Clark provides a comprehensive list of philological seminars from the mid-eighteenth century to 1838. On the much later establishment of the philosophy seminar, see Ulrich Johannes Schneider, "The Teaching of Philosophy at German Universities in the Nineteenth Century," *History of Universities,* 12 (1993), 199–338. Citing nineteenth-century sources, Schneider characterizes the seminar as evolving from a method of "conversational teaching," rather than placing the primary emphasis on research as Clark does. On the various false starts in founding historical seminars before Ranke's took hold, see Max Lenz, *Geschichte der Königlichen Friedrich-Wilhelms-Universität zu Berlin,* 3 vols. (Halle: Wisenhaus, 1910), III, 246–248. The literature on Ranke is enormous. Two recent helpful books are Georg G. Iggers and James M. Powell, eds., *Leopold von Ranke and the Shaping of the Historical Discipline* (Syracuse: Syracuse University Press, 1990); and Wolfgang J. Mommsen, ed., *Leopold von Ranke und die moderne Geschichtswissenschaft* (Stuttgart: Klett-Cotta, 1988). See also David Aaron Jeremy Telman, "Clio Ascendant: The Historical Profession in Nineteenth-Century Germany," Diss., Cornell University, 1993.

7. Herbert Baxter Adams, "New Methods in the Study of History," *Journal of Social Science,* 18 (May 1884), 255.

8. Ephraim Emerton, "The Historical Seminar in American Teaching," quoted ibid., 246.

9. Walter Prescott Webb, "The Historical Seminar: Its Outer Shell and Its Inner Spirit," *Mississippi Valley Historical Review,* 42 (1955–1956), 9.

10. The seminar of the nineteenth century as discussed in this chapter is not exactly the same as its offspring, the contemporary seminar. Today's seminar often discusses recent books, rather than scrutinizing primary sources as a way of checking secondary works.

11. Wilhelm von Giesebrecht, *Gedächtnissrede auf Leopold von Ranke* (Munich: Akademie der Wissenschaften, 1887), 14–15. Seminar participants in the first half of the century tended to use the word "workshop"; those in the latter half more often used the word "laboratory."

12. Letter to Heinrich Schreiber, August 11, 1840, in *The Letters of Jacob Burckhardt*, ed. and trans. Alexander Dru (London: Routledge and Kegan Paul, 1955), 57.

13. *Autobiography of Andrew Dickson White* (New York: Century, 1907), 39. See Günter Berg, *Leopold von Ranke als academische Lehrer* (Göttingen: Vanderwoeck and Ruprecht, 1968), which establishes this point.

14. Letter to Albrecht Wolters, July 20, 1843, in *The Letters of Jacob Burckhardt*, 82–83. Burckhardt did not like Ranke as a person but appreciated his seminar teaching.

15. Charles Seignobos, who visited an array of German universities late in the 1870s, made the same observation with regard to a particular history professor, comparing his skill in seminars and his abysmal performance in lectures, where he gave "a prolix lesson, confused and without life. It is hardly believable that someone could explain things he knows so well so badly." Seignobos, "L'enseignement de l'histoire en allemagne," *Revue internationale de l'enseignement*, 1 (January–June 1881), 575.

16. Examples of the enormous literature on the relationship between philological methods and the development of historical science are Anthony Grafton, *Defenders of the Text: The Traditions of Scholarship in an Age of Science, 1450–1800* (Cambridge, Mass.: Harvard University Press, 1991), 214–243; and Suzanne Marchand, *Down from Olympus: Archeology and Philhellenism in Germany, 1750–1970* (Princeton: Princeton University Press, 1996). William Clark traces a longer road to professionalization within the academy in "On the Ironic Specimen of the Doctor of Philosophy," *Science in Context*, 5, no. 1 (1992), 92–137, which argues that it was the changing nature of the doctoral degree itself that launched research.

17. Paul Frédéricq, "De l'enseignement supérieur de l'histoire," *Revue de l'instruction publique en Belgique*, 25 (1882), 45.

18. See, for example, the report by Charles Kendall Adams on his seminar, which he began in the 1860s at the University of Michigan; quoted in Herbert Baxter Adams, "New Methods of Study in History," *Journal of Social Science*, 18 (May 1884), 249–250. Charles Adams said that contrary to the usual practice in German seminars, he had experimented by letting the students themselves choose a topic, with excellent results.

19. Giesebrecht, *Gedächtnissrede auf Leopold von Ranke*, 14.

20. Emerton, "The Practical Method in Higher Historical Instruction," 34–35.

21. On the importance of women to the salon, see, for instance, Dena Goodman, *The Republic of Letters* (Ithaca: Cornell University Press, 1994); Deborah Hertz, *Jewish High Society in Old Regime Berlin* (New Haven: Yale University Press, 1988). On the role of middle-class women in ordinary social interchange, see, for example, Leonore Davidoff, *Family Fortunes* (Chicago: University of Chicago Press, 1987); and Bonnie G. Smith, *Ladies of the Leisure Class: The Bourgeoises of Northern France in the Nineteenth Century* (Princeton: Princeton University Press, 1981).

22. Frédéricq, "De l'enseignement supérieur de l'histoire," 26.

23. For the U.S. case, see Jurgen Herbst, *The German Historical School in American Scholarship: A Study in the Transfer of Culture* (Ithaca: Cornell University Press, 1965), esp. chs. 3–5.

24. Letter to Mrs. David Little, April 28, 1887, cited in F. M. Powicke, *Modern Historians and the Study of History* (London: Oldhams, 1955), 76.

25. Letter from Charles Gross, quoted in Herbert Adams, "New Methods of Study in History," 234.

26. For one description, see the Julia Garnett Pertz Papers, Houghton Library, Harvard University, 1304.2, Folder 52, letter to Mrs. Taylor, April 28, 1842, in which Julia Pertz describes G. H. Pertz's receiving room and library. An important analysis of men's scholarship in relation to urban household space and household authority can be found in Gabor Gyani, "Domestic Material Culture of the Upper-Middle Class in Turn-of-the-Century Budapest," Paper presented at the Hungarian-American IREX conference on Material Culture, New York, January 1993.

I am not claiming here that this was the first time teaching took place at home. Rather, I am trying to capture the texture of that experience as it affected students.

27. Paul Frédéricq, "L'enseignement supérieur à Paris," *Revue internationale de l'enseignement* (June 15, 1883).

28. Keylor, *Academy and Community*, 71.

29. Charles Seignobos, "L'enseignement de l'histoire en allemagne," *Revue internationale de l'enseignement,* 1 (January–June 1881), 591, n. 1.

30. Daniel Coit Gilman to Herbert Baxter Adams, July 15, 1883, in W. Stull Holt, ed., *Historical Scholarship in the United States, 1876–1901, as Revealed in the Correspondence of Herbert B. Adams* (Baltimore: Johns Hopkins University Press, 1938), 69.

31. Henry Adams, *The Education of Henry Adams* (New York: Modern Library, 1931; orig. pub. 1918), 303.

32. William Clark maintains that non-"showy" proceedings were characteristic of the German philological seminar of the late eighteenth century. These contrasted with traditional displays of academic prowess in *disputationes* and earlier kinds of seminars. See William Clark, "From the Medieval *Universitas Scholarium* to the German Research University: A Sociogenesis of the German Academic," Diss., University of California at Los Angeles, 1986, 525–527, 543–550.

33. Ernest Lavisse, "Concours pour l'agrégation d'histoire et de géographie," *Revue internationale de l'enseignement,* 1 (January–June 1881), 119.

34. Gabriel Monod, "Georges Waitz et le séminaire historique de Goettingue," *Portraits et souvenirs* (Paris: Calmann-Lévy, 1897), 102–103.

35. Frédéricq, "De l'enseignement supérieur de l'histoire," 28.

36. William Stubbs, "Inaugural Lecture," in Stubbs, *Seventeen Lectures on the Study of Medieval and Modern History* (New York: Fertig, 1967; orig. pub. 1886), 12.

37. Letter from Charles H. Levermore, January 29, 1887, in Holt, ed., *Historical Scholarship*, 94. Military metaphors were also common but not incongruous, given the republican ideology of "armed virtue" and military involvement in imperialism at the time.

38. Ernest Lavisse, *Souvenirs* (Paris: Calmann-Lévy, 1988; orig. pub. 1912), 223, 234–235.

39. Lavisse, "Concours pour l'agrégation," 130.

40. Francis Cornford, quoted in Webb, "The Historical Seminar," 23.

41. Keylor, *Academy and Community*, 71 and 265, n. 58.

42. Gabriel Hanotaux, *Mon temps*, 3 vols. (Paris: Plon, 1933–1940), I, 229.

43. Emerton, "The Practical Method," 35.

44. Arthur Newton, quoted in Margaret Spector, "A. P. Newton," in Herman Ausubel, J. Bartlet Brebner, and Erling M. Hunt, eds., *Some Modern Historians of Britain: Essays in Honor of R. L. Schuyler* (New York: Dryden Press, 1951), 293.

45. Webb, "The Historical Seminar," 10. Webb is incorrect in referring to the French word *semen*, which does not exist. The actual word is *sperme*. Elizabeth Vincentelli (personal communication) pointed out this error in Webb's analysis.

46. Charles Forster Smith, *Charles Kendall Adams: A Life-Sketch* (Madison: University of Wisconsin Press, 1924), 22. In a letter to Herbert Baxter Adams, February 9, 1886, C. K. Adams places his first seminar in 1869 (Holt, ed., *Historical Scholarship*, 79). This is not to say that women did not have their own fantasies about the seminar, or that the male metaphors absolutely excluded them. The words "seminar" and "seminary" were used interchangeably in the nineteenth century. Many institutions of higher education for women were founded as "seminaries" and enjoyed wide appeal. I am indebted to Carl Schorske for this point.

47. Johann Gustav Droysen, *Historik: Vorlesungen über Enzyklopädie und Methodologie der Geschichte* (Munich: R. Oldenbourg, 1958), 411.

48. Ibid., 411–415.

49. The complicated story of scientific history in Britain is summarized in J. M. Kenyon, *The History Men* (London: Weidenfeld and Nicolson, 1983). Alfred Pollard and others outside Oxford and Cambridge conducted well-known seminars, while a long list of scholars at the older institutions called for their regularization. One interpretation for the persistence of the tutorial system can be found in Linda Dowling, *Hellenism and Homosexuality in Victorian Oxford* (Ithaca: Cornell University Press, 1994). On Maitland's various seminars, see C. H. S. Fifoot, *Frederic William Maitland: A Life* (Cambridge, Mass.: Harvard University Press, 1971), 98.

50. See Charles E. McClelland, "Republics within the Empire: The Universities," in Jack R. Dukes and Joachim Remak, eds., *Another Germany: A Reconsideration of the Imperial Era* (Boulder: Westview, 1988), 169–180.

51. On republican rhetoric and values, see, among many works, Jean Starobinski, *Jean-Jacques Rousseau: La transparence et l'obstacle* (Paris: Plon, 1957); J. G. A.

Pocock, *The Machiavellian Moment: Florentine Political Thought and the Atlantic Republican Tradition* (Princeton: Princeton University Press, 1975); Lynn Hunt, *Politics, Culture, and Class in the French Revolution* (Berkeley: University of California Press, 1984). See also Rogers Brubaker, *Citizenship and Nationhood in France and Germany* (Cambridge, Mass.: Harvard University Press, 1992). On the way in which the construction of politics and the public sphere excluded what were designated feminine qualities, see Joan Landes, *Women and the Public Sphere in the Age of the French Revolution* (Ithaca: Cornell University Press, 1988).

52. Accounts of the nationalistic impulses of professionalizing historians in the nineteenth century are legion, and can be found in primary sources such as Holt, *Historical Scholarship* passim; in older surveys such as Keylor, *Academy and Community*, passim; and in new monographs such as Robert Southard, *Droysen and the Prussian School of History* (Lexington: University of Kentucky Press, 1995).

53. On Bachofen's quarrels with professionalization, see especially Lionel Gossman, *Orpheus Philologus: Bachofen versus Mommsen on the Study of Antiquity* (Philadelphia: American Philosophical Society, 1983).

54. See Felix Gilbert, "Jacob Burckhardt's Student Years: The Road to Cultural History," *Journal of the History of Ideas*, 47 (1985), 249–274; Werner Kaegi, *Jacob Burckhardt: Eine Biographie*, 5 vols. (Basel: B. Schwabe, 1947).

55. One example was the academic in-fighting over the editorship of the *Monumenta Germaniae Historica;* see David Knowles, *Great Historical Enterprises: Problems in Monastic History* (London: Thomas Nelson, 1963). Roger Chickering, *Karl Lamprecht: A German Academic Life, 1856–1915* (Atlantic Highlands, N.J.: Humanities Press, 1993), describes the ostracism of Karl Lamprecht, who controlled the Leipzig seminar. The letters and papers of nineteenth-century historians bear ample witness to the struggle for place, the personal vendettas, and the intense rivalries that shaped the profession.

56. Information on Salmon can be found in Louise Fargo Brown, *Apostle of Democracy: The Life of Lucy Maynard Salmon* (New York: Macmillan, 1943); and in the Lucy Maynard Salmon Papers, Vassar College Archives (the fan manuscript is in box 13, 50–51). Beatrice Berle, in an interview on October 12, 1985, described Salmon's seminar; see also Beatrice Berle, *A Life in Two Worlds* (New York: Walker, 1983). J. B. Ross provided other important insights into Salmon's methods and teaching at Vassar (interview, May 1985).

57. Letter to Bettina von Arnim, February 6, 1828, in Leopold von Ranke, *Das Briefwerk,* ed. Walther Fuchs (Hamburg: Hoffmann und Campe, 1949), 139.

58. Léon de Laborde, *Les archives de la France: Leur vicissitudes pendant la Révolution, leur régéneration sous l'empire* (Paris: Vve. Renauard, 1867), 63–64 and passim. I thank Jennifer Milligan for pointing out this passage. This chapter does not explore the complex history, ongoing debates, and rivalries (to which Laborde

refers) among proponents of archives and proponents of libraries. It considers interest in manuscript rooms of national libraries and in rare bound volumes as part of the research commitment.

59. Decree of 7 Messidor, Year II, quoted in Henri Bordier, *Les archives de France* (Paris: Dumoulin, 1855), 6. On this history, see also Laborde, *Les archives de la France*, 1–156.

60. Baron von Stein invoked the ideology of the fetish in its non-Western form when he complained: "The history of the Pharaohs, the life of the gazelles and monkeys is studied, but nothing is done for the history of our people." Cited in Gooch, *History and Historians*, 66–67.

61. On som. of the most important compilations, see especially Knowles, *Great Historical Enterprises*.

62. *Choix de lettres de Eugène Burnouf* (Paris: Champion, 1894), passim.

63. Letter to Heinrich Ritter, October 4, 1827, in Ranke, *Das Briefwerk*, 114–115.

64. Letter to E. A. Freeman (n.d. [1870]), in *Letters of John Richard Green*, ed. Leslie Stephen (New York: Macmillan, 1901), 259.

65. Letter to Heinrich Ritter, October 28, 1827, in Ranke, *Sämmtliche Werke*, LIII–LIV, 175.

66. Letter to Ferdinand Ranke, November 11, 1836, in Leopold von Ranke, *Neue Briefe*, ed. Bernhard Hoeft and Hans Herzfeld (Hamburg: Hoffmann und Campe, 1949), 230.

67. Charles-Victor Langlois and H. Stein, *Les archives de l'histoire de France* (Paris: Alphonse Picard, 1891), 1.

68. Hanotaux, *Mon temps*, II, 8.

69. Bordier, *Les archives de France*, 26–48.

70. Heinrich von Sybel, *Vorträge und Abhandlungen* (Munich: R. Oldenbourg, 1897), 365.

71. Owen Chadwick, *Catholicism and History: The Opening of the Vatican Archives* (Cambridge: Cambridge University Press, 1978).

72. Hanotaux, *Mon temps*, II, 63, 36.

73. George Eliot, *Middlemarch: A Study of Provincial Life*, 3 vols. (London: Blackwood, n.d.), II, 219, 14.

74. Robert Browning, "The Grammarian's Funeral," in *The Poems and Plays of Robert Browning* (New York: Modern Library, 1934), 172.

75. Augustin Thierry, *Dix ans d'études historiques*, 6th ed. (Paris: Furne, 1851), 23.

76. Otfried Müller, *Lebensbild in Briefen*, quoted in Gooch, *History and Historians*, 40.

77. Theodor von Sickel, *Römische Erinnerungen* (Vienna: Universitum, 1947), 45–46, 133–137, 170–171, 184–185.

78. Paul Lacroix Jacob, *Les amateurs de vieux livres* (Paris: Edouard Rouveyre, 1880), 49. This is not the only period in which people had an obsession with books and manuscripts. For instance, a fascinating fourteenth-century work—Richard de

Bury, *Philobiblon,* trans. E. C. Thomas (Oxford: Oxford University Press, 1970; orig. pub. 1345)—touts the importance of books. This is a general topos in literature, but I contend that the amount of fiction calling attention to maniacal behavior in the nineteenth century is much greater. Even if it weren't, the topos needs to be examined (as does any other long-standing phenomenon such as the state or the economy) for its historical specificity.

79. Charles Nodier, *Le Bibliomane* (Paris: L. Conquet, 1894; orig. pub. 1834); Gustave Flaubert, "Bibliomanie" [1837], in Flaubert, *Oeuvres complètes* (Lausanne: Rencontre, 1964), I, 78–83.

80. *Lettres de Léopold Delisle: Correspondance adressée à Louis Blancard* (Paris: Imprimerie Jacqueline, 1912), xiii, n. 3.

81. On this question, literary scholars and anthropologists can offer important background to the historiography of the concept: William Pietz, "The Problem of the Fetish, I," *Res,* 9 (Spring 1985), 5–17; William Pietz, "The Problem of the Fetish, II: The Origin of the Fetish," *Res,* 13 (Spring 1987), 23–45; William Pietz, "The Problem of the Fetish, III: Bosman's Guinea and the Enlightenment Theory of Fetishism," *Res,* 16 (Autumn 1988), 105–123; Emily Apter, *Feminizing the Fetish* (Ithaca: Cornell University Press, 1992); W. J. T. Mitchell, *Iconology: Image, Text, Ideology* (Chicago: University of Chicago Press, 1986); Emily Apter and William Pietz, eds., *Fetishism as Cultural Discourse* (Ithaca: Cornell University Press, 1993); and Laura Mulvey, "Some Thoughts on Theories of Fetishism in the Context of Contemporary Culture," *October,* 65 (Summer 1993), 3–20.

82. Pietz, "The Problem of the Fetish, IIIa," 111 passim. According to Pietz, Westerners as early as the eighteenth century were also condemning African fetishism for its unenlightened standard of beauty and misguided notions of sexual potency.

83. "Prefatory Note," *English Historical Review,* 1 (1886), 5;Reviews of S. Gardiner, *History of the Commonwealth and Protectorate 1649–1660,* and of Georg Busolt, *Handbuch der griechischen Geschichte,* in *English Historical Review,* 13 (1898), 167, 125. See also Lord Acton's praise for Ranke's writing "without adornment," in John Emerich Edward Dalberg Acton, *Lectures on Modern History* (New York: Meridian, 1961; orig. pub. 1906), 39; and "Gardiner's Personal Government of Charles I," *Saturday Review,* 22 December 1877, 774.

84. Richard Hildreth, *History of the United States of America,* 6 vols. (New York: Harper, 1849–1852), IV, vii.

85. Maury's work includes histories of classical Greece and Rome and several histories of learned societies in France from the seventeenth to the nineteenth century, but he also wrote serious accounts on less scholarly topics. See his books *Magic and Astrology in Antiquity and the Middle Ages* (1860) and *Sleep and Dreams* (1861), which went through many editions.

86. Alfred Maury, *La magie et l'astrologie dans l'Antiquité et au Moyen Age; ou, Etude sur les superstitions païennes,* 4th ed. (Paris: Didier, 1877), 353, 370. Maury, in the name of science, constantly eroded the position of scientific scholars. When writing about fetishism, shamanism, and other magical practices, he maintained that shamans were "attentive observers of humans and of all their weaknesses, adept at penetrating from the surface to the depths of one's conscience." Fetish priests were often "organized into a powerful and respected caste, and possessed, like the Chaldeans, secrets for working prodigies that could astonish the imagination." Once these priests and shamans acquired the skills for summoning up truths about the dead, even for summoning the dead themselves, "they become the object of public esteem" (ibid., 17, 19, 39, 20). Maury's work pointed to an anxiety about truth that had not existed in such foundational works as Wilhelm Humboldt's, in which the imagination was to fill in essential connections that were missing from documents.

87. For an account of this controversy, as well as an extensive bibliography, see Herbert Butterfield, *Man on His Past* (Cambridge: Cambridge University Press, 1955), 191–201.

88. Michèle Le Doeuff, *The Philosophical Imagination,* trans. Colin Gordon (London: Athlone, 1989), 92.

89. Hanotaux, *Mon temps,* II, 36–37.

90. Gabriel Hanotaux, *Les Bibliophiles* (Paris: A. Ferroud, 1924), 36.

91. Charles-Victor Langlois and Charles Seignobos, *Introduction aux études historiques* (Paris: Hachette, 1898).

92. Letter from Thierry to Claude Fauriel, June 1829, quoted in Rulon Nephi Smithson, *Augustin Thierry* (Geneva: Droz, 1973), 22.

93. For elaboration, see Robert A. Nye, *Masculinity and Male Codes of Honor in Modern France* (New York: Oxford University Press, 1993), ch. 6.

94. Alfred Binet, "Le fétichisme dans l'amour: Etude de psychologie morbide," *Revue philosophique,* 24 (1887), 143–167.

95. Letter of August 19, 1863, in *A Memoir of the Right Hon. William Edward Hartpole Lecky* (London: Longmans, Green, 1909), 38.

96. Letter to Bettina von Arnim, February 6, 1828, in Ranke, *Briefwerke,* 139. This is a common allusion among researchers.

97. See, for instance, Knowles, *Great Historical Enterprises,* on the many intrigues over controlling various sections of the *Monumenta Germaniae Historica.*

98. Wilhelm von Humboldt, "On the Historian's Task" [1821], in Leopold von Ranke, *The Theory and Practice of History,* ed. Georg G. Iggers and Konrad von Moltke, trans. Wilma A. Iggers and Konrad von Moltke (Indianapolis: Bobbs-Merrill, 1973), 8–9.

99. Charles Seignobos, "Les conditions psychologiques de la connaissance en histoire," *Revue philosophique,* 24 (July 1887), 8–9.

100. Humboldt, "On the Historian's Task," 8.

101. Jules Michelet, "Préface de 1869," in Michelet, *Histoire de France,* 18 vols. (Paris: A. Lacroix, 1876), I, xxxvi.

102. Letter to Prévost-Paradol, March 2, 1849, in *Hippolyte Taine: Sa vie et sa correspondance,* 4 vols. (Paris: Hachette, 1902–1907), I, 51.

103. Letter to Heinrich Ranke, November 1827, in Leopold von Ranke, *Sämmtliche Werke,* LIII–LIV, 179.

104. *Life and Letters of Mandell Creighton, D.D.,* ed. Louise Creighton, 2 vols. (London: Longmans, Green, 1906), I, 80–83.

105. See Apter, *Feminizing the Fetish,* 39–40.

106. John Emerich Edward Dalberg Acton, Letter to contributors to the *Cambridge Modern History,* in Acton, *Lectures on Modern History* (London: Macmillan, 1950), 315–316.

107. Arnold J. Toynbee, *A Study of History: The Inspiration of Historians* (New York: Oxford University Press, 1963), 24–41.

108. James Bryce, *Studies in Contemporary Biography* (New York: Macmillan, 1903), 386.

109. In stressing the complexity of the practices of objectivity, I take my cue from Megill, *Rethinking Objectivity,* 1–20, a collection devoted to scientific practices in a number of fields. Another exploration of the conflict between gender and the democratic aspirations of U.S. historians can be found in Joan W. Scott, "American Women Historians, 1884–1984," in Scott, *Gender and the Politics of History* (New York: Columbia University Press, 1988), 178–198.

5 MEN AND FACTS

1. Michel de Certeau, *The Writing of History,* trans. Tom Conley (New York: Columbia University Press, 1988), 26.

2. Benedict Anderson, *Imagined Communities: Reflections on the Origins and Spread of Nationalism* (London: Verso, 1983).

3. Jürgen Habermas, *The Structural Transformation of the Public Sphere: An Inquiry into a Category of Bourgeois Society,* trans. Thomas Burger (Cambridge, Mass.: MIT Press, 1989); Craig Calhoun, ed., *Habermas and the Public Sphere* (Cambridge, Mass.: MIT Press, 1992).

4. Friedrich Schlegel, *Kritische Ausgabe,* ed. Ernst Behler (Paderborn: Schöningh, 1958), XII, 123, quoted in Azade Seyhan, *Representation and Its Discontents: The Critical Legacy of German Romanticism* (Berkeley: University of California Press, 1992), 73.

5. Ephraim Emerton, "The Historical Seminary in American Teaching," quoted in Herbert Baxter Adams, "New Methods in the Study of History," *Journal of Social Science,* 18 (May 1884), 246.

6. See, for instance, Ludmilla Jordanova, *Sexual Visions: Images of Gender in Science and Medicine between the Eighteenth and Twentieth Centuries* (Madison: University of Wisconsin Press, 1989).

7. Londa Schiebinger, *Nature's Body: Gender in the Making of Modern Science* (Boston: Beacon, 1993).

8. Friedrich Schlegel, *Philosophical Fragments,* trans. Peter Firchow (Minneapolis: University of Minnesota Press, 1991), 81.

9. Ernest Renan, *L'avenir de la science,* in Renan, *Oeuvres complètes,* ed. Henriette Psichari (Paris: Calmann-Lévy, 1949; orig. pub. 1890), III, 897.

10. Numa Fustel de Coulanges, "De l'analyse des textes historiques," *Revue des Questions Historiques,* 41 (January 1887): 20.

11. Michel Foucault, *Discipline and Punish: The Birth of the Prison,* trans. Alan Sheridan (New York: Pantheon, 1977).

12. Leopold von Ranke, "On the Character of Historical Science" [manuscript of the 1830s], in Ranke, *The Theory and Practice of History,* ed. Georg G. Iggers and Konrad von Moltke, trans. Wilma A. Iggers and Konrad von Moltke (Indianapolis: Bobbs-Merrill, 1973), 36–39.

13. Ibid., 33.

14. Wilhelm von Humboldt, "On the Historian's Task" [1821], in Ranke, *The Theory and Practice of History,* 10.

15. Ibid., 14.

16. Charles Seignobos, "Les conditions psychologiques de la connaissance en histoire," *Revue philosophique,* 24 (June–December 1887), 7.

17. F. W. Maitland to Henry Jackson, March 5, 1904, in *The Letters of Frederic William Maitland,* ed. C. H. S. Fifoot (Cambridge: Cambridge University Press, 1965), 299.

18. Eugène Burnouf to his father, April 14, 1835, in *Choix de lettres de Eugène Burnouf* (Paris: Champion, 1894), 208.

19. Numa Fustel de Coulanges, "De l'analyse des textes historiques," *Revue des Questions Historiques,* 41 (January 1887), 33.

20. *Enzyklopädie und Methodologie der philologischen Wissenschaften* (Hamburg: Felix Meiner, 1959), quoted in Lionel Gossman, *Orpheus Philologus: Bachofen versus Mommsen on the Study of Antiquity* (Philadelphia: American Philosophical Society, 1983), 73.

21. Mark Pattison, *Essays,* ed. Henry Nettleship, 2 vols. (New York: Burt Franklin, 1965; orig. pub. 1889), I, 365.

22. Ernest Renan, *L'avenir de la science,* in Renan, *Oeuvres complètes* (Paris: Calmann-Levy, 1949), III, 733.

23. Theodor Mommsen, *Römische Geschichte,* 3 vols. (Berlin: Weidmann, 1868), I, 28.

24. See Michel Foucault, *The Birth of the Clinic: An Archaeology of Medical Perception,* trans. Alan Sheridan (New York: Pantheon, 1973); Jordanova, *Sexual Visions,*

passim; Barbara Duden, *The Woman beneath the Skin: A Doctor's Patients in Eighteenth-Century Germany*, trans. Thomas Dunlap (Cambridge, Mass.: Harvard University Press, 1991).

25. Ranke, "On the Character of Historical Science," 39.

26. Humboldt, "On the Historian's Task," 10.

27. Ibid., 6.

28. Renan, *L'avenir de la science*, 888.

29. Richard Hildreth, *History of the United States of America*, 6 vols. (New York: Harper, 1849–1852), IV, vii.

30. "Prefatory Note," *English Historical Review*, 1 (1886), 5.

31. Reviews of S. Gardiner, *History of the Commonwealth and Protectorate, 1649–1660*, and Georg Busolt, *Handbuch der griechischen Geschichte*, in *English Historical Review*, 13 (1898), 167, 125. See also Lord Acton's praise for Ranke's writing "without adornment," in Acton, *Lectures on Modern History* (New York: Meridian, 1961), 39.

32. "Gardiner's Personal Government of Charles I," *Saturday Review*, December 22, 1877, 774.

33. Quoted in Peter Novick, *That Noble Dream: The "Objectivity Question" and the American Historical Profession* (Cambridge: Cambridge University Press, 1988), 193.

34. On the body as an entity that is in one way or another assigned a sex, see Judith Butler, *Bodies That Matter: On the Discursive Limits of "Sex"* (New York: Routledge, 1993); and Anne Fausto-Sterling, "The Five Sexes," *The Sciences*, 33 (March–April 1993), 20–24.

35. See Novick, *That Noble Dream*, for an example of the way in which the debased female body continues to serve, along with the debased black body, as an indicator of the inferiority side of the equation. This interpretation takes its direction from Butler, *Bodies That Matter*.

36. Renan, *L'avenir de la science*, 948.

37. Humboldt, "On the Historian's Task," 6.

38. Ibid., 10.

39. Ibid., 25–26.

40. Renan, *L'avenir de la science*, 862–863.

41. For examples of the ways in which scholars have demonstrated the relationship between the body and the gendering of logic, philosophy, science, and other fields of inquiry, see Andrea Nye, *Words of Power: A Feminist Reading in the History of Logic* (London: Routledge, 1990); Genevieve Lloyd, *The Man of Reason: "Male" and "Female" in Western Philosophy* (Minneapolis: University of Minnesota Press, 1984); Linda Alcoff and Elizabeth Potter, eds., *Feminist Epistemologies* (New York: Routledge, 1993); Ann Garry and Marilyn Pearsall, *Women, Knowledge, and Reality: Explorations in Feminist Philosophy* (Boston: Unwin Hyman, 1989); Michèle

Le Doeuff, *Hipparchia's Choice: An Essay concerning Women, Philosophy, etc.*, trans. Trista Selous (Oxford: Blackwell, 1991); Sandra Harding, *The Science Question in Feminism* (Ithaca: Cornell University Press, 1986); Donna Haraway, *Primate Visions: Gender, Race, and Nature in the World of Modern Science* (New York: Routledge, 1989).

42. On this point, see Jonathan Crary, *Techniques of the Observer: On Vision and Modernity in the Nineteenth Century* (Cambridge, Mass.: MIT Press, 1990), passim.

43. For one elaboration of this point, with Madame Bovary used as the example of such a reader, see Rita Felski, *The Gender of Modernity* (Cambridge, Mass.: Harvard University Press, 1995), 79–87.

44. Humboldt, "On the Historian's Task," 18.

45. "Fustel de Coulanges," *Revue historique,* 41 (1900), 278.

46. Thomas Babington Macaulay, quoted in John Clive, *Macaulay: The Shaping of a Life* (New York: Knopf, 1973), 38.

47. Renan, *L'avenir de la science,* 928.

48. Ignaz von Döllinger, *Fables Respecting the Popes in the Middle Ages,* trans. Alfred Plummer (London: Rivingtons, 1871), 48.

49. Humboldt, "On the Historian's Task, 6.

50. Renan, *L'avenir de la science,* 921.

51. Humboldt, "On the Historian's Task," 6.

52. Ibid., 10.

53. Fustel de Coulanges, "De l'analyse des textes historiques," 35.

54. See Maurice Merleau-Ponty, *Le visible et l'invisible,* ed. Claude Lefort (Paris: Gallimard, 1964); Laura Mulvey, *Visual and Other Pleasures* (Bloomington: Indiana University Press, 1989), 14–29.

55. Susan McClary, discussing the sonata form, sees in its general structure (a departure from the original key through ever-ascending chords) a drive toward excess and competition. This drive, introduced by the composer, is resolved only in the return to the original key. See McClary, *Feminine Endings: Music, Gender, and Sexuality* (Minneapolis: University of Minnesota Press, 1991).

56. G. P. Gooch, *History and Historians in the Nineteenth Century* (London: Longman's, Green, 1913), 69.

57. The term "congealing," and the idea of a mutation of facts into values and vice versa, come from the work of Joel Kupperman ("How Facts Congeal into Values," paper presented at the City University of New York Graduate Center, New York, January 1997). I am very grateful for his help on this central analytic point of the chapter.

58. Anthony Ashley Cooper, third earl of Shaftesbury, *Characteristics of Men, Manners, Opinions, Times,* ed. John M. Robertson (Indianapolis: Bobbs-Merrill, 1964; orig. pub. 1711), 338.

59. Phillips Payson, quoted in Michael Warner, *The Letters of the Republic: Publication and the Public Sphere in Eighteenth-Century America* (Cambridge, Mass.: Harvard University Press, 1990), 122.

60. Quoted in John Craig, *Scholarship and Nation-Building: The Universities of Strasbourg and Alsatian Society* (Chicago: University of Chicago Press, 1984), 45.

61. Michel de Certeau, *L'écriture de l'histoire* (Paris: Gallimard, 1975), 118.

62. Ernest Renan, "What Is a Nation?" trans. Martin Thom, in Homi Bhabha, ed., *Nation and Narration* (London: Routledge, 1990), 8–21.

63. Numa Fustel de Coulanges, *Histoire des institutions politiques de l'ancienne France*, 2 vols. (Paris: Hachette, 1875).

64. Benedict Anderson, *Imagined Communities: Reflections on the Origins and Spread of Nationalism* (London: Verso, 1983); Jean-Luc Nancy, *The Birth to Presence*, trans. Brian Holmes et al. (Stanford: Stanford University Press, 1993), 143–167.

65. Augustin Thierry, *Considérations sur l'histoire de France* (Paris: Furne, 1840), 140–143.

66. Gabriel Hanotaux, "Au temps de l'Ecole des Chartes," in Hanotaux, *Sur les chemins de l'histoire*, 2 vols. (Paris: Champion, 1924), 7.

67. G. W. F. Hegel, *Philosophy of History*, trans. J. Sibree (New York: Willey Book Co., 1944), 60; and idem, *The Phenomenology of Mind*, trans. J. B. Baille (New York: Harper and Row, 1967), 496–497. Lucien Febvre, *Combats pour l'histoire* (Paris: Armand Colin, 1953), 40.

68. Lucien Febvre, *Michelet* (Paris: Trois Collines, 1946), 58. Numa Fustel de Coulanges, *The Ancient City: A Study of the Religion, Laws, and Institutions of Greece and Rome* (Garden City: Doubleday, 1955; orig. pub. 1864), 132.

69. Fustel de Coulanges, "De l'analyse des textes historiques," 35.

70. Ranke, *The Theory and Practice of History*, 58–59.

71. Henri Berr, *Peut-on refaire l'unité morale de la France?* (Paris: Armand Colin, 1901), 20.

72. On the triumph of masculine time over feminine space, see also Johann Gustav Droysen, *Historik: Vorlesungen über Enzyklopädie und Methodologie der Geschichte* (Munich: R. Oldenbourg, 1958), 411–415.

73. Ernst Bernheim, *Lehrbuch der Historischen Methode und der Geschichtsphilosophie* (Leipzig: Duncker und Humblot, 1908; orig. pub. 1889), 312.

74. Leopold von Ranke, *Die römischen Päpste, ihre Kirche und ihr Staat*, 3 vols. (Berlin: Duncker und Humblot, 1854), I, 50.

75. The procedural language of history was similarly agonistic and strife-laden. In doing research the historian struggled with "those passages that raised difficulties in his way"; he "set up masters (including people, facts, and principles) whom . . . he could obey." Interrogating authors and sources led to finding "masters." Historians duplicated this authoritarian rhetoric in setting up the subfield of historiography, where they struggled in the same way that great political figures did.

Their agon was about historical method and historiographic accomplishment, and they struggled with other men for distinction. In their case, however, the emplotment of historiography, because the method of history was vital and alive, set up strings of these historians as "masters," as authoritative figures "to obey." The language of history, flowing from the state as subject of historical research and as source of historical information and from scientific historians engaged in seminar work on politics, was one of authority, power, and mastery—the characteristics of rule mostly attributed to men. By distributing these individuals, nations, and great historians in a professional narrative, according to a sequence that was generally agreed-upon as accurately portraying historical time, professionals further constructed a science of the real that was the story of men's importance.

76. Mommsen, *Römische Geschichte*, 28–33. Progressive interpretation bears the marks of a primal dream of merged identities, unindividuated from a forebear (especially the mother), during which growth and progress entail advancing from a material state of nature, pleasure, and the arts (the Greeks) to a more abstract one that bears the traces of masculine law in the nation-state and its realism in world conquest. The ideal of a modern, developmental man, whose perceptive powers grow incrementally, was embedded in another ideal according to which the nation-state emerges as masculine values differentiate from and triumph over those of a nature-bound, physical, and thus femininely defined primitive state, whether that of a common Indo-European language or of a common classical heritage such as that of a feminized Hellenism.

77. Carol Pateman, *The Sexual Contract* (Stanford: Stanford University Press, 1988).

78. The example is Elizabeth Anscombe's (see her essays "Modern Moral Philosophy" and "On Brute Facts"), cited in Kupperman, "How Values Congeal into Facts," 22–24.

79. Alain Viala, *Naissance de l'écrivain: Sociologie de la littérature à l'âge classique* (Paris: Minuit, 1985), 55–70, 115–116.

80. Elizabeth Deeds Ermarth, *Realism and Consensus in the English Novel* (Princeton: Princeton University Press, 1983).

81. Seignobos, "La connaissance en histoire," 21.

82. Ibid., 22–23.

83. Richard Hildreth's six-volume *History of the United States of America* (New York: Harper, 1849–1852) was little read by the public when it first appeared, but his expressions of scientific commitment won him this kind of praise from professionals. See James Baldwin, *An Introduction to the Study of English Literature and Literary Criticism*, 2 vols. (Philadelphia: Potter, 1883), II, 83; and Henry T. Tuckerman, "A Sketch of American Literature," in Thomas B. Shaw, *Outlines of English Literature* (Philadelphia: Lea, 1852), 450, as cited in Donald E. Emerson, "Hildreth, Draper, and 'Scientific History,'" in Eric F. Goldman, ed., *Historiography and Urbanization: Essays in Honor of W. Stull Holt* (Port Washington, N.Y.:

Kennikat Press, 1968), 143. See also *Littell's Living Age* [Boston], 23 (1849), 365, cited ibid., 145.

84. Ermarth, *Realism and Consensus,* 16–37.

85. Ranke, *Die römischen Päpste,* I, xi.

86. "Preface" to *History of the Popes,* in Ranke, *The Theory and Practice of History,* 139.

87. Seignobos, "De la connaissance en histoire," 20–21.

88. Brooks Adams, quoted in Novick, *That Noble Dream,* 38, n. 26; *R. H. Tawney's Commonplace Book,* ed. J. M. Winter and D. M. Joslin (Cambridge: Cambridge University Press, 1972), 42.

89. "'On the edge of the cliff': this image, which Michel de Certeau used to describe the work of Michel Foucault, seems to me appropriate for all intellectual approaches having at their heart relations between the products of discourse and social practices." Roger Chartier, *On the Edge of the Cliff: History, Language, and Practices,* trans. Lydia G. Cochrane (Baltimore: Johns Hopkins University Press, 1997), 1.

90. This conclusion is influenced by the writings of Hayden White and Nancy Armstrong.

6 HIGH AMATEURISM AND THE PANORAMIC PAST

1. Susan Reynolds Williams, "In the Garden of New England: Alice Morse Earle and the History of Domestic Life," Diss., University of Delaware, 1992.

2. Jackson Lears, *No Place of Grace: Antimodernism and the Transformation of American Culture, 1880–1920* (New York: Pantheon, 1981).

3. For instance, Antoinette Burton, *Burdens of History: British Feminists, Indian Women, and Imperial Culture, 1865–1915* (Chapel Hill: University of North Carolina Press, 1994). For a different interpretation, see Billie Melman, *Women's Orients: English Women and the Middle East, 1718–1918* (Ann Arbor: University of Michigan Press, 1995).

4. See, for instance, Rosalind Williams, *Dream Worlds: Mass Consumption in Late Nineteenth-Century France* (Berkeley: University of California Press, 1982).

5. See Mary Chalmers, "Harnessing Revolutionary Passions: The French Academy of Moral and Political Sciences, 1832–1848," Diss., University of Rochester, 1995. See also William Reddy, *The Rise of Market Culture: The Textile Trade and French Society, 1750–1900* (Cambridge: Cambridge University Press, 1984).

6. Recent literature on feminism, social science, and progressive reform groups includes Kathryn Kish Sklar, *Florence Kelley and the Nation's Work: The Rise of Women's Political Culture* (New Haven: Yale University Press, 1995); Eileen Yeo, *The Contest for Social Science: Relations and Representations of Gender and Class* (London: Rivers Oram, 1996); Evelyn Brooks Higginbotham, *Righteous Discon-*

tent: The Women's Movement in the Black Baptist Church, 1880–1920 (Cambridge, Mass.: Harvard University Press, 1993).

7. Some recent literature on women's statistical work includes Judith Coffin, *The Politics of Women's Work: The Paris Garment Trades, 1750–1915* (Princeton: Princeton University Press, 1996), 201–228; Ellen Fitzpatrick, *Endless Crusade: Women Social Scientists and Progressive Reform* (New York: Oxford University Press, 1990); Bonnie G. Smith, "Writing Women's Work," European University Institute, Working paper no. 91/7, 1991; Martin Bulmer, Kevin Bales, and Kathryn Kish Sklar, eds., *The Social Survey in Historical Perspective* (Cambridge: Cambridge University Press, 1991).

8. Amelia B. Edward Papers, Somerville College Archives, Oxford University, Catalogue of library, box 5, 423–431; clipping from Amelia B. Edwards, letter to the editor, *The Academy* [London], September 23, 1878, box 4, 348–422. For an account of earlier women's polyvalent historical imaginings, see Daniel Woolf, "A Feminine Past: Gender, Genre, and Historical Knowledge in England, 1500–1800," *American Historical Review,* 102 (June 1997), 645–679.

9. Caroline Jebb, *Life and Letters of Sir Richard Claverhouse Jebb* (Cambridge: Cambridge University Press, 1907), 163–165. I am grateful to Kali Israel for this reference. For more on Pattison, who would become Lady Emilia Dilke, see Kali Israel, "Drawing from Life: Art, Work, and Feminism in the life of Emilia Dilke," Diss., Rutgers University, 1992.

10. Ricarda Huch, *Erinnerungen an das eigene Leben* (Cologne: Kiepenheuer und Witsch, 1980), 163–176, 391–401.

11. See the Vernon Lee collection at Somerville College, Oxford, for details of this situation and for indications that Vernon Lee had an inkling of the special preparations made for her visits.

12. Quoted in Peter Gunn, *Vernon Lee: Violet Paget, 1856–1935* (London: Oxford University Press, 1964), 105, 139.

13. Mary Robinson to Vernon Lee, September 1930, Bibliothèque Nationale manuscripts, Fonds anglais 243, fol. 106.

14. Letters to Vernon Lee, March 17, 1927, and June 17, [1929?], Bibliothèque Nationale manuscripts, Fonds anglais 243, fols. 70, 73.

15. Letters of Vernon Lee to Théodore Bentzon (Thérèse Blanc), October 22, 1892, and March 26, 1887, Bibliothèque Nationale manuscript NAF 12993, fols. 38–42, 14.

16. *A Bright Remembrance: The Diaries of Julia Cartwright, 1851–1924,* ed. Angela Emanuel (London: Weidenfeld and Nicolson, 1989), 124.

17. Maria Grever, *Strijd tegen de stilte: Johanna Naber (1859–1941) en de vrouwenstem in geschiedenis* (Hilversum, Netherlands: Verloren, 1994).

18. See her letters to Vilhjalmur Stefansson, Dartmouth College Library, quoted in Jean Barman, "'I Walk My Own Track in Life and No Mere Man Can Bump Me Off It': The Historical Career of Constance Lindsay Skinner," in Beverly Boutilier

and Alison L. Prentice, eds., *Creating Historical Memory: English-Canadian Women and the Work of History* (Vancouver: University of British Columbia Press, 1997).

19. Matilde Serao to Gaetano Bonavenia, June 1878, quoted in Anthony Gisolfi, *The Essential Matilde Serao* (New York: Las Americas Publishing, 1968), 19 (my translation). On Serao, see also Zygmunt G. Baranski and Shirley W. Vinall, eds., *Women and Italy: Essays on Gender, Culture and History* (New York: St. Martin's, 1991).

20. Margaret Oliphant, *The Autobiography of Mrs. Oliphant*, ed. Mrs. Harry Coghill (Chicago: University of Chicago Press, 1988; orig. pub. 1899), 67.

21. Ibid., 36.

22. See Steward Weaver, *A Marriage in History: The Lives and Work of J. H. and Barbara Hammond* (Stanford: Stanford University Press, 1997).

23. Ibid. J. L. Hammond railed against the researcher's inadequacies.

24. Oliphant, *Autobiography*, 74.

25. "Arvède Barine" was the pseudonym of Louise-Cécile Vincens, whose psychological histories included *Névrosés: Hoffmann, Quincey, Edgar Poe, Gérard de Nerval* (Paris: 1898); and *Portraits de femmes: Mme Carlyle, George Eliot, Une détraquée, Un couvent de femmes en Italie au XVIe siècle, Psychologie d'une sainte* (Paris, 1887). She also wrote many histories of women, and articles for a variety of Parisian journals. Her papers are in the Bibliothèque Nationale manuscript collection, as well as in the Bibliothèque Marguerite Durand in Paris.

26. The series *Women of Colonial and Revolutionary Times*, published in the 1890s by Scribner's, consisted of six volumes: Mary Gay Humphreys, *Catherine Schuyler* (1897); Alice Morse Earle, *Margaret Winthrop* (1895); Harriet Horry Ravenel, *Eliza Pinckney* (1896); Anne Hollingsworth Wharton, *Martha Washington* (1897); Alice Brown, *Mercy Warren* (1896); and Maud Wilder Goodwin, *Dolly Madison* (1896). The series *Famous Women*, published by Roberts Brothers of Boston in the 1880s, included Mathilde Blind, *George Eliot* (1893); Mary Robinson, *Emily Brontë* (1883); Bertha Thomas, *George Sand* (1883); Anne Gilchrist, *Mary Lamb* (1883); Emma Pitman, *Elizabeth Fry* (1884); Vernon Lee, *The Countess of Albany* (1884); Elizabeth Robins Pennell, *Mary Wollstonecraft* (1884); Mathilde Blind, *Madame Roland* (1886); Florence Miller, *Harriet Martineau* (1884); and Bella Duffy, *Madame de Staël* (1887). These works were republished in England by William Allen as the *Eminent Women* series. A. Carette [née Bouvet] edited a French version, in ten volumes, between 1890 and 1905. Carette's series included biographies and selected writings of Anne de Montpensier, Marguerite-Jeanne de Staël-Delaunay, Jeanne de Campan, Laure d'Abrantes, Félicité de Genlis, Marie-Jeanne Roland, Madame de La Fayette, Françoise de Motteville, Louise-Elisabeth Vigée-LeBrun, and George Sand.

27. On Hopkins, see Jane Campbell, "Pauline Elizabeth Hopkins," in Darlene Clark Hine, ed., *Black Women in America: An Historical Encyclopedia*, 2 vols. (Brooklyn, N.Y.: Carlson, 1993), 1: 577–579; Kevin Gaines, *Uplifting the Race: Black Lead-*

ership, Politics, and Culture in the Twentieth Century (Chapel Hill: University of North Carolina Press, 1996), passim.

28. Oliphant, *Autobiography*, 67.

29. Clara Erskine Clement, *The Queen of the Adriatic; or, Venice, Medieval and Modern* (Boston: Estes and Lauriat, 1893), 2, 370. On modernist use of water imagery, see Marianne DeKoven, *Rich and Strange* (Princeton: Princeton University Press, 1993).

30. Julia Cartwright, *Beatrice d'Este, Duchess of Milan, 1475–1497: A Study of the Renaissance,* 2nd ed. (London: J. M. Dent, 1903; orig. pub. 1899), 89.

31. Ibid., v.

32. Mildred Lewis Rutherford, "Historical Sins of Omission and Commission" [1915], quoted in Jacqueline Goggin, "Politics, Patriotism, and Professionalism: American Women Historians and the Preservation of Southern Culture, 1890–1940," paper presented at the annual meeting of the American Historical Association, 1989, 1.

33. Goggin, "Politics, Patriotism, and Professionalism," passim; Oona Schmid, "Mammy Stories: Constructing an Aedifice of Ladyhood," unpublished paper, 1996.

34. James-Martin Skidmore, "History with a Mission: Ricarda Huch's Historiography during the Weimar Republic," Diss., Princeton University, 1993; Audrey Flandreau, "Ricarda Huch's *Weltanschauung* as Expressed in Her Philosophical Works and in Her Novels," Diss., University of Chicago, 1948.

35. Ricarda Huch, *Die Geschichten von Garibaldi,* 2 vols. (Leipzig: Insel, 1925), passim.

36. Julia Cartwright, *Sacharissa: Some Account of Dorothy Sidney, Countess of Sunderland, Her Family and Friends, 1617–1684,* 4th ed. (New York: E. P. Dutton, n.d.).

37. On railway travel and the panorama, see Wolfgang Schivelbusch, *The Railway Journey: The Industrialization of Time and Space in the Nineteenth Century* (Berkeley: University of California Press, 1986), 52–69.

38. Vernon Lee, *Euphorion: Being Studies of the Antique and Medieval in the Renaissance,* 2nd ed. (London: T. Fisher Unwin, 1885; orig. pub. 1884), 10–23.

39. Ibid., 11.

40. Ibid., 12.

41. Violet Paget [Vernon Lee] to Bernard Berenson, January 25, [1895?], Bernard Berenson Archive, Villa I Tatti, Harvard University Center for Italian Renaissance Studies, Florence.

42. Violet Paget [Vernon Lee] to Bernard Berenson, January 8, [1894?], ibid.

43. Ibid.

44. I would like to thank Patience Hartwell Smith for first suggesting the connection between trauma, the disbelieved amateur, and the attempt to develop a believable story.

45. There are some good studies of the way in which amateur work—much of it best-selling—was read during this period. Anne-Marie Chartier and Jean Hébrard, *Discours sur la lecture, 1880–1980* (Paris: Centre Georges Pompidou, 1989), covers discussions of school reading. Mary Kelley's study of women's reading in the early part of the century remains exemplary; see Kelley, "Reading Women / Women Reading: The Making of Learned Women in Antebellum America," *Journal of American History* 83 (September 1996), 401–424. See also James Smith Allen, *In the Public Eye: A History of Reading in Modern France, 1800–1940* (Princeton: Princeton University Press, 1991).

46. Vernon Lee, *Euphorion*, 353; Vernon Lee, *The Countess of Albany* (Boston: Roberts Brothers, 1897), 74.

47. Lina Eckenstein to Karl Pearson, April 27, 1887, University of London, University College Archives, Karl Pearson Papers, 680/3. For one appreciation of the Men and Women's Club, see Judith Walkowitz, *City of Dreadful Delight: Narratives of Sexual Danger in Late-Victorian London* (Chicago: University of Chicago Press, 1991), 135–170.

48. F. M. Powicke, quoted in R. B. McDowell, *Alice Stopford Green: A Passionate Historian* (Dublin: Allen Figgis, 1967), 86.

49. See Reddy, *The Rise of Market Culture;* Chalmers, "Harnessing Revolutionary Passions"; Joan Scott, *Gender and the Politics of History* (New York: Columbia University Press, 1988); and Judith Ann DeGroat, "The Working Lives of Women in the Parisian Manufacturing Trades, 1830–1848," Diss., University of Rochester, 1991.

50. Marie-Claire Hoock-Demarle, "Les écrits sociaux de Bettina von Arnim, ou Les débuts de l'enquête sociale dans le Vormärz prussien," *Le Mouvement Social,* 110 (January–March 1980), 25–26.

51. Virginia Woolf, "Introduction," in Margaret Llewelyn Davies, ed., *Life as We Have Known It: By Co-operative Working Women* (London: Hogarth, 1931), xxvi.

52. The central source for this interpretation is Anna Davin, "Imperialism and Motherhood," *History Workshop Journal,* 5 (Spring 1978), 9–65.

53. Caroline Dall, *"Woman's Right to Labor"; or, Low Wages and Hard Work* (Boston: Walker, Wise, 1860), ix. Dall dedicates her book to Anna Jameson. On the early appeal of the social sciences to Dall and other women in the United States, see William Leach, *True Love and Perfect Union* (New York: Basic Books, 1980); as well as the literature in note 7, above.

54. For general information on Augusta Moll-Weiss, see Bibliothèque Marguerite Durand, Paris, DOS MOL. Augusta Moll-Weiss, *Les écoles ménagères à l'étranger et en France* (Paris: A. Rousseau, 1908), xii. Alice Salomon and Marie Baum, *Das Familienleben in der Gegenwart* (Berlin: F. A. Herbig, 1930). Salomon had received a doctorate in economics *(Nationalökonomie)* in 1906 from the University of Berlin, with a dissertation on the causes of wage differentials between men and women ("Die Ursachen der ungleichen Entlöhnung von Männer- und Frauenar-

beit"). See Annette Vogt, "Findbuch [Index-Book]: Die Promotionen von Frauen an der Philosophischen Fakultät von 1898 bis 1936 und an der Mathematisch-Naturwissenschaftlichen Fakultät von 1936 bis 1945 der Friedrich-Wilhelms-Universität zu Berlin sowie die Habilitationen von Frauen an beiden Fakultäten von 1919 bis 1945," Preprint 57, Max-Planck-Institut für Wissenschaftsgeschichte (Berlin), n.d., 4.

55. Dall, *"Woman's Right to Labor,"* ix.

56. For some of the context of Austrian research, see Helmut Gruber, *Red Vienna: Experiment in Working-Class Culture, 1919–1934* (New York: Oxford, 1991).

57. On the beginning of the Fabian Women's Group, see Fabian Society, *Three Years' Work, 1908–1911* (London: G. Standring, 1911); and Polly Beals, "Fabian Feminism: Gender, Politics, and Culture in London, 1880–1930," Diss., Rutgers University, 1989. On the Section d'Etudes Féminines of the Musée Social, see Bibliothèque Marguerite Durand, Paris, DOS 396/MUS.

58. Salomon and Baum, *Das Familienleben in der Gegenwart,* 7ff.

59. Magdalen Pember Reeves, *Round About a Pound a Week* (London: G. Bell, 1913), 10.

60. Ibid., 15.

61. See, for instance, Caroline Milhaud, *Enquête sur le travail à domicile dans l'industrie de la fleur artificielle* (Paris: Imprimerie Nationale, 1913); Alice Clark, *The Working Life of Women in the Seventeenth Century* (New York: A. M. Kelley, 1968; orig. pub. 1919).

62. Adelheid Popp, *The Autobiography of a Working Woman,* trans. E. C. Harvey (Chicago: F. G. Browne, 1913), 14–15. See Mary Jo Maynes, *Taking the Hard Road: Life Course in French and German Workers' Autobiographies in the Era of Industrialization* (Chapel Hill: University of North Carolina Press, 1995).

63. Hélène Elek, *La Mémoire "Hélène"* (Paris: Maspero, 1977).

64. Popp, *Autobiography,* 17. Popp adds that her father died "without a word of reconciliation."

65. Jeanne Bouvier, *Mes mémoires; ou, 59 années d'activité industrielle, sociale, et intellectuelle d'une ouvrière, 1875–1935* (Paris: Maspero, 1983; orig. pub. 1936), 18–19.

66. Ibid., 213, 215.

67. See the introduction to the 1983 edition of her memoirs. The trouble professionals have with worker-writers is discussed in Jacques Rancière, *La nuit des proletaires* (Paris: Fayard, 1981).

68. Undated letter to Franklin Roosevelt [ca. 1933], in Bouvier, *Mes mémoires,* 236.

69. See Frederick S. Boas, "Charlotte Carmichael Stopes: Some Aspects of Her Life and Work," in *Essays by Divers Hands: Transactions of the Royal Society of Literature of the United Kingdom,* new series (London: Oxford University Press, 1931), X, 77–95; Gwendolen Murphy, "A Bibliographical List of the Writings of Charlotte Carmichael Stopes," ibid., 96–108.

70. Luise Büchner, *"Gebildet, ohne gelehrt zu sein"*: *Essays, Berichte, Briefe,* ed. Margarete Dierks (Darmstadt: Justus von Liebig, 1991); Luise Büchner, *Deutsche Geschichte, 1815–1870* (Leipzig: Theodor Thomas, 1875); Luise Büchner, *Die Frauen und ihr Beruf* (Frankfurt: Meidinger Sohn, 1855). Florence Griswold Buckstaff, "Married Women's Property in Anglo-Saxon and Anglo-Norman Law, and the Origins of the Common-Law Dower," *Annals of the American Academy of Political and Social Science,* 4 (July 1893–June 1894), 233–264.

71. Buckstaff, "Married Women's Property," 264.

72. See the rich correspondence of Lina Eckenstein in University of London Archives, Maria Sharpe and Karl Pearson Papers.

73. On the history and fate of the International Archive for the Women's Movement in the Netherlands, see Maria Grever, "Controlling Memories: Gender and the Construction of Scientific History," *Annali dell'Istituto Storico Italo-Germanico in Trento,* 23, no. 2 (1997), 385–400.

74. See Nancy Cott, ed., *A Woman Making History: Mary Ritter Beard through her Letters* (New Haven: Yale University Press, 1991).

75. On some of these, see Maïté Abistur, "Catalogue du Fonds Bouglé," typescript, Bibliothèque historique de la ville de Paris, 14–18, 24.

76. Interview with Marie-Louise Bouglé, in *Minerva* (1932), quoted ibid., 24.

77. Amelia B. Edwards, Commonplace book, Amelia B. Edwards Papers, Somerville College Archives, Oxford University, Box 5.

7 WOMEN PROFESSIONALS: A THIRD SEX?

1. I would like to thank my colleagues Dee Garrison and Mary Hartman for sharing their memories of Margaret Judson, whom they both admired.

2. Dominick LaCapra, *Representing the Holocaust: History, Memory, Trauma* (Ithaca: Cornell University Press, 1994), introduction.

3. W. Stull Holt, "The Idea of Scientific History in America," *Journal of the History of Ideas,* 1 (1940), 352.

4. On Tawney, see Stewart Weaver, *A Marriage in History: The Lives and Work of Barbara and J. L. Hammond* (Stanford: Stanford University Press, 1997).

5. On the professional situation of women holding doctorates in history in the United States, see Jacqueline Goggin, "Challenging Sexual Discrimination in the Historical Profession: Women Historians and the American Historical Association, 1890–1940," *American Historical Review,* 97, no. 3 (June 1992), 769–802. Among recent works on professional historians or professionally trained women in the United States generally, see Joan Scott, *Gender and the Politics of History* (New York: Columbia University Press, 1988), 178–198; Patricia Palmieri, *In Adamless Eden: The Community of Women Faculty at Wellesley* (New Haven: Yale University Press, 1995); Ann Firor Scott, ed., *Unheard Voices: The First Historians of Southern Women* (Charlottesville: University of Virginia Press, 1993); Rosalind Rosenberg,

Beyond Separate Spheres: Intellectual Roots of Modern Feminism (New Haven: Yale University Press, 1982).

On women in Canada, see Beverly Boutilier and Alison L. Prentice, eds., *Creating Historical Memory: English-Canadian Women and the Work of History* (Vancouver: University of British Columbia Press, 1997).

6. For some recent literature covering professional historians or professionally trained women in Europe, see Janet Sondheimer, *Castle Adamant in Hampstead: A History of Westfield College, 1882–1982* (London: Westfield College, University of London, 1983); Carol Dyhouse, *No Distinction of Sex? Women in British Universities, 1870–1939* (London: UCL Press, 1995); Jo Burr Margadant, *Madame le Professeur: Women Educators in the Third Republic* (Princeton: Princeton University Press, 1987); Anne Schlüter, ed., *Pionierinnen, Feministinnen, Karrierefrauen? Zur Geschichte des Frauenstudiums in Deutschland* (Pfaffenweiler: Centaurus, 1992). See also Vera Brittain, *Women at Oxford: A Fragment of a History* (New York: Macmillan, 1960).

7. Maxine Berg, "The First Women Economic Historians," *Economic History Review*, 45, no. 2 (1992), 308–329; W. H. Beveridge and Graham Wallas, "Professor Lilian Knowles, 1870–1926," *Economica*, 6 (June 1926), 119–122; C. M. Knowles, "Professor Lilian Knowles," in L. C. A. Knowles, *The Economic Development of the British Overseas Empire*, 2 vols. (London: Routledge, 1930), II, vii–xxii.

8. Helen Maud Cam, "Eating and Drinking Greek," *Girton Review*, 184 (1969), 12. Many useful Cam manuscripts are on deposit in the archives of Girton College.

9. Patrick Geddes and J. A. Thomson, *The Evolution of Sex* (London: Walter Scott, 1889); Herbert Spencer, *Principles of Biology* (London: Williams and Norgate, 1867). See Carol Dyhouse, *Girls Growing Up in Late Victorian and Edwardian England* (London: Routledge and Kegan Paul, 1981), 139–175; Lynn Gordon, *Gender and Higher Education in the Progressive Era* (New Haven: Yale University Press, 1990).

10. The classic study is Karen Offen, "Depopulation, Nationalism, and Feminism in Fin-de-Siècle France," *American Historical Review*, 89 (June 1984), 648–676.

11. Conference of the Society of Oxford Women Tutors with the Association of Head Mistresses, February 23, 1917, typescript of minutes, Lady Margaret Hall Archives, Eleanor Lodge Papers, box 1.

12. Much of the information on Harrison in this chapter comes from the Jane Ellen Harrison Papers at Newnham College, Cambridge. On Harrison, see especially Sandra Peacock, *Jane Ellen Harrison: The Mask and the Self* (New Haven: Yale University Press, 1988); and Jessie Stewart, *Jane Ellen Harrison: A Portrait from Letters* (London: Merlin, 1959). The literature on Harrison and the Cambridge "ritualists" is extensive.

13. See Eleanor Lodge, *Terms and Vacations*, ed. Janet Spens (Oxford: Oxford University Press, 1938); Louise Fargo Brown, *Apostle of Democracy: The Life of Lucy*

Maynard Salmon (New York: Macmillan, 1943; Palmieri, *In Adamless Eden,* 137–142.

14. The fact that in the late 1800s and early 1900s many Western countries had a "surplus" of single women has not been clearly explained. The excess may have been due to male migration, service in imperial armies, women's longer life expectancy, or other factors. The carnage of World War I exacerbated the trend. See (for England) Martha Vicinus, *Independent Women: Work and Community for Single Women, 1850–1920* (Chicago: University of Chicago Press, 1985).

15. Unless otherwise cited, details on Power's life come from Maxine Berg, *A Woman in History: Eileen Power, 1889–1940* (Cambridge: Cambridge University Press, 1996).

16. Eileen Power to Bertrand Russell, October 21, 1921, quoted in Berg, *A Woman in History,* 141.

17. Edith Hamilton and Alice Hamilton, "Students in Germany," *Atlantic Monthly,* 2, no. 3 (March 1965), 130–131; Rita McWilliams-Tulberg, *Women at Cambridge: A Men's University—Though of a Mixed Type* (London: V. Gollancz, 1975), 207.

18. Berg, "The First Women Economic Historians," 309; Marjorie Chibnall, "Eleanora Mary Carus-Wilson, 1897–1977," *Proceedings of the British Academy* (London: Oxford University Press, 1982), 503–520; Goggin, "Challenging Sexual Discrimination in the Historical Profession," 776, n. 14. See, among Helen Sumner Woodbury's other works, her pioneering *History of Women in Industry in the United States* (Washington: Bureau of Labor Statistics, 1910).

19. Hope Mirrlees, "Outline of a Life," manuscript III, Jane Ellen Harrison Papers, Newnham College Archives, Cambridge University.

20. Marcel Prou, *L'Ecole des Chartes* (Paris: Société des Amis de l'Ecole des Chartes, 1927), 20. I am grateful to Jennifer Milligan for providing me with this work.

21. See, for example, Lora D. Garrison, *Apostles of Culture: The Public Librarian and American Society* (New York: Free Press, 1979); Mary Niles Maack, "Women Librarians in France: The First Generation," *Journal of Library History,* 18 (Fall 1983), 407–449. American woman archivists, notably Margaret Cross Norton, fought for professional recognition for decades.

22. Society of Oxford Women Tutors and Association of Head Mistresses, Typescript of conference, February 23, 1917, Lady Margaret Hall, Eleanor Lodge Papers, box 1. See also Ada Elizabeth Levett, "The University Woman and the War," *Atheneum,* 4613 (January 1917).

23. Berg, *A Woman in History,* 181–182.

24. See Annette Vogt, "Findbuch [Index-Book]: Die Promotionen von Frauen an der Philosophischen Fakultät von 1898 bis 1936 und an der Mathematisch-Naturwissenschaftlichen Fakultät von 1936 bis 1945 der Friedrich-Wilhelms-Universität zu Berlin sowie die Habilitationen von Frauen an beiden Fakultäten von 1919 bis 1945," Preprint 57, Max-Planck-Institut für Wissenschaftsgeschichte (Berlin),

n.d.; Fritz Fellner, "Frauen in der österreichischen Geschichteswissenschaft," *Jahrbuch der Universität Salzburg* (Salzburg: Die Universität, 1984).

25. Margaret Judson, *Breaking the Barrier: A Professional Autobiography by a Woman Educator and Historian before the Women's Movement* (New Brunswick: Rutgers University Press, 1984), 30, 34, 109, 92.

26. Quoted in Alison Prentice, "Laying Siege to the History Professoriate," in Boutilier and Prentice, eds., *Creating Historical Memory*. See also Michael Hayden, ed., *So Much To Do, So Little Time: The Writings of Hilda Neatby* (Vancouver: University of British Columbia Press, 1983).

27. Jane Ellen Harrison to Gilbert Murray, January 2, 1903, in Newnham College Archives, Cambridge University, Jane Ellen Harrison Papers, box 1. See also Hope Mirrlees, "Outline of a Life.". On Power in London clubs: personal communication from Sir Jack Plumb, Cambridge, 1985. Wallas, "Professor Lilian Knowles," 119.

28. Charles K. Webster, "Eileen Power, 1889–1940," *Economic Journal,* 50, no. 200 (1940), 572.

29. Quoted in Kathleen Major, "Helen Maud Cam," *Dictionary of National Biography, 1961–1970,* ed. E. T. Williams and C. S. Nicholls (Oxford: Oxford University Press, 1981), 166–167.

30. See Goggin, "Challenging Sexual Discrimination in the Historical Profession," passim; Brown, *Apostle of Democracy,* passim.

31. F. W. Maitland to Henry Jackson, December 2, 1906, in *The Letters of Frederic William Maitland,* ed. C. H. S. Fifoot (Cambridge: Cambridge University Press, 1965), 388. Maitland's eulogies to Bateson were deeply moving. See *The Cambridge Review,* December 6, 1906; and *Selected Historical Essays of Frederic William Maitland,* ed. Helen Maud Cam (Cambridge: Cambridge University Press, 1957), 277.

32. The Lucy Maynard Salmon Papers in the Vassar College Archives contain many folders pertaining to this affair. I have also relied on Elizabeth Adams Daniels, "Lucy Maynard Salmon and James Baldwin: A Forgotten Episode," paper prepared for the Evalyn A. Clark Conference, Vassar College, October 12–13, 1984.

33. Madeleine Wallin to George C. Sykes, September 23, 1894, Smith College Archives, Wallin Collection, folder 6.

34. Mirrlees, "Outline of a Life."

35. Quoted in Leona C. Gabel, *From Slavery to the Sorbonne and Beyond: The Life and Writings of Anna J. Cooper* (Northampton, Mass.: Smith College, Department of History, 1982), 79. For an interpretation of Cooper's thought in the context of African-American intellectual life, including its class and gender dimensions, see Kevin K. Gaines, *Uplifting the Race: Black Leadership, Politics, and Culture in the Twentieth Century* (Chapel Hill: University of North Carolina Press, 1996), 128–151.

36. Anna J. Cooper, *A Voice from the South: By a Black Woman of the South* (Xenia, Ohio: Aldine, 1892), 77.

37. Letter of August 5, 1985.

38. J. B. Ross, personal communication, May 1985. I am grateful for the abundant information Dr. Ross provided in the course of several interviews.

39. I acknowledge, with thanks, the generous information provided by Janet Sondheimer on many women historians, including Helen Maud Cam and Caroline Skeel, in personal conversations in 1985. On Skeel, see Caroline Skeel Papers, Westfield College Archives, University of London. On Ada Elizabeth Levett, see H. M. Cam, M. Coate, and L. S. Sutherland, eds., *Studies in Manorial History* (Oxford: Oxford University Press, 1938), which contains biographical information as well as her inaugural lecture. See also the Ada Elizabeth Levett Papers, Westfield College Archives, University of London. On the medievalist Maude Violet Clarke, who died in 1935 at the age of forty-three, see Clarke, *Fourteenth Century Studies*, ed. L.S. Sutherland and M. McKisack (Oxford: Clarendon, 1937), with a biographical sketch by E. L. Woodward. See also the Maude Violet Clarke Papers, Lady Margaret Hall Archives.

40. See, for instance, Alice Zimmern, "Women in European Universities," *Forum* (April 1895), 187–199. Zimmern noted that German universities had generally gone backward, depriving women of their traditional right to attend lectures. Zimmern also reported on French lycées for women, women's clubs, housing for women, and the position of the governess. Some papers are available in the archives of Girton College.

   Lucy Maynard Salmon Papers, Vassar College Archives, contain manuscripts of articles Salmon wrote on European universities and on the current state of education in history.

41. *Selected Historical Essays of F. W. Maitland*, 277–278.

42. Interview with J. B. Ross, Washington, D.C., May 1985. On the domestic ideal in college dormitories, see Helen Horowitz, *Alma Mater: Design and Experience in the Women's Colleges from their Nineteenth-Century Beginnings to the 1930s* (New York: Knopf, 1984).

43. Sondheimer, *Castle Adamant in Hampstead*, 10–24.

44. Palmieri, *In Adamless Eden*, passim.

45. Caroline Ware, paper prepared for the Evalyn A. Clark Conference, Vassar College, October 1985.

46. See Judith Bennett, "Medievalism and Feminism," *Speculum*, 68 (April 1993), 309–331.

47. Margaret Hastings and Elisabeth G. Kimball, "Two Distinguished Medievalists: Nellie Neilson and Bertha Haven Putnam," *Journal of British Studies*, 18, no. 2 (Spring 1979), 142–159.

48. Mabel C. Buer, *Health, Wealth, and Population in the Early Days of the Industrial Revolution* (London: Routledge, 1926), ix.

49. Janet Sondheimer, Personal communication, July 30, 1985.

50. Caroline Skeel Papers, Westfield College, University of London, file labeled "Welsh Cloth–Cattle."

51. Thomas Frederick Tout, "Mary Bateson," *Dictionary of National Biography*, Supplement, 1901–1911 (London: Smith Elder, 1912), 110.

52. Mary Bateson, "History of the Double Monasteries," *Transactions of the Royal Historical Society*, new series, 13 (1899), 137–198.

53. Eileen Power, *Medieval English Nunneries, circa 1275 to 1535* (Cambridge: Cambridge University Press, 1922).

54. Jane Ellen Harrison, *Alpha and Omega* (London: Sidgwick and Jackson, 1915), 206, 207.

55. Jane Ellen Harrison to Gilbert and Mary Murray, August 14, 1902, Newnham College Archives, Cambridge University, Jane Ellen Harrison Papers, box 1.

56. Jane Ellen Harrison, *Themis: A Study of the Social Origins of Greek Religion*, 2nd ed. (Cambridge: Cambridge University Press, 1927; orig. pub. 1912), xii.

57. Harrison, *Alpha and Omega*, 141.

58. Harrison, *Themis*, 267.

59. Lewis Farnell, *Oxford Magazine* (1912), quoted in Peacock, *Jane Ellen Harrison*, 212.

60. Harrison, *Alpha and Omega*, 152.

61. Lucy Maynard Salmon, *Domestic Service* (New York: Macmillan, 1897).

62. Quoted in Brown, *Apostle of Democracy*, 157.

63. For an appreciation of Salmon's connections with architecture and urbanism, see Nicholas Adams, "Lucy Maynard Salmon: A Lost Parent for Architectural History," *Journal of the Society of Architectural Historians*, 55, no. 1 (March 1996), 4–5, 108.

64. Lucy Maynard Salmon, *Historical Material* (New York: Oxford University Press, 1933), 157.

65. Lucy Maynard Salmon, "History and Historical Study," unpublished manuscript, Vassar College Archives, Lucy Maynard Salmon Papers, Hollinger box 13.

66. James Monroe Taylor to Lucy Maynard Salmon, November 16, 1904, Lucy Maynard Salmon Papers, Hollinger box 3, folder 15.

67. Elizabeth Adams Daniels, "Lucy Maynard Salmon and James Baldwin: A Forgotten Episode," paper prepared for the Evalyn A. Clark Conference, Vassar College, October 12–13, 1984, provides an account of this failed attempt to unseat Salmon. See also Brown, *Apostle of Democracy*.

68. Lucy Maynard Salmon, "The Historical Museum," *Educational Review* (February 1911), 144–160.

69. Henry Canby to Lucy Maynard Salmon, March 1, 1912, Vassar College Archives, Lucy Maynard Salmon Papers, Hollinger box 10.

70. Lucy Maynard Salmon, *Progress in the Household* (Boston: Houghton Mifflin, 1906), vii.

71. Ibid., xiv, xii.

72. Lucy Maynard Salmon, *The Newspaper and the Historian* (New York: Oxford University Press, 1923), v; Lucy Maynard Salmon, *The Newspaper and Authority* (New York: Oxford University Press, 1923), v.

73. Power, *Medieval Nunneries*, 50.

74. Harrison, *Themis*, 261–262.

75. G. G. Coulton, *Fourscore Years: An Autobiography* (New York: Macmillan, 1944), 265.

76. For a summary of the positions for and against the disruptive force of the carnivalesque, see Peter Stallybrass and Allon White, *The Politics and Poetics of Transgression* (Ithaca: Cornell University Press, 1986), 1–26. On the carnivalesque in general, see Mikhail Bakhtin, *Rabelais and His World*, trans. T. F. Rable (Cambridge, Mass.: Harvard University Press, 1968); and idem, *The Dialogic Imagination*, trans. Caryl Emerson and Michael Holquist (Austin: University of Texas Press, 1981).

77. A. E. Levett, "English Manorial History in the Fourteenth Century," manuscript, Westfield College, University of London, Levett Papers, box 1, Deposit 26/2.

78. Salmon, *Progress in the Household*, 11.

79. Lucy Maynard Salmon, "The Teaching of History in Academies and Colleges," in Anna C. Brackett, ed., *Woman and the Higher Education* (New York: Harper, 1893), 161.

8 MODERNISM, RELATIVISM, AND EVERYDAY LIFE

1. See Dorothy Ross, ed., *Modernist Impulses in the Human Sciences* (Baltimore: Johns Hopkins University Press, 1994); and Allan Megill, "'Grand Narrative' and the Discipline of History," in Frank Ankersmit and Hans Kellner, eds., *A New Philosophy of History* (Chicago: University of Chicago Press, 1995), 151–173.

2. Quoted in Ray Billington, *Frederick Jackson Turner: Historian, Scholar, Teacher* (New York: Oxford University Press, 1973), 101.

3. Direction for some of my arguments on modernism, masculinity, historical writing, and artistic modernism comes in part from Rita Felski, *The Gender of Modernity* (Cambridge, Mass.: Harvard University Press, 1995); Marianne DeKoven, *Rich and Strange: Gender, History, Modernism* (Princeton: Princeton University Press, 1991); Kaja Silverman, *Male Subjectivity at the Margins* (London: Routledge, 1992); and Peter Middleton, *The Inward Gaze: Masculinity and Subjectivity in Modern Culture* (London: Routledge, 1992).

4. Benedetto Croce, *An Autobiography*, trans. R. G. Collingwoood (Freeport, N.Y.: Books for Library Press, 1970; orig. pub. 1927), 50–51.

5. Ibid., 51–52.

6. Henri Berr, *Hymne à la vie* (Paris: Albin Michel, 1945), 59.

7. R. G. Collingwood, *An Autobiography* (Oxford: Oxford University Press, 1951; orig. pub. 1939), 150–154.

8. J. B. Bury, *Selected Essays of J. B. Bury,* ed. Harold Temperley (Cambridge: Cambridge University Press, 1930), 22. Trevelyan advanced the position in "Clio: A Muse," an essay of 1903 which was later (1913) reprinted in a book of the same name, and reformulated it along the way. He drew the distinction among the scientific, artistic, and philosophical aspects of history most clearly in "Bias in History" (1947), reprinted in G. M. Trevelyan, *An Autobiography and Other Essays* (London: Longmans, Green, 1949), 68–81.

9. Berr, *Hymne à la vie,* 58.

10. Ibid., 197. Although this book was published during World War II, Berr maintained that much of it had been written in his early years. The story is set in the years after 1880.

11. Henri Berr, *L'histoire traditionnelle et la synthèse historique* (Paris: Félix Alcan, 1921), v.

12. See also Henri Berr, *Peut-on refaire l'unité morale de la France?* (Paris: Armand Colin, 1901).

13. Roger Chickering, *Karl Lamprecht* (Atlantic Highlands, N.J.: Humanities Press, 1993), 82–83.

14. The term "lifeless" fills historical criticism from the end of the nineteenth century on; the term "scissors-and-paste men" is Collingwood's.

15. R. G. Collingwood used the phrase "scissors-and-paste men" to categorize the old practitioners of scientific history (*The Idea of History,* passim), while the charge of doing "lifeless" or "dry" history was deployed by most of the modernizers, from Lamprecht to Bloch and Febvre.

16. Lord Acton, manuscript Add. 5528, Cambridge University Library, fols. 190b–193a, quoted in Herbert Butterfield, *Man on His Past* (Cambridge: Cambridge University Press, 1955), 87.

17. James Harvey Robinson, *The New History: Essays Illustrating the Modern Historical Outlook* (Springfield, Mass.: Walden Press, 1958; orig. pub. 1912), 36.

18. Berr, *Hymne à la vie,* 46.

19. Berr, *L'histoire traditionnelle et la synthèse historique,* 16.

20. Berr, *L'histoire traditionnelle et la synthèse historique,* 21.

21. Henri Berr, *Vie et science: Lettres d'un vieux philosophe strasbourgeois et d'un étudiant parisien* (Paris: Armand Colin, 1894), 150.

22. Ibid.

23. Ibid., 158.

24. Wassily Kandinsky, *Concerning the Spiritual in Art,* trans. M. T. H. Sadler (New York: Dover, 1977; orig. pub. 1911), 7–18. The language of history mirrored that of the artistic movements acmeism and purism.

25. François Guizot to Pauline de Meulan Guizot, in Charles Pouthas, *Une famille de bourgeoisie française de Louis XIV à Napoléon* (Paris: Félix Alcan, 1934), 67.

26. See Walter Goetz, *Historiker in Meiner Zeit* (Cologne: Böhlau, 1957), 256–258.

27. Berr, *Lettres,* 141–142.

28. Karl Lamprecht, *What Is History? Five Lectures on the Modern Science of History,* trans. E. A. Andrews (New York: Macmillan, 1905), 12.

29. Robinson, *The New History,* 64.

30. Max Lazard, *François Simiand, 1873–1935: L'homme, l'oeuvre* (Paris: Domat Montchrestien, 1936), 35.

31. Lamprecht, *What Is History?* 12–13.

32. Charles Beard, "Written History as an Act of Faith," *American Historical Review,* 39 (January 1934), 219–229.

33. Robinson, *The New History,* 15–16.

34. Marc Bloch, *The Historian's Craft,* trans. Peter Putnam (New York: Vintage, 1953), passim.

35. Ibid., 71.

36. Friedrich Meinecke, *Autobiographische Schriften,* ed. Eberhard Kessel (Stuttgart: K. F. Koehler, 1969), VIII, 3.

37. Robinson, *The New History,* 57.

38. Berr, *Peut-on refaire l'unité morale de la France?* 20.

39. Robinson, *The New History,* 64, 136.

40. The information in this paragraph comes from Ernest Samuels, *Henry Adams* (Cambridge, Mass.: Harvard University Press, 1989), passim.

41. Henry Adams, *Mont-Saint-Michel and Chartres* (New York: Mentor, 1961; orig. pub. 1904). Pages numbers are indicated in the text.

42. Rita Felski, *The Gender of Modernity* (Cambridge, Mass.: Harvard University Press, 1995), 201.

43. Samuels, *Henry Adams,* 209.

44. Ibid., 276.

45. See Susan W. Friedman, *Marc Bloch, Sociology and Geography: Encountering Changing Disciplines* (Cambridge: Cambridge University Press, 1996); Bertrand Miller, ed., *March Bloch, Lucien Febvre et les "Annales d'Histoire Economique et Sociale": Correspondance, 1928–1933* (Paris: Fayard, 1994).

46. Marc Bloch, "Les plans parcellaires: L'avion au service de l'histoire agraire en Angleterre," *Annales d'Histoire Economique et Sociale,* 2 (1930), 557–558.

47. Samuels, *Henry Adams,* 199.

48. This tribute was first made when Power received an honorary doctorate at the University of Manchester; it was subsequently published by Tawney in his obituary notice of her. Quoted in Berg, *A Woman in History,* 256–257.

49. Lucy Maynard Salmon, "The Family Cookbook," *Vassar Quarterly,* 11 (March 1926), 104–105. Like most of her other manuscript work on the topic that is dated in the first decade of the twentieth century, this article was probably written much earlier than the publication date indicates.

50. At the Evalyn Clark Conference at Vassar College, October 1985, Lucy Maynard

Salmon was vividly remembered as the person who had provided the distinctive traits that still characterized the teaching of history at Vassar.

51. This analysis is suggested by the work of Rosalind E. Krauss. See, notably, Krauss, *The Originality of the Avant-Garde and Other Modernist Myths* (Cambridge, Mass.: MIT Press, 1985), 8–22; and idem, *The Optical Unconscious* (Cambridge, Mass.: MIT Press, 1994), esp. 48–58.

52. Mary Beard, *On Understanding Women* (New York: Longmans, Green, 1931), 11–12.

53. Ricarda Huch, *Gesammelte Werke,* 11 vols. (Cologne: Kiepenheuer und Witsch, 1966), VII, 649–650.

54. Beard, *On Understanding Women,* 5.

55. Mary Beard, *America through Women's Eyes* (New York: Macmillan, 1933), 245–249, 258–265, 252–258, 480–498; Beard, *On Understanding Women,* 515, 513.

56. From Persis Greely Anderson, "To a Minor Corporation," in Martha Bensley Bruere and Mary Ritter Beard, eds., *Laughing Their Way: Women's Humor in America* (New York: Macmillan, 1934), 113.

57. Mary Beard to Una Winter, August 13 and May 1, 1947, Henry E. Huntington Library, San Marino, Calif., Una Winter Collection, box 13.

58. See, for example, Lydia Maria Child, *The History of the Condition of Women in Various Ages and Nations,* 2 vols. (Boston: J. Allen, 1835). The first volume covers women of Asia and Africa; the second covers Europe, Native Americans, and women of the South Sea Islands.

59. The point that history is the moralizing of the past comes from Hayden White, *The Content of the Form* (Baltimore: Johns Hopkins University Press, 1987), 20–21.

60. Beard, *On Understanding Women,* 514.

61. Ibid., 13.

62. Maud Violet Clarke, notes for "Methods of Thinking about Historical Problems," Somerville College, Oxford University, Maud Violet Clarke Papers.

63. Two important anthologies on Beard are Nancy Cott, ed., *A Woman Making History: Mary Ritter Beard through her Letters* (New Haven: Yale University Press, 1991); and Ann Lane, ed., *Mary Ritter Beard: A Sourcebook* (New York: Schocken, 1977). For a fuller treatment of Mary Beard's modernism, see Bonnie G. Smith, "Seeing Mary Beard," *Feminist Studies,* 10 (Fall 1984), 399–416.

64. Harrison, *Themis,* 18.

65. David Hollinger, "The Knower and the Artificer" and "Postscript 1993," in Dorothy Ross, ed., *Modernist Impulses in the Human Sciences* (Baltimore: Johns Hopkins University Press, 1994), 26–54.

66. See not only P. J. Kenyon's *The History Men,* but even works like Peter Novick's *That Noble Dream.* The tendency is to acknowledge women as being currently in the profession but to erase the thousands who wrote before the 1970s.

67. Mary Williams to James A. Robertson, December 30, 1919, quoted in Jacqueline Goggin, "Challenging Sexual Discrimination in the Historical Profession: Women Historians and the American Historical Association, 1890–1940," *American Historical Review*, 97, no. 3 (June 1992), 784.
68. This argument is based on Dominick LaCapra, *Representing the Holocaust: History, Theory, Trauma* (Ithaca: Cornell University Press, 1994).

Index

Index

Index